THE

LIFTING

OF THE VEIL

ACTS 15:20-21

AVRAM YEHOSHUA

Trafford
PUBLISHING™

All quotes from *Unger's Bible Dictionary* used by permission.

Order this book online at www.trafford.com/07-0724
or email orders@trafford.com

Most Trafford titles are also available at major online book retailers.

Note for Librarians: A cataloguing record for this book is available from Library
and Archives Canada at www.collectionscanada.ca/amicus/index-e.html

Printed in Victoria, BC, Canada.

ISBN: 978-1-4251-2328-4

*We at Trafford believe that it is the responsibility of us all, as both individuals
and corporations, to make choices that are environmentally and socially sound.
You, in turn, are supporting this responsible conduct each time you purchase a
Trafford book, or make use of our publishing services. To find out how you are
helping, please visit www.trafford.com/responsiblepublishing.html*

*Our mission is to efficiently provide the world's finest, most comprehensive
book publishing service, enabling every author to experience success.
To find out how to publish your book, your way, and have it available
worldwide, visit us online at www.trafford.com/10510*

 Trafford PUBLISHING www.trafford.com

North America & international
toll-free: 1 888 232 4444 (USA & Canada)
phone: 250 383 6864 ♦ fax: 250 383 6804 ♦ email: info@trafford.com

The United Kingdom & Europe
phone: +44 (0)1865 722 113 ♦ local rate: 0845 230 9601
facsimile: +44 (0)1865 722 868 ♦ email: info.uk@trafford.com

10 9 8 7 6

This book is dedicated to Messiah Yeshua,
whose Spirit and Word
have shown me the Way of Life.
May its words glorify You my Lord.

And to my wife Ruti, whose love for Yeshua
has been a beacon Light for me
in this world of darkness.
Thank you my love.

Just as a veil has been over the eyes of the Jewish people
concerning Yeshua the Messiah
(2nd Cor. 3:14-16)

A similar veil is over the eyes of the Bride of Christ
concerning the Law of Moses
(Dan. 7:25)

THE LIFTING OF THE VEIL
ACTS 15:20-21

Table of Contents

Abbreviations

ALGNT	Analytical Lexicon of the Greek New Testament
AHCL	The Analytical Hebrew and Chaldee Lexicon
ARA	A Rabbinic Anthology
CED	Collins English Dictionary
DBI	Dictionary of Biblical Imagery
GELNT	A Greek-English Lexicon of the New Testament And Other Early Christian Literature
IBD	The Illustrated Bible Dictionary
ISBE	The International Standard Bible Encyclopedia
JNTC	Jewish New Testament Commentary
KJV	King James Version Bible
NAGL	The New Analytical Greek Lexicon
NASB	New American Standard Bible
NBDBG	The New Brown, Driver, Briggs, Gesenius Hebrew and English Lexicon
NGEINT	The New Greek-English Interlinear New Testament
NIV	New International Version
NKJV	New King James Version
NRSV	New Revised Standard Version
TDNT	Theological Dictionary of the New Testament
TDOT	Theological Dictionary of the Old Testament
TLOT	Theological Lexicon of the Old Testament
TWOT	Theological Wordbook of the Old Testament
UBD	Unger's Bible Dictionary
WBC	The Wycliffe Bible Commentary
WNCD	Webster's New Collegiate Dictionary

Acknowledgements

I'm indebted to Hannah Cooperman, Ruti Yehoshua and Avimelech ben Avraham for their tireless efforts in proofreading the manuscript, as well as their keen insights. Many mistakes were corrected because of them. If there are any typographical errors, it's my responsibility as I revised the book after they read it.

INTRODUCTION

The book of Acts forms an indispensable bridge between the Gospels and the letters of Peter, Paul, James and John. Without Acts we'd be at a great loss as to what happened in Jerusalem after the Resurrection with the subsequent giving of the Holy Spirit on Pentecost. We wouldn't know of the many thousands of Jewish people that came to believe in Messiah Yeshua (the Hebrew name for Jesus).[1] We also wouldn't realize what Peter, Stephen and Philip did or how Paul came to believe in Yeshua. And we wouldn't have any idea how the question of Gentile salvation, circumcision and the Law was settled in Acts 15.

For 1,900 years the Church has taught that the Law of Moses was nullified by the sacrificial death of Jesus. The Feasts of Israel, the dietary laws and the Seventh Day Sabbath are only for the Jews who rejected Jesus and are still 'under the old Law.' Christians are under Grace and free from the Law or as F. F. Bruce writes, Christianity is a 'law-free gospel.'[2] Acts 15 is one of the major places in Scripture that the Church points to in order to prove their position. The chapter deals with the issue of whether Gentile believers needed to be circumcised and keep the Law in order to be saved.

Salvation is based on faith in Jesus plus nothing else. In other words there's no law or good deed that one can do that transforms their nature into that of Messiah's. It's a gracious work of God the Father through His Son for forgiveness, sanctification and final glorification.

The Church wrongly misinterprets the four rules of James (Acts 15:20) thus laying the groundwork for a major heresy. They believe the rules apply to table fellowship and that these are the only rules or laws for Christians. Their anti-Law theology supports this false perception and sets up their inability to correctly discern the meaning of the next verse where James comments on Gentile believers already going to the synagogues to learn the Law of Moses and assumes they'd continue.[3]

F. F. Bruce speaks of the Council of Acts 15 as 'epoch-making.'[4] Howard

---

[1] Some places in Acts where Jews believed in Jesus are: Acts 2:41, 47; 4:14; 5:14; 6:1, 7; 9:31, 35, 42; 13:43; 14:1; 17:1-4, 11; 18:8, 17; 21:20.

[2] F. F. Bruce, Author; Gordon D. Fee, General Editor, *The New International Commentary on the New Testament: The Book of the Acts* (Grand Rapids, MI: William B. Eerdmans Publishing Company, 1988), p. 285.

[3] Church theology on the Law has been challenged in the last 40 years by E. P. Sanders (*Paul and Palestinian Judaism*; 1977), James Dunn (*The Theology of Paul the Apostle*; 1998), and N. T. Wright (*Paul: In Fresh Perspective*; 2005) to name a few people. Equating the Law with legalism is finally being seen as a caricature of God's holy Law.

[4] Ibid., p. 282.

Marshall agrees and states that,

> 'Luke's account of the discussion regarding the relation
> of the Gentiles to the law (sic) of Moses forms the center
> of Acts both structurally and theologically.'[5]

The Book of Acts is extremely important and Acts 15 is the theological center for properly understanding the Law in the New Testament. It's at this fulcrum point that the Law is declared valid for every believer. God ordained James to officially authorize the Law for every Christian. And it's at this crucial theological point that the Church has failed. It's created a theological veil that has kept Christians from their ancient Hebraic heritage and also led them into pagan celebrations in the Name of Jesus and anti-Semitism. This is something that Jesus and Paul never intended.

Almost two thousand years ago all the believing Jewish Elders and Apostles of Jerusalem assembled to debate the matter of Gentile conversion to the Jewish Messiah (Acts 15:6). They needed to know exactly what constituted salvation for the Gentile. Paul, Barnabas and others from the congregation of Antioch were there that day too. The Jewish leadership in faraway Antioch (modern day southern Turkey) had requested a ruling. Acts 15:1-2 states,

> 'Some men came down from Judah and began teaching
> the brethren, "Unless you are circumcised according to
> the custom of Moses you cannot be saved." And when
> Paul and Barnabas had great dissension and debate with
> them, the brethren determined that Paul and Barnabas and
> some others of them should go up to Jerusalem to the
> Apostles and Elders concerning this issue.'[6]

The men from Judah wanted the Gentiles to be circumcised which meant becoming a Jew. They'd then be part of the people that God was redeeming (Israel) and they'd be told to keep the Law to insure their eternal life.

God's intent though was that the Gentile would be saved the same way as

---

[5] I. Howard Marshall, M.A., B.D., Ph.D., Professor R.V.G. Tasker, M.A., B.D., General Editor, *Tyndale New Testament Commentaries: Acts* (Leicester, England: Inter-Varsity Press, 2000), p. 242.

[6] *Bible Master 3.0: NAS Computer Bible* (Anaheim, CA: Foundation Press Publications, 1992). Many Scripture quotes are taken from the New American Standard Bible. Changes have also been made to texts where the Hebraic perspective (translation) seems more suitable. Unless otherwise stated, *italics* are my way of emphasizing a word or phrase. Also, proper nouns are capitalized (e.g. Aaron the High Priest, the Law, the Temple, etc.), and the Name of the God of Israel (Yahveh) is written instead of the ubiquitous term, 'the LORD.'

the Jew was; by their faith in Yeshua as the Redeemer of Mankind. In other words by God's gracious action toward us in Messiah (Acts 2:37-40; 15:11). And then in the aftermath of this, four rules were issued (v. 20). Proper interpretation of them is vital in determining what James and the Council, and therefore what the Messiah through them, intended for the Gentile believers *after* they had entered into the Kingdom of Jesus.

What the Holy Spirit issued through James for the Gentile was conceptually no different than what God did for Israel through Moses when He brought Israel out of Egyptian slavery. The Hebrews were not saved by circumcision or the Law but by the blood of the lamb (Ex. 12).[7]

It follows that the Gentile wouldn't be saved by circumcision or the Law either. But after Hebrew deliverance or salvation from Egypt, Yahveh brought Israel to Mt. Sinai to learn of His Ways; *Who* was this God that had just brought Egypt, the mightiest nation in the world at that time, to its knees? What was pleasing and right in His eyes? What did He consider wrong or sin? And what sins would cost them their life if they disobeyed Him?

Yahveh didn't set them free to do their own thing, willing to accept whatever any Hebrew thought was right in his own heart. He gave them His holy Law (Dt. 4:5-8; Rom. 7:12) so they'd know right from wrong and He'd be able to dwell among them. Why would it be different in Christ? Why would His holy Ways be invalid for the Gentile?

Some might say, 'But the only thing we need to do is to love God and neighbor.' This is the *heart* of the Law (Dt. 4:5-6; Lev. 19:18). And this is how Yeshua spoke of summing up the Law but He didn't do away with the *other* commandments and statutes (Mt. 22:40).

Others might say, 'But we have the Spirit to guide us in God's will.' Yet it's the *express* purpose of the Spirit to write the Law of God upon the heart of every believer (Jer. 31:33; Ezk. 36:26-27; Heb. 8:10). How is it that many who have this Spirit balk at the very Law the Spirit desires to

---

[7] Alfred Edersheim, *The Temple: It's Ministry and Services* (Peabody, MA: Hendrickson Publishers, 1994), pp. 183-184. Edersheim writes that the sacrifice of the Passover lamb in Egypt was a picture of the Sacrifice of Yeshua. No other sacrifice 'could so suitably commemorate His death, nor yet the great deliverance connected with it, and the great union and fellowship from it.' It 'had been instituted and observed before Levitical sacrifices existed; before the Law was given; nay, before the Covenant was ratified by blood (Ex. 24). In a sense, it may be said to have been the cause of all the later sacrifices of the law (sic) and of the Covenant itself.' The Jew was not saved from Egyptian slavery by either circumcision or the Law but by the blood of the lamb; the Grace of Yahveh to Israel.

place upon their heart? If the Law of God was truly written on the heart, wouldn't believers want to keep Passover and God's Sabbath day holy?

The Gentile who was saved by the Blood of the Lamb was to learn about his new Family (Israel) that he was now a part of (John 10:16; Rom. 11:24; Eph. 2:13) and God's holy ways. He would do this by going to the synagogue on the Sabbath and learning about Jesus and the Law of God (Acts 15:21). The Law would teach the Gentile Who the God of Israel was, his new Family history and what God required of him that he might walk in those ways in the Power and Love of the Spirit, just as Jesus did. After all, if Jesus kept the Sabbath, dietary laws and Passover, and we want to be like Him, shouldn't we be keeping those same things too?

It's not without a compelling truth that the Lord uses the expression Born from Above (or Born Again; Jn. 3:3, 7) to indicate one's birth or entry into His Kingdom by His Spirit. An infant is born into a family without keeping any of the family rules 'by the grace of the parents.' Does this mean that the child will not be required to keep the family rules when it comes of age? Does it matter if the child obeys the father and does the father's will? Or should the will of the child overrule the will of the father? Would the father be pleased if the child brought in rules that contradicted his own values? Knowing the will of the Father and doing it are central to being a son or daughter of God. Yeshua said,

> 'Not everyone who says to Me, 'Lord, Lord' will enter
> the Kingdom of Heaven but he who does the will of My
> Father who is in Heaven will enter.' (Matt. 7:21 see also
> 12:50)

What is the will of God in relation to the Law? Many in the Church say, 'The Law has been done away with.' Yet Marshall, before he theologizes the Law away, says the Law of Moses is the will of God our Father.[8] And God gave those rules and laws to Israel *after* they were *saved* from Egyptian slavery. The same holds true for the (saved) believer today.

Jesus says that love is the basis for all the laws of Moses (Mt. 22:34-40) and so Christians are keeping the core of the will of God. Unfortunately the Church teaches against everything in the Law except what they perceive to be the moral laws. Therefore many believers are ignorant of the specifics of God's Law and horrified to even consider it.

The mere mention of 'the Law' as part of God's will brings puzzled looks, fear or contempt to the faces of many, who in their pride and ignorance,

---

[8]   Marshall, *Acts*, p. 242. What 'evidence was there that the law, which *represented the will of God* for his covenant people, had been repealed?'

4

think they rightly understand Law and Grace. Unfortunately those same facial expressions could be seen on the Pharisees who boasted of their own righteousness (Lk. 18:9-14) and proper interpretation of the Word of God (Mt. 15:1-20) while rejecting the understanding of God the Son who stood before them.

On the other hand, some extremists in the Law Camp say that Christians who don't keep Sabbath and Passover, etc., are going to Hell. This is totally wrong. Anyone who loves Jesus and their neighbors, are keeping the heart of the Law (Dt. 4:5-6; Lev. 19:18; Lk. 10:25-28). These extremists fail to realize that even if a Christian is keeping Sunday and eating ham, if they have a living relationship with Jesus they'll be forgiven of those sins (1st Pet. 4:8). His Sacrifice is that great (Acts 13:38-39). But a believer walking in those sins is not what the Holy Spirit wants for them today. And their committing those sins has its negative effect upon them as well as others. Striving to reflect His pure and undefiled Truth, and be an example to others, is a divine goal.

Of course there are Christians who hear that eating pig won't send them to Hell so they're not concerned about the Law. But sinning against God is no light matter. And building a theological house on sand is much more disastrous than building a real house on it (Mt. 7:24-27). Reading into Acts 15 (and other passages of Scripture) that the Law has been done away with is a false interpretation of the text. And false theology leads to false and sinful lifestyles. This distorts the picture of the true Jesus that godly believers want to emulate and present to others.

It also offends many Jews who understand, and correctly so, that the Messiah wouldn't do away with the Law of Moses. Jews know that the only true God is the God of Israel and that He gave the Law to Moses. And Yahveh Himself warns them in the Law that if anyone entices them to follow something else, they're to be stoned (Dt. 13:1-5; 17:2-13). At this point a 'Jesus who has done away with the Law' becomes a salvation issue for the entire Jewish community. Placing this major stumbling block in the way of the Jewish people is nothing less than satanic.

Most Israelis are taught in grade school that Jesus started another religion; Christianity. Is that really what Jesus did? It can't be found in the entire Book of Acts. And that this religion hates the Law of Moses and the Jewish people. The last 1,900 years of Church history confirms this sinister attitude toward the Jewish people. At the foundation of this attitude is how the Church views the Law of Moses, the last forty years of loving Christian outreach not making a dent in the mind of the average Jew.

In the New Covenant whenever salvation is pitted against the Law (or

5

circumcision, which implied that the Gentile was to become a Jew[9] and keep the Law for salvation), it's rightly rejected as a means of obtaining and maintaining the new birth and the new life. Paul's emphasis of non-circumcision for the Gentile (1st Cor. 7:17-19) was always against the keeping of the Law *for salvation* which circumcision implied (e.g. Gal. 2:16, 19, 21; 5:3, 6).

One cannot add anything to the finished Work of Messiah Yeshua. But once that is established, the Law rightfully comes to the forefront in the New Testament for how one should live out this new life. It's the guideline for what is right or wrong in God's eyes. In other words, Sabbath, Passover and dietary laws, etc., are still in effect for the believer today. Christian scholar David Williams writes, 'for Paul, the law remained the authoritative guide to Christian living.'[10] All the Jewish believers kept the Law (Acts 21:20) including Paul (Acts 21:23-24, 26; 23:1-5; 25:8) who commanded his followers to keep it also (Rom. 3:31; 7:7, 12, 14; 1st Cor. 7:19). And if Paul wrote to Gentile believers 'to follow him as He followed Christ' (1st Cor. 4:14-17; 11:1; Phil. 3:15-17; 4:9; 1st Thess. 1:6-7; 2nd Thess. 3:7, 9) shouldn't the Gentile believer be keeping the laws that pertain to him from just this perspective?

How can it be that the ancient faith community of believers loved the Law and adhered to it while the modern faith community teaches against it? Are there two different faith communities in the one Flock of Jesus (Jn. 10:16)?

The Church is adamant though...the Law doesn't pertain to them. Even within the so-called Messianic Jewish Community today there's division over the observance of the Law of Moses (Torah) for the Jewish and Gentile believer. Very few Jewish believers think that they or the Gentile must

---

[9]   E. P. Sanders, *Wikipedia: The Free Encyclopedia* at http://en.wikipedia.org/wiki/E._P._Sanders), first raised Christian awareness that circumcision meant the Gentile was to become part of the (supposedly eternally saved) Chosen People; a Jew. And that one stayed 'in the Covenant' by keeping the Law. (See Scot McKnight, *Jesus Creed* at http://www.jesuscreed.org/?p=2686). David Stern, *Jewish New Testament Commentary* (Clarksville, MD: Jewish New Testament Publications, 1992), p. 273. Circumcision for the Gentile meant the circumcision party (Acts 15:1) was requiring the Gentile to become a proselyte (i.e. 'in every sense' a Jew). Stern adds that their becoming Jews is also clearly seen in Acts 15:5 which phrase, 'to observe the Law of Moses' meant that the Gentile was to keep both the written Law and the Oral Law (Talmud) for salvation.

[10]   David J. Williams; W. Ward Gasque, New Testament Editor, *New International Biblical Commentary: Acts* (Peabody, MA: Hendrickson Publishers, 1999), p. 261.

keep Torah even though Messianics assemble on the Sabbath and do Passover ceremonies, etc. Unfortunately the celebrating of Sabbath and Feasts are often only 'window dressing' to impress the *unbelieving* Jewish community that Messianic Jews are 'still Jewish.'[11] These Messianics allow themselves to meet on the Sabbath, etc., because they're 'under Grace' and so they can meet on Saturday too. But they don't see the Law as the holy commandments of God that everyone should observe.

This theology also allows them to maintain their relationship with the 'Law-free' Church. But this is extremely confusing to many Gentiles that come to them, who desire to learn about the Law. Why would any Gentile raised and nurtured in the Church want to keep the Law of Moses?

While the Church and much of the Messianic community steer away from the Law for believers, the Spirit of Jesus is leading many Gentile and Jewish believers all over the world into observing the Law of Moses. In these last days, the Holy Spirit is using the Law as a filter to see who will walk where Jesus is leading them, even if it goes against 1,900 years of staunch Church opposition. In this it's not unlike the controversy that surrounded Yeshua as He confronted some of the Synagogue teachings of His day (Mt. 15:1-20, etc.), or any new move of the Spirit of God since the days of Moses or Paul.

Resisting the Work of the Holy Spirit is an all too common phenomenon among God's people (Ps. 95:6-11; 2nd Cor. 1:23; 12:21; 13:2, 10). But those who realize that the oasis they're at is not the final one, will be open to the leading of the Holy Spirit to the next oasis, even if the path appears dangerous.

With the writings of E. P. Sanders, James Dunn and N. T. Wright, the way is also being cleared at the scholarship level. This will filter down through the ranks. Even though none of these men are advocating observance of the Law of Moses, within a generation, because of the new position concerning the Law (that it isn't legalism but *God's will* on how to live a righteous life)[12] many believers will read past the findings of these men and walk into Torah, to the glory of God. The proper interpretation of Acts 15:20-21 will help lead the way.

---

[11] Please see *Goodbye Messianic Judaism!* at http://www.seedofabraham.net/gmesjud.html for why the Messianic Community has disappointed many believers.

[12] McKnight, www.jesuscreed.org/?p=2689. Aug. 8th, 2007. The site sums up the position of Sanders, Dunn and Wright as agreeing on a number of things, one of which is that 'God gave the Torah' to the Jews to show them 'how to live before God in righteousness.'

Millions of believers love Jesus with all their heart but are enslaved to Church theology and traditions that nullify the Word of God and don't even realize it. Great is the power of Satan to deceive, even and especially the Bride of Christ (Dan. 7:25; Rev. 12:17).

Once the Gentiles in the days of Peter and Paul, came into the Kingdom of Messiah by the Grace of God, they was expected to learn and follow all the commandments of Moses that applied to them.[13] *The Lifting of the Veil* will reveal this, and the Bride will be able to see her Bridegroom clearer than ever before, walking in ways that are pleasing to Him.

---

[13]   Not all the commandments of Moses apply to everyone and some aren't done now. Some apply only to priests and aren't done today in the Jewish community because there is no Temple. Some commandments only apply to women and others only to farmers, etc. One must know the commandments in order to observe those that apply to them (e.g. Sabbath, Feast days and dietary laws, etc.).

THE FOUR RULES

The Church correctly understands Acts 15 to be a place where God declared that the Gentile didn't have to be circumcised and keep the Law of Moses for justification. But it points to the four rules of v. 20 and erroneously says that these are the only rules the Gentile has to be aware of[14] (other than love of God and neighbor).[15]

Christian interpretation explains the four rules as 'an expression of Christian charity' toward 'the weaker brother'[16] (the Jewish believer).[17] This is alleged because the Jewish believer hadn't realized yet that he was set free from the Law. But could all the Jewish Apostles not realize this? Didn't Jesus speak of the Law's demise in His 40 days with them *after* the Resurrection, when He taught them about the Kingdom (Acts 1:1-3)?

Scholars recognize that all the Jewish believers, including Peter and Paul, continued to 'live by the Jewish law.'[18] Were *all* the Jewish believers wrong? According to the Church they were. But so as not to offend Jewish sensibilities, the Gentiles were asked to walk in the four rules.[19] This way there could be 'a basis for fellowship' with the Jews since the Jews were 'in every city' (v. 21).[20]

---

[14] Marshall, *Acts*, p. 242: The Gentile was saved 'without accepting the obligations of the Jewish law'; p. 243: 'no more than these minimum requirements' (the four rules) 'should be imposed upon the Gentiles.'

[15] This contradicts the New Testament. Leaving aside moral rules (e.g. stealing and murder, etc., for the Church teaches that the 'moral law' passes into the New Testament), what makes something like homosexuality wrong (Lev. 18:22; 20:13; Rom. 1:27)? In other words, if a Greek man said that homosexuality for him was 'loving his neighbor as himself,' how could Paul say he was wrong? The Apostle could only turn to the Law. One point here is that the four rules cannot be the only rules for the Gentile.

[16] Marshall, *Acts*, p. 242.

[17] Charles F. Pfeiffer, Old Testament, Everett F. Harrison, New Testament, *The Wycliffe Bible Commentary* (Chicago: Moody Press, 1977), p. 1152.

[18] Marshall, *Acts*, p. 243. *WBC*, p. 1152 states, 'the Jewish Christians' *continued 'the practice of the Old Testament Law'*; p. 1150: 'It is apparent that *no Jewish believers gave up their Jewish practices* when they became Christians.' Williams, *Acts*, p. 256 states, the 'law *remained determinative for their lives.* They had no clear teaching from the Lord to the contrary'.

[19] Marshall, *Acts*, p. 253. 'Gentiles should abstain from certain things which were repulsive to Jews.'

[20] Pfeiffer, *WBC*, p. 1152. 'The decree was issued…as a basis for fellowship' so as not to 'offend the weaker brother'.

Bruce explains that the rules centered around 'table fellowship'[21] between Jew and Gentile because they think that three of the rules fall under the category of dietary regulations. In other words, they seem to have been given by James so that the Gentile believer would be able to eat and fellowship with the Jewish believer (who still kept the dietary laws). The four rules in Acts 15:20 are, to keep away from,

> 'the pollution of idols and of
>
> sexual immorality and of
>
> things strangled and of
>
> blood.'

Scholarship is unanimous that the first rule, 'pollution of idols' deals with eating meat sacrificed to an idol. The meat was either eaten at the sacrifice or sold at the marketplace.[22]

Things strangled was interpreted to mean the Gentile shouldn't eat meat from a strangled animal. It should be slaughtered properly, draining the blood. And blood, the last rule, was said to refer to blood which might be found in meat that wasn't properly drained, or cooked long enough. (The Law prohibits the eating of blood.) The Church, *interpreting* these rules said that, out of consideration for Jewish sensibilities, they wouldn't break them.[23]

The second rule, 'sexual immorality' (which the King James Version and the New Revised Standard Version call fornication), is generally seen as any kind of illicit sex such as adultery, homosexuality, pre-marital sex or incest, etc. Marshall translates it as unchastity, 'variously understood as

---

[21] Bruce, *The Book of the Acts*, p. 285. Bruce states that after the decision that Gentiles needn't be circumcised, the Apostles and Elders 'turned to consider terms on which table fellowship between Jewish and Gentile Christians might become acceptable.' Marshall, *Acts*, p. 243 states this is 'the question of how Jewish Christians, who continued to live by the Jewish law could have fellowship at table with Gentiles who did not observe the law'.

[22] Marshall, *Acts*, p. 253. Also, *WBC*, p. 1152: 'Often meat purchased in the market places had been sacrificed in pagan temples to heathen deities. The eating of such meat was offensive to sensitive Jewish consciences, for it smacked of taking part in the worship of the pagan deity.'

[23] Marshall, *Acts*, p. 253. 'The third element was meat which had been killed by strangling, a method of slaughter which meant that the blood remained in the meat, and the fourth item was blood itself.' 'Nevertheless, some kind of compromise was necessary in order not to offend the consciences of the strict Jewish Christians, and he proposed that the Gentiles be asked to refrain from food dedicated to idols, from unchastity, and from meat containing blood' (p. 243).

illicit sexual intercourse or as breaches of the Jewish marriage law (which forbade marriage between close relatives, Lev. 18:6-18).'[24]

The Wycliffe Bible Commentary is not certain as to what James, the half brother of Jesus, meant. It follows Marshall as to illicit intercourse but adds that it could point specifically to cult prostitution:

> 'fornication may refer either to immorality in general or to *religious prostitution* in pagan temples. *Such immorality was so common* among Gentiles that it merited special attention.'[25]

Without realizing it, *Wycliffe* hit upon the key to unlocking the proper interpretation of Acts 15:20 with *religious prostitution*. The first rule, meat sacrificed to idols, falls under sacrificial idolatry. The second rule should have been seen as part of sacrificial idolatry also, from just its word usage in the Bible, and it being rampant in the Gentile world. The second rule speaks of cult prostitution. With these two rules we have the major part of a pagan ceremony on sacrificial-sexual idolatry.

The fourth rule of *blood* is easily incorporated into this understanding and *things strangled* follows suite. Unfortunately it would be a long time before anyone presented the second rule as cult harlotry, with the four rules pertaining to sacrificial-sexual idolatry. Yet it should have been realized immediately.

As to where James got these four rules from and what they meant to the Gentile, R. J. Knowling writes that some think the rules come from the seven laws of Noah. But he correctly sees that even though,

> 'there are points of contact' 'it would seem that there are certainly four of the Precepts' (of Noah) 'to which *there is nothing corresponding* to the Decree.'[26]

Knowling goes on to relate that some say the rules were part of what was given to the 'stranger' dwelling in Israel (the ger toshav). But he understand that this 'would be far from satisfactory' as the Jewish Christians who kept all the Law (Acts 21:20) would be seen as superior, and only when the Gentile would keep the whole Law would he have 'full privilege of the Christian Church and name.'[27]

---

[24] Ibid.

[25] Pfeiffer, *WBC*, p. 1152.

[26] R. J. Knowling, D.D; W. Robertson Nicoll, M.A., LL.D., Editor, *The Expositor's Greek Testament, vol. two: The Acts of the Apostles* (Peabody, MA: Hendrickson Publishers, 2002), p. 335.

Knowling writes that others consider the rules coming from Lev. 17–18 but this too is awkward for him as it makes the 'written law' 'the source of the Jewish prohibitions.'[28] He states that attempts have been made to present the rules as 'binding upon proselytes in the wider sense, i.e. upon the uncircumcised' that existed in the days of the Apostles but 'of direct evidence' 'there is none.'[29] He writes,

> 'the difficulty is so great in supposing Paul and Barnabas could have submitted to the distinction drawn between the Jewish Christians and the Gentile Christians that it led to doubts as to the historical character of the decree.'

Doubting the event, some state the decree was 'formulated after Paul's departure.' 'But this view cannot be maintained' in light of Acts 16:4,

> 'where Paul is distinctly said to have given the decrees to the Churches to keep.'[30]

Knowling adds though, that W. M. Ramsay, following John Lightfoot,

> thought 'it impossible to suppose that St. Paul would have endorsed a decree which thus made mere points of ritual compulsory.'[31] He says that to enforce 'the Decree' in the Gentile churches would 'have been a cause of perplexity, a burden too heavy to bear, the source of a Christianity maimed by Jewish particularism.'[32]

All these views, from table fellowship to Noahide Law to thinking that Paul would never accept it, rest upon the assumption that the Law of Moses was done away with. Yet David Williams says,

> 'those who argue that Paul could not have endorsed the decrees as they appear in the accepted text' don't 'show any appreciation of the situation in the church of the first century or of Paul's own attitude toward the law. There is considerable evidence that the decrees as we have them were not only issued but observed in the Gentile churches for many years after their promulgation.'[33]

---

[27] Ibid.

[28] Ibid.

[29] Ibid., p. 336.

[30] Ibid.

[31] Ibid.

[32] Ibid., p. 337.

The Church contends that the Law of Moses doesn't apply to them. But when the four rules are properly interpreted, the Church's premise will be seen as false, and the 'problem' with Paul accepting them clears up.

The four rules are the filter, and the first rules, the pagan Gentile convert needed to be aware of. The rest of the 'rules' of Moses followed as they grew in Christ, and went to the synagogue on the Sabbath day to learn of 'Moses' (Acts 15:21). Why these four rules first? Because of Gentile propensity to add gods to the gods they already had, and to continue in their sacrificial-sexual idolatry (in honor of the gods and goddesses).

The four rules weren't made so the Gentile believer could fellowship with the Jewish believer, as important as that is, but so the Gentile could *retain his salvation*. The Gentile needed to know the boundaries of the Covenant he had entered into. He had to realize what was permissible for him and what wasn't.

The four rules of James are an inherent 'whole.' They are a package or a unit on sacrificial-sexual idolatry. This pagan practice had to stop immediately, if Gentile faith in Jesus was to be recognized as genuine.

The second rule is commonly translated as sexual immorality or fornication but there's overwhelming evidence to support the understanding that cult prostitution is specifically what James meant. Translating it as sexual immorality is very unfortunate because it not only hides the meaning of the second rule, but helps to distort the proper interpretation of what the Decree means.

Rule one forbids the Gentile from eating the meat of the pagan sacrifice (at the sacrifice). Rule two prohibits cult prostitution after the eating of the sacrifice. Rule three, strangled, speaks of a pagan sacrifice where the neck was strangled. And rule four forbids the drinking of the fresh raw blood from the pagan sacrifice which is the satanic counterpart to the drinking of Messiah's Blood from the Third Cup of Passover.[34] The four rules specifically deal with sacrificial-sexual idolatry, something every Gentile in the

---

[33] Williams, *Acts*, p. 268. He cites as further evidence for the observance of the Decree, 'Rev. 2:14, 22; Justin Martyr, *Dialogue* 34:8; Minucius Felix, *Octavius* 30:6; Eusebius, *Ecclesiastical History* 5.1.26; Tertullian, *Apology* 9:13; *Pseudo-Clementine Homilies* 7.4.2; 8:1, and 19—perhaps also Lucian, *On the Death of Peregrinus* 16, who says that Christians broke with Peregrinus because 'he was discovered...eating one of the things which are forbidden to them.'

[34] See *Passover* at http://www.seedofabraham.net/feasts2.html for the meaning of the Third Cup, and why Yeshua chose this one to represent His Blood.

ancient world fully understood, and many practiced.

These rules had nothing to do with table fellowship. They were designed to filter out gross idolatry. *That* would be very offensive to the God of Israel and cost the Gentile his life; his eternal life. One might think in terms of Christianity today; that anyone coming to Jesus wouldn't imagine they could worship Jesus and Zeus too, but Gentiles in the days of the Apostles believed they could have as many gods as they wanted.

Their culture and souls were permeated with that view. 'Adding Jesus' to their pantheon wouldn't be blasphemous as far as many of them were concerned. Of course this would be an abomination in God's eyes. This is why James gave the four rules. He wanted the Gentiles to know there were red lines that couldn't be crossed, even under Grace.

Once it's understood that the four rules dealt with cultic idolatry and weren't rules chosen for 'table fellowship' to appease the 'weaker' Jewish believer, the theological door opens that leads to the observance of the Law for the Gentile (Acts 15:21). The four rules become the filter that the Gentile had to pass through, in order for his salvation to be seen as authentic, and not some rules that he voluntarily observed in condescension to Jewish believers.[35] It'll become apparent that these four rules weren't the 'only ones' for the Gentile but the first of many that God gave to His people Israel, both Jewish and Gentile believer.

The Church takes the Wind of the Holy Spirit out of the sails of Acts 15:20 in presenting their interpretation of table fellowship. Even with sexual immorality (or fornication KJV) being addressed as cult prostitution, without all four being seen as a unit on cultic idolatry, one is able to assume that the four rules are just random selections on the part of James toward Jewish sensibilities that have little relevance for us today.[36]

---

[35]   It seems the height of ignorance and arrogance to present the new Gentile believers as the stronger in the faith of the two groups. All the Apostles had been walking for many years with the Holy Spirit, and as is attested (Acts 21:20; 22:12; 24:14; 25:8, etc.) kept the Law all their lives. But the Church says the Apostles were wrong. Could it be that the Church is wrong?

[36]   Stern, *JNTC*, p. 278. In commenting on a possible interpretation of the four rules, Stern says that if 'these food laws were given only as practical guides to avoid disruption of fellowship between believing Jews and Gentiles in the social context of the first century' then 'the issue is irrelevant, and there is no need for Gentile Christians to obey a command never intended as eternal.' He adds, 'Messianic Jews today are a small minority in the Body of Messiah and few if any of them take umbrage' at Gentile eating habits. But this logic is flawed, and not only because the rules have nothing to do with food laws. Contrary to what Stern writes, there are many believing Jews today who are

The Church hasn't been able to understand this 'unit of cultic idolatry' because of its perception and vilification of the Law of Moses. The Church sees anyone that keeps the Law as being in bondage. But teaching that the Law is a bondage makes the God who gave it to Israel a malicious Ogre. Did Yahveh set the Hebrews free from Egyptian slavery only to shackle them 'to the accursed Law'? No wonder many Christians think 'the God of the Old Testament' is very cruel and different from 'the loving Jesus.'

The Law, far from being a curse, is the basis for understanding not only Who the God of Israel is and what He has done and will do for Israel, but what He thinks is sin and what is pleasing to Him (Ex. 31:12-17; Lev. 23; Dt. 4:5-8; Rom. 3:20; 7:7, 12, 14; 1st Jn. 5:2-3, etc).[37] The one who is cursed is the one not observing it.[38] What that means today for many Christians who don't observe the Sabbath and who eat pig, etc., is that at these specific points, they are breaking God's Law and sinning. They're not following God's will for their lives in these areas. Whether they understand it as such or not, they are suffering the consequences of sin.

One doesn't have to understand (or even acknowledge) the laws of proper nutrition in order to be adversely effected by poor eating. Lack of knowledge or ignorance of a law is never a proper defense, whether in a court of law or before the Heavenly Tribunal.[39]

---

offended by Gentile eating habits (i.e. unclean meats). The only condition that has changed since James gave the ruling is that now there are more Gentile believers than Jewish believers. But as Paul said, 'if food causes my brother to stumble, I will never eat meat again so that I will not cause my brother to stumble' (1st Cor. 8:13). Stern's position also doesn't speak of the example that Gentile Christians are supposed to be toward Jews that don't believe (Rom. 11:13-14). What kind of an example is it to a Jew who doesn't know the Jewish Messiah yet, for a Gentile Christian to tell him that he can eat pork, when the Jew knows that *God forbids such things* (Lev. 11:7; Dt. 12:8)?

[37] Leland Ryken, James Wilhoit and Tremper Longman III, General Editors, *Dictionary of Biblical Imagery* (Leicester, England: InterVarsity Press, 1998), p. 489. Under 'Law' it states, 'The law expresses God's expectations for the moral and spiritual conduct of Israel, the guidelines God has given to Israel to enable them *to live life as he created it to be lived.*' They write, 'there is general agreement that it' (the Law) 'bears the connotations of guidance, teaching and instruction.'

[38] Dt. 27:26: "'Cursed is he who does not confirm the words of this Law by doing them.' And all the people shall say 'Amen!'"

[39] Hos. 4:6: 'My people are destroyed for lack of knowledge. Because you have rejected knowledge, I will also reject you from being My priest. Since you've forgotten the Law of your God, I will also forget your children.' (See Lev. 4:2; 5:17-19, the sacrifice for the sin of ignorance and Lk. 12:47-48. If some-

Today everyone has Bibles and the Holy Spirit to teach them His ways. The problem is that most have been blinded by the tradition of the Church which nullifies the Law of Moses. In this the Church is very Pharisaic. It presents a doctrine they say is from God, but in reality, it nullifies and makes void God's teaching in this vital area (Mt. 15:3, 7, 9; Rom. 3:31).

All God's commandments are for our blessing and wisdom, and reveal to us how much He loves us (Dt. 4:5-8; Mt. 22:35-40). When we fail to walk in any of them that pertain to us, whether intentionally or out of ignorance, we are the ones to suffer. That's why it's so important to properly understand what God says about the Law in the New Testament.

Acts 15:20 is the filter through which the ancient Gentile had to leave all his others gods and goddesses behind him. It's not the magic wand that makes the Law disappear, but quite the contrary, it precedes the verse that establishes the Law in the life of every Gentile believer (Acts 15:21).

Being 'free in Christ' is not a license to sin. True freedom is walking in His will. By understanding that all four rules center around sacrificial-sexual idolatry, Yakov (James in English but more properly Jacob), was giving the Gentiles what Yahveh gave Israel, when Israel was about to enter into the Promised Land. Yahveh sternly warned Israel about worshiping Him, and Him only. In Dt. 4–9 and 12–13, Yahveh admonished Israel concerning idolatry and its consequences. In the Ten Commandments Yahveh says,

> '*You must have no other gods except Me.* You must not make for yourself an idol or any likeness of what is in the Heavens above or on the Earth beneath or in the waters under the Earth. You must not worship them or serve them for I, Yahveh your God, am a jealous God, visiting the iniquity of the fathers on the sons to the third and the fourth generations of those who hate Me.' (Dt. 5:7-9)

There were to be no other gods for the Sons of Israel. They weren't to serve (worship or sacrifice to) them. The Gentiles, entering into the Promised One (Yeshua), were being warned in the very same way by the Holy Spirit, through the head of the Assembly, Yakov.

Just as God didn't expect Israel to learn all the Law in one day, so too with the Gentiles. But the Gentile was to be *immediately* aware of the most important things (not to practice cultic idolatry)[40] and then they

---

one breaks the Law in ignorance, it's still a sin and has its consequences.)

[40] Idolatry is not isolated to pagan altars. Burning incense to the gods, astrology and Tarot cards are also idolatrous and exclude 'believers' from the Kingdom

would learn the rest of the Law as they went to the synagogues, where Moses was taught every Sabbath in all the cities of the world (Acts 15:21). Just as a child adopted into a family gradually learns all the family rules and values, so too would the Gentile come to know all the Law of Moses that applied to him, as seen through the eyes of Jesus (and not the Rabbis or Pharisees, etc).

This understanding for Acts 15:20, that Yakov gave the Gentiles 'a package deal' on sacrificial-sexual idolatry, significantly hinges on the definition of the second rule. With this rule it either stands or falls.

The Greek word for the second rule is πορνεια (por-nay-ah).[41] It's usually translated in Acts 15:20 as 'sexual immorality' or 'fornication.' But if it means cult prostitution and not the vague term 'sexual immorality' or illicit sex, adultery, pre-marital sex or even common prostitution, the traditional Church teaching of 'table fellowship' disintegrates.

Once the four rules are seen as a conceptual unit on sacrificial-sexual idolatry, the idea that 'the Law has been done away with' collapses. The rules can't be seen as the 'only ones' but the first of many from the Law for the Gentile believer. The Law's proper place in the life of every Christian will then be re-established (Rom. 3:31), and Jesus will be glorified.

Acts 15:20 is the anointed admonition of Yakov to the Gentiles to break off with all pagan sacrificial rites. These four rules were the litmus test to the Gentile for their biblical salvation. Yakov then adds v. 21, *knowing from past experience,* that Gentiles were already learning the Law at the synagogues (which will be seen as both a term for the traditional synagogue, and a place like the 'church' at Antioch). These Gentiles were growing in the awareness of what kind of a lifestyle the God of Israel desired for them.

This understanding shatters the Church's doctrine of the Law of Moses. It'll no longer be able to use Acts 15 to theologically veil the eyes of believers from this vital aspect of their Messiah. Properly understood, the text reveals God's desire for all His people to walk in the Law, by the wisdom and power of the Spirit of Yeshua.

(Gal. 5:19-21), but James is specifically addressing pagan *sacrificial* rites.

[41] Unless otherwise stated, Greek words used will be identical for both the Textus Receptus and the United Bible Societies' Greek New Testament, Third Corrected Edition. The latter is the Greek text for the NRSV, NASB (and other Bibles). This means the KJV and the NRSV, etc., have the same Greek word here. When there's a difference it'll be noted.

THE FIRST RULE: SACRIFICIAL MEAT

Breaking up Acts 15:20 into the four rules, Yakov admonishes the Gentile believers to keep away from,

1. 'the pollution of idols
2. and of sexual immorality
3. and of the thing strangled[42]
4. and of blood.'[43]

The Greek phrase for the first rule (pollution of idols) is αλισγημάτων των ειδωλων (ah-lis-gay-mah-tone tone ae-doe-lone). Wesley Perschbacher says the word for pollution (ah-lis-gay-mah-tone) means 'pollution, defilement, Acts 15:20'.[44] Bauer says it means to 'make ceremonially impure' and that the plural, pollutions (which is written in v. 20), 'denotes separate acts.'[45] Literally it's 'the pollutions of idols.' Timothy Friberg agrees.[46] It's something that *defiles* and can be done *repeatedly*.

Perschbacher states that the word for idols (ae-doe-lone) means, 'a form, shape, figure; image or statue; hence, an idol, image of a god, Acts 7:41, et al.; meton.[47] a heathen god, 1st Cor. 8:4, 7'.[48] Friberg states it's 'an object resembling a person or animal and worshiped as a god idol, image'.[49] Bauer concurs, adding that it's a 'false god.'[50]

---

42 The literal Greek rendering of this phrase is, 'and of the strangled'. 'Thing' is not in the text but it can be translated as 'the thing(s) strangled.'

43 Robert K. Brown and Philip W. Comfort, Translators; J. D. Douglas, Editor; *The New Greek-English Interlinear New Testament* (Wheaton, IL: Tyndale House Publishers, 1990), p. 472. Taken from the English of the *Interlinear*.

44 Wesley J. Perschbacher, Editor, *The New Analytical Greek Lexicon* (Peabody, MA: Hendrickson Publications, 1990), p. 15.

45 Walter Bauer, augmented by William F. Arndt, F. W. Gingrich and Frederick Danker, *A Greek-English Lexicon of the New Testament and Other Early Christian Literature* (London: The University of Chicago Press, 1979), p. 37.

46 Timothy Friberg, Barbara Friberg and Neva Miller, *Analytical Lexicon of the Greek New Testament* (Grand Rapids, MI: Baker Books, 2000), p. 43.

47 J. M. Sinclair, General Consultant; Diana Treffry, Editorial Director, *Collins English Dictionary*, Fourth Edition (Glasgow, Scotland: HarperCollins Publishers, 1998), p. 980. The abbreviation 'meton.' means 'by metonymy'. It means 'the substitution of a word referring to an attribute for the thing that is meant'. An example of this is, 'the use of the crown to refer to a monarch.'

48 Perschbacher, *NAGL*, pp. 118-119.

49 Friberg, *ALGNT*, pp. 130-131.

The four rules are mentioned twice more in Acts after Yakov initially declares them in 15:20 (15:29; 21:25), and this further clarifies what he meant for the first rule. Luke uses a very specific Greek word for idols in the last two cites. It's ειδωλοθυτων (ae-doe-lo-thu-tone).[51]

Perschbacher says it's an animal 'sacrificed to an idol' 'the remains of victims sacrificed to idols, reserved for eating; Acts 15:29; 21:25.'[52] Friberg writes almost the same thing saying, it was 'the remains of victims sacrificed to an idol and reserved for eating' 'Acts 21:25'.[53] And David Williams also states it was an animal 'sacrificed to idols'.[54]

Bruce comments that the Gentiles were 'directed to avoid food which had idolatrous associations.'[55] This is vague, as no time frame is indicated when the person was eating the sacrificial meat (at the sacrifice or somewhere else). This will allow Bruce to think that the rules were part of the Noahide Laws and given for table fellowship, even though he believes that the Gentiles didn't have to follow the four rules.[56]

David Stern is also vague on when the meat was eaten. He says the rule meant to stay away from 'food sacrificed to false gods'.[57] Howard Marshall says the 'pollutions of idols' referred,

> 'to meat offered in sacrifice to idols and then eaten in a
> temple feast or sold in a shop.'[58]

Bauer states it's meat sacrificed to an idol and eaten at the pagan temple in honor of the god with the remains (if any) sold at the marketplace. He says,

> it's 'meat offered to an idol, an expression which' 'was
> possible only among Jews' 'and Christians.' (For what
> Gentile would call his god an idol?) 'It refers to sacrificial
> meat, part of which was burned on the altar, part was eat-

---

50 Bauer, *GELNT*, p. 221.

51 Brown, *NGEINT*, p. 472.

52 Perschbacher, *NAGL*, p. 118.

53 Friberg, *ALGNT*, p. 130.

54 Williams, *Acts*, p. 267.

55 Bruce, *The Book of the Acts*, p. 295.

56 Ibid., p. 285. Bruce states, 'the last thing that would have occurred to him' (Paul) 'would be to quote a decision of the Jerusalem church as binding on Gentile Christians.'

57 Stern, *JNTC*, p. 277.

58 Marshall, *Acts*, p. 253.

en at a solemn meal in the' (pagan) 'temple and part was sold in the market' 'for home use'[59] if there was anything leftover.

Ben Witherington III says it means 'something given, dedicated, even sacrificed to idols' '*in a temple.*'[60] He rightly states that the theme of the four rules is only seen when the first rule of Acts 15:20, the 'pollutions of idols' is understood to be a sacrifice '*eaten in the presence of the idol.*'[61] Witherington says that it's crucial for a proper interpretation of what James ruled, to see that it's 'more than just a meat' or a food issue, but points directly to sacrificial meat eaten in a pagan temple *at the time of the sacrifice.*

Why is he correct? Why can't it also be the meat sold in the market? Because the four rules center around *sacrificial*-sexual idolatry, and not the possible eating of the sacrificial meat 'leftovers' from the market. The Apostle Paul will address the issue of meat sold in the market. He will allow pagan sacrificial meat to be consumed by believers *when taken from the market* (or another's dinner table), as long as it wasn't made known to the buyer (or guest), that it was meat sacrificed to an idol. But he will not allow a believer to eat the sacrificial meat at the site of the sacrifice (1st Cor. 10:21, 25, 27-28), as that would make them part of the worship of an idol (i.e. idolaters). There wasn't any disagreement between Yakov and Paul. The Apostle to the Gentiles upheld Yakov's rules (Acts 16:4).

The primary, and only meaning, of Yakov's first rule centered around the eating of the sacrificial meat at the time of the sacrifice and not any excess meat that might be sold to, or be at, the marketplace. The eating of the meat at the temple of the god or goddess would certainly pollute and defile the Gentile Christian, as many times as he would do it.

This brings 'pollutions of idols' into much sharper focus. It wasn't just some meat that was somehow tainted with an idolatrous association, or excessive sacrificial meat sold in the market. It was animal meat sacrificed to the god at the pagan temple and eaten there at the time of the sacrifice by the Gentile in honor of his god or goddess. The first rule falls squarely under sacrificial idolatry and points to the theme for the other rules.

Assertions that the rule was given because eating meat sacrificed to pagan

---

[59]   Bauer, *GELNT*, p. 221.

[60]   Ben Witherington III, *The Acts of the Apostles: A Socio-Rhetorical Commentary* (Grand Rapids, MI: William B. Eerdmans Publishing Company, 1998), p. 461.

[61]   Ibid., pp. 462-463.

gods would offend 'Jewish sensitivities,' begs the question of whether or not Jesus would have been offended. What would He think if His Gentile followers sacrificed a bull to Zeus and ate the sacrificial meat in honor of Zeus? Yakov's main concern in issuing rule number one was that the Gentile believer wouldn't eat the meat of an idolatrous sacrifice at the time of the sacrifice. He didn't go into an area that Paul would later address.

No believer today would possibly think that it'd be alright with Jesus if they participated in a pagan sacrifice to Artemis, Diana or Baal and ate the meat thereof. But in Revelation this is exactly what some Gentile believers did in two of the assemblies (2:14, 20). Jesus Himself had to rebuke them for this *and* for cult prostitution. Paul too had to warn many of his Gentile Christians about these idolatrous practices and their consequences.

Yakov was not writing about meat sold in the marketplace that had been offered to idols. His first rule, to keep away from 'the pollutions of idols'[62] is directed against believing Gentiles participating in sacrificial idolatry. It specifically speaks of the eating of meat sacrificed to the idol at the time of the sacrifice.

---

[62] 'Pollutions' in the plural means that one was defiled by going to the pagan temples and eating of the sacrificial meat on many different occasions. The Gentile world was infested with many gods and goddesses, most of whom demanded animal sacrifice. Yakov was making reference to going to them on more than one occasion; and not the different stages of the sacrificial meat (at the sacrificial site and at the marketplace). As Bauer, *GELNT*, p. 37 brings out, the plural 'denotes separate acts' and as such, would entail the different times a pagan would go 'to worship,' each time polluting himself. See also Mt. 15:19.

THE SECOND RULE:
CULT PROSTITUTION

The second rule is cult prostitution. It was the 'high point' of the sacrificial event and what attracted many pagans: sexual idolatry. Satan knows how to lure Man away from God; just equate worship with sex. The symbolic meaning of the animal sacrifice was union with the pagan god or goddess which found 'fulfillment' through the temple priest or priestess (cult harlot).

The New Greek-English Interlinear New Testament uses the term 'sexual immorality' to translate the Greek word πορνεια (pornay'ah), the second rule of Yakov. The New Revised Standard Version translation (on the side of the page) offers the word 'fornication.'[63] Nothing unusual, as different Bibles use various words to convey the meaning of a Greek or Hebrew word. But what is sexual immorality? What is fornication? Are they interchangeable? And do either of them represent what Yakov meant?

In the New Testament and Old Testament (via the Septuagint), the Greek word pornay'ah has the basic meaning of prostitution, either cultic or common. The concept of selling one's self (prostitution), is then figuratively expanded in a variety of ways (e.g. to criticize Israel for making treaties with other nations while not relying upon Yahveh; or of a person who sells himself for monetary gain or worldly ambition; or for one who practices magic, selling himself to it instead of Yahveh, etc.). It will also be used as the derogatory epithet of an adulteress, when the nation of Israel, as Yahveh's unfaithful Wife, deserts Him for another god; and for a woman who has intercourse with a man other than her husband.

Yakov was a Jew and spoke Hebrew, not Greek, at the Jerusalem Council in Acts 15.[64] Therefore his thoughts and words would have lined up with

---

[63] Brown, *NGEINT* uses the New Revised Standard Version translation (on the side of each page) as an aid to the reader. Some other Bibles that translate the Greek word as 'fornication' include the KJV and the NASB.

[64] See David Bivin and Roy Blizzard's, *Understanding the Difficult Words of Jesus* (Shippensburg, Pennsylvania: Destiny Image Publishers, 2001). Biblical scholarship has had to take into account many recent (20th century) findings that have determined that Hebrew was the spoken language. For centuries many thought that it was Aramaic but even renowned Aramaic scholars like Matthew Black and Max Wilcox concede that 'Hebrew was' the 'living language' and the 'normal vehicle of expression' (pp. 12-13). This understanding rests on a number of findings in different fields. One is the discovery of the bar Kochba letters dated at 134–135 A.D. in which Hebrew is the language.

the Hebrew definitions of the word he used. The Greek word will confirm this. The Hebrew word Yakov spoke that day was זְנוּת (zih-nute).[65] After

_____

Also, much of the literature of Qumran is in Hebrew and not Aramaic (pp. 14, 20-21). The ratio of Hebrew to Aramaic is 'nine to one' and it's most likely that the Aramaic found, was written much earlier when Aramaic was popular (p. 29). There's also the witness of the early Church Father Papias, Bishop of Hierapolis in Turkey (150–170 A.D.) who wrote, 'Matthew put down the words of the Lord in the Hebrew language' (pp. 23-24).

The three Synoptic Gospels upon being translated into Hebrew from the Greek text (for Israelis today), contain many places where the Greek words form perfect Hebrew syntax and idiomatic expressions (pp. 53-65). This confirms Papias. Of the 215 ancient coins at the Israel Museum covering a period of roughly 450 years, from the fourth century B.C. until 135 A.D., '99 have Hebrew inscriptions' and 'only one has an Aramaic inscription' (p. 33; the other 115 coins are Roman).

Early Rabbinic literature was all written in Hebrew (p. 43). The New Testament declares Hebrew to be the language of Yeshua and the Apostles. Unfortunately, scholars and translators have said that what the New Testament 'meant' was Aramaic. That Aramaic was used is not to be denied. But just as an Englishman can say, 'Bon appetite,' without anyone suggesting that all Britain speaks French as their primary language, so too could Yeshua use Aramaic words and phrases (Mk. 5:41; 7:34; Jn. 1:42).

The New Testament speaks of the inscription over the head of Yeshua being in *Hebrew*, Latin and Greek (Jn. 19:20); and of Mary addressing Him in Hebrew (Jn. 20:16). Paul tells us that Yeshua spoke to him in Hebrew (Acts 26:14); and that Paul spoke to the crowd at the Temple in Hebrew (Acts 21:40; 22:2). There are other references specifically to the Hebrew language (Jn. 5:2; 19:13, 17; Rev. 9:11; 16:16).

Geoffrey W. Bromiley, General Editor; Everett F. Harrison, Roland K. Harrison and William Sanford LaSor, Associate Editors, *The International Standard Bible Encyclopedia*, vol. one (Grand Rapids, MI: William B. Eerdmans Publishing Company, 1979), p. 233 (IV. Aramaic and the NT.). With the finding of the Dead Sea Scrolls (1947f.), 'it became obvious that Hebrew was indeed' the language of Yeshua.

They also write, "In a compelling article on '*Hebrew in the Days of the Second Temple*' (JBL, 79 [1960], 32-47), J. M. Grintz has offered...evidence to show that Hebrew, rather than Aramaic, lay behind the Gospel of Matthew. A number of expressions in the Gospel can only be explained on the basis of Hebrew...like the use of 'Israel' (Aram. regularly uses 'Jews'), and 'gentiles' (Aram. has no word like 'goyim')" etc. The common language of Jesus and the Apostles was Hebrew, not Aramaic. Yakov spoke Hebrew at the Council of Acts 15.

[65] תורה נביאים כתובים והברית החדשה (*Torah, Prophets, Writings and The New Covenant*) (Jerusalem: The Bible Society of Israel, 1991), pp. 170-171, 180. The Greek pornay'ah of Acts 15:20 is translated into Hebrew as miz-nute מִזְנוּת ('from prostitution'). It's the same for Acts 21:25. When the letter is

examining it and some derivatives, along with places where it's used in the Bible, we'll turn to the Greek perspective on it. By examining the meaning of the word and surveying the practice of cult prostitution in Israel, and in the ancient world, it'll become clear as to what Yakov was dealing with, and why the second rule speaks of cult harlotry.

The Hebrew Noun: Zih-nute (Prostitution)

It's important to present what the lexicons (ancient foreign language dictionaries) say about Yakov's word, whether in Hebrew or in Greek. This way the true meaning for Acts 15:20 can be seen. Is it cult prostitution, sexual immorality or something else? In his classic Hebrew lexicon, Francis Brown states that zihnute means 'fornication.' He lists three categories and Scripture cites:

1. 'sexual' Hosea 4:11,

2. 'international' Ezekiel 23:27 and

3. 'religious' Numbers 14:33; Jeremiah 3:2, 9; 13:27; Ezk. 43:7, 9; Hosea 6:10.[66]

What does Brown mean by 'fornication'? The texts cited deal first and foremost with cult prostitution. A secondary figurative meaning comes when God denounces Judah for her whoring after Egypt (which entailed both figurative as well as literal cult prostitution).

Brown's 'sexual' for Hosea 4:11 speaks of harlotry. Immediately in the next verse (v. 12), this 'harlotry' is seen as cult harlotry. Yahveh says, 'My people consult their *wooden idol*' (with harlotry and harlot also appearing in the verse). The consulting of wooden idols, aligned with harlotry, can only mean cult prostitution. In Hos. 4:13 Yahveh says, 'They offer *sacrifices*' which again speaks of the harlotry as cult harlotry and not common harlotry. This is specifically confirmed in v. 14 as God states through the Prophet that they 'offer *sacrifices* with *temple* prostitutes'. And in v. 17 the Lord says, 'Ephraim is joined to *idols*. Let him alone!' Obviously this 'fornication' of Brown's that he describes as 'sexual' is

---

written in 15:29, it's ou-min hahz-nute וּמִן הַזְּנוּת ('and from [the] prostitution'). The Hebrew word Yakov spoke that day was זְנוּת zihnute (harlotry).

66 Dr. Francis Brown, Dr. S. R. Driver, Dr. Charles A. Briggs, based on the lexicon of Professor Wilhelm Gesenius; Edward Robinson, Translator and E. Rodiger, Editor, *The New Brown, Driver, Briggs, Gesenius Hebrew and English Lexicon* (Lafayette, IN: Associated Publishers and Authors, Inc., 1978), p. 276.

specifically cult prostitution and nothing else, for they are performing this harlotry in the midst of their idols with cult prostitutes.

The KJV translates the word in Hosea 4:11 as 'whoredom' and the NASB as 'harlotry' (continuing this translation in their other verses as well). Both the words whoredom and harlotry are synonyms for prostitution. The Hebrew word can mean common prostitution but the two Bibles would immensely improve their translations by using either 'cult whoredom' or 'cult harlotry' to distinguish it from common harlotry.

For 'international' Brown lists Ezk. 23:27. The KJV has 'your whoredom brought from the land of Egypt'. It's not hard to imagine what *kind* of 'whoredom' they picked up in Egypt. Only three verses later we read of cult harlotry:

> 'I will do these things unto thee because thou hast gone a whoring after the heathen and because thou art polluted with their *idols*.' (Ezk. 23:30 KJV)

This can only be cult prostitution that Ezekiel is referring to. The NASB confirms this when it translates the verse as,

> 'These things will be done to you because you have *played the harlot* with the nations because you have defiled yourself with their *idols*.' (Ezk. 23:30 NASB)

Hebrew parallelism is 'not a repetition of the same sound, but a repetition' 'of the same thought.'[67] It's 'the placing of two synonymous phrases or sentences side by side'.[68] The biblical quote in Ezekiel, 'played the harlot' parallels 'their idols.' The 'harlot' must be a cult harlot. Brown's 'international fornication' specifically means cult prostitution too.

Brown refers to Israel's unfaithfulness to Yahveh (Num. 14:33) as 'religious' fornication. Israel refused to believe that God would bring them into the Promised Land, choosing to believe the lie of the ten spies instead (Num. 13:25–14:4). There's no actual or literal prostitution here, cultic or common. The idea is that Israel chose not to believe Yahveh's word to them. This is a figurative meaning for prostitution (unbelief).

Brown also cites Jer. 3:9 and 13:27 which specifically deal with the cult prostitution of Judah and her idols. Israel as the Wife of Yahveh, is also metaphorically seen to be adulterous:

> 'Because of the lightness of her harlotry, she polluted the

---

67 Bivin, *Understanding the Difficult Words of Jesus*, p. 89.
68 Ibid.

land and committed *adultery with stones and trees.'*

'As for your adulteries and your lustful neighings, the
lewdness of your prostitution *on the hills* in the field, I
have seen your abominations. Woe to you, Oh Jerusalem!
How long will you remain unclean?!'

On 'the hills' is a reference to where Judeans would go to engage in cult
harlotry. The 'adultery with stones and trees' can't mean individual
Judeans committing common adultery, but is a reference to Judah with its
cult harlotry; the worship of idol gods using cult harlots.

Judah was in covenant with Yahveh, figuratively married to Him and Him
only (Is. 54:5; Jer. 3:14, etc.). Therefore their worship of *other* gods was
termed adultery. They copied the pagans around them, setting up stones
and trees (wooden images) to their gods and that's where they would sacrifice and commit cult harlotry, to their eternal shame. It's only in this
metaphorical sense that adultery will ever be used to describe Israel and
Judah's whoring after other gods. Israel was in covenant with Yahveh and
the closest earthly parallel to that was the marriage of a man to a woman.

In Brown's category on 'religious', 'figurative' is used (Num. 14:33) to
describe Israel's unfaithfulness or disloyalty to Yahveh. Alongside it was
cult prostitution in Jeremiah. He lists two other passages in Ezekiel (43:7,
9), but these also relate to idolatrous harlotry, both the specifics of cult
prostitution and the selling of one's soul to the idols of wood and stone.
What Brown classifies as 'religious' turns out to be Israel whoring after
other gods, another case of literal cult prostitution (except for Num.
14:33). And under Brown's cite for Hosea, the NASB reads,

'In the House of Israel I have seen a horrible thing!
Ephraim's harlotry is there, Israel has defiled itself!'
(Hosea 6:10)

One could try and make a case that this harlotry is common prostitution as
the verse doesn't give a specific form, one way or the other. But Hosea's
theme is not against common prostitution. It's against the northern kingdom of Israel *steeped* in sacrificial-sexual idolatry. The verse reflects cult
prostitution. This is noted by the *Theological Dictionary of the Old Testament* when it states that Israel,

'associated with the syncretistic cult at Gilgal and Beth-
aven; this cult was harlotry in a double sense, since *actual
sexual intercourse was part of the cult* (4:13f.) and its
idolatry meant *faithlessness* toward Yahweh (4:15).'[69]

TDOT's 'sexual intercourse' and 'idolatry' can only be cult prostitution.

The cite of Hosea 4:15 was also a part of the passage connected to Hosea 4:11 that Brown listed above:

> 'Though you, Israel, *play the harlot*, do not let Judah become guilty. Also do not go to Gilgal or go up to Bethaven and take the oath, "*As Yahveh lives!*"' (Hosea 4:15 see also 1st Kings 12:25-33; 13:1-10)

This speaks of the practice of cult harlotry 'in the Name of Yahveh' ('As Yahveh lives!'). In Rev. 2:14, the same perverse sin happens 'in the Name of Jesus.' *TDOT* goes on to state that in Hosea 9:1, 'Israel's harlotry' 'in forsaking Yahweh (sic) is associated with the *fertility cult*'.[70] These fertility cults with their 'sacred prostitutes' are primarily the 'cause' or *the theme of the prophets* in speaking out against both the faithlessness of the northern kingdom of Israel (2nd Kgs. 17:1-23) and the southern kingdom of Judah (Jer. 7:25; 35:15).

Commenting on Hos. 4:15, C. F. Keil writes that Yahveh was telling Judah not to become like her northern neighbor Israel or else she too would share in her guilt. The reference to Gilgal here 'is not the Gilgal in the valley of the Jordan' (where Joshua first led Israel into the Promised Land; Josh. 4:20; 5:9-10), but 'northern Gilgal upon the mountains'.[71] This Gilgal had once been home to 'a school of the prophets' in the days of Elijah and Elisha (2nd Kgs. 2:1; 4:38), but now was the 'seat of one form of idolatrous worship'.[72] Keil writes,

> 'Bethaven is not the place of that name mentioned in Josh. 7:2' 'but, as Amos 4:4 and 5:5 clearly show, a name which Hosea adopted from Amos 5:5 for Bethel' 'to show that Bethel, the house of God, had become Bethaven, a house of idols, through the setting up of the golden calf there' (1st Kgs. 12:29). 'Swearing in the name of Jehovah (sic) was commanded in the law' (Dt. 6:13; 10:20), 'but this oath was to have its roots in the fear of Jehovah'. 'Going to Gilgal to worship idols, and swearing by Jehovah cannot go together. The confession of Jehovah in the mouth of an idolater is hypocrisy'.[73]

---

[69] Botterweck, *TDOT*, vol. IIII, p. 102.

[70] Ibid.

[71] C. F. Keil and F. Delitzsch, *Commentary On The Old Testament*, vol. 10: *Minor Prophets* (Peabody, MA: Hendrickson Publishers, 2001), p. 55.

[72] Ibid.

[73] Ibid., pp. 55-56.

The northern kingdom of Israel was a land and a people defiled with cult prostitution, as Hosea spoke of in the verses just before 4:15. It's here we find the famous passage, 'My people are destroyed for lack of knowledge' (Hos. 4:6) because they had chosen to forget that the Law of their God prohibited cult harlotry. Hosea 4:12 says that the 'people consult their wooden idol' and have a 'spirit of harlotry.' Keil writes,

> this 'spirit of harlotry' 'includes both *carnal* and spiritual whoredom, since idolatry, especially the Asherah worship, was connected with *gross licentiousness*.'[74]

Brown's category of 'religion' that he put Hosea 4:15 in, can only be speaking of Israel walking in cult harlotry when Scripture presents them as playing the harlot. His three categories all dovetail into cult harlotry.

Benjamin Davidson in his lexicon says that zihnute means 'whoredom'.[75] He doesn't list any cites but says it can apply to *idolatry* also.

R. L. Harris in the *Theological Wordbook of the Old Testament* writes that zihnute means 'fornication.'[76] Unfortunately he doesn't list any cites either. Davidson and Harris will flush out their meaning of 'whoredom' and 'fornication' respectively, when they speak of the verb that zihnute comes from.

The Hebrew term that James used in Acts 15:20 for the second rule, zihnute, which Brown translates as 'fornication,' overwhelmingly means cult prostitution (from the cites he listed). It was also used once in a figurative sense as Israel's unfaithfulness to Yahveh (Num. 14:33), a theme in Israel's history that was not confined to that cite.

From its Hebrew context and usage, the word that Yakov used in Acts 15:20 conveys the idolatrous sin of cult prostitution. In Hosea the context revealed it's idolatrous meaning. This principle of context will apply to the four rules of James also. The placement of zihnute within the framework of three rules on sacrificial idolatry can only mean that James was speaking of cult prostitution and not common prostitution (nor adultery, incest or any other form of illicit sex).

The Hebrew verb will broaden the understanding of the word that James

---

[74] Ibid., p. 54.

[75] Davidson, *The Analytical Hebrew and Chaldee Lexicon* (Grand Rapids, MI: Zondervan Pub. House, 1979), p. 240.

[76] R. L. Harris, Editor; Gleason Archer, Jr. and Bruce Waltke, Associate Editors, *Theological Wordbook of the Old Testament*, vol. I (Chicago: Moody Press, 1980), p. 246.

used that day. It was understood by all the Jewish believers there as cult prostitution. This, despite the fact that other forms of unlawful sex can be associated with it's secondary meaning.

The Hebrew Verb: Zah-nah (To Prostitute)

Hebrew nouns generally come from the verbs. Zihnute is derived from the Hebrew verb זָנָה (zah-nah).[77] Francis Brown says it means,

> to 'commit fornication, be a harlot' 'be or act as a harlot' 'Gen. 38:24' 'Dt. 22:21' 'improper intercourse with foreign nations' 'intercourse with other *deities*, considered as harlotry, sometimes involving *actual prostitution*' 'Ex. 34:15-16; Dt. 31:16; Lev. 17:7' 'especially of Israel, Judah and Jerusalem' 'figuratively of a lewd woman, Ezk. 16:15' 'moral defection, Is. 1:21'.[78]

Brown's primary meaning is prostitution ('fornication' 'harlot') and sexual idolatry (cult harlotry; 'actual prostitution' 'especially Israel, Judah and Jerusalem'). To 'commit fornication' for Brown means prostitution, specifically cult prostitution as will be seen. (Brown's use of 'harlot' for Gen. 38:24, is actually a cult harlot, as *Judah and Tamar* will reveal.)

Dt. 22:21 speaks of a new bride being accused of not being a virgin. She's classified as a harlot because she acted like a harlot (in having sex outside of marriage). Her punishment for not being a virgin was death by stoning. God takes promiscuity very seriously and this would speak of either cult or common prostitution.

Brown's cite of Ex. 34:15-16 shows Yahveh speaking of actual cult prostitution. God says,

> 'otherwise you might make a covenant with the inhabitants of the land and they would *play the harlot with their gods* and *sacrifice* to their gods and someone might *invite you to eat of his sacrifice* and you might take some of his daughters for your sons and his daughters might play the harlot with their gods and cause your sons also to play the harlot with their gods.'

Obviously these harlots are cult harlots ('gods' 'eat of his sacrifice'). In *Israel and Baal Peor* Israel engages in cult prostitution before they even

---

[77] Davidson, *AHCL*, p. 240.

[78] Brown, *NBDBG*, p. 275.

reach the Promised Land. Brown's Deuteronomy passage (as well as his cite in Leviticus) is similar in nature:

> 'Yahveh said to Moses, "Behold! You are about to lie
> down with your fathers and this people will arise and play
> the harlot with the *strange gods* of the land, into the midst
> of which they are going, and will forsake Me and break
> My Covenant which I have made with them."' (Dt. 31:16)

These cites all deal with cult prostitution, not only on the physical, sexual level, but also on the spiritual or covenantal level. Brown goes on to relate how Israel, Judah and Jerusalem could be called a harlot in their going after other gods, which also centers on cult prostitution. He uses the figurative or derogatory description of a 'lewd woman' but this 'woman' is none other than Judah herself in her sin of sexual idolatry: cult prostitution. Ezk. 16:15 states,

> 'But you trusted in your beauty and played the harlot be-
> cause of your fame and you poured out your harlotries on
> every passer-by who might be willing.'

The historical understanding of why Judah was taken into captivity was because of their worship of other gods: sacrificial and sexual idolatry. Fertility cults and cult harlotry went hand in hand.

In Isaiah 1:21, the Prophet uses the verb zanah to describe Jerusalem and her ungodly behavior; from murder, rebellion and thievery to abandoning the cause of the widow and the orphan. All this falls under desertion of the Covenant with respect to Mosaic Law. Here zanah is used in a figurative sense, Jerusalem having sold herself to things of unrighteousness.

Francis Brown's 'fornication' is primarily cult prostitution. This is the verb base for Yakov's noun.

Benjamin Davidson states that zanah means, 'to commit whoredom, play the harlot; frequently also to commit *spiritual whoredom* or idolatry'.[79] Israel was committing spiritual whoredom in seeking other gods and physical whoredom by joining themselves to the cult prostitutes.

According to the *Theological Lexicon of the Old Testament* the basic meaning of zanah is 'to whore, commit harlotry (of the woman; Num. 25:1 of the man).'[80] It also says that originally it referred to 'unregulated,

---

[79] Davidson, *AHCL*, p. 240.

[80] Ernst Jenni and Claus Westermann, Authors; Mark E. Biddle, Translator, *Theological Lexicon of the Old Testament*, vol. 1 (Peabody, MA: Hendrickson Publishers, 1997), p. 389.

illicit sexual behavior between man and woman'.[81] This last phrase is an unfortunate definition as adultery can fall within their parameters. An adulteress can be called a harlot but only in a derogatory sense. Adultery is not prostitution. When the Scriptures speak of harlotry, the context determines if it's common or cult harlotry. The overwhelming majority of the references to prostitution bear out that it's cultic.

TLOT also says that a Hebrew who committed harlotry was 'an abomination in Israel' (Lev. 19:29) and that the word is used in a figurative sense 'to describe apostasy from Yahweh and conversion to other gods.'[82] It states, 'To whore away from Yahweh is synonymous with adultery'.[83] This is true but only on a spiritual level. Israel would be Yahveh's unfaithful Wife for many centuries. Literally though, as a nation, they were practicing cult prostitution. That doesn't mean that common prostitution was unheard of, but idolatry mixed with sex was the gross sin of the day. This is supported by what *TLOT* says concerning Jeremiah (and Hosea):

> 'The high hills, mountains, and green trees (2:20; 3:6) are named as the sites of the harlotry (as already in Hosea 4:13), apparently specific *Baalistic cultic* sites.'[84]

Speaking of Jeremiah, *TDOT* states that harlotry 'frequently uses the symbolism of *marriage*.' Referring to Canaanite cult practices it says, 'Upon every high hill and under every green tree you bowed down as a *harlot*' (Jer. 2:20).'[85] When they report that Jeremiah compares the apostasy to adultery (Jer. 3), they again relate that Israel 'participates in the syncretistic *cult*.'[86] In Jeremiah 5, the adultery of Israel is linked with *idols* which can only mean cult prostitution 'under every high hill' (Jer. 3:6-9, 13). This is Baal worship. Over and over again Israel is admonished and rebuked for sacrificial-sexual idolatry in her unfaithfulness as Yahveh's Wife. Israel was heavily involved in cult prostitution. She's only called an adulteress because of her spiritually figurative marriage to Yahweh.

The *Theological Wordbook of the Old Testament* says zanah means, to 'commit fornication, be a harlot, play the harlot.'[87] Again the linking of the English word 'fornication' with the meaning of the Hebrew word be-

---

[81] Ibid.

[82] Ibid.

[83] Ibid.

[84] Ibid.

[85] Botterweck, *TDOT*, vol. IIII, pp. 102-103.

[86] Ibid., p. 103.

[87] Harris, *TWOT*, vol. I, p. 246.

ing defined as harlotry and whoredom reveals how 'fornication' is used by some academics. *Nowhere* has it meant actual adultery between two human beings. Only in terms of its figurative usage does it relate to Israel as the adulteress.

As for 'biblical' fornication being translated as 'sexual immorality' in an English Bible (for Acts 15:20), one would be hard pressed to understand that it specifically means cult harlotry. This is the problem with placing 'sexual immorality' or 'illicit sex' into the slot for the second rule of Acts 15:20. The Hebrew word and its verb base speak of either a harlot (cult or common prostitute), or someone who acts like a harlot; either a person or a nation.

The *Theological Dictionary of the New Testament* states that the Hebraic meaning for prostitution can be used in figurative ways. Conceptually it can display the surrender of one's heart to something other than Yahveh. People or nations can sell themselves to something other than God:

> 'In a few instances זנה' (zanah, to commit prostitution) 'is used figuratively in a different sense for the commerce which woos other peoples and the political devices which ensnare them. Thus Isaiah 23:15-18 refers to Tyre' as 'the forgotten harlot' while Nahum 3:1-7 speaks of the whore Nineveh who 'enmeshed the peoples with her harlotry and the nations with her magical arts, v. 4.'[88] It can also be used as a warning 'against surrender to the alien secular wisdom of Greece.'[89]

The soul can be prostituted to many things other than the God of Israel. William Wilson summarizes zanah and says it means,

> 'to commit fornication, to play the whore or harlot; properly and chiefly spoken of a female, whether married or unmarried.' 'Rarely this verb is applied to men' but he does list Num. 25 as an example of such. 'Trop. of idolatry;[90] the relation existing between God and' Israel 'being everywhere shadowed forth by the prophets under the emblem of the conjugal union, see Hos. 1–2; Ezek. 16; 23, so

---

[88] Gerhard Kittel and Gerhard Friedrich, Editors; Geoffrey W. Bromiley, Translator and Editor, *Theological Dictionary of the New Testament*, vol. 6 (Grand Rapids, MI: Wm. B. Eerdmans Publishing Company, 1999), p. 587.

[89] Ibid., p. 586.

[90] Sinclair, CED, p. 1637. 'Trop.' is an abbreviation for trope which means, 'a word or expression used in a figurative sense.'

that in worshipping other gods' they 'are compared to a harlot and adulteress. It is also said of superstitions connected with idolatry, Lev. 20:6, as to consult wizards, etc.' 'to depart from the faith and trust due to God' 'whoredom, fornication' or 'any breach of fidelity towards God, e.g. of a murmuring and seditious people' 'metaph. for idol worship.'[91]

The verb, both from Hebrew and Greek, can be used figuratively for things that are not literally prostitution (e.g. consulting a witch, etc.). But all the literal definitions of zanah speak of harlotry, a harlotry that biblically is overwhelmingly cultic. This is how all the ancient peoples worshipped their gods and what enticed Israel.

One cannot scripturally say that adultery is equal to harlotry. But because the harlotry of Israel involved other gods, this made Israel both a cult harlot and an 'adulteress.' As *TDOT* states,

'Because Jerusalem' 'committed fornication even though Yahweh made a covenant with her, her fornication is equivalent to adultery.'[92]

Here fornication is both cult prostitution and used figuratively (in Israel's unfaithfulness to Yahveh). *TDOT* misses it though when they speak of figurative applying to most of the times it's mentioned, even though they have within their statement the truth of the matter:

'Most of the occurrences of zanah and its derivatives, however, have figurative meaning, referring to Israel's faithlessness toward Yahweh and *worship of other gods* (Lev. 17:7; 20:5f; Num. 14:33; 15:39; 25:1;' etc.).[93]

In saying that 'most' of the time zanah is 'figurative' they err. But when they write that it's 'worship of other gods' they don't seem to realize, or at least they don't speak of it, that pagan worship of other gods centered around cult prostitution. And yet they go on to say,

'The verb zanah designates primarily a sexual relationship outside of a formal union. Because the woman is subordinate to the man, she is always the subject of zanah'.[94]

---

[91] William Wilson, *Wilson's Old Testament Word Studies* (Peabody, MA: Hendrickson Publishers, no publishing date given), p. 480.

[92] Botterweck, *TDOT*, vol. IIII, p. 104.

[93] Ibid., p. 99.

[94] Ibid., p. 100.

The analysis of Ezekiel by *TDOT* as an 'example' of zanah contradicts their understanding as it overflows with literal cult prostitution, something that is much more specific than their definition. They state that chapters,

> '16 and 23 in particular use *sexual terminology* to depict
> the *apostasy* of the people.'

In these two chapters, zanah and some derivatives occur 42 times. In all the Tanach (Old Testament), the terms occur only 134 times.[95] In other words more than 31% of its use occurs in these two chapters of Ezekiel. The Prophet was decrying Israel for her cult prostitution. This is what sent Judah into Babylonian captivity.

TDOT says the sections deal with the sexual apostasy of the people but fail to plainly state that cult harlotry was at the core of it. Cult harlotry was rampant in Judah before the Babylonians destroyed Jerusalem and *TDOT*, in a roundabout way affirms this, saying Judah 'gave herself over to the worship of Canaanite gods' (Ezekiel 16:16).[96] For Ezk. 23 they say,

> 'Samaria bestowed her harlotries' 'on Assyria and her
> idols' 'as well as Egypt (vv. 7f.)'[97] with the apostasy in-
> volving the 'idolatry of Jerusalem.'

All these speak of cult prostitution. *TDOT* ends by saying that the idolatry was 'adultery with disgraceful idols'[98] another less than direct affirmation of Judah's cult prostitution.

Francis Brown's 'fornication' and 'harlotry' meant cult harlotry. *TDOT*'s presentation of zanah revealed a vast picture of cult prostitution. It's unfortunate that neither Brown nor *TDOT* were more specific in their choice of words (e.g. to use cult harlotry instead of harlotry or adultery).

Both the Hebrew noun and the verb reveal that Yakov's word primarily means cult harlotry. Cult harlotry, placed after Yakov's first rule on sacrificial meat at the pagan shrine, sets up a more than reasonable assumption that the next two rules would belong to the category of sacrificial-sexual idolatry also.

The Hebrew feminine participle will round out the meaning of the word and its usage in the Hebrew language. It'll also reveal that adultery and unchastity, etc., cannot possibly be what Yakov meant that day.

---

[95] Jenni, *TLOT*, vol. 1, p. 389.

[96] Botterweck, *TDOT*, vol. IIII, p. 103.

[97] Ibid.

[98] Ibid., p. 104.

The Hebrew Participle: Zo-nah (Prostitute)

The Hebrew word used to describe the person who commits zihnute (noun: fornication, common or cult harlotry), and who practices zanah (verb: to fornicate, to commit common or cult harlotry), is זוֹנָה (zo-nah). In English the meaning of zonah revolves around three synonymous words: harlot, whore and prostitute, and only these. Francis Brown describes the women as 'harlots'[99] and Davidson calls her a 'harlot.'[100] Context will determine if cult or common harlot is meant. Speaking of the verb, *TDOT* states zanah,

> 'is the usual word for the activity of a harlot or prostitute; she is even called a zonah. It is used of Tamar (Gen. 38), Rahab (Josh. 2:1; 6:17, 22, 25), the mother of Jephthah (Judges 11:1), etc.'[101]

Note well that there's no mention of an adulteress, just common or cult harlots. For their definition of the participle zonah they write,

> it 'designates a woman who has sexual intercourse with someone with whom she does not have a formal covenant relationship. Any sexual relationship of a woman outside the marriage bond or without a formal union is termed fornication. When there is a formal union and the sexual association is formed outside this union, zanah becomes synonymous with ni-eph, 'commit adultery' (ni-eph being thus a narrower term than zanah).'[102]

This is a very general definition (i.e. any sexual relationship outside of marriage), with no cites from Scripture to understand how they got to it. They say that when adultery is committed the adulteress can also be called a zonah (a whore or harlot), but they give the Hebrew term for adultery (ni-eph). This is the specific term for who she is, an adulteress (while harlot or zonah would be the derogatory term).

Immediately after this quote they present Ezekiel 16 and 23, which is specifically cult prostitution and Israel's unfaithfulness to Yahveh. In this, Israel was both cult harlot and adulteress. Her adultery was spiritual. Her

---

[99] Brown, *NBDBG*, p. 275. From the Hebrew; house of harlotry (Jer. 5:7), and women harlots (1st Kings 3:16).

[100] Davidson, *AHCL*, p. 240.

[101] Botterweck, *TDOT*, vol. IIII, p. 99. All three appear to be cult harlots.

[102] Ibid., p. 100.

harlotry was literal and idolatrous; cult prostitution with worship and sacrifice to other gods.

The biblical meaning of zonah speaks of a cult or common prostitute. Though an adulteress could be called a whore, it's only in a derogatory sense and not in the actual definition of her action.

The Hebrew word Yakov used that day (zihnute; prostitution) means cult prostitution. This is the word's primary use in the Old Testament (as seen from the lexicons, etc.), and very little is spoken about common harlotry. Coming immediately after the first rule on sacrificial idolatry, it reinforces cult prostitution as what Yakov meant. With this, *blood* and *things strangled* will easily enter the category of sacrificial idolatry to form Yakov's basic unit on sacrificial-sexual idolatry.

This takes the foundation out from under those who translate Yakov's word as 'sexual immorality' or any other kind of sexual intercourse outside of marriage. And not even common prostitution can be what Yakov meant as it doesn't fit into the category of sacrificial-sexual idolatry.

This shows how unwarranted the spurious argument is that the four rules were given because the 'weaker Jewish brethren' clung to the 'outdated' Law and didn't know any better. The Council of Acts 15 was called to decide on *what constituted salvation for the Gentile*. Acts 15:20 with its four rules underscored that concern. It has nothing to do with table fellowship.

As for the unfounded idea that the Jewish brethren were weaker or lacked the true understanding of the faith concerning the Law of Moses, is it really possible that all the Jewish Apostles somehow missed the Lord on His understanding of the Law for them, *so many years after the Resurrection* (Mt. 13:10-11; Acts 1:1-3)? Or is it possible that the Church is deceived with their paradigm of a 'Law-free Gospel'?

Judah and Tamar will further confirm that zonah is a definition for a cult harlot, even when it might seem to speak of a common harlot. *Israel and Baal Peor* will reveal Israel's carnal and lustful heart before they entered the Promised Land, and *Cult Prostitution in Ancient Israel* will make known how widespread a phenomenon cult prostitution was in both Judah and Israel for many centuries. These will present Yakov's Family history and why he gave the four rules on sacrificial-sexual idolatry to the Gentile believers...first.

JUDAH AND TAMAR

The story of Judah and Tamar (Gen. 38) shows the term zonah (female prostitute), is not only used for a cult prostitute but is conceptually the same as the specific Hebrew word for a cult prostitute קְדֵשָׁה (kih-day-shah). The text uses these two different words for Tamar, but at first it's impossible to know if Judah thought she was a common or a cult prostitute. This is because the text around zonah isn't descriptive enough to determine what kind of a harlot he was speaking of. Further on in the story though, his understanding is clearly brought out with the specific use of the term for a cult harlot.

Tamar had veiled herself and sat by the road. She made herself to look like a prostitute in order to deceive Judah. Not recognizing that it was his daughter-in-law, Judah saw her as a zonah, a prostitute (לְזוֹנָה lih-zonah, to be a prostitute; Gen. 38:15). What kind of a prostitute (common or cultic), can't be determined from just this verse.

After three months, Tamar is found to be pregnant. She's charged with being a harlot and being with child by whoredom (KJV from zanah, v. 24 twice). Did it mean that Judah now thought that Tamar was a cult prostitute? From this verse also it can't be determined because the context doesn't describe it or reveal what Judah was thinking. There are three possibilities: one, Judah thought she became pregnant by common prostitution. Two, that she had 'slept around' and Judah was using the word in a derogatory sense for her whoring heart, but she hadn't committed literal prostitution as she didn't receive payment for it. Or three, he thought that Tamar became pregnant by cult prostitution.

The only way to tell what kind of prostitute Judah thought he had encountered that day is from vv. 21-22. When Judah's friend tries to locate the harlot, to bring her the wages, he can't find her. But he's told by the men of the area that there wasn't any *cult* prostitute at the place where Judah had been with Tamar.

Three times the specific word for a female cult harlot (kih-day-shah) is used (v. 21 twice; v. 22 once). Davidson explains that the kih-day-shah is a 'prostitute' 'devoted to prostitution *in honor of idols.*'[103] The NASB calls her a '*temple* prostitute' and the NIV a '*shrine* prostitute.

The use of the specific Hebrew word for a female cult prostitute (kih-day-shah), speaking of the same person that is also described as a harlot in

---

[103] Davidson, *AHCL*, p. 654.

Gen. 38:15 (and v. 24) reveals that zonah (harlot) is *interchangeable* with the specific Hebrew word for a female *cult* harlot. When Judah spoke of a harlot in vv. 15, 24 we know he meant a cult harlot and not a common one. Davidson, the NASB and the NIV confirm this from vv. 21-22. Brown's 'harlot' of Gen. 38:24 (p. 29 above), proves to be a cult harlot.

The Illustrated Bible Dictionary also affirms that zanah refers to cult prostitution and is interchangeable with it. They write,

> 'Tamar is described as both a harlot (Gen. 38:15) and a cult prostitute (Gen. 38:21, RSV mg.). The two Heb. words are used as parallels in Ho. 4:14.'[104]

The use of zonah for a cult prostitute is almost 4,000 years old. In other words, it was ancient in the days of James 2,000 years ago. He could speak of 'prostitution' and *everyone* would know he meant cult prostitution. The use of the Greek word for harlotry will also equate harlot with the cult harlot right through to the book of Revelation.

The word for a prostitute (zonah) is conceptually the same as the specific term for a female cult prostitute. *TWOT* also confirms this when it writes about *temple* prostitutes saying, 'the usage may be extended to refer to prostitution in general.'[105]

The primary emphasis in both Scripture and in authoritative definitions of the Hebrew words for prostitution and prostitute reveal its overwhelming cultic use. With Tamar there's no question that what the KJV translates as 'harlot' means cult harlot. When a Jew like Yakov spoke of prostitution, having begun with his first rule on *sacrificial* idolatry, there was no need for him to elaborate about what kind of prostitution he meant. Everyone knew he meant cult prostitution. The theme of Acts 15 is Gentile salvation. As wicked as going to a common prostitute is, it doesn't mean loss of salvation, but using a temple prostitute would, as *Jesus and Divorce* will reveal.

The four rules of Acts 15:20 are a conceptual unit. Yakov was warning the new Gentile believers that sacrificial-sexual idolatry would endanger their salvation. To assign the second rule to something other than cult prostitution cannot be supported by the usage of the word in the Old Testament. *Israel and Baal Peor* will further support this.

---

[104] J. D. Douglas, M.A., B.D., S.T.M., Ph.D., Organizing Editor, *The Illustrated Bible Dictionary*, Part 3 (Leicester, England: Inter-Varsity Press, 1998), p. 1289.

[105] Harris, *TWOT*, vol. II, p. 788.

ISRAEL AND BAAL PEOR

Even before the Hebrew people entered the Land that Yahveh promised to them, Israel disgraced herself in cult prostitution. *Webster's* assigns the 'honor' of orgies to the Greeks or Romans.[106] But the Assyrians and Babylonians who preceded them[107] had orgies as part of their idolatrous worship, as did the Moabites. The story of Israel at Baal Peor is a story of idolatrous lust unchecked:

> 'While Israel remained at Shittim the people began to *play the harlot* with the daughters of Moab. For they invited the people *to the sacrifices of their gods* and the people *ate* and bowed down to their gods. So Israel *joined themselves* to Baal of Peor and Yahveh was angry with Israel. Yahveh said to Moses,'

> 'Take all the leaders of the people and execute them in broad daylight before Yahveh so that the fierce anger of Yahveh may turn away from Israel.'

> 'So Moses said to the judges of Israel, 'Each of you slay his men who have joined themselves to Baal of Peor.' Then behold, one of the Sons of Israel came and brought to his relatives a Midianite woman in the sight of Moses and in the sight of all the Congregation of the Sons of Israel while they were weeping at the doorway of the Tent of Meeting.'

> 'When Phineas the son of Eleazar, the son of Aaron the Priest saw it, he arose from the midst of the Congregation and took a spear in his hand and he went after the man of Israel into the tent and pierced both of them through, the man of Israel and the woman, through the body. So the plague on the Sons of Israel was checked. Those who died by the plague were 24,000. Then Yahveh spoke to Moses saying,'

> 'Phineas the son of Eleazar, the son of Aaron the Priest has turned away My wrath from the Sons of Israel in that he was jealous with My jealousy among them so that I did

---

[106] Henry Bosley Woolf, Editor in Chief, *Webster's New Collegiate Dictionary* (Springfield, MA: G. & C. Merriam Co., 1980), p. 802.

[107] Alexander Hislop, *The Two Babylons*, 2nd American edition (Neptune, NJ: Loizeaux Brothers, 1959), pp. 22, 48-49, 71-80.

not destroy the Sons of Israel in My jealousy. Therefore say,'

'Behold! I give him My Covenant of Peace and it shall be for him and his descendants after him a covenant of a perpetual priesthood because he was jealous for his God and made atonement for the Sons of Israel.' (Num. 25:1-13)

In commenting on what Pinhas (Phineas) did, *The Chumash* states:

'Pinhas...saved them from calamity' and 'put an end to the devastating plague that had taken 24,000 lives in retribution for the orgy[108] *of immorality* with the Moabite and Midianite women.'[109] The Hebrews had fallen into 'debauchery[110] and *idolatry*.'[111]

The worship of Baal Peor entailed this, as did the worship of many other pagan gods. The sacrifices the Sons of Israel offered to Baal Peor *bonded* them to the god. They ate the sacrificial meat (and possibly drank the sacrificial blood although no mention is made of this), bowed down and worshiped this god, engaged in sexual orgies with the women and so *joined* themselves to Baal Peor (Num. 25:3). Yahveh was so angry that He was ready to destroy the whole Congregation of Israel, so great was the offense (Num. 25:11). This is biblical fornication and expressly what Yakov didn't want believing Gentiles doing in their pagan temples.[112]

The name Baal Peor means that it was the god Baal, associated with the top of a mountain called Peor. The god was also known as just Baal (Lord) or Molech (King) and originally signified Nimrod deified, the first King of Babylon.[113] To the Greeks Baal was known as Bacchus. The Philistines knew Baal as Dagon. He had many other names in different

---

[108] Woolf, *WNCD*, p. 802. Orgy: '1: secret ceremonial rites held in honor of an ancient Greek or Roman deity and usually characterized by ecstatic singing and dancing 2a: drunken revelry b: an excessive, sexual indulgence (as a wild party)'.

[109] Rabbi Nosson Scherman & Rabbi Meir Zlotowitz; General Editors, *The Chumash*, 2nd edition: 2nd impression (Brooklyn, NY: Mesorah Publications, Ltd., Feb. 1994), p. 876.

[110] Woolf, *WNCD*, p. 289. Debauchery: '1a: an extreme indulgence in sensuality, b: orgies, 2a: archaic: seduction from virtue or duty.'

[111] Scherman, *The Chumash*, p. 876.

[112] This kind of pagan 'worship' was going on all over the world in Yakov's day. Biblical fornication is sexual idolatry. Paul had to deal with this same issue in Corinth (1st Cor. 6:15-19; 10:21).

[113] Hislop, *The Two Babylons*, pp. 230-231.

countries and different times but his licentious worship rites remained basically the same:

> 'The sun, as the great source of light and heat, was worshiped under the name of Baal.'[114] (This is one of the reasons why the mountains and the high places were used for worship.) '*Infants* were the most acceptable offerings at his altar' 'with the priest of Baal *eating of the human sacrifice.*'[115]

It's not mentioned that Israel sacrificed their infants in Num. 25 but all too often the Bible confirms such monstrous events.[116] If it happened at Baal Peor, it would only be an additional reason for Yahveh's anger against Israel.

In Num. 25:1, the Hebrew verb זָנָה (zanah) is seen. It means 'to commit whoredom, play the harlot; *frequently*' of 'idolatry.'[117] Israel was certainly playing the harlot. All idolatry is sin but not all idolatry involves cult prostitution. Zanah in the context of idolatry *always* speaks of apostasy and not the vague term 'sexual immorality.' King David in his adultery with Bathsheba didn't apostatize, as great as his sin was. He slept with another man's wife. He committed adultery, not cult prostitution. (In the section *Jesus and Divorce* it'll be apostasy in the form of cult prostitution that constitutes a biblical divorce between two believers, not adultery.)

One could say that cult prostitution falls under the general term 'sexual immorality.' But how would anyone know that cult prostitution was what James meant if the English translation of the second rule is 'sexual immorality'? It's not possible.

Unfortunately even with translations that use fornication, the problem arises of it being defined by the popular misunderstanding instead of the 'biblical definition.' The difference amounts to placing what Israel did under a heading that is very general ('sexual immorality' as most define fornication today), as opposed to the specific understanding of the spirit and practice in which they engaged: sexual idolatry. This revealed their faithless and perverse hearts. This is apostasy and Israel will be guilty of it many times in her history.

---

[114] Ibid., p. 226.

[115] Ibid., pp. 231-232.

[116] Dt. 12:31; 2nd Kings 16:3; 17:17; 21:6, 10; 2nd Chron. 28:3; 33:6; Jer. 7:31; Ezk. 20:31; 23:37, etc.

[117] Davidson, *AHCL*, p. 240.

In Num. 25:3 the Hebrew verb that states that Israel joined herself to Baal Peor is צָמַד (tzah-mahd). It means 'to be bound to, joined to.'[118] The noun means a 'pair, couple, yoke (of oxen, mules, horsemen).'[119] The verb also means, 'specif. of (a) *girl with two lovers*', to 'be attached, *attach oneself*, specif. be (religiously) devoted.'[120] The Sons of Israel, eating of the idolatrous sacrifice, solemnized a spiritual marriage to Baal Peor. The orgies consummated it. This wasn't common harlotry.

Here was Israel, Yahveh's Bride, with another lover, Baal Peor, while the Groom was still in the House! The Shekinah Glory Cloud, the visible expression of Yahveh was continually over the Holy of Holies in the Wilderness (except when it led them to another camp; Ex. 40:34-38; Num. 10:33-34). Keil says,

> 'the people began to commit whoredom with the daughters of Moab: they accepted the invitations of the latter to a sacrificial festival of their gods, took part in their sacrificial meals, and even worshipped the gods of the Moabites, and indulged in the licentious worship of Baal-Peor'. 'זָנָה' (zanah) 'construed with אֶל' ('el' as we find in Num. 25:1) 'as in Ezek. 16:28, signifies to incline to a person, to attach one's self to him, so as to commit fornication. The word applies to carnal and spiritual whoredom.'

> 'The lust of the flesh induced the Israelites to approach the daughters of Moab and form acquaintances and friendships with them, in consequence of which they were invited by them 'to the slain-offerings of their gods,' i.e. to the sacrificial festivals and sacrificial meals, in connection with which they also 'adored their gods,' i.e. took part in the idolatrous worship connected with the sacrificial festival.'

> 'These sacrificial meals were celebrated in honor of the Moabite god Baal-Peor, so that the Israelites joined themselves to him. 'צָמַד' (tzah-mahd) 'in the Niphal, to bind one's self to a person. Baal-Peor is the Baal of Peor, who was worshipped in the city of Beth-Peor (Dt. 3:29; 4:46; see at chapter 23:28), a Moabite Priapus,[121] in honor of

---

[118] Ibid., p. 646.

[119] Ibid.

[120] Brown, *NBDBG*, p. 855.

42

whom women and virgins prostituted themselves. As the god of war, he was called Chemosh'.[122]

Those 24,000 Israelis and Baal Peor were walking hand in hand. And yet if you would have asked any one of them if they still believed in Yahveh, they would have said 'Of course!' But there can be no 'pairing up' of Yahveh's people with another god. For in doing this those Israelis weren't worshiping the One True God and Him only (see Jer. 16:10f.). This was biblical fornication or cult harlotry and was dealt with by Yahveh, Pinhas rescuing the rest of Israel from certain destruction. Would God's attitude toward other gods and cult harlotry change when the Gentiles came to believe in His Son? Of course not (Ex. 22:20; 34:12-16; Mal. 3:6; Heb. 13:8; Rev. 18:4-5).

The Hebrew verb in Num. 25:11 that Yahveh used to describe what He was going to do to Israel if Pinhas had not intervened is כָּלָה (kahl-lah) in the Piel form. It means 'to complete, finish, end' 'to waste, ruin, destroy' and 'to cause to vanish.'[123] Yahveh was angry with those Hebrews because of their whoring hearts. Israel was God's Wife and the Lord was ready to annihilate the whole Camp. Everyone was effected by their sin.

Unger's Bible Dictionary states,

> 'the worship of Baal-Peor was a *temporary apostasy* brought about by the temptations to licentious indulgence[124] offered by the rites of that deity.'[125]

It's not without dry wit that they write of a *temporary apostasy* because all who took part in it were killed. Note well the seductiveness of pagan worship with its appeal to the lust of the flesh (the orgies). The Moabites were not unusual in their 'sexual indulgence' but representative of pagan worship *all over the world*. Yahveh abhorred it for His people Israel and so would Yakov in Acts 15:20. Israel was only a tiny island in an ocean of cult prostitution and sadly enough, they all too often drank from the same filthy waters as the peoples around them.

A number of times in the Old Testament God calls Israel adulterous or a

---

[121] Sinclair, *CED*, p. 1226. Priapus: '(in classical antiquity) the god of the male procreative power and of gardens and vineyards.'

[122] Keil, *The Pentateuch*, pp. 790-791.

[123] Davidson, *AHCL*, p. 379.

[124] Woolf, *WNCD*, p. 657. Licentious: '1: lacking legal or moral restraints; esp: disregarding sexual restraints.'

[125] Merrill F. Unger, *Unger's Bible Dictionary* (Chicago: Moody Press, 25th printing, 1976), p. 514.

prostitute (harlot)[126] because Israel went after other gods. This related to their idolatry, not their personal marriage relationships (although that was effected too). In other words adultery is used of Israel as a people married to Yahveh and so when unfaithful to Him, He can call them adulterous. But their adultery literally consisted in cult harlotry. Adultery isn't used of an individual who practices cult or even common prostitution.

The *Dictionary of Biblical Imagery* explains there were times that the word 'harlot' or 'harlotry' could be used for a wicked person or people, but that *cult* harlotry was *the chief meaning* of it:

> "Individuals and the Israelite nation as a whole are ac-
> cused of harlotry when they seek security from mediums
> and spiritists (Lev. 20:6), military might (Nahum 3:1-4),
> political alliances (Ezek. 23:5-6) or commerce (Is. 23:17).
> *Because they value material gain too highly*, Israelites
> who accept bribes and abandon God's plan of social jus-
> tice are also considered harlots (Is. 1:21-23). *Above all
> these however, idolatry* stands as the most common cause
> for the epithet 'prostitute.'"[127]

There are many times in the history of God's people, in the Land that He gave to them, where Yahveh rebuked Israel through His servants the Prophets. From just after Yehoshua's (Joshua's) death, till the captivity in Babylon, Scripture abounds with Yahveh grieving and being angry with His people for their cult prostitution. He wasn't speaking of individuals committing adultery but the nation committing apostasy through sacrifi-cial, sexual and spiritual idolatry.[128] Sometimes it would include worship of Yahveh whereas at other times it wouldn't. But at all times it was very offensive to God, and those in Israel who were righteous (1st Kgs. 19:18).

Many sons of Israel were involved in cult prostitution at Baal Peor. They had sexual orgies and bound themselves to another god, having eaten of the sacrifices (Num. 25:2). This directly attacked and severed the covenant marriage relationship they had with Yahveh. To eat the meat of the sacri-fice was to be *one with the god* to whom it was sacrificed to. This is the first rule of Acts 15:20, 'to keep away from the pollutions of idols' (i.e. the eating of sacrificial meat offered to the idol at the time of the sacri-

---

126 Jer. 2:20; 3:1; Ezek. 16:1-31, etc.

127 Ryken, *DBI*, p. 677.

128 In Malachi 2:10-16, Yahveh remonstrates Judah for not only cult prostitution but adultery as well. This doesn't mean they're one and the same but that some were committing one while others were committing both.

fice). The eating of the sacrificial meat went hand in hand with the idolatrous ceremony of cult prostitution. That's what an orgy is, a feast of flesh, both animal and human. The sexual orgy crudely symbolized union with Baal Peor, another name for Satan.

In the Mosaic sacrificial system the eating of the sacrifice was only done by the common Israeli upon entry into the Covenant (Ex. 12:3-10); for the official ratification of the Covenant by the Elders (Ex. 24:4-11); and for the Sacrifice of Shalom (peace, communion, union). It was at the Shalom Sacrifice that the Israeli, his family and friends, sat down with the priest and ate some of the meat of the sacrifice (Lev. 3:1-17).[129] This spoke of *oneness* with Yahveh and of God being pleased with them. In pagan rituals the symbolism was the same, just counterfeit.

In Acts 15:20, James was concerned with the Gentiles continuing to practice sacrificial-sexual idolatry. They, like Israel before them, could think that worship of Jesus and Diana was compatible and acceptable, but Yahveh wouldn't share that view with them. The danger that Yakov envisioned for the new Gentile believers was that they might not think it wrong to maintain their previous gods, along with Jesus. With its appeal to the lust of the flesh, it would destroy the Gentile believer's relationship with Jesus. This is why James gave the second rule: no cult prostitution.

James was emphasizing the spiritual relationship the Gentile had with Yeshua and what would break it. Those who insist the word should be translated as sexual immorality or unchastity, etc., do a grave injustice to the Word of God and a gross disservice to English readers of the Bible. Why place a word or term that actually has no specific meaning (sexual immorality), when the Hebrew word has such a specific and powerful primary meaning?

By using the general term 'sexual immorality' instead of cult prostitution, many classify this most abhorrent sin of sexual apostasy with other non-apostasy related (sexual) sins like premarital sex or adultery, etc. This of course has tremendous theological ramifications for Acts 15:20 as well as other implications (i.e. the understanding of marriage and what constitutes a biblical divorce when Jesus says a biblical divorce cannot take place 'except for fornication' [Mt. 5:32], which the Church has traditionally interpreted as adultery).

---

[129] Unger, *UBD*, pp. 948-949. 'The sacrificial feast' enjoyed by both priest and offerer alike symbolized God and Man at table. In the Middle East, no stronger picture of fellowship, union, peace, security and of being in the 'Kingdom of God' on Earth could be displayed.

From the Hebrew word meanings, from Gen. 38, and now from Israel's apostasy at Baal Peor, the use of Yakov's word has consistently meant cult prostitution. With the first rule also speaking of sacrificial idolatry, two strong points have been established for the concept that Yakov's rules speak of sacrificial-sexual idolatry. The other two rules are part of it also. The four rules are various aspects of sacrificial-sexual idolatry.

Israel's history is filled with the sacrificial-sexual worship of other gods. Cult prostitution was devastating to ancient Israel and one more reason why Yakov gave these four rules to the Gentiles...first.

CULT PROSTITUTION
IN ANCIENT ISRAEL

A brief survey of cult prostitution and how it effected Israel will reveal what Yakov, and every Jew, knew in relation to their own history. It'll again confirm why Yakov's second rule should be understood the way the Hebrew defines zanah (and also the way the Greek will define pornay'ah) as cult prostitution, and not the vague term 'sexual immorality' which is a very general term and totally distorts Yakov's ruling.

Throughout the Tanach there are many references to cult prostitution and its sway upon Israel. Yahveh forbids His people from practicing it or becoming cult prostitutes. *TDNT* states,

> 'The Deuteronomic Law unconditionally forbids cultic prostitution. No girl is to be a temple devotee, no man a קָדֵשׁ' (kah-daish, the specific term for a male temple prostitute) '23:17. Profits derived' (from cult harlotry) 'are not to be used on behalf of'[130] God's Temple.

God wasn't interested in tithes or anything else 'earned' from a cult prostitute. The term 'dog' was a loathsome epithet for the male cult prostitute but this didn't stop some in Israel from becoming one. *The Illustrated Bible Dictionary* states,

> 'In Dt. 23:17-18, the contemptuous phrase, 'dog' evidently refers to a male cult prostitute. In Rehoboam's time' (935–919 B.C.) 'the presence of such male prostitutes became widespread (1st Kings 14:24). Asa, Jehoshaphat and Josiah attempted to root out this abomination (1st Kings 15:12; 22:46; 2nd Kings 23:7).'[131]

The reason why these men were called 'dogs' is because of the way they performed their sexual idolatry on other men. Keil writes that the ka-daish 'received his name for the dog-like manner in which the male' 'debased himself'.[132]

Here is cult prostitution as homosexual idolatry. The term 'dogs', used as late as the last chapter of Revelation (22:15), reveals the practice was still observed as 'worship' in the final days of the Apostle John (95 A.D.).

---

[130] Kittel, *TDNT*, vol. VI, p. 586.

[131] Douglas, *IBD*, Part 3, p. 1289.

[132] Keil, *The Pentateuch*, p. 949.

Both male and female cult prostitution was widespread in Canaan before the Hebrews got there. Yahveh prohibited Israel from engaging in idolatry because of its effect upon their covenant relationship and the souls of His people. *UBD* states,

> 'Israel was in covenant with Yahveh, married to God, pledging herself to Him and Him only (Ex. 19:3; 20:2, etc.). *Idolatry* was 'a political crime of the gravest nature, *high treason against the King.* It was a transgression of the covenant (Dt. 17:2-3), *the evil*' (emphasis theirs) 'pre-eminently in the eyes of Jehovah (1st Kings 21:25). Idolatry was a great wrong because of the licentious rites associated with it (Rom. 1:26-32), thus debauching[133] the morals of its adherents.'[134]

Male cult prostitutes were designated by the specific word קָדֵשׁ (kadaish). The female cult prostitute was known as קְדֵשָׁה (kih-day-shah, the feminine form of the word). This is who Tamar made herself out to be (Gen. 38:21-22). Some might ask,

> 'If Yakov's second rule spoke of cult prostitution, why didn't he just use the specific words for them?'

Yakov used the basic word for cult prostitution. This was more than sufficient as it covered both male and female prostitutes. He didn't need to use the specific words for male and female cult prostitutes. Also, his four rules weren't a theological dissertation on cult harlotry but four short rules concerning sacrificial-sexual idolatry. *Because* of their shortness, we know that everyone knew what they meant. Witherington states, 'all four items in the decree were *shorthand* for things that took place in pagan temples'.[135] Tim Hegg adds a valuable insight when he says that the rules must have been very well known among both Gentiles and Jews. He cites the use of the Greek article (the) 'before each item in the initial listing' saying, 'they represented well-known entities' and both peoples would have been able to identify the meanings by the 'single terms.'[136] The Gentiles knew exactly what Yakov meant.

---

[133] Woolf, *WNCD*, p. 289. Debauch: '1a: archaic: to make disloyal, b: to seduce from chastity, 2a: to lead away from virtue or excellence, b: to corrupt by intemperance or sensuality.'

[134] Unger, *UBD*, p. 949.

[135] Witherington, *The Acts of the Apostles*, p. 463 note 420.

[136] Tim Hegg, *The Letter Writer: Paul's Background and Torah Perspective* (Israel: First Fruits of Zion, 2002), p. 272.

The history of Israel is one sad commentary after another as the people and their leaders indulged in cult harlotry year after year, century after century. There are those who see the 'God of the Old Testament' as a wrathful angry God 'out to get you!' as soon as you make a mistake. But the love and *long-suffering* God of the Old Testament is abundantly evident in the many centuries He didn't destroy the generations of Israelis that committed cult harlotry. He pleaded with them through His Prophets but most of the time Israel was deaf to the One who created and loved her (2nd Kgs. 17:1-23; Jer. 26:5; 35:15).

After Joshua, the problem of cult prostitution manifested itself among the people of God and kept them in chains of darkness. Israel wouldn't be rid of this abomination until the northern kingdom of Israel was obliterated by Assyria in 721 B.C. One hundred and thirty-five years later (586 B.C.) the southern kingdom of Judah was decimated and taken into captivity by the Babylonian king. *ISBE* states,

> 'In the period of the Judges' (about 1300–1080 B.C.) '*religious prostitution* was one of the basic causes of the degradation of the people (Judges 2:17). They came to worship both the priestly ephod and certain Baals by means of *sacred prostitution* (8:27-35).'[137]

The terms 'religious prostitution' and 'sacred prostitution' obviously speak of cult prostitution in the days of the Judges. *ISBE* goes on to state this, and the reason for the destruction of both kingdoms:

> 'The captivity of the half-tribe of Manasseh resulted from their participation in the *religious prostitution* connected with the Canaanite gods (1st Chron. 5:25). The same can be said of the fall of both the northern and southern kingdoms as the idolatrous practices they followed included such rites (Ezk. 16:16-58).'[138]

After the days of King Solomon, his son Rehoboam assumed the Throne (935 B.C.), but foolishness was in his heart. He wouldn't relieve the heavy taxes that his father had placed upon the people. Instead he told them they 'hadn't seen anything yet.' This caused the Israelis in the north to rebel, thus tearing David's Kingdom in two (1st Kings 12).

Rehoboam's propensity for idolatry was another indication of his foolishness. Son of an Ammonite (pagan) mother, he 'perpetuated the worst fea-

---

[137] Bromiley, *ISBE*, vol. one, p. 617.

[138] Ibid.

tures of Solomon's idolatry (1st Kings 14:22-24).'[139] The 'worst features' of idolatry means he indulged in cult harlotry and sacrificed his infants.

From Rehoboam to the Babylonian captivity (935–586 B.C. approximately 350 years), Judah would more often than not, walk against the Torah or Instruction[140] of God. Hezekiah, a righteous king (715–686 B.C.) would restore and purify the Temple,

> 'which was *dismantled and closed* during the latter part of his' father's reign (2nd Chron. 28:24; 29:3). 'But the reform extended little below the surface (Isaiah 29:13). Idolatry spread fearfully in the last times of the kingdom of Judah, until it brought down on the people the punishment of captivity in Babylon.'[141]

It's hard to imagine that the Temple of Yahveh in Jerusalem would be closed because the people were more interested in pagan gods and goddesses (i.e. cult prostitution) than Yahveh. The reform of Hezekiah didn't last because the hearts of the people were very lustful. Cult prostitution was an immense problem for the people of Judah…and for Yahveh.

King Josiah began his reign in 640 B.C. and was another righteous king.[142] When he ascended the Throne, male cult homosexuality was socially acceptable in the Kingdom and was even being practiced in the Temple of Yahveh! *TDNT* states,

> 'Josiah's sharp attack, under which the houses of the kedeshim' (male and female cult prostitutes) 'in the Temple were destroyed, shows that the evil had made its way even into the Temple cultus in Jerusalem, 2nd Kings 23:7.'[143]

Cult prostitution would sever the covenant protection between Yahveh and His people and open them up to enemies within and without. Sacrificial-sexual idolatry was seen as unfaithfulness on the part of Israel; an un-

---

[139] Unger, *UBD*, p. 514.

[140] The word Torah means to teach, instruct or direct and therefore is not 'law' per se but the Teaching of Yahveh for Israel. Davidson, *AHCL*, p. 346: The verb means 'to teach, instruct' and the noun means 'instruction, direction, precept'.

[141] Ibid.

[142] There were righteous kings before Hezekiah, like Asa (911–870 B.C.) and Jehoshaphat (870–848 B.C.) but their attempts at reform didn't last any longer than Hezekiah's (2nd Chron. 14:1-15:19; 17:1-20:23).

[143] Kittel, *TDNT*, vol. VI, p. 586.

faithfulness that would sever them from their God. It was apostasy and yet Yahveh didn't immediately act upon it as He had at Baal Peor. It didn't mean the people escaped unscathed though. *ISBE* writes,

> 'The degradation of the human being through religious prostitution becomes a figure for the spiritual infidelity that Israel and Judah show to God. The Old Testament pictures Yahweh as the husband of Israel. For example, Israel and Judah are depicted as faithless sisters who play the harlot, being unfaithful to their Beloved (see esp. Jer. 3:1-3 and Ezk. 23). The deep religious significance of such a figure is apparent when we see the *close connection between idolatry and religious prostitution*. To demonstrate the faithlessness of Israel, Yahweh commanded the prophet Hosea to take a wife who had been a harlot. Unable to break the habit of her former life, she became a living representation of Israel's faithlessness to Yahweh. Hosea filled the role of God, who was always willing to forgive.'[144]

God's faithfulness and forgiveness have been from the Beginning. It didn't begin with Jesus. It's amplified and culminates in Him.

The Hebrew language and perspective are very concrete and therefore very simple. The abstract is brought into the physical realm so that all can plainly understand what God is speaking about. Yahveh remonstrates His people for worshipping idols of wood and stone. This can only be cult prostitution. *TDNT* states,

> "In Isaiah 1:21, the 'city of Jerusalem, once faithful and the refuge of the righteous, has now become a harlot.' In Jer. 3:1-4:4, the prophet 'accuses Israel and Judah of playing the harlot with many lovers (3:2), of committing adultery with wood and stone' '(3:9), and of defiling the Land by their πορνειαι'" (Greek: por-nay-ai; cult harlotry).[145]

The *Dictionary of Biblical Imagery* explains,

> 'Israel chose to follow the cults God had warned against (Psalm 106:35-39). Through Jeremiah, God notes the nation's resulting brazen and degraded state in his accusation: On every high hill and under every spreading tree,

---

[144] Bromiley, *ISBE*, vol. two, p. 617.

[145] Kittel, *TDNT*, vol. VI, p. 587. The Greek word comes from the Septuagint.

> you lay down as a prostitute. How can you say, "I am not
> defiled, I have not run after the Baals?" You are a swift
> she-camel running here and there, a wild donkey accus-
> tomed to the desert, sniffing the wind in her craving; in
> her heat who can restrain her? (Jer. 2:20, 23-24, NIV)'[146]

Can there be any doubt as to the devastating effect cult prostitution had
upon ancient Israel? Both the northern and southern kingdoms were obliterated because of it. Even though Gentiles would come to believe in Jesus,
would they be excluded from personal catastrophe if they indulged in cult
prostitution? In First Corinthians, as well as other letters, Paul addressed
this very issue with them.

Hosea ministered to the northern kingdom from 760–722 B.C. Isaiah
served the Lord from 740–700 B.C. And Jeremiah was sent to the southern kingdom of Judah which fell to Babylon. He ministered from 626–586
B.C. *TDNT* says,

> 'In *Jeremiah as in Hosea* the charge of infidelity goes
> hand in hand with an uncompromising rejection of the
> practice of *sacral prostitution* as this was found in the
> Canaanite cult, Jer. 2:20; 3:6; cf. Hos. 4:12-14.[147]

Time after time Yahveh sent His Prophets to plead and to warn the people
against their sacrificial-sexual apostasy. But it was to little avail. This
didn't take God by surprise (Dt. 28:49-68; 31:16), and shouldn't be used
by some to denote God's permanent severing of Israel (Jer. 16:14-16;
33:6-26; Hos. 1:10-11; Joel 2:18-19; Zeph. 3:8-20; Rom. 9–11, etc.).

Many ancient peoples would leave their female babies by the roadside because they were seen as a liability to raise (food and clothing, etc.). Pagan
priests would come along and raise them for cult prostitution. In contrast
to many in the ancient pagan world abandoning their female babies,
Yahveh speaks to Judah through Ezekiel, saying He found Israel aban-
doned like that but had mercy upon her. As she grew to womanhood she
betrayed her Husband and lusted after other gods. This both saddened and
angered Yahveh. God's anger toward Israel, because of her impenetrable
heart and idolatrous prostitution, is seen in Ezk. 16. His love and pain for
her can also be felt:

> Ezk. 16:4-6: 'As for your birth, on the day you were born,
> your navel cord was not cut nor were you washed with

---

[146] Ryken, *DBI*, p. 677.

[147] Kittel, *TDNT*, vol. VI, p. 587.

water for cleansing. You weren't rubbed with salt or even wrapped in cloths. No eye looked with pity upon you to do any of these things for you, to have compassion upon you. Rather you were thrown out into the open field, for you were abhorred on the day you were born. When I passed by you and saw you squirming in your blood, I said to you while you were in your blood, "Live!" Yes, I said to you while you were in your blood, "Live!"'

Ezk. 16:7-8: '"I made you numerous like plants of the field. Then you grew up, became tall and reached the age for fine ornaments; your breasts were formed and your hair had grown. Yet you were naked and bare. Then I passed by you and saw you and behold! You were at the time for love so I spread My skirt over you and covered your nakedness. I also swore to you and entered into a Covenant with you so that you became Mine" declares the Lord Yahveh.'

Ezk. 16:9-10: 'Then I bathed you with water, washed off your blood from you and anointed you with oil. I also clothed you with embroidered cloth and put sandals of badger skin on your feet, and I wrapped you with fine linen and covered you with silk.'

Ezk. 16:11-13: 'I adorned you with ornaments, put bracelets on your hands and a necklace around your neck. I also put a ring in your nostril, earrings in your ears and a beautiful crown on your head. Thus you were adorned with gold and silver and your dress was of fine linen, silk and embroidered cloth. You ate fine flour, honey and oil so you were exceedingly beautiful and advanced to royalty.'

Ezk. 16:14-16: 'Then your fame went forth among the nations on account of your beauty for it was perfect because of My splendor which I bestowed upon you' declares the Lord Yahveh. 'But you trusted in your beauty and played the harlot because of your fame and you poured out your *harlotries* on every passer-by who might be willing. You took some of your clothes, made for yourself colorful *shrines* and *played the harlot*. Nothing like this has ever been or ever shall be.'

Ezk. 16:17: '"You also took your beautiful jewels made

of My gold and of My silver, which I had given you, and made for yourself *male images* that you might *play the harlot with them*. Then you took your embroidered cloth and covered them, and offered My oil and My incense before them. Also My bread which I gave you, fine flour, oil and honey with which I fed you, *you would offer before them* for a soothing aroma. So it happened" declares the Lord Yahveh.'

Ezk. 16:20-21: 'Moreover *you took your sons and daughters* whom you had borne to Me and *sacrificed* them to idols to be devoured. Were your harlotries so small a matter? You slaughtered My children and offered them up to idols by causing them *to pass through the fire*.'

Ezk. 16:22-23: 'Besides all your abominations and harlotries you did not remember the days of your youth, when you were naked, bare and squirming in your blood. Then it came about after all your wickedness. "Woe! Woe to you!" declares the Lord Yahveh,'

Ezk. 16:24-25: 'that you built yourself a *shrine* and made yourself *a high place* in every square. You built yourself a high place at the top of every street and made your beauty abominable and you spread your legs to every passer-by to multiply your whoredom.'

The charges against Judah are unfaithfulness, sacrificial idolatry, cult harlotry and child sacrifice. As the door opened to cult harlotry and sacrificial idolatry, it also led to the casting of their infants into the fires of the pagan gods (vv. 20-21). This is something so wicked that it's sickening to imagine. It was rampant. They played the harlot in following all the nations, and murdered their sons and daughters (Ezk. 16:15-16, 18-22, 24-25).

Yahveh gave life to Israel and set her on high as a free woman but she chose to cleave to another husband. The things that Yahveh gave here (oil, flour and clothes, etc.), would be given as offerings to other gods. Left unchecked, the abomination spread like wildfire through most of the communities, Tribes and nation. Yahveh had to deal with her. Both kingdoms were destroyed because of cult harlotry.

Sacrificial-sexual idolatry caused Yahveh to annihilate the northern kingdom, and He decimated the southern kingdom and brought them into Babylonian captivity. The punishment seems to have impressed itself upon the remnant that was left of the kingdom of Judah. After the Baby-

54

lonian captivity (586–516 B.C; see Jer. 29:10 and also 25:11-12) never again do the Jewish people engage in sacrificial idolatry, cult prostitution or infant sacrifice.

God finally brought judgment upon His people. He severely punished them for cult prostitution. They walked in the ways of the nations around them and found out that there was a price to pay. This historical background figures prominently into why Yakov gave the four rules to the Gentile believers.

Yakov's use of zihnute (prostitution), means cult prostitution. The context, word definitions, and history of Israel point directly to this and nothing else. That's not to say that common harlotry was non-existent, but the rule that Yakov presented to the Gentile believer *specifically* dealt with cult prostitution. Any other suggestion as to it's meaning (e.g. sexual immorality, unchastity, adultery, etc.), negates the historical reality of cult harlotry within Israel, the biblical usage of the word, and the use of zihnute right after the first rule on sacrificial idolatry (not to eat meat sacrificed to an idol at the time of the sacrifice). With the first two rules speaking of sacrificial-sexual idolatry, is it unreasonable to assume that the third and fourth rules would also?

Yakov was concerned about Gentile believers thinking they could worship Jesus on the Sabbath, and go to the temple of Diana on Sunday. The Apostle Paul would deal with cult prostitution among the Corinthians and other congregations he established. And Jesus would use the Apostle John to speak against it in Revelation.

What happened in Israel was happening among the Gentile believers. If it could happen in ancient Israel, where God called them to be holy and commanded them not to do the things the Gentiles did (Dt. 12:28-32), it could certainly happen in pagan Greece and Rome which knew no God like Yahveh.

Yakov knew all about the Hebrew word meanings for cult prostitution, *Judah and Tamar*, *Israel and Baal Peor* and *Cult Prostitution in Ancient Israel*. Most likely the Holy Spirit was bringing all this to his recollection. On one hand, it doesn't have anything to do with 'what the Gentiles must do to be saved.' On the other hand, it has everything to do with it. *Cult Prostitution in the Ancient World* will seal this understanding of how infested cult harlotry was among the pagans, and reinforce how Yakov saw the situation before him.

CULT PROSTITUTION
IN THE ANCIENT WORLD

A brief sketch of cult prostitution in the ancient world will yield more understanding and depth as to the extent of idolatry in the Gentile world. It'll also help to explain why Yakov wanted the converted pagan Gentiles to stay away from their former places of 'worship.'

One of Alexander Hislop's themes in *The Two Babylons* is that all the pagan religions had their prototype in ancient Babylon. The names of the gods and the goddesses would change over time and with each nation but their pagan rites would basically remain the same. Because of this they could be linked to each other and back to Babylon. It was in Babylon that cult prostitution began and would spread all over the Earth:

> 'The Chaldean Mysteries can be traced up to the days of Semiramis who lived only a few centuries after the Flood and who is known to have impressed upon them the image of her own depraved and polluted mind. That beautiful but abandoned Queen of Babylon was not only herself a paragon of unbridled lust and licentiousness, but in the Mysteries which she had a chief hand in forming, she was worshipped as Rhea, the great 'Mother' of the gods, with such atrocious rites as identified her with Venus, the Mother of all impurity and raised the very city where she had reigned to a bad eminence among the nations, as the grand seat at once of idolatry and consecrated prostitution.'[148]

Semiramis, known as both the Queen of Heaven and Ishtar (where Easter comes from), allowed for the worst lusts within man to surface and be validated as worship. Cult prostitution in the ancient world was not only rampant, it was an accepted, noble and 'godly' fixture of life. *ISBE* states,

> 'The Code of Hammurabi allowed female prostitutes at any temple. The Gilgamesh Epic pictures such a woman in connection with the temple of Ishtar'.[149]

Hammurabi was King of Babylon when Abraham was alive (around the 18th century B.C.).[150] One of the practices of the Babylonian religion con-

---

[148] Hislop, *The Two Babylons*, p. 5.

[149] Bromiley, *ISBE*, vol. two, p. 617.

[150] Sinclair, *CED*, p. 699.

sisted in *every teenage daughter* losing her virginity in 'honor' of the Babylonian Venus. *ISBE* states,

> 'the Babylonians compelled every native female to attend the temple of Venus once in her life and to prostitute herself in honor of the goddess.'[151]

TDNT adds,

> it 'was a national custom in' 'which even daughters of prominent families followed and to which no shame attached.[152]

This was the ancient world, carnal and deceived. Hislop writes,

> "We find from Herodotus that the peculiar and abominable institution of Babylon in prostituting virgins in honor of Mylitta was observed also in Cyprus in honor of Venus. But the positive testimony of Pausanias brings this presumption to a certainty. 'Near this,' says that historian, speaking of the temple of Vulcan at Athens, 'is the temple of Celestial Venus, who was first worshipped by the Assyrians and after these by the Paphians in Cyprus and the Phoenicians who inhabited the city of Ascalon in Palestine.'"[153]

The Assyrians who 'gave' Venus to Athens actually 'took' their Venus from Babylon. Hislop states,

> 'the Assyrian Venus' 'the great goddess of Babylon, and the Cyprian Venus were one and the same'.[154]

Pausanias didn't realize that Celestial Venus was worshipped before the time of the Assyrians in the land of Babylon. But such was the case as the Assyrian religion was modeled after the Babylonian. Hislop writes,

> 'Tarsus, the capital of Cilicia, was built by Sennacherib, the Assyrian king, *in express imitation of Babylon*. Its religion would naturally correspond'.[155]

Mylitta whom Herodotus speaks of, was just another name for Venus or the Babylonian Queen deified.[156] One of the great goddesses of ancient

---

[151] Bromiley, *ISBE*, vol. two, p. 617.

[152] Kittel, *TDNT*, vol. VI, p. 581.

[153] Hislop, *The Two Babylons*, p. 157.

[154] Ibid.

[155] Ibid.

Greece was Aphrodite but she was just the Babylonian Queen by another name:

> 'This Babylonian queen' (Semiramis) 'was not merely in character coincident with the Aphrodite of Greece and the Venus of Rome but was in point of fact, the historical original of that goddess that by the ancient world was regarded as the very embodiment of everything attractive in female form and the perfection of female beauty; for Sanchuniathon assures us that Aphrodite or Venus was identical with Astarte, and Astarte being interpreted is none other than, 'The woman that made towers or encompassing walls' (i.e. Semiramis).[157] The Roman Venus, as is well known, was the Cyprian Venus and the Venus of Cyprus is historically proved to have been derived from Babylon.'[158]

> 'On the testimony of Augustine, himself an eye-witness, we know that the rites of Vesta, emphatically 'the virgin

---

[156] Ibid., p. 304. 'This, then, was the case with the goddess recognized as Astarte or Venus, as well as with Rhea. Though there were points of difference between Cybele, or Rhea, and Astarte or Mylitta the Assyrian Venus, Layard shows that there were also distinct points of contact between them. Cybele or Rhea was remarkable for her turreted crown. Mylitta, or Astarte, was represented with a similar crown. (Layard's *Nineveh*, vol. ii. p. 456). Lions drew Cybele or Rhea; Mylitta, or Astarte, was represented as standing on a lion (Ibid.). The worship of Mylitta, or Astarte, was a mass of moral pollution (Herodotus, lib. i. cap. 199, p. 92). The worship of Cybele, under the name of Terra, was the same (Augustine, *De Civitate*, lib. vi. cap. 8, tom. ix., p. 203).'

Page 310: 'We have evidence, further, that goes far to identify this title as a title of Semiramis. Melissa or Melitta (Appolodorus, vol. i. lib. ii. p. 110)—for the name is given in both ways—is said to have been the mother of Phoroneus, the first that reigned, in whose days the dispersion of mankind occurred, divisions having come in among them, whereas before, all had been in harmony and spoke one language (Hyginus, fab. 143, p. 114). There is no other to whom this can be applied but Nimrod; and as Nimrod came to be worshipped as Nin, the son of his own wife, the identification is exact. Melitta, then, the mother of Phoroneus, is the same as Mylitta, the well known name of the Babylonian Venus; and the name, as being the feminine of Melitz, the Mediator, consequently signifies the Mediatrix.'

[157] Ibid., see pp. 30-32, 296-297, 318. The encompassing walls signified her association with her husband Nimrod who was the first to make walled cities. This provided men with protection from the wild animals and human enemies, and being grateful for that, submitted to him as the first human king.

[158] Ibid., pp. 74-75.

goddess of Rome,' under the name of Terra, were exactly the same as those of Venus, the goddess of impurity and licentiousness (Augustine, *De Civitate Dei*, lib. ii. cap. 26). Augustine elsewhere says that Vesta, the virgin goddess, "was by some called Venus."'[159]

The pagan mindset saw cult prostitution as the highest form of religion, authorized by their gods. Only the God of the tiny Hebrew nation would come against this worship of lust.

Many times, because of the passing of a name from one language to another, the original name could be detected. An example of this is the Greek goddess Hestia and the Roman version Vesta. Hislop notes,

'In Greece she' (Semiramis) 'had the name of Hestia, and amongst the Romans, Vesta, which is just a modification of the same name.'[160]

Each city-state in ancient Greece had its founding god or goddess as well as the importation of other gods and goddesses. *ISBE* states,

families 'worshiped Hestia, goddess of the hearth, Zeus as protector of the courtyard and their own gods and heroes.'[161] 'Each state worshiped Hestia and also the god credited with its founding. Therefore, Athenians worshiped Athena but Spartans venerated Zeus.'[162]

For a Gentile to worship more than one god was not uncommon, it was *normal*.

Cult prostitution was everywhere but Corinth was noted for it:

'the temple of Aphrodite with its 1,000 hierodules[163] was famous and an inscription recalls that the goddess answered their prayers for the threatened fatherland in a critical hour.'[164]

Cult prostitution thrived in Corinth. This is important in understanding the

---

[159] Ibid., p. 76 note §.

[160] Ibid., p. 77.

[161] Bromiley, *ISBE*, vol. two, p. 563.

[162] Ibid.

[163] Sinclair, *CED*, p. 728: '(in ancient Greece) a temple slave, esp. a sacral prostitute', 'from Greek hierodoulos'. From hiero + doulos (slave). Hiero: 'holy or divine' that is to say, a holy slave.

[164] Kittel, *TDNT*, vol. VI, p. 582.

Apostle Paul when he writes about fornication (cult prostitution) in his letter to the Corinthians (1st Cor. 5, 6 and 10).

Of course Aphrodite was not the only goddess or god that offered cult prostitution in Greece and other lands:

> 'Dionysus was worshiped sometimes in orgiastic frenzy'.
> 'His attributes that guaranteed fertility closely parallel those of Demeter, who also seems to have controlled agricultural cycles.'[165] Demeter was the mother goddess.[166]

TDNT states that prostitution,

> 'was practiced by the class of hierodules whose payment accrued to the goddess. This type of prostitution was *widespread in Asia Minor* in cults of mother deities; it is also found, however, *in Syria and Egypt*. Through the *Canaanite cults* (Baal, Astarte), it penetrated into the religion of Israel.'[167]

> '*Numerous* nude female figurines found throughout the Near East depict the goddesses who were venerated in sacred prostitution.'[168]

This was cult prostitution in the ancient world. In that world women usually had no rights. Perhaps this, along with satanic deception and the fact that carnal lust is a powerful urge of human nature, explains why there were so many cult prostitutes.

The ancient peoples had a very perverse understanding of life, according to God's standard. Sex, like the appetites of hunger and thirst, was not seen to need any restraints.[169] And as for the value of female babies in the ancient *civilized* world, they were seen as liabilities to be gotten rid of:

> 'Many cultures devalued female babies, so infant girls were often left to die and then picked up by people who raised them for prostitution.'[170]

Cult prostitution not only exploited females but men as well. Greece and Canaan weren't the only places where cult homosexual prostitution was

---

[165] Bromiley, *ISBE*, vol. two, p. 563.

[166] Ibid.

[167] Kittel, *TDNT*, vol. VI, pp. 581-582.

[168] Douglas, *IBD*, Part 3, p. 1289.

[169] Kittel, *TDNT*, vol. VI, p. 582.

[170] Ryken, *DBI*, p. 677.

practiced and condoned. *The Illustrated Bible Dictionary* speaks of it being found in Syria and Phoenicia also:

> 'In the Ugaritic texts of temple personnel we find the qdsm' (kih-dih-sheem, masculine plural for the singular, kih-daish) 'who were...male cult prostitutes. Explicit references to sacred prostitution in Syria and Phoenicia are found in the late texts of Lucian's De Dea Syria (2nd century AD). The prostitution of women in the service of Venus at Heliopolis (Baalbek) is attested as late as the 4th century AD.'[171]

Yet ancient Canaan *seemed to outdo the other lands* in terms of heterosexual as well as homosexual cult prostitution. Perhaps that's what Yahveh meant when He spoke to Abraham about *the sin of the land* not being filled up yet (Gen. 15:16; Lev. 18:6-25), and why Joshua and the conquering Hebrews weren't to take any captives (Dt. 20:16-18). *Unger's* states,

> 'Fertility cults *nowhere controlled people more completely* than in Canaan.'[172]

The people of Canaan were totally degenerate and given over to wickedness. *DBI* explains the perverse symbolism behind cult prostitution:

> 'Fertility cults that worshiped Baal advocated intercourse between worshipers and religious prostitutes, both male and female, to encourage the gods to bestow greater fertility on land, livestock and people.'[173]

TDOT confirms that cult prostitution was part of the ancient lifestyle, both of the pagans and of Israel:

> 'In Canaanite culture, extramarital relationships in connection with the fertility cult were common. Through sacral prostitution the harlot and her lover became consecrated individuals'.[174] And that,

> 'Apostasy from Yahweh was frequently connected with participation in the Canaanite fertility cult with its sacral prostitution.'[175]

---

[171] Douglas, *IBD*, Part 3, p. 1289.

[172] Unger, *UBD*, p. 512.

[173] Ryken, *DBI*, p. 677.

[174] Botterweck, *TDOT*, vol. IIII, p. 101.

[175] Ibid., p. 100.

Unger's and *IBD* declare that Canaan was infested with cult prostitution and that it would of course, effect the very life of Israel:

> 'The inhabitants of Canaan were addicted to Baal worship, which was conducted by priests in temples and in good weather, outdoors in fields and particularly on hilltops called 'high places.' The cult included *animal sacrifice, ritualistic meals* and licentious dances. Near the rock altar was a sacred pillar or massebah, and close by the symbol of the asherah, both of which apparently symbolized human fertility' (ancient pornography). 'High places had chambers for sacred prostitution by male prostitutes (kedishim) and sacred harlots (kedeshoth) (1st Kings 14:23-24; 2nd Kings 23:7).'[176]

> 'We may assume that the worship of the major Canaanite goddesses, Ashera, Astarte and Anath, involved sacred prostitution'.[177]

Canaan was saturated with this form of lustful worship. The reason given to justify cult prostitution had to do with 'helping the gods' to bring life-giving rain and therefore, food to the people to live. To a people ignorant of the true ways of God (i.e. His Law), this might seem reasonable:

> 'The rainfall of winter and the drought of summer were believed to indicate that Baal had died and that there was a need for him to be brought to life again by magic rites.'[178]

> 'Similarly, the Canaanites believed that the gods could be helped to bring about fertility of the soil *if the people fertilized one another* in the places of worship. Therefore, there was a crude sexuality in the name of religion. *Every Canaanite sanctuary* had its own prostitutes for that purpose.'[179]

> 'Their votaries believed that they could stimulate the fertility of their crops by sympathetic magic when they engaged in intercourse.'[180]

---

[176] Unger, *UBD*, p. 413.

[177] Douglas, *IBD*, Part 3, p. 1289.

[178] Ralph Gower, *The New Manners and Customs of Bible Times* (Chicago: Moody Press, 1987), p. 335.

[179] Ibid., p. 334.

'In the Baal cult, spring festivals dramatized, in act, the mating of Baal with the goddess of fertility. Archaeological discoveries have revealed that the devotees of Baal practiced prostitution as a part of their worship.'[181]

By linking Man's need for food (life), to cult prostitution, Satan elevated lust to a divine duty. The Gentiles didn't have the knowledge of the God of Israel and His standard concerning moral behavior so there was no restraining moral guide to their 'religious' behavior. So completely different were Yahveh's requirements that, for many centuries, His own people ran to the sin of sacrificial-sexual idolatry, copying the pagans around them.

In the days of Yakov, the third largest city in the Roman Empire was Antioch, located in what was known as Syria and now in what is southernmost Turkey.[182] It was from this city that Paul and Barnabas were sent to Jerusalem to determine what the Gentiles were to do in order to be saved (Acts 15:2-3, 22, 30, 35). Then it was known as Syrian Antioch, to distinguish it from Pisidian Antioch, in what is now central Turkey (Acts 13:14; 14:19, 21). In speaking about Syrian Antioch, F. F. Bruce, in typical British understatement writes,

'The city's reputation for moral laxity was enhanced by the cult of Artemis and Apollo at Daphne, five miles distant, where the ancient Syrian worship of Astarte and her consort, with its ritual prostitution, was carried on under Greek nomenclature.'[183]

The repugnancy of this 'moral laxity' was dryly noted by the Roman satirist Juvenal when he wrote, 'the sewage of the Syrian Orontes has for long been discharging itself into the Tiber.'[184] Even Rome, no paragon of virtue, could smell the stench of orgiastic cult prostitution that was pervading its Empire from the East.

James Pritchard describes the sensuality of Astarte from the Ras Shamra texts found in Ugarit (Syria):

---

[180] Douglas, *IBD*, Part 3, p. 1289.

[181] Pfeiffer, *WBC* (Chicago: Moody Press, 1977), p. 145.

[182] Bruce, *The Book of the Acts*, p. 224. 'Antioch on the Orontes (modern Antakya in the Hatay province of Turkey), situated some eighteen miles upstream, was founded 300 B.C. by Seleucus Nicator, first ruler of the Seleucid dynasty, and was named by him after his father Antiochus.'

[183] Ibid.

[184] Ibid.

The 'holy trees, symbols of the life force' 'show stylized trees growing out of the navel or the pudenda of a formalized goddess. Sexual intercourse under these holy trees was thought to transmit the potency and vitality of the goddess (Hos. 4:13-14).'

'The female deity Asherah is referred to in the Bible as the consort of Baal (Judg. 3:7; 2nd Kgs. 23:4). These Asherahs and Astartes are often described as fertility goddesses. However, the female partner of the weather god appears to bare her breasts in an erotic pose rather than in a maternal gesture. Ancient Syrian seals which depict her surrounded by stars as the queen of the heavens, baring her breasts to the weather god striding across the hills, seem to confirm this.'

'It is quite clear that prostitution was connected with the cult of Asherah (cf. 2nd Kgs. 23:7). In the same way, the goddess figurines found in' Israel 'from the 10th–6th centuries BC (described in the Bible as 'teraphim'), are to be regarded not only as 'nourishing goddesses' 'but also as symbols of eroticism (see Prov. 5:19).'[185]

Turning west to Rome, the 'center of civilization' at the time of Yakov and Acts 15, it seems that all the gods of the conquered lands, had conquered the citizens of Rome. The city was a mixture of 'Italian, Etruscan, Greek, Egyptian and oriental' (i.e. Babylonian and Syrian, etc.) gods and goddesses.[186] *ISBE* states,

'The mysterious religion of Etruria first impressed the Roman mind, probably giving them the trinity of the Capitol (Jupiter, Juno, Minerva), which had come from Greece'. 'Latium contributed the worship of Diana (from Aricia) and a Latin Jupiter. Two Latium cults, Hercules and Castor' were there and 'the Sibylline Books' were treated as 'sacred scriptures for the Romans.'

'The Greek trinity of "Demeter, Dionysus, and Persephone under the Latin names of Ceres, Liber, and Libera"' was there 500 years before Yeshua was born in Bethlehem, with Apollo coming about 50 years later.

---

[185] James B. Pritchard, *The Harper Atlas of the Bible* (New York: Harper & Row, Publishers, 1987), pp. 101-103.

[186] Bromiley, *ISBE*, vol. four, p. 212.

'Mercury, Asclepius, Dis, and Proserpina' were relatively new arrivals in the '3rd cent. B.C.' But the 'craving for more sensuous worship' had the Greek deities entering 'wholesale and were readily assimilated' 'in the 2nd cent. B.C. Hebe entered as Juventas, Artemis as Diana, Ares as Mars.'

'It was the Orient, however, that supplied what they really wanted. In 204 B.C. Cybele, known as the great Mother, came from Pessinus' (modern day Anatoli; central western Turkey, near biblical Pisidian Antioch). 'Her coming gave an impetus to the wilder and more orgiastic cults and the mysterious glamor that captivated the common mind. It struck a fatal blow at the old Roman religion. Bacchus with his gross immorality soon followed.' Although the 'educated classes sank into skepticism' concerning belief in the gods, 'the populace' was enthralled by 'superstition' and the pantheon of gods and goddesses.'[187]

The entire 'civilized' world was enmeshed in sacrificial-sexual idolatry. The book of Acts attests to this also. After proclaiming Yeshua as the Messiah (Acts 14:8-18), Paul sees a man in Lystra who was lame from his mother's womb. Paul heals him and the people of the town rejoice and want to offer sacrifice to Paul and Barnabas as gods!

Of course the two of them try as hard as they can to restrain the people from doing so, and just barely succeed. This same crowd though, later led by some instigators, turns on Paul and actually stones him, leaving him for dead! The point of this is that in Paul's day, the reality of paganism was saturated upon the hearts and minds of the Gentile peoples; *all* the Gentile peoples. This must be taken into account regarding Acts 15:20.

Going through Athens, one of the most cultured and sophisticated cities of the world then, Paul observed that it was 'full of idols' (Acts 17:16). Confirming this lifestyle of idolatry and cult prostitution, the Scriptures declare that all Asia and the world worshiped Artemis (Diana). Demetrius, a silversmith who made silver idols of Artemis (Acts 19:24), speaks of how Paul's preaching of Messiah Yeshua as the one and *only* way, negatively effected his business, and the worship of the goddess:

'And not only is there danger that this trade of ours fall into disrepute but also that the temple of the great goddess Artemis will be despised, and that she whom all of Asia

---

[187] Ibid., pp. 212-213.

and the world worship should even be dethroned from her magnificence.' (Acts 19:27)

This glimpse into the ancient world has revealed that cult prostitution was a major reality in every land, and morally upheld as proper. Into this milieu comes the God of Israel in Jesus Christ whose standard was quite radical, and as Demetrius attests to, quite repulsive to many of the natives.

How many new Gentile believers in the days of the Apostles would even consider cult prostitution a sinful act? Yakov was making sure they understood what would be required of them immediately, or their very salvation would be in jeopardy.

Today Western man doesn't go to temples to worship this way. He's thrown off the wooden idols for 'living idols' (Hollywood movies, television, Playboy magazine, Internet pornography, etc.). It feeds the same sexual lust and draws the same demons. This kind of 'worship' is openly flaunted and embraced by the Western world. Not much has changed since the days of ancient Canaan, Greece and Rome. Lustful sensuality is the religion of modern man and seen as alright because 'everyone does it.' And the truth is, most everyone does do it, following the ancient lustful mentality in how they dress and act.

The Greek Perspective on the Second Rule will parallel the Hebraic. It'll confirm that Yakov's second rule specifically addressed cult harlotry and that all four rules are a conceptual package against sacrificial-sexual idolatry, not some random rules given for table fellowship. With table fellowship being seen as a false interpretation, the foundation is taken out from under those who teach that the Law isn't for the Gentile. This is because the four rules are a reflection of commandments found in the Law. If the Law had been done away with, Yakov couldn't have given the rules, as Knowling pointed out (pp. 11-12 above).

These four rules were the first of many for the Gentile believers; the beginning of a new lifestyle for them. In learning Torah they would come to know the *entire* spectrum of Yeshua's will for their life:

> '*All Scripture* is inspired by God and is profitable for teaching, for reproof, for correction and for training in righteousness so that the man of God may be perfect, fully equipped for every good work.' (2nd Tim. 3:16-17)

THE GREEK PERSPECTIVE
ON THE SECOND RULE

The Hebraic perspective on the second rule in Acts 15:20 revealed that James was speaking of cult prostitution. But even though Yakov spoke Hebrew at the Council, years later Luke wrote it down in Greek.[188]

Looking at the Greek word that Luke penned, and two variations of it, will bring out the scope of how the word is used. It'll present the basic and primary meaning of the word for the New Testament prostitution (as it was for the Hebrew word). Context will speak of cult prostitution. The Greek noun for the second rule is 'prostitution' while the verb means 'to prostitute.' Another noun will speak of the person who is a prostitute. Context and ancient pagan reality will again play an important part in determining if cult or common prostitution is meant.

At the very least, the second rule of Yakov should be translated into English as prostitution. And as the other three rules relate to sacrificial idolatry, the only proper interpretation for the second rule is cult prostitution. Biblical fornication in the Old Testament is first and foremost cult prostitution. This carries over into the New Testament also.

Unfortunately the use of the term fornication for English translations must be ruled out specifically for Acts 15:20, and in general for all other texts, because its biblical definition is not understood today. Many wrongly think the term relates to adultery or illicit sex.

Placing fornication or sexual immorality or adultery, etc., into Acts 15:20, totally obscures what James meant for the second rule and for his theme of sacrificial-sexual idolatry. The second rule should be translated as cult prostitution or cult harlotry. The meaning of the Greek words will bring this out.

---

[188] Yeshua, the Apostles, and all the Jews in Judah and Galilee spoke Hebrew as their native language (see p. 22 note 64 above). It also seems that half the Book of Acts was originally taken from a Hebrew source. Bivin, *Understanding the Difficult Words of Jesus*, p. 5, states, 'The first 15 chapters of Acts show some of the same textual evidence as the Synoptic Gospels of being originally communicated in Hebrew. They deal with events in Jerusalem and are recounted in a Hebrew context. In Acts 15:36 there is a shift to Greek as Luke himself begins to describe Paul's missionary journeys.' It seems that Yakov spoke Hebrew at the gathering and that the first half of Acts was originally recorded in the Hebrew language. This only emphasizes that the word should first be recognized as coming from a Hebraic context, with Greek confirming the meaning of the word to be cult prostitution.

The Greek Noun: Por-nay-ah (Prostitution)

The Greek word for the second rule in Acts 15:20 is πορνειας (por-nay'ahs). It's in the genitive form. Genitive speaks of possession and in English is seen by either the word *of* or an apostrophe s ('s) at the end of a word. For example, in the phrase 'the cane of John' the word *of* tells us whose cane it is. We could also say 'John's cane.'

In Greek a possessive form is seen in the final ending ς (sigma) or 's' sound placed at the end of the word. It's the 's' sound in pornay'ahs that literally declares '*of* (the) prostitution' for v. 20. When the possessive ending is taken off the word, it's πορνεια (pornay'ah) prostitution.

Walter Bauer's classic Greek lexicon defines πορνεια (pornay'ah) as,

> 'prostitution, unchastity, fornication, of every kind of un-lawful sexual intercourse' 'of sexual unfaithfulness of a married woman Mt. 5:32; 19:9'.[189]

Pornay'ah (in Acts 15:20) is variously translated in most Bibles as 'sexual immorality' 'fornication' or 'unchastity' but never cult prostitution. Yet the very first word Bauer uses to define pornay'ah is prostitution. English Bible translators don't use prostitution because they may want to give por-nay'ah as wide a definition as possible. They don't realize the other three rules deal with sacrificial idolatry. They also don't understand the theolog-ical dilemma they place themselves in by declaring pornay'ah to mean 'every kind of unlawful sexual intercourse' or 'sexual immorality.'

If Yakov meant the last two definitions, what would be the criteria for es-tablishing what was lawful and immoral, and what wasn't? In ancient Greece, homosexuality was very lawful, common and morally upheld by the society,[190] as it sadly is today in Western countries. What standard

---

[189] Bauer, *GELNT*, p. 693.

[190] Kittel, *TDNT*, vol. VI, p. 593, states, 'In the shameful vices of *unnatural* sex relations, *which spread like a plague* in the Graeco-Roman world of his day, Paul sees the outworking of a severe judgment of God' Rom. 1:18f. Homo-sexuality or incest might not be frowned upon just because someone 'believes in Christ.' There are 'Christians' today who live lifestyles of homosexuality. Some denominations of the Church even condone such lifestyles by the ca-nard that they were 'born that way' and that 'we mustn't judge people but only love them.' The Torah condemns such 'lifestyle choices' and so did Paul. Torah is where Paul, the greatest proponent of Grace, takes his warnings against homosexuality and incest from. He also says we must judge those in the congregation, and specifically says that homosexuals will not inherit the

would be used to define lawful and moral? If we leave it up to each country, community or person, there's going to be a very wide range and diversity of what constitutes 'lawful and moral,' much of what God calls sin.

The criteria that establishes what is lawful and moral in God's eyes is the Law of Moses (as understood, defined and interpreted by Yeshua, not the Pharisees or the Rabbis). Theologians and translators, offering the widest possible definition for pornay'ah in Acts 15:20, place themselves in a tremendous theological bind. If the Law has been done away with, as they teach, *there's no moral standard or law to condemn homosexuality.* Someone might say, 'but Paul writes that it's wrong in Romans.' Was Paul making up his own rules, or presenting them from the Law (Lev. 18:22; 20:13, etc.)? And if he was presenting it from the Law, doesn't that mean that the Law was still in effect for Paul, and those he was writing to?

Isn't it interesting that homosexuality and adultery are sins in the Old Testament *and* the New Testament? Where did the New Testament get these from? Someone might say, 'If it's repeated in the New Testament then we have to abide by it.' But the point is that it's *established* in the Law of Moses, and written of in the New, because of Gentile sins. If Gentiles weren't sinning in homosexuality and cult prostitution, etc., these things might not have appeared in the New. Then someone could say, 'If it's not in the New, it's not a sin.' Just because a commandment like the Sabbath isn't specifically re-commanded in the New, it doesn't mean that God has abolished it. Paul's moral compass for sin was the Law of Moses.

Paul also spoke of Mosaic Law when the need arose to justify a point he wanted to make.[191] If the Law was done away with, he couldn't do that.

The Church teaches that the moral laws weren't done away with. Aside from the fact that nowhere in the New Testament does it say the moral law is the only thing that 'passes over' into the New Testament, we're right back at our starting point: who defines the moral law? Who defines what is lawful and what is sin? God or Man?

If 'everyone is free and under Grace' there's no standard that proclaims sin except perhaps the New Testament. This isn't bad but for things the New Testament doesn't seem to command, things like Sabbath, Passover and dietary laws,[192] the Church has made its own laws (Sunday, Easter and

---

Kingdom of God (1st Cor. 6:1-11).

[191] See p. 99 note 263 below, for places in 1st Corinthians where Paul does this.

[192] A careful and accurate reading of the New Testament confirms that the Sabbath, Passover and dietary laws, to name a few major areas, are still valid. For more understanding see *Law 102* at www.seedofabraham.net.

ham, etc.), *to take the place* of God's laws. If morality is defined by obedience to God, then it's certainly immoral not to keep the Sabbath day holy.

Man-made standards will vary for each Christian denomination. Many groups such as Pentecostals, Methodists and Baptists, etc., condemn the mere drinking of a glass of wine as sin. While others, such as Catholics and Episcopalians, etc., uphold it. Who sets the standard? The Church or the Bible?

Alcohol isn't condemned in the Bible but alcoholism is. Many mistake the two for the same thing but they're not. To drink alcohol is not a sin and doesn't make one an alcoholic. If it were sin, it would be stated as such somewhere in the Bible (Lk. 7:33-34; 1st Tim. 5:23). The point here is that without the Law of Moses, the Church makes up her own laws for sin, many of which contradict and nullify the Word of God (Dt. 14:26). Isn't this *exactly* what Yeshua came against with the Pharisees and Scribes (Mt. 15:1-20; Lk. 11:52)?

There are five basic categories of sexual practices that are forbidden in the Law of Moses:

1. Prostitution (common and cultic; Lev. 21:9: for the daughter of a priest that plays the harlot, death by fire. For the daughter of a common Israeli, death by stoning).

2. Adultery (Lev. 20:10: death as the punishment).

3. Homosexuality (Lev. 20:13: death as the punishment).

4. Incest (Lev. 18:6-29: cut off, i.e. death; see Lev. 20:3-5).

5. Sex outside of marriage (Dt. 22:20-21: death by stoning).[193]

As sinful as all these are in God's eyes, only cult prostitution is unforgivable today, as it severs the believer from Yeshua.[194] All other sexual sins are forgivable through His Blood, revealing the depth of God's grace toward His creation (Jn. 8:2-11; Acts 13:38-39). One who says they believe in Jesus, but plays the cult harlot, has severed her covenant relationship with Yeshua. She's cut herself off from Yeshua by this sexually idolatrous act. She's chosen to worship, and joined herself to, another god.

Bauer states that pornay'ah can be defined as fornication. But what does

---

[193] An exception to this is if a man rapes a virgin who is not engaged to another man (Dt. 22:28-29). He must pay her father fifty silver shekels and marry her (and cannot divorce her), if the father consents. See also Lev. 19:20.

[194] This only speaks of one who is already a believer in Christ. If a cult harlot comes to believe in Yeshua, her sins will be forgiven and she'll walk into new life with Him.

he mean by fornication? Is it conceptually the same as prostitution, which was his first word, or is it defined by him as 'every kind of unlawful sexual intercourse' which immediately follows fornication? It's hard to tell.

The Companion Bible: The Authorized Version of 1611 uses fornication for Acts 15:20. It means cult prostitution for them. Fornication at one time seems to have meant, or included, cult prostitution. Their comment on it for the second rule states,

> 'In many cases the rites of *heathenism* involved uncleanness as an act of worship. Compare Num. 25:1-15.'[195]

Heathenism alerts us to idolatry. In their comment on Num. 25:1 they say that Israel committed *whoredom* with the daughters of Moab in honor of the pagan god Baal Peor. This idolatry must be of a sexual nature. In their note to Num. 25:3, they state the Israelis *prostituted* themselves to the god. Fornication for them, specifically for Acts 15:20, is cult prostitution.[196] *The Companion Bible* links pornay'ah in Acts 15:20 to cult prostitution by using the word fornication. It's possible that Bauer was defining it the same way but it's not clear.

Another word Bauer uses to describe pornay'ah is unchastity. Unchastity is the opposite of chaste which means,

> 'not having experienced sexual intercourse; virginal' 'abstaining from unlawful or immoral sexual intercourse.'[197]

Unchastity is a term for one who has had unlawful sexual intercourse and is no longer a virgin. It's one who's done something immoral or lawfully wrong. The use of unchastity opens itself up to being seen as any kind of sexual immorality, or as Bauer states, 'every kind of unlawful sexual intercourse.' Pornay'ah now is being used in a very broad general sense to describe, perhaps in a derogatory way, one who goes beyond the biblical sexual norms. The Hebrew word also had this for secondary meanings. It primarily spoke of prostitution but could be used in a general way to describe an adulteress or a wizard or anyone who sold themself to something other than God. This is the general derogatory sense of the word.

Even though a cult prostitute would be unchaste, it wouldn't define what Yakov meant, for just in and of itself, no one would be able to understand

---

[195] *The Companion Bible: The Authorized Version of 1611* (Grand Rapids, Michigan: Kregel Publications, 1990), p. 1617.

[196] In the section *Israel and Baal Peor*, this prostitution was specifically seen as cultic, centering around the worship of Baal (Num. 25).

[197] Sinclair, *CED*, p. 273.

that Yakov spoke of cult prostitution. Unchastity is therefore a false and misleading word when placed as the English translation for Yakov's second rule. This also holds true for 'sexual immorality.'

Another grave theological problem arises when Bauer states that pornay'ah is 'sexual unfaithfulness of a married woman, Mt. 5:32; 19:9'. This of course is an adulteress. One could call an adulteress a harlot but this only speaks of her in a derogatory way. It's not an actual description of what she did. What Bauer defines as adultery for both cites (pornay'ah; Mt. 5:32; 19:9), doesn't mean adultery at all but cult prostitution.[198] Bauer falls into the same deep pit that most theologians do when they think that Jesus is declaring that 'only for adultery,' can a biblical divorce take place. But this isn't what Jesus said or meant. More on this in the section *Jesus and Divorce*.

In his initial definition, Bauer unfortunately gives no indication that the word can mean cult prostitution. He only presents 'prostitution.' It's veiled however in a comment further on in the lexicon. There he speaks of 'idolatry' 'pagan cults' and 'sexual debauchery' and so cult prostitution could indeed be a part of his definition for fornication or pornay'ah:

> 'fig., in accordance w. an OT symbol of apostasy from God, of idolatry; from the time of Hosea the relationship betw. God and his people was regarded as a marriage bond. This usage was more easily understandable because *many pagan cults* (Astarte, Isis, Cybele, et al.), were connected with *sexual debauchery* (cf. Hosea 6:10; Jer. 3:2, 9; Rev. 19:2).'[199]

The Greek word pornay'ah lines up with its Hebraic counterpart for both forms of prostitution; cultic and common. *Sexual idolatry* was the grand form of pagan worship. This is cult prostitution. Bauer speaks of 'sexual debauchery' and links it with pagan cults (Isis and Cybele, etc.). When Israel did this they severed themselves or apostatized from Yahveh, as we saw in *Israel and Baal Peor* and *Cult Prostitution in Ancient Israel*.

This is what Yakov wanted the new Gentile believers to be aware of. Paul too admonished the Gentiles in Corinth about this very thing, using the example of Israel at Baal Peor. He said to them that it was written for *their instruction* or benefit. *TDNT* states,

> 'The judgment which smote the Israelites, the fore-fathers

---

[198]   The two Greek words of Mt. 5:32 and 19:9 are spelled differently because one is singular and the other is plural. They're the same Greek word.

[199]   Bauer, *GELNT*, p. 693.

72

of Christians (1 C. 10:1), in the wilderness when they fell victim to idolatry and lust, and thus tempted God, took place as an example' '10:8, 11.'[200]

The reference *TDNT* makes to 1st Cor. 10:8 is the sacrificial-sexual idolatry of the Baal Peor affair. Paul, writing about fornication (KJV), points directly to that specific orgy:

> '*Now these things were our examples*, to the intent we should not lust after evil things, as they also lusted. Neither be ye *idolators*, as were some of them; as it is written, The people sat down to eat and drink, and rose up to play. Neither let us commit *fornication*, as some of them committed, and fell in one day three and twenty thousand.' (1st Cor. 10:6-8 KJV)

'Fornication' in 1st Cor. 10:8 should read cult prostitution. Paul was admonishing the Corinthians, 'Neither let us commit cult prostitution!' It was a major problem among a number of Gentile believers. How could it not be?

Other lexicons also confirm prostitution as the primary meaning of pornay'ah, which becomes cult prostitution for most New Testament texts. In his lexicon, Wesley Perschbacher writes that pornay'ah in Acts 15:20 means whoredom:

> 'fornication, whoredom, Matt. 15:19; Mark 7:21; Acts 15:20, 29' 'adultery, Matt 5:32; 19:9; incest, 1st Cor. 5:1'
> 'from the Hebrew, put symbolically for idolatry, Rev. 2:21; 14:8'.[201]

Fornication here is used with prostitution (whoredom), as Bauer did. Perschbacher notes that it should be translated as fornication or whoredom, at least for our cite. It's a shame that translators don't follow suite and place 'whoredom' there. Even though it wouldn't be specifically what James had in mind, it would be light years ahead of 'fornication', 'sexual immorality' or 'unchastity.' Again though, as with Bauer, it's hard to understand what Perschbacher means by fornication, although with whoredom following it, it would seem to suggest that it's similar.

Perschbacher also notes the Hebraic connection in Revelation, 'symbolically' speaking of idolatry. Unfortunately, Perschbacher also thinks the Greek word can be used for the term adultery, citing Matt. 5:32 and 19:9.

---

[200] Kittel, *TDNT*, vol. VI, p. 593.

[201] Perschbacher, *NAGL*, p. 340.

He falls into the same pit that Bauer did before him. It's not that an adulteress couldn't be called a whore or a harlot in a derogatory way. The
Greek definition expands to include those who are incestuous, adulterous
or homosexual, etc., but only as a degrading slur upon them. Perschbacher
is wrong for translating pornay'ah to mean adultery in Matthew. There's
not one cite in the New Testament to validate the use of it as adultery.

Paul used πορνεια (pornay'ah) in 1st Cor. 5:1 to describe the man who
slept with his father's wife. Most theologians describe it as incest. It certainly was incestuous but there's a twist to it. More on this in the section
Incest in Corinth.

Timothy Friberg's lexicon states that pornay'ah is,

> 'generally, of every kind of extramarital, unlawful, or un-
> natural sexual intercourse, fornication, sexual immorality,
> prostitution'. As 'a synonym for μοιχεια (moi-kay-ah),
> (marital) unfaithfulness, adultery (Mt. 5:32)'; 'metaphori-
> cally, as apostasy from God through idolatry (spiritual)
> immorality, unfaithfulness (Rev. 19:2)'.[202]

For Friberg it's a general 'free for all' in that the word can mean any number of different things, with prostitution coming at the end (of his first sentence). That pornay'ah can be used to describe things other than prostitution ('every kind…unnatural sexual intercourse'), has been shown, in
that it can be a derogatory description of a lewd person, etc., but this is not
the primary meaning of the word in the New Testament.

To understand what James meant when he said it, it's essential to take the
primary meaning of the word, as no secondary or tertiary meaning can be
inserted without proving that the primary meaning wasn't meant. But
translators haven't followed this elementary rule. Friberg too falls into the
same crowded pit that Bauer and Perschbacher are in. He thinks that adultery constitutes a biblical divorce ('Mt. 5:32') or as he states, is 'a synonym for' adultery.

Revelation is a book that gives examples of actual cult prostitution among
believers. Friberg only mentions it in a 'metaphorical' way but includes
both 'apostasy' and idolatry. This of course is the literal reality of pornay'ah as cult prostitution. (Common prostitution is not idolatrous.) In the
second chapter of Revelation, Jesus deals with cult prostitution in two assemblies in what is now western Turkey (Rev. 2:14, 21). *Theological Dictionary of the New Testament* fumbles on pornay'ah also, stating it,

---

[202] Friberg, *ALGNT*, p. 323.

'occurs only 3 times' (in Acts), 'in verses recording the prohibitions of the apostolic decree, 15:20, 29 and 21:25.' 'There is no insistence on the Jewish Law, only on the observance of minimal requirements for the interrelationships of Jewish and Gentile Christians, 15:28. Among these is the prohibition of fornication.'[203]

'The whole decree is thus presented, not as a ritual order, but as a short moral catechism which mentions negatively the three chief sins (idolatry, murder and fornication').[204]

'The surprising combination of πορνεια' (pornay'ah, fornication: Acts 15:20), 'with dietary regulations is due to the fact that the four prohibitions are based on Lv. 17 and 18. πορνεια' (pornay'ah) 'here is marrying within the prohibited degrees, which acc. to the Rabbis was forbidden "on account of fornication." Lv. 18:6-18.'[205]

TDNT presents *their theology* of the passage as though it were the only possible interpretation. James made the decree as 'a short moral catechism' that had *no bearing on Gentile observance* of the Law ('There is no insistence on the Jewish Law'). And yet they mention Lev. 17–18 (commandments from the Law), *as the basis for the rules*. Welcome to theological gymnastics class 101.

Not marrying one's sister or aunt, etc., are very specific laws within the Law of Moses (Lev. 18:6-18). Witherington rightly *rejects any connection* to these prohibited marriages because the term pornay'ah 'is not used to describe these sexual sins' in the Septuagint.[206] *TDNT* doesn't have a valid basis for linking pornay'ah in Acts 15:20 with the forbidden relationships of Lev. 18.

TDNT presents table fellowship (interrelationships between Jewish and Gentile believers), as the reason why James gave the rules. Unfortunately they're interpreting the rules in a way that Yakov never intended.

TDNT also states that the three major rules (minus strangling), speak of idolatry, murder and fornication. But murder, as we'll see, can't be what Yakov meant by blood, and so this negates that interpretation also. More

---

[203] Kittel, *TDNT*, vol. VI, p. 592.

[204] Ibid., p. 593.

[205] Ibid.

[206] Witherington, *The Acts of the Apostles*, p. 465.

on this in the section *The Third Rule: Blood.*

Bauer listed prostitution first, and might have used it for translating Yakov's word. Perschbacher actually listed 'whoredom' as the definition of the word in Acts 15:20. Although these aren't fully accurate, they're better than what Bibles have now. Friberg muddied the waters by 'throwing in everything' about pornay'ah so that all sexual sins were on an equal footing (e.g. 'every kind of extramarital' sex). It's only at the end of his definitions that prostitution appears, and that it seems, like an 'add on.' Unfortunately none of them presented *cult* prostitution as a primary definition, although it was mentioned by both Bauer and Perschbacher.

TDNT tried to link pornay'ah (fornication) with the forbidden marriages of Lev. 18 but if that was correct, Yakov would have mentioned more relating to a possible marriage partner. At the very least, that a believer should be married to another believer (1st Cor. 7:39). And as Witherington revealed, pornay'ah is never used in speaking of the forbidden marriages in the Septuagint. Incestuous relationships wasn't the meaning for Yakov's second rule. And *TDNT*'s theology of table fellowship, along with their interpretation that blood relates to murder (in Acts 15:20), wasn't what Yakov meant either.

The Companion Bible was accurate. From its cite in Acts 15:20 it pointed directly to the Baal Peor fiasco in Num. 25, exposing fornication as sexual idolatry (cult prostitution). This also brought out that at one time, fornication properly related to what pornay'ah meant.

The definitions of the lexicons will become very specific when they speak of the *person* who practices pornay'ah. It has nothing to do with adultery, incest, common homosexuality or promiscuity, etc. This will confirm the primary meaning of Yakov's word as prostitution (either common or cultic).

Incest, adultery and pre-marital sex are sins that can be forgiven but cult prostitution theoretically cannot be. The only sins that cannot be forgiven are blasphemy against the Holy Spirit and apostasy (1st Tim. 4:1; Heb. 6:4-6). These are direct frontal attacks on the work of the Holy Spirit. Believers who become, or use, cult prostitutes severe themselves from the covenant they have with the Father. They have intentionally chosen to fall, or run away from, the faith, severing their relationship with Yeshua. Yet even in this, God may extend mercy.

The Greek Verb: Por-nu-oh (To Prostitute)

Walter Bauer says the Greek verb πορνευω (por-nu-oh) means 'to prostitute, practice prostitution or sexual immorality'.[207] Using pornu'oh for 'sexual immorality' is more of a general 'catch-all' than an actual description of what a person might do. But Bauer describes the root of the word when he says it means 'to prostitute, practice prostitution.'

Perschbacher is more focused with his definition. He writes that it means,

> 'to commit fornication or whoredom, 1st Cor. 6:18; 10:8'
> 'from the Hebrew, to commit spiritual fornication, practice idolatry'.[208]

He opts for two descriptions of pornu'oh which are the primary biblical meanings. With him having 'fornication or whoredom' it seems that fornication for him is harlotry. His including it for 1st Cor. 6:18 and 10:8 misses that it's 'cult whoredom' instead of just 'whoredom.' 1st Cor. 6:18 speaks of cult harlotry and 10:8 is the Baal Peor catastrophe. Thousands of Hebrews lost their lives because they ate the meat sacrificed to the god and committed cult prostitution.

Perschbacher also brings in the 'spiritual' aspect. This relates directly to God and a person's walk with Him and any number of other things (e.g. magic, astrology, unfaithfulness, etc.). But 'from the Hebrew' relates primarily to Israel whoring after other gods through cult harlotry which is evident from them practicing 'idolatry'.

Friberg states that pornu'oh means,

> to 'generally practice sexual immorality, commit fornication, live without sexual restraint (1st Cor. 6:18)' 'metaphorically practice idolatry (Rev. 17:2)'.[209]

Friberg again presents a broad definition with 'sexual immorality' and to 'live without sexual restraint.' One is hard pressed to understand that prostitution is the root of the word. His 'living without sexual restraint' also misses the point as the biblical phrase 'to prostitute' points primary to cult prostitution.

Turning to the Greek noun will cement it's definition as prostitution.

---

[207] Bauer, *GELNT*, p. 693.

[208] Perschbacher, *NAGL*, p. 340.

[209] Friberg, *ALGNT*, p. 323.

The Greek Noun: Por-nay (Prostitute)

Pornay πορνη (por-nay) is the Greek noun that's associated with Yakov's second rule. This is the description of a person who commits prostitution; a prostitute. The lexicons become very specific now. Bauer says it's,

> a 'prostitute, harlot. 1 Cor. 6:15. fig. (Is. 1:21; 23:15f; Jer. 3:3; Ezk. 16:30f); as the designation of a government hostile to God and his people, Rev. 17:15f.'[210]

There's no reference to an adulteress or someone promiscuous or anything else that might be mistakenly placed into the category of 'sexual immorality' or a 'sexual sin of any kind.' His definition, although limited here in not mentioning a cult prostitute, give us the primary meaning of pornay'ah (prostitution) as one who is a prostitute.

Perschbacher agrees with Bauer, adding 'whore' (which is the same as a prostitute or harlot), but then unfortunately writes 'an unchaste female.' This clouds the issue for anyone looking at his definition but when his cite is looked up, this 'unchaste female' is none other than a prostitute (and not an adulteress, etc.). He defines pornay as,

> 'a prostitute, whore, harlot, an unchaste female, Matt. 21:31-32; from the Hebrew, an idolatress, Rev. 17:1, 5, 15.'[211]

The 'unchaste female' that Perschbacher speaks of in 'Matt. 21:31-32' are actually prostitutes (NASB) or harlots (KJV):

> 'Which of the two did the will of his father?' They said, 'The first.' Jesus said to them, 'Truly I say to you that the tax collectors and *prostitutes* will get into the Kingdom of God before you. For John came to you in the way of righteousness and you did not believe him; but the tax collectors and *prostitutes* did believe him; and you, seeing this, did not even feel remorse afterward so as to believe him.' (NASB)

In translating pornay in Mt. 21:31-32 as an unchaste female, Perschbacher completely misses the point as to who Yeshua was speaking about. These women were prostitutes or harlots as both the NASB and KJV bring out. 'Unchaste' describes their immoral character but doesn't say who they

---

[210] Bauer, *GELNT*, p. 693.

[211] Perschbacher, *NAGL*, p. 340.

were. He does recognize though that 'from the Hebrew, the woman is an idolatress'. This speaks of sexual idolatry (harlot plus idolatry), which is cult harlotry. His idolatress is linked to the Harlot of Babylon (Rev. 17:1, 5) which is certainly a reference to sexual idolatry or cult harlotry (along with other forms of 'harlotry').

The biblical noun should not be watered down to include an adulteress or an unchaste female. L. Ryken speaks of the difference between a prostitute and an adulteress:

> 'A prostitute, also called a harlot, is a person who provides sexual activity in exchange for material security. Generally a woman, she is distinguished from an adulteress by her lack of discrimination in partner choice.'[212]

It's the harlot's job to corral as many men as she can. And she certainly wouldn't say that she was choosing a partner. She calls attention to herself by the way she dresses and acts that she may attract as many as she can.

On the other hand, the adulteress is not looking for anyone to detect her adultery. The adulteress usually confines herself to one adulterer in any given period in her life.

An adulteress shouldn't be labeled a prostitute except in a derogatory way. This is the way the Scriptures speak of Israel in relation to Yahveh. When Israel goes into cult prostitution she's called an adulteress by Yahveh because she's in covenant marriage with Him. But the actual practice of what she did was cult prostitution in the midst of sacrificial idolatry.

Friberg writes that pornay means,

> to 'sell' 'literally, a woman who practices sexual immorality as a means of making a living; harlot, prostitute, whore, 1st Cor. 6:15)'.[213]

Even though he again takes the broadest possible path (one 'who practices sexual immorality'), Friberg can only offer the terms harlot, prostitute and whore for pornay. There's no mention of an adulteress or common homosexual, etc.

Please note how the various definitions of all three men narrow considerably when they speak of the person acting in the way of pornay'ah (prostitution). They become very specific in their nomenclature. This was true for the Hebrew word also.

---

[212] Ryken, *DBI*, p. 676.

[213] Friberg, *ALGNT*, p. 324.

The Greek lexicons, once broken down, present πορνεια (pornay'ah) and two other Greek words associated with it, primarily as prostitution (cult or common), or those who practice it. An adulteress can be classified under pornay'ah but only as a derogatory term for her.

The primary meaning of the verb meant 'to prostitute' and the specific and only meaning of the person who walked in pornay'ah was a prostitute. The primary meaning of the Greek word for Yakov's second rule is prostitution from both Greek and Hebrew sources. With the other rules speaking of idolatry, this 'prostitution' and 'prostitute' must be cultic. For Yakov to have meant anything else he would have had to specifically say it.

SCHOLARSHIP AND THE SECOND RULE

The understanding of the four rules specifically addressing sacrificial-sexual idolatry primarily rests upon the second rule being seen as cult prostitution. Four scholars believe that the second rule means cult prostitution (Knowling, Bivin, Witherington and Hegg), while others consider it a possibility (Williams, *Wycliffe* and Stern).

It's very telling though that scholars in the caliber of F. F. Bruce and Howard Marshall don't even mention it. Bruce believes that fornication relates to unlawful marriages in Torah. The second rule for him means that Gentiles 'should conform to the Jewish code of relations between the sexes instead of remaining content with the pagan standards.'[214] He tries to explain how the Gentiles could be commanded to walk in the commandments of Moses by saying that they did it, not because they had to but 'voluntarily' for table fellowship. But this 'slight of hand' theology is unacceptable. First, Gentiles had no say in the forming of the Decree. And second, one can't be seen as doing something voluntarily if it's commanded of them.

Howard Marshall believes that the second rule should be translated as,

> 'unchastity, variously understood as illicit sexual intercourse or as breaches of the Jewish marriage law (which forbid marriage between close relatives, Lv. 18:6-18).'[215]

TDNT presented the same understanding for the second rule[216] as Marshall but Witherington dismantled their interpretation by noting that the Septuagint never refers to those prohibited marriages as pornay'ah.[217] And Knowling brought up the theological conundrum that taking rules from the Law would entail a less than full membership among the Jewish believers. He also questioned the rules coming from the Noahide Laws as four of the seven laws of Noah weren't covered in the Decree.[218]

David Williams mentions the possibility that the second rule could mean cult prostitution and that it might be linked to the first rule. But he obscures it by saying it's 'idolatry' that 'often involved immorality' and that

---

214 Bruce, *The Book of the Acts*, p. 295.

215 Marshall, *Acts*, p. 253.

216 Kittel, *TDNT*, vol. VI, p. 592 and p. 75 above.

217 Witherington, *The Acts of the Apostles*, p. 465. Also p. 75 above.

218 Knowling, *The Expositor's Greek Testament, vol. two: The Acts of the Apostles*, p. 335. Also pp. 11-12 above.

the second rule might pertain to the forbidden marriages of Lev. 18:

> 'there may have been an intended connection between
> these two' (pollutions of idols and sexual immorality) 'for
> idolatry often involved immorality; but immorality is
> sometimes taken to mean marriage within the forbidden
> decrees (cf. Lev. 18:6-18)'.[219]

David Stern clouds the issue by listing *all* the possibilities, including cult
prostitution, when he says that the second rule,

> is 'any form of sexual immorality' 'sexual unions outside
> of marriage' along with homosexual behavior, temple
> prostitution and other improper practices.'[220]

Wycliffe sees cult prostitution as a possibility and says it was very common in the world at that time:

> 'fornication may refer to immorality in general or to reli-
> gious prostitution in pagan temples. Such immorality was
> so common among Gentiles that it mentioned special
> attention.'[221]

Some scholars recognize that Yakov could have been speaking about cult
prostitution. But R. J. Knowling, who lived about a hundred years ago,
presented the second rule squarely as such. He stated,

> 'the heathen view of impurity was' very 'lax throughout
> the Roman empire.'[222]

His 'impurity' referred to cult harlotry. He related how some thought the
second rule referred to the forbidden marriages of Mosaic Law but didn't
accept that interpretation because of the way the word was used *throughout* the New Testament:

> 'An attempt has been made to refer the word here to the
> sin of incest, or to marriage within the forbidden decrees,
> rather than to the sin of fornication...but others take the
> word in its general sense *as it is employed elsewhere in
> the N.T.*' 'from the way in which women might be called
> upon *to serve impurely in a heathen temple* (to which reli-

---

[219] Williams, *Acts*, p. 266.

[220] Stern, *JNTC*, p. 277.

[221] Pfeiffer, *WBC*, p. 1152.

[222] Knowling, *The Acts of the Apostles*, p. 324; 'cf. Horace, *Sat.*, 1:2, 31; Terence,
       Adelphi 1:2, 21; Cicero, *Pro Caelio* 20'.

gious obligation, as Zockler reminds us, some have seen a reference in the word here') 'we see the need and the likelihood of such a specific enjoinder against the sin of fornication.'[223]

Fornication for Knowling meant cult prostitution. This was evident to him from the way the word was used throughout the New Testament and from how Gentile women were called upon to present themselves for service at the 'heathen temple.' It's also seen in his statement that the pagan religious obligation as such, dictated 'a specific enjoinder against the sin of' cult prostitution. This could only be religious if it were cult prostitution (vs. common prostitution).

David Bivin, even though he thinks that 'blood and strangled' speak of dietary regulations, believes that pornay'ah in Acts 15:20 should be,

> 'cult prostitutes.' 'Unchastity" is a poor translation. The Hebrew equivalent of the Greek noun *primarily* has to do with prostitution.'[224]

Witherington also says the basic meaning of pornay'ah is prostitution:

> 'the term πορνεια' (pornay'ah) 'in its most basic meaning refers to prostitution, including so-called sacred prostitution.'[225]

Witherington writes that if James meant adultery he would have used the Greek word for adultery μοιχεια (moi-kay-ah).[226] Hegg also believes that pornay'ah refers to cult prostitution.[227]

Witherington and Hegg understand Yakov's second rule as cult prostitution *and* that the rules are a unit on sacrificial-sexual idolatry. It's very sad though that over the last 1,900 years, only a few have been able to see the second rule as cult prostitution and only two have understood the rules as pertaining to sacrificial-sexual idolatry. But this opens the theological door for the Law to come through, even though Witherington doesn't see it.

The majority of Christian scholars don't realize that pornay'ah in Acts 15:20 is cult prostitution. It certainly can't be for lack of definitions in the

---

[223] Ibid.

[224] Bivin, *Understanding the Difficult Words of Jesus*, p. 109 and note *.

[225] Witherington, *The Acts of the Apostles*, p. 463.

[226] Ibid.

[227] Hegg, *The Letter Writer: Paul's Background and Torah Perspective*, p. 279.

Hebrew and Greek lexicons. It's because of their preconceived theology that 'the Law isn't anymore.' This excludes prostitution and especially cult prostitution from their radar screen of possibilities. And even among those that understand pornay'ah as cult prostitution, their theology prohibits them from understanding the four rules as a package deal on sacrificial-sexual idolatry. Knowling and Bivin fall into this category.

It's understandable because Church teaching on the Law creates a thick veil over the eyes of most theologians. These scholars are experts in their field and yet they don't realize the error they believe and propagate. The power of heretical tradition is deception that leads to false practice. And this is why Messiah Yeshua came against it so strongly among His own people (Mt. 15:1-20).

It's a massive theological shift to think about, let alone accept, that the Law of Moses is still valid. Only Hegg has understood this and that the Law wasn't done away with by the decision of James and his four rules. The Law is still in effect for both Jewish and Gentile believers.

The second rule of James has nothing to do with prohibited marriages, adultery, pre-marital sex or common homosexuality, etc. Prostitution is the correct general definition for the second rule from both Hebrew and Greek word meanings. In terms of both its ancient reality and word usage in the Bible, it relates directly to cult prostitution. Some scholars have seen this.

Popular Definitions of Fornication

Although fornication is the biblical term that the KJV, NASB and NRSV use for Acts 15:20, and it can be said to mean cult prostitution, it becomes very clouded when one looks up the definition in some popular sources (and even in scholarly sources as we've seen). *Unger's Bible Dictionary* defines fornication as,

> 'The worship of idols is naturally mentioned as fornication (Rev. 14:8; 17:2, 4; 18:3; 19:2) as also the defilement of idolatry as incurred by eating the sacrifices offered to idols (Rev. 2:21).'[228]

> 'At the present time, adultery is the term used of such an act when the person is married, fornication when unmarried'.[229]

Unger's is much too general and totally misses the biblical reality by saying that the 'worship of idols' and the 'eating of sacrifices' constitutes fornication as there's no mention of sexual idolatry as the basis for it. Their second paragraph states that at 'the present time' sexual intercourse outside of marriage is 'fornication' ('fornication when unmarried'). This seems to be how many people use it today.

UBD's definition excludes married people from the ability to commit fornication as they classify that as adultery. This doesn't line up with the biblical definition at all. Nowhere is that distinction seen. In other words, it doesn't matter if a person is married or not, they can still commit fornication (common or cult prostitution).

Unger's says that fornication can only be applied to single people ('when unmarried') but this also contradicts Yeshua. He says that only for fornication (Mt. 5:32; 19:9 KJV), can a biblical divorce between two believers take place. Obviously the fornicator can be married.

Unfortunately for *Unger's* there's no mention of prostitution. As this is the primary meaning of the word, their definition falls far short and is very misleading. They also give a definition for 'the present time' (adultery), that doesn't match the biblical reality. This is unacceptable for a biblical dictionary on something this major.

Webster's Dictionary is another source that people might turn to in order to understand what fornication in their English Bible means. At this point though *Webster's* lacks biblical credibility. Fornication for them is sexual

---

[228] Unger, *UBD*, p. 378.

[229] Ibid.

intercourse between persons other than a man and his wife.[230] This would include both married and single people but doesn't speak specifically of prostitution. Actually fornication for *Webster's* is either adultery or sex outside of marriage. The reality that fornication is primarily cult or common prostitution is absent. The word has taken on a 'popular definition.'

A third source affirms the failure of the first two. *Collins English Dictionary* states that fornication is 'voluntary secular intercourse outside marriage' 'between two persons of the opposite sex, where one is or both are unmarried.'[231] Again a definition that rests on sexual intercourse outside of marriage which can be adultery or promiscuity. There's no mention of prostitution, and cult prostitution cannot fall into their framework as they speak of '*secular* intercourse'. They go on to say that fornication is 'sexual immorality in general, esp. adultery.'[232]

According to the Internet encyclopedia *Wikipedia*, the term fornication comes from the Latin word *fornicationis*. It means 'an archway or vault.' In 'Rome, prostitutes could be solicited there' and so the word became a 'euphemism for prostitution.'[233] But even with this they define fornication,

> as 'a term which refers to sexual intercourse between consenting unmarried partners. In contrast adultery is consensual sex where one or both of the partners are married to someone else.'[234]

Fornication may have been an accurate English representation at one time but not for today. The common definitions make the use of the word problematic and misleading and excludes fornication from being used in an English Bible because there's no link to cult prostitution. Of course for the same reason, illicit sex, sexual immorality and unchastity, as some Bibles translate the second rule, are also unacceptable.

It's to the discredit of these sources that they don't present the biblical definition of fornication somewhere in their definitions. This creates a serious problem for understanding what the KJV, NRSV or NASB mean when they place fornication as the second rule of Acts 15:20. And this is why all English Bibles should use the precise term 'cult prostitution' (or cult harlotry) for Yakov's second rule.

---

[230]   Woolf, *WNCD*, p. 448.

[231]   Sinclair, *CED*, p. 602.

[232]   Ibid.

[233]   *Wikipedia* at http://en.wikipedia.org/wiki/Fornication.

[234]   Ibid.

JESUS AND DIVORCE

Over the centuries the chief, if not only grounds for biblical divorce in the Church, has been adultery. This position was primarily based on Matthew 5:32 where Jesus said,

> 'whosoever shall put away his wife, saving for the cause of *fornication* (πορνεια pornay'ah) causeth her to commit adultery.' (μοιχευθηναι moi-ku-thay-nay 'to commit adultery') (KJV)

R. T. France states that the cause of divorce, pornay'ah (fornication KJV; unchastity, NASB and NRSV) 'means adultery'.[235] Robert Mounce agrees by saying it 'undoubtedly refers in this context to an adulterous liaison'.[236] *The Wycliffe Bible Commentary* believes that adultery is 'the one cause for divorce allowed by Christ.'[237] And David Stern sees pornay'ah as adultery, stating that a marriage,

> 'must not be dissolved for anything less than the most direct insult to its one-flesh integrity, adultery.'[238]

The most obvious questions to ask are, 'If Jesus meant that only for adultery a divorce could take place, why isn't the Greek word for adultery used as the *reason* for divorce? Why is the word, whose primary meaning is prostitution, written as the reason? This is very troubling especially when the Lord uses the word adultery in the very same sentence to speak of the one who is divorced for anything less than pornay'ah.

It's very clear in whatever language is used. If Yeshua taught adultery as the reason for a biblical divorce, it'd have been written in the Greek New

---

[235] R. T. France, M.A., B.D., Ph.D., Author; The Rev. Leon Morris, M.Sc., M.Th., Ph.D., General Editor, *Tyndale New Testament Commentaries: Matthew* (Leicester, England: Inter-Varsity Press, 2000), p. 123.

[236] Robert H. Mounce, Author; W. Ward Gasque, New Testament Editor, *New International Biblical Commentary: Matthew* (Peabody, MA: Hendrickson Publishers, 1995), p. 47.

[237] Pfeiffer, *WBC*, p. 938. Wycliffe places an appendage on the theme of adultery saying it could also mean 'unfaithfulness during the betrothal period' a time amounting to about a year in ancient Israel. In the Law (Dt. 22:23-27), if the woman was found to have had sex with another during this period, it would have been seen as adultery because the two were legally married (even though they hadn't consummated it yet). Betrothal was officially a part of marriage. One betrothed to another was seen as married, so much so that if they wanted to break the betrothal a divorce would be necessary (Mt. 1:18-25).

[238] Stern, *JNTC*, p. 59.

Testament (reflecting the Hebrew word for adultery).[239] The Greek has Yeshua saying it's only for pornay'ah (prostitution) that a divorce can take place (not μοιχευω moi-ku-oh, adultery).

TDNT states the Greek word for adultery specifically means adultery, unlike the word pornay'ah which can have other meanings:

> 'μοιχευω' (moi-ku-oh adultery) 'is narrower than πορ-
> νεια' (pornay'ah prostitution), 'and refers solely to adul-
> tery.'[240]

Bauer too says that pornay'ah is to be, 'Distinguished from μοιχευειν' (moi-ku-ain) 'commit adultery'.[241] If moikuoh refers solely to adultery then why would Yeshua use pornay'ah (prostitution), if he wanted to convey that only for adultery a divorce could take place?

The Septuagint reveals that the Hebrew and Greek understanding for the words prostitution and adultery remained very constant. TDNT states,

> 'In the LXX' (Septuagint) 'the group πορνευω' (por-nu-
> oh) 'to play the harlot' 'is normally used for the root זנה'
> (zanah), 'while with equal consistency μοιχευω' (moi-
> ku-oh) 'is used for נאף' (nah-ahf; adultery).[242]

The distinction between prostitution and adultery is not only found in Hebrew and Greek but in English as well. A prostitute is not an adulteress and an adulteress is not a prostitute. These distinctions are self-evident and clear. Adultery cannot arbitrarily be forced into Yeshua's reason for divorce (or Yakov's second rule for the Gentile).

ISBE contrasts the harlot and cult prostitute with an adulteress:

> 'Harlot; play the harlot...zana' (Hebrew; to prostitute);
> 'porne' (pornay, the Greek word for a prostitute), 'whore,
> commit fornication' 'common whore, prostitute, temple-
> prostitute. A harlot is a woman who uses her sexual ca-
> pacity either for gain or for pagan religious purposes. In
> contrast to the adulteress she is promiscuous and usually
> shows no regard for who her mate might be.'[243]

---

[239] Also interesting to note is what Yeshua says of a woman who is divorced for anything less than pornay'ah (Mt. 19:9). She becomes an adulteress, not a prostitute. In other words she's still married to the original partner. This is also true for the man that puts her away for anything less than pornay'ah.

[240] Kittel, TDNT, vol. VI, p. 581.

[241] Bauer, GELNT, p. 693.

[242] Kittel, TDNT, vol. VI, p. 584.

ISBE notes that 'temple prostitution' is associated with both the Hebrew and the Greek word for prostitution. It also states there's a difference between a prostitute and an adulteress, something that is very obvious but seems to have eluded the attention of the Church and most theologians at Mt. 5:32.

Some scholars though blur the distinction between prostitution and adultery. *TDNT* actually uses Scripture that doesn't support their position:

> 'Examples show that זנה' (zanah, to prostitute), 'can be used of the married woman who is unfaithful to her husband (Hos. 1–2; Ezk. 16, 23), or of the betrothed who by law already belongs to her husband, Gen. 38:24. In content πορνευω' (pornu'oh, to prostitute) 'here is equivalent to' 'μοιχευω' (moi'kuoh, adultery).[244]

TDNT is completely inaccurate when it states that prostitution 'is equivalent to' adultery. It aligns the concept of spiritual adultery (the nation's unfaithfulness to Yahveh), with common adultery among individuals.

In Ezekiel 16 and 23 Judah is accused by God of literally practicing sexual idolatry (cult harlotry), and worship of (sacrifice to) pagan gods. She had severed herself from her Husband Yahveh. God would correct her through destruction of Judah and captivity in Babylon for the remnant.

Hosea's wife was a cult prostitute before Hosea married her.[245] Her 'adultery' consisted in returning to cult prostitution. Gomer continued in her profession while married to Hosea and symbolically pictured Israel's unfaithfulness to Yahveh. Stating that she was an adulteress ('unfaithful') fails to recognize that her sin wasn't primarily adultery but cult prostitution. Also her whoring spirit pictured the cult harlotry of Israel that gave itself 'upon every high hill' to the pagan deities. Yahveh's wife was symbolically seen as an adulteress but the *practice* the Israelis committed was

---

[243] Bromiley, *ISBE*, vol. two, p. 616.

[244] Kittel, *TDNT*, vol. VI, p. 584.

[245] Hosea's message of repentance was to the northern kingdom of Israel, steeped in cult prostitution and sacrificial idolatry. For the parallel to be complete it would only seem reasonable that Gomer, reflecting Israel, would be a cult prostitute. This is hinted at in her name. Keil, *Minor Prophets*, p. 27 relates how her name means 'perfection, completion in a passive sense' and 'that the woman was thoroughly perfected in her whoredom, or that she had gone to the furthest length in prostitution.' The name of her parent, Diblaim, also is telling as it occurs in 'Moabitish places in Num. 33:46' and we know that the Moabites worshiped their gods through cult prostitution.

cult harlotry. Israel would be obliterated because of it (2nd Kgs. 17:1-23).

Gomer is a symbol of Israel in its cult harlotry. And Judah in Ezk. 16 and 23 is literally practicing cult harlotry as a nation. For *TDNT* to present these two examples as 'adultery' defies the rules of scholarship and common sense.

TDNT's 'betrothed' of Gen. 38:24 is Tamar. But the biblical verse in question says she 'had played the harlot' and was pregnant by 'prostitution.' Nowhere does it suggest that adultery was the cause of her pregnancy (as was brought out in the section on *Judah and Tamar*).

TDOT presents their theological difference between zanah (Hebrew: to prostitute), and na-af (Hebrew: to commit adultery) saying,

> 'Certain distinctions exist between zana and the parallel root na-af 'to commit adultery.' 'Na-af' (adultery) 'connotes sexual intercourse between a married person and someone other than his/her spouse (Lev. 20:10). The two words are set in significant contrast in Hos. 4:13-14, where 'daughters' are said to 'commit whoredom' (ASV and RSV 'play the harlot,' zana) and 'spouses' to 'commit adultery' (na-af).'[246] Zana also refers figuratively to Israel as committing national harlotry (Ezk. 16:26-28).[247]

Contrary to what *TDOT* says, it's not 'in significant contrast' that whoredom and adultery are seen. The adultery that Hosea spoke of was spiritual adultery (i.e. cult harlotry), the theme of Hosea. But *TDOT* does speak of the specific word for adultery in both Hebrew and Greek.

It should be noted that by the time of Yeshua, the word זָנָה zanah (to play the harlot; to prostitute oneself) had come to encompass a number of different sins in the eyes of the Rabbis. But this was not an actual definition of the sins, but a general derogatory 'catch-all' for the word:

> 'Later Judaism gradually broadened the original usage to include adultery, incest, unnatural vice (e.g. sodomy), and unlawful marriages.'[248]

Even though these sins fall under the heading of harlotry in Rabbinic Judaism, it didn't mean that the adulteress would actually be doing the work of a prostitute or that the one who committed homosexuality was actually

---

[246] Harris, *TWOT*, vol. I, p. 246. The adultery here is again figurative as the wives were involved in cult harlotry just as much as their husbands were.

[247] Ibid.

[248] Kittel, *TDNT*, vol. VI, p. 587.

a zonah (prostitute). In the eyes of the Rabbis the people committing sodomy, etc., would be seen as walking at a similar level of unfaithfulness to Yahveh as that of a prostitute. But even with this, ancient Judaism knew that fornication involved '*especially* the sin of *paganism*'.[249]

Rabbinic Judaism's primary meaning for zanah was cult prostitution (and that even over common prostitution). The hearers of Yeshua that day fully understood that He was referring to cult prostitution. It would be the same for those who heard Yakov give the second rule.

Bauer and Perschbacher, etc., weren't accurate in linking adultery with pornay'ah for Mt. 5:32 (and 19:9). And France, Mounce, *Wycliffe* and Stern didn't pick up on the obvious difference between pornay'ah (harlotry), and moi'kuoh (adultery), as the reason for divorce. Pornay'ah in these cites (Mt. 5:32 and in 19:9)[250] cannot be defined as adultery. It defies common sense that Yeshua would use adultery as how the person would be labeled, and use an entirely different word as the cause for divorce, if the meaning was supposed to be identical. He could well have used adultery as the cause for divorce *if He meant adultery*. To place the meaning of adultery upon pornay'ah totally distorts what Yeshua was teaching.

Also, a major theological problem arises if adultery is seen as the grounds for divorce among believers. Adultery is a very grievous sin, especially to the spouse offended. But what of the sacrificial love and forgiveness of Jesus? Is not the Blood of Jesus able to forgive the adulteress and to heal the husband? What makes adultery 'the unforgivable sin'? Didn't Yahveh forgive King David for adultery (2nd Sam. 12:1-15)? Didn't Yeshua forgive the woman caught in adultery (Jn. 8:2-11)? If so, then why would it be any less for those in His Kingdom (Acts 13:38-39)?

As both believing partners struggle to find Him in all this, the one offended can offer forgiveness to the repentant offender. And the offender, if truly repentant, will be humbled and brought back into the fold. Why should adultery be seen as severing the marriage?

When a believing spouse commits cult prostitution, then there is biblical grounds for divorce. Why cult prostitution and not common prostitution? Because common prostitution, like incest, common homosexuality and

---

[249] Ibid., p. 588.

[250] In Matt. 19:9 Jesus says, 'And I say unto you, whosoever shall put away his wife, except it be for fornication, and shall marry another, committeth adultery: and whoso marrieth her which is put away doth commit adultery' (KJV). Fornication here (immorality NASB) is the Greek pornay'ah. The Greek for adultery here is moi-kah-tie, the same word used in Matt. 5:32. The same argument that is used for Matt. 5:32 applies to Mt. 19:9 also.

even adultery is a sin that can be forgiven by the Blood of Yeshua. To not forgive these sins by a believing spouse (for a believing spouse), defies the concept of forgiveness that Yeshua heralds.

On the other hand, cult prostitution (the worship of another god through sexual intercourse), severs the believing spouse from God first, and then from the spouse. Divorce becomes just the official recognition of this.

Yeshua used the word for prostitution to declare that His idea of marriage between two believers[251] can only be severed by cult harlotry (i.e. sexual idolatry which reveals apostasy). When a believer divorces his believing wife for anything less than cult harlotry, he is committing adultery if he marries another and causing her to be adulterous if she marries another.

Robert Mounce sees the superficiality of interpreting pornay'ah as adultery. He says that Jesus, in declaring adultery to be the only grounds for divorce in Matthew 5, *lacks spiritual punch*:

> 'Some writers consider this section the third antithesis' of
> what Jesus had been saying previously, but it's not 'clear
> in what way Jesus *intensifies* the law on divorce.'[252]

There was and still is a belief in traditional Jewish thinking that when Messiah would come, He'd reveal the commandments to Israel on a deeper level. It's interesting that Yeshua's teaching on divorce comes on the heels of some very powerful and radical ways of looking at the commandments (e.g. if you hate your brother you've already broken the commandment of murder). Mounce correctly discerns that the way Messiah's view on divorce is understood today, is not much different from the view of the world.

Indeed Yeshua intensified His generation's understanding of the commandments as only the Messiah could. The Torah is the love of God in verbal form. It's the written reflection of Yahveh's awesome deeds and holy character (Rom. 7:12, 14). There's a tremendous amount of grace in the Torah (the promises to the Fathers, Passover, Exodus, Red Sea, the Commandments and the subsequent fulfillment of the blessed life in Canaan). Yeshua is *the* Word of God (Jn. 1:1-3; Rev. 19:13) and as such, He is the *Living* Torah. And now the Father extends through the Son a greater promise...eternal life in the New Jerusalem. And because Yeshua is the Living Torah, He was able to explain the depths of the Torah in a way that no one else could. In His Teaching on the Mount, Yeshua re-

---

[251] Yeshua is speaking of life in His Kingdom. His Standard is for all in His Kingdom.

[252] Mounce, *Matthew*, pp. 46-47.

vealed the *essence* of the Torah: 'Love your enemies' and 'turn the other cheek' (Ex. 16:1-5; 17:1-7; 23:4-5; 32:1-6, 30-32; Lev. 19:17-18; Num. 12:1-15). This is such a radical concept that many say,

> 'It can only apply in Heaven. No one can seriously consider living like that here on Earth.'

But who will hit you on the cheek in Heaven? And what enemies will you have there to love? His words must apply to His followers today as He Himself demonstrated. But His words are so far from the accepted norm, so against our carnal nature, that many find themselves not able to fathom how to walk in them. Mounce correctly questions that if Yeshua's position on divorce is that of the world's, how can it be God's perfect standard?

All those who say pornay'ah in Mt. 5:32 (and 19:9) means adultery, line up with the Jewish sage Shammai. He lived a generation before Yeshua and in seeking to understand what God meant by listing 'uncleanness' as the cause of divorce in Dt. 24:1 ('uncleanness' KJV; 'indecency' NASB) he stated that only for adultery could a man divorce his wife.

His opponent in this and many other debates was Hillel. By the time of Yeshua the view of Hillel had been adopted over that of Shammai. Hillel said that 'even if she burns his toast' the husband has biblical grounds for divorce[253] as this could make the wife unclean in his eyes.[254] The point is that there is no intensification of the grounds for divorce on Yeshua's part if one thinks that adultery justifies divorce. Yeshua would just have been affirming Shammai.

Yeshua though, was stating something much more radical than Shammai (and the interpretation the Church has given it), and more in line with His other foundational concepts of Torah. Isn't this understanding also hinted at with the Apostles' response, the second time it's recorded in Matthew?

> 'And I say unto you, Whosoever shall put away his wife,
> except it be for fornication (pornay'ah) and shall marry

---

[253] In this area Hillel was right. Not that burnt toast was cause for divorce but the *attitude* in back of it. The reason is obvious. Mosaic Law commanded the stoning to death of any adulteress (Lev. 20:10). Divorce wouldn't be necessary. How 'indecency' from Dt. 24:1 should be understood is when a woman had an attitude and actions which were not in line with holiness. If a woman was vengeful, contentious, flirtatious or dressed provocatively, these are Mosaic grounds for divorce. This was a concession to their hard hearts (both men and women) because they hadn't been given the Holy Spirit. With the Spirit though, one can pray for the spouse, and one's heart is softened toward the other, something that just might cause the other to repent.

[254] Stern, *JNTC*, p. 59. From the Mishna: *Gittin* 9:10.

another, committeth adultery (moi-kah-tai, to commit
adultery) and whoso marrieth her which is put away doth
commit adultery.' (Mt. 19:9)

'His disciples say unto Him, 'If the case of the man be so
with his wife, it is not good to marry.' (Mt. 19:10)

Yeshua declared that except for cult prostitution a man (in His Kingdom)
couldn't get divorced. This meant the Apostles were stuck with their
wives! In the days of Yeshua, many, like today, were tossing their spouses
away 'for burning their toast' so they could marry the next slice of bread
that came along.

Why would the Apostles think it wasn't good? Because they were still
only carnal men. They hadn't been filled with the Holy Spirit yet. The
Scriptures speak of their hearts being hard (Mk. 6:52; 8:17). This is seen
in their quarreling among themselves as to who was the greatest among
them (Luke 22:24-27). It's seen in their thinking that Yeshua was talking
about physical bread when He told them to beware of the leaven of the
Pharisees and Sadducees (Matt. 16:5-12). It's seen in their telling the
blind man to stop pestering Jesus as He walked by (Luke 18:35-43). And
it's seen in Yeshua's stern rebuke to Peter, and immediately after that, His
warning to the others about dying to self if they wanted to follow Him
(Matt. 16:22-38). It's also pointedly seen in their unbelief at being told
that Yeshua was risen from the dead (Mk. 16:9-15; Lk. 24:11).

Cult prostitution is the very simple and yet profound explanation for what
pornay'ah means. It reveals Yeshua's radical concept of marriage and divorce (and why the Apostles were so shook up). And it's very consistent
with what He requires of people in His Kingdom: *sacrificial* love, repentance, forgiveness and full reconciliation.

Some might question the specific use of cult prostitution over common
prostitution as pornay'ah can mean either one. Is it common prostitution,
cultic, or both that Yeshua speaks of? It has to be the one that's idolatrous.
If a believer is a cult prostitute she has already cut herself off from the
covenant with God (apostasy), and severed her relationship with her earthly partner. It's not as though God couldn't theoretically forgive the person
but when a person reaches that state, God knows they will never repent;
they've gone over a red line. The official act of divorce just ratifies what
has already happened; high-handed rebellion against Yeshua, and the tearing apart of the one flesh (Gen. 2:24).

This kind of sin stands in a class all by itself. The person has willfully
bound himself or herself to another god. There's no longer union with

Yahveh or His people and this is why the plague in Num. 25 took 24,000 sons of Israel. When one has a believing partner that is into cult prostitution, divorce is not only justified, it's absolutely necessary.[255]

Common prostitution doesn't fall under this category. As awful as it is, it can be forgiven because it doesn't involve the sexually idolatrous worship of, and joining to, another god. All *sexual* sins can be forgiven except the one that involves idolatry. If a believer becomes a common prostitute there is still hope for restoration as the heart has not merged with another god. Just as there is hope for a believer who commits adultery, incest or common homosexuality.

Another reason why Yeshua is referring only to cult prostitution is because of the infrequent use of pornay'ah by Him. *TDNT* writes,

> 'the question of πορνεια' (pornay'ah) 'is seldom dealt with in the preaching of Jesus and the primitive community, it arises more frequently in Paul. As compared with the different judgment of the Greek world and ancient syncretism, the concrete directions of Paul bring to the attention of Gentile Christians the incompatibility of πορνεια' (pornay'ah; cult prostitution) 'and the kingdom of God.'[256]

Why the difference between Jesus, the 'primitive community' (the community of Jews in Jerusalem that believed in Yeshua) and Paul? The only reason Yeshua mentions it is to display the radical standard of marriage and divorce for believers. R. T. France affirms that divorce was all too freely practiced by his (Yeshua's) 'contemporaries.'[257] Yeshua was declaring His sole criteria for divorce.

Yeshua wasn't warning His Jewish followers about practicing cult harlotry but showing them the Kingdom standard. That's why the Apostles were worried. They wanted to be able to divorce their wives if they didn't like them. With Yeshua's standard they realized they didn't have that option. And neither do believers today if they're married to a believer.

The only reason why pornay'ah is mentioned three times in the Jewish

---

[255] This helps to understand Paul's teaching on the marriage of an unbeliever and a believer in 1st Cor. 7:12-16. The unbeliever who is *pleased* to dwell with the believer is not continuing in pagan practices which would corrupt the believer, isn't fighting the believer as he walks in the things of the Lord and is certainly not physically or emotionally abusing him, etc.

[256] Kittel, *TDNT*, vol. VI, p. 593.

[257] France, *Matthew*, p. 280.

'primitive community' is as a warning *to the Gentile believer* (in the Book of Acts). It's actually the same warning, Acts 15:20 being replicated in 15:29 and 21:25. The Jewish believers didn't need to be reminded of what cult harlotry would do to their relationship with God the Father and Yeshua the Son. They knew all too well their terrible Family history concerning cult harlotry and what it had done to their Fathers. But it seems that the Gentile believers needed to be warned and this is exactly what Acts 15:20 is all about. Yakov was warning the Gentiles that if they practiced cult prostitution, their faith in Jesus would be null and void.

On the other hand, Paul addresses the issue *many times* because cult prostitution was actually taking place among his Gentile *believers*. Paul rebuked his Gentile believers for practicing cult harlotry (1st Cor. 6:13-20; 10:7-8; 2nd Cor. 12:21; Gal. 5:19-21 KJV) saying that 'those who practice such things will not inherit the Kingdom of God (Eph. 5:3-5; Col. 3:5; 1st Thess. 4:3-8 KJV).

Yeshua's sole cause for divorce among His followers was cult prostitution and not adultery, as these four reasons bring out:

1. No intensification: Yeshua intensified and revealed the depth of the commandments of Torah and in essence, the very nature of God. Having adultery as the grounds for divorce does not intensify the criteria for divorce and presents God as not wanting to, or not able to, forgive the adulteress.

    - It also doesn't allow God to redeem the sin in the life of both the adulteress and the offended spouse so they can struggle with forgiveness and become 'more like Jesus.' This is called the furnace of affliction or God's refining Fire and the Holy Spirit uses it to make believing hearts more like the heart of their Master.

2. Word usage: Pornay'ah primarily means prostitution not adultery. This, coupled with Yeshua's use of adultery in the same sentence as the description of the wife divorced for anything less than pornay'ah also excludes pornay'ah from meaning adultery. He could not have meant adultery as justification for divorce between two believers.

3. The Blood of forgiveness: The adulteress (or adulterer) can be forgiven. The believer who is a cult prostitute cannot be restored to fellowship. (Although one must follow the leading of the Holy Spirit in this too.) She has left the covenant for another god. In this Yeshua is *conceptually* spring-boarding off of Dt. 13:6-11 ('wife of your bosom' 'to go serve other gods' 'you must surely kill her').

4. The rare use of pornay'ah: Both Yeshua (and the primitive Jewish believing community), by their infrequent use of pornay'ah, as contrasted with Paul, reveal that cult prostitution was not a common sin in Judah or Galilee among the Jewish people at that time. Yeshua's use of it presented the Kingdom standard for biblical divorce, a very radical concept.

The sexually idolatrous worship of another god severs the covenant with the God of Israel made by the believer. The difference between Mosaic divorce, or that of Shammai and the Church today, is that Yeshua's standard is *infinitely* higher. Yeshua wants us to realize our own hard hearts and our need for Him in the mist of this world of darkness. Only with His heart and power can we walk in His Kingdom.

Under Mosaic Law a man could divorce his wife for 'uncleanness' (Dt. 24:1-4; see also Prov. 12:4). It was variously interpreted in the days of Yeshua as to what exactly constituted uncleanness. That it couldn't have been sexual idolatry is understood from Mosaic Law in that the punishment for cult (or common prostitution) was death (and therefore divorce wasn't necessary).[258] Yeshua says the reason why God gave divorce to Israel through Moses was because of the hardness of their hearts:

> 'He said to them, "Because of your hardness of heart, Moses permitted you to divorce your wives. But from the beginning, it wasn't this way."' (Mt. 19:8; also Mk. 10:5)

In other words, they weren't able to forgive their wives for the 'uncleanness' they saw in them. It could have been something as serious as a rebellious heart toward her husband or God, or as innocent as an inability to please a hard husband. But this hardness gives way to life in the Spirit where one is saved to serve his wife and to pray for forgiveness in one's heart toward her for any 'uncleanness.' But for cult prostitution there is no recipient to forgive as the wife has intentionally severed her covenant with God and her husband. All that is left for the husband to do is to officially and spiritually divorce her. The relationship is already severed.

One must enter a marriage upon due reflection that it's of God, and for life, so that in the midst of troubles, one has no option for divorce unless the spouse is a cult harlot. In other words, marriage among believers in Messiah should never end in divorce. That's what the new heart is all

---

[258] Ex. 34:15-16; Lev. 20:1-6; Num. 25:1-9f; Dt. 31:16-17 and by inference, Lev. 20:10 and Dt. 22:18, 20, 22, 25. That the uncleanness wasn't adultery is seen in that the punishment for adultery was also death (Dt. 22:22). Shammai was wrong, and so is the Church.

about (Ezk. 36:26). The theme of the parable of the unjust steward who wasn't able to pay his master (Lk. 16:1-13) clearly shows us to what extent Yeshua wants us to forgive others. Because his master forgave him much it would be unthinkable for him not to forgive one who owed him much less. If our spouse sins by being adulterous, who are we, lustful creatures that we are, to withhold forgiveness? Yeshua has forgiven us for so much more. It's in this life that we must seek the Lord for His heart that is able to forgive, even those who crucify us. That's why bad things happen to us...so we can see our heart and cry out for His heart.

Yeshua forbids divorce except upon the grounds of cult prostitution. The bar has been raised to the highest of Heavens. This opens up a new understanding concerning what constitutes biblical grounds for a divorce among professed believers.[259] In Yeshua, reconciliation of all differences can take place...all differences except that of having another god and sexually acting it out.

Theologically, divorce can only take place between two believers when one partner permanently severs their relationship from Yeshua. Such is the case with cult prostitution (and of course apostasy, which although possibly harder to recognize, also severs the covenant with God).[260] All other sins are forgivable for the believer.[261]

---

[259] Yeshua's statements relate to two believers in His Kingdom. When the Apostle Paul deals with divorce between a believer who is married to an unbeliever the criteria changes for this situation (1st Cor. 7:12-16).

[260] Apostasy is the falling away from Yahveh, never to return. It's not that the person has back-slidden or has become a prisoner of Satan but on the contrary, it implies that the person is now working for Satan. It doesn't mean that they will automatically relinquish their 'tag' of 'Christian' either. Some will keep it to deceive believers and family members.

[261] One should separate from a believing partner that is a habitual offender in things like adultery, incest, physical abuse, emotional abuse, etc. Separate but don't divorce. Separation should be used as a chastisement of teaching toward the offender, with an eye to having them set their life in order with the King and not to be enslaved to those carnal passions. It's also a time for the one who separated, to pray and intercede for their spouse, until deliverance and healing come.

CULT PROSTITUTION
IN THE CORINTHIAN ASSEMBLY

The letters of the Apostle Paul are not only filled with rich theological gems but also stern rebukes to local believers for sins they were committing.[262] Sometimes the Gentile believers weren't even aware of it (1st Cor. 10:21-22), or if they were they didn't exhibit anything that led them to change (1st Cor. 5:1-2). Many of those problems would never have arisen if they had a foundational knowledge in the Law of Moses. That's not to say that they weren't being taught the Law.[263] But just as mature belief in Messiah Yeshua doesn't happen overnight, so too it takes a while for the Law to become part of a believer's understanding and walk. That's why Yakov gave the initial filter of the four rules (Acts 15:20), and spoke of Gentiles going to the synagogues every Shabat (Hebrew for Sabbath), to learn Torah (Acts 15:21).

There are three texts in First Corinthians that speak of cult harlotry, two of which aren't normally associated with it (5:1; 6:12-20), although the word pornay'ah is used in both. The third text is chapter ten where Paul specifically speaks of pornay'ah in relation to the cult harlotry of Num. 25. Translators generally see 1st Cor. 5:1 as only incest, and 6:12-20 as common harlotry. These two texts have been overlooked as places where the Apostle addressed cult prostitution.

---

[262] Some problems Paul wrote of in his letter to the Corinthians were: divisions and strife (1:10-13; 3:1-9); pride (4:7-21); the Elders not rebuking a man who slept with his father's wife (5:1-8); lawsuits against one another (6:1-9); cult prostitution (6:18; 10:8); idolatry (8:1); the worship of demons (10:20); the eating of sacrifices to demons and the drinking of the blood (10:21); men who would completely cover their heads in the assembly and women who would not (11:4-16); their perverse way of taking the Lord's Supper (11:17-22); their lack of discernment for His Body (11:29-30); chaos in the assembly when the Spirit would manifest (14:1-19, 27-28, 33-34); etc.

[263] There are four places in First Corinthians where Paul uses the Law to make his points valid. This meant the Law was still in effect, and that the Corinthians were learning it: 1. Paul encourages the Corinthians to keep 'the Feast' (1st Cor. 5:6-8). This can only be Passover as he's just spoken about unleavened bread (Ex. 12:14-20; Lev. 23:6). 2. He sums up his ability to receive funds from them by citing the Law (9:8-9). 3. He tells them that women shouldn't speak in the assembly, again citing the Law (14:34-35). 4. In 16:8 Paul speaks of staying at Ephesus till Pentecost. Pentecost is the Greek word for the Mosaic holy day of Shavuot in Lev. 23:15-22. Why would Paul note 'time' by an outdated Jewish feast and that, to Gentiles, unless he still kept the Law and taught it to them (Phil. 3:17)?

Corinth, capital of Roman Greece was the fourth largest city in the Roman Empire in the days of Paul.[264] With a population of approximately 650,000 people (400,000 of which were slaves), Corinth was a very significant city where Paul founded the Corinthian assembly.[265]

The city was steeped in cult harlotry. Many 'gods' inhabited the city. There was Poseidon the sea god and Isis from Egypt along with Serapis, etc., but Aphrodite was the favorite and with good reason. She satisfied the lust of the flesh. So common was this 'worship' that to 'Corinthicize' someone was seen as a 'euphemism for whoredom.'[266]

Shrines of Aphrodite 'were everywhere' in Corinth.[267] Aphrodite was seen as the 'patroness of harlots'[268] and was known for her 'great army of prostitutes'.[269] At her *main* temple which 'crowned the Acrocorinthus' there were over a thousand cult priestesses (i.e. temple prostitutes) to accommodate the Corinthians in their fervor 'to worship' the goddess.[270]

There doesn't seem to have been a great need for a 'theological education' to be a cult priestess either. Whenever the city was in danger or in matters of 'grave importance' common prostitutes were pressed into the service of the goddess to gratify the need for beseeching her favor.[271]

Paul's Gentile converts seem to have made up the bulk of the congregation in Corinth.[272] They would come from those very people immersed in the mindset of paganism; both slave and free. That's why Paul had so many problems with the Corinthian believers. G. G. Findlay notes that many of the Gentile *believers* were '*steeped* in pagan vice' and bound-up 'with idolatry'.[273]

---

[264] G. G. Findlay, B.A., Author; W. Robertson Nicoll, Editor, M.A., LL.D., *The Expositor's Greek Testament*, vol. two: *St. Paul's First Epistle to the Corinthians* (Peabody, MA: Hendrickson Publishers, 2002), p. 730.

[265] Leon Morris, The Rev. Canon, M.Sc., M.Th., Ph.D., *Tyndale New Testament Commentaries: 1 Corinthians* (Leicester, England: Inter-Varsity Press, 2000), p. 18 note 5.

[266] Findlay, *St. Paul's First Epistle to the Corinthians*, p. 734.

[267] Morris, *1 Corinthians*, p. 18 note 3.

[268] Ibid.

[269] Ibid.

[270] Findlay, *St. Paul's First Epistle to the Corinthians*, p. 734.

[271] Morris, *1 Corinthians*, p. 18 note 3. (See also Num. 31:1-4, 12-18 for ordinary women being 'pressed into' the service of cult harlotry.)

[272] Findlay, *St. Paul's First Epistle to the Corinthians*, p. 730.

We know that Paul also had a number of Jewish converts in Corinth[274] but they wouldn't be involved in cult prostitution because they knew the Law of Moses. Unfortunately, as in modern congregations today, they wouldn't or couldn't effect the behavior of many of the Gentiles in the congregation, especially the ones who wanted to continue in their pagan ways.

Some of the Corinthians would radically change their understanding of cult prostitution and Jesus when they heard Paul's letter. But some of them would continue to practice cult harlotry as is seen from what Paul writes in 2nd Cor. 6:14-18 (12:21 and 13:5).

Habits learned over a lifetime and sanctified by one's culture are not only very hard to break but all too often seen as 'normal and right.' Because of this 'normalcy' we catch a rare glimpse of a young congregation where the gross sin of cult prostitution walks hand in hand with 'belief in Jesus.' What James warned Gentiles against in Acts 15:20, Paul actually had to battle!

In presenting these three sections of Paul's first (preserved) letter to the Corinthians (1st Cor. 5:9-11), the Apostle didn't outline it with chapter and verse numbers. His raising of a concern or concept in one section may continue in another form in a later section as he thinks of further things to support his previous words.

The internal problem of cult prostitution is first specifically addressed in chapter five. Then in chapter six there's a general discourse against it, which is further developed in chapter ten, using the history of Israel. There he speaks not only of cult harlotry but also of the table and cup of demons. Three of the four prohibitions of Yakov are actually being practiced by Gentile believers in Corinth, as chapter ten brings out:

1. the drinking of the raw blood of the sacrifice,

2. the eating of the sacrificial meat at the time of the sacrifice in the pagan temple,

3. and the 'worship' of the god or goddess through the cult harlots, all in the Name of Jesus.

---

[273] Ibid., p. 731.

[274] In Acts 18:8 Crispus, the leader of the Jewish synagogue, and his household, left the synagogue and assembled with the believers. It's not unreasonable to assume that a number of Jews followed him. See 1st Cor. 1:14, 16 where Paul immersed not only Crispus but Gaius and Stephanas who may have been Jewish too. Also, Paul was in Corinth for a year and a half (Acts 18:11) reasoning with the Jews about Yeshua being the Messiah (Acts 18:4).

Incest in Corinth: 1st Cor. 5:1-5

Most bible commentators take pornay'ah in 1st Cor. 5:1 to mean 'incest' as the Gentile Christian man had intercourse with his stepmother. So Morris ('Paul draws attention to a case of incest'),[275] and Findlay (the 'Case of Incest'),[276] and *Wycliffe* ('the fornication was incest').[277]

It certainly was an incestuous affair but most likely something much more: incestuous cult prostitution. This is based upon Paul's own words and the use of pornay'ah (fornication). Commentators have failed to pick up on its uniqueness. Paul writes,

> 'It is reported commonly that there is fornication among you, and *such fornication as is not so much as named among the Gentiles*, that one should have his father's wife.' (1st Cor. 5:1 KJV)[278]

When Paul states this fornication was such that it was 'not so much as named among the Gentiles,' it must have been a very exceptional case. But the woman wasn't even related to the man by blood. She wasn't his mother but his stepmother, or more properly as Paul speaks of it, his father's wife.

The father most likely married her later in life when his son was already a man. The wife wouldn't be a stepmother who raised him but just 'another woman' to him. There would be no childhood emotions attached to this woman, as might be found with a step-mother, which would make their sin 'that much less' incestuous.

In most incestuous relationships there is a blood relationship between the two parties which makes it truly incestuous. But for there *not* to be one here would make it a far less exceptional case than otherwise. It's hard to believe that Paul would think that this kind of incest was so unique as to exclaim that it wasn't found even among the Gentiles. It should be obvious that it wasn't because the woman was his father's wife.

---

[275] Morris, *1 Corinthians*, p. 83.

[276] Findlay, *St. Paul's First Epistle to the Corinthians*, p. 807.

[277] Pfeiffer, *WBC*, p. 1236.

[278] Substituting 'cult prostitution' for fornication, it becomes clearer as to what Paul was addressing: 'It is reported commonly that there is *cult prostitution* among you, and such *cult prostitution* as is not so much as named among the Gentiles, that one should have his father's wife.' (1st Cor. 5:1)

She was most likely a cult harlot. This would account for Paul's use of pornay'ah (prostitution) and make the incestuous relationship part of an idolatrous sexual rite. If she were 'only' a common harlot, again, it wouldn't make it so exceptional. Her being a cult harlot would not only be unique but also part of the theme of cult prostitution that Paul will further develop and speak against in chapters six and ten.

It's unique in that this is a man who is supposed to be a Christian and here he is worshipping another god through a cult prostitute who is his father's wife. This must have been a first for the Apostle.

With Paul's use of the Greek word for prostitution (pornay'ah) and his astonishment of the actual deed, along with his punishment,[279] it suggests that the woman was indeed a cult harlot and that she had intercourse with the son of the man she was married to at one of the pagan shrines.[280] If this is the case then the only place in the New Testament where pornay'ah has been seen as incest (and only incest) vanishes. For then it would become incestuous cult prostitution, a truly unparalleled sin.

Of course common prostitution cannot be ruled out either. But because of the uniqueness of the event in Paul's eyes, and the fact that he addresses cult harlotry just a little further on in the letter, the woman must have been a cult harlot.

Cult prostitution with the wife of the believer's father must have been a first for Corinth too ('not so much as named among the Gentiles'). What a horrendous 'witness for Christ' this must have been to the believers in the assembly as well as many unbelievers in Corinth.

This is a problem with 'freedom in Christ' when it's not coupled to God's restraining boundaries; His Law (Lev. 18:8; 20:11; Dt. 22:30; 27:20). People don't understand His will. And this is why Yakov's second rule prohibits cult harlotry and why he gave the four rules to the Gentiles...first.

---

[279] Paul speaks of handing him over to Satan to deal with his flesh (1st Cor. 5:5). He would be severed from Yeshua and the only fellowship in town, and if unrepentant, spend eternity in Hell. The punishment seems to have had the desired effects (2nd Cor. 2:3-11).

[280] Whether the husband was alive or not cannot be determined from the text although Paul doesn't say she was a widower. The father doesn't seem to be a Christian. If he were alive, which seems likely, he may have even initiated and affirmed the event. It might have seemed good in his pagan eyes. Perhaps that's why the Christian man did it? To honor his father?

Cult Prostitution in Corinth: 1st Cor. 6:12-20

In 1st Cor. 6:12-20 Paul speaks about what appears to be the sin of cult prostitution among the Gentile believers at Corinth. He initially tackles the Gnostic libertine heresy that says free men can do whatever they want. Because the Corinthian believers were 'free in Christ' some united the two beliefs, logically seeing no need for sexual restraint. This reveals a problem with those who espouse freedom in Christ and don't want to realize that it's freedom from sin, not license to sin. What is the Standard? It's the Law of Moses lived out through Jesus.

Many consider the harlot that Paul mentions twice (6:15-16), and the harlotry he speaks of three times (vv. 14, 18 twice), to be of the common variety. But can this be considering that Corinth was known throughout the ancient world for its cult harlots? Can Paul be writing about harlotry in Corinth and it had nothing to do with pagan temples and cult harlots? There's nothing in the Greek words for harlot or harlotry, and nothing in the context of this passage to the Corinthians, that means that this harlot has to be only a common harlot and not a cult harlot. If anything, those who think her to be a common harlot have the burden of responsibility to prove it. They should present clear evidence that the Apostle was speaking about common harlotry and common harlotry only. But this can't be done.

Morris states that the philosophy behind the average Corinthian was a 'man who recognized no superior and no law but his own desires.'[281] In other words, he thought he could do whatever he wanted to do. Enter now some of them who accept Christ as their Savior. Would their thought pattern change in this area? For some Gentiles, no.

Paul begins his argument against this freedom by declaring that he too is free. Then he tells them what true freedom really is: putting Jesus ahead of self:

> 1st Cor. 6:12: 'All things are lawful unto me, but all things are not expedient: all things are lawful for me, but I will not be brought under the power of any. 13. Meats for the belly and the belly for meats: but God shall destroy both it and them.'

> 14: 'Now the body is not for *fornication*, but for the Lord; and the Lord for the body. And God hath both raised up the Lord, and will also raise up us by his own power.

---

[281] Morris, *1 Corinthians*, p. 19.

15. Know ye not that your bodies are the members of Christ? Shall I then take the members of Christ and make them the members of an *harlot*? God forbid!'

16-17: 'What? Know ye not that he which is *joined to an harlot* is one body? For two, saith he, shall be one flesh. But he that is joined unto the Lord is one spirit.'

18: 'Flee *fornication!*[282] Every sin that a man doeth is without the body; but he that committeth fornication sinneth against his own body. 19. What? Know ye not that your body is the *temple* of the Holy Ghost which is in you, which ye have of God, and ye are not your own?'

20: For ye are bought with a price: therefore glorify God in your body and in your spirit, which are God's.' (1st Cor. 6:12-20 KJV)

Paul states that 'All things are lawful' to him and many take this as a cue that the Law has been done away with.[283] But the phrase obviously can't mean 'every–thing.' This is seen from the fact that this passage has Paul coming against harlotry in Corinth, and he's just spoken against thieves and adulterers, etc. (6:9-11). Therefore 'all things' doesn't mean '*every* thing.' Paul would never lie, or break the Sabbath commandment, etc.

The phrase can be equally translated to mean 'All things are possible' or 'All things are permitted' for me.[284] It seems to imply that Paul was speaking *rhetorically* saying, 'I can do what you're doing too if I wanted to!' Paul wasn't addressing the Law of Moses. David Stern thinks the phrase wasn't a part of Paul's teaching but that he was echoing a Gnostic libertine concept that was 'in use among a group of Corinthians.'[285] This ver-

---

[282] The NASB has 'Flee immorality.' This totally distorts the meaning that Paul was trying to get across.

[283] Paul uses the phrase twice here in v. 12. It's also used twice in 10:23 where there's a natural link to the cult harlotry that Paul is speaking about in chapter six. In 10:23 Paul deals with cult harlotry, the eating of the meat of the pagan sacrifice at the time of the idolatrous act and the drinking of the blood from the sacrifice. This would also seem to align the two texts concerning what *type* of harlotry Paul was primarily speaking of here; cult harlotry.

[284] William D. Mounce, *The Analytical Lexicon to the Greek New Testament* (Grand Rapids, Michigan: Zondervan Publishing House, 1993), p. 194. Friberg, *ALGNT*, p. 155. It denotes 'that there are no hindrances to an action or that the opportunity for it occurs, it is possible' 'predominately as denoting that an action is not prevented by a higher court or by law it is permitted, it is lawful, it may be done'. Roman law permitted cult prostitution and this is quite possibly the freedom that Paul was speaking of.

sion of Gnostic philosophy espoused that anything and everything sensual was permissible to free men. And even slaves were now 'free in Christ.' This attracted many with no moral compass and no desire 'to curb the flesh.'[286] They weren't interested in understanding what was right or wrong if it inhibited their sinful lifestyle. Just how many believers in Corinth walked this way isn't known. If it was only one person, Paul would have addressed it as such, as he did in chapter five with the man who had intercourse with his father's wife. Instead it seems to be aimed at a group in the congregation (see 2nd Cor. 12:21).

Paul qualified 'all things' (παντα pahn-tah) and the qualification was all things that edify and don't imprison one ('I will not be brought under the power of any' v. 12). Obviously if one sins it's not edifying ('expedient'), and not a 'freedom' but an enslavement. The Apostle confined himself to the realm of a godly lifestyle. Just as God can do 'any–thing' but restricts Himself to righteousness, so too Paul. He was free to do whatever he thought best in any situation that he found himself in, but he wouldn't use his freedom in Christ to justify sin.

Stern believes that Paul incorporates another libertine phrase[287] when he writes in v. 13: 'Meats for the belly, and the belly for meats'.[288] This speaks of the specific justification that the libertines used for unrestrained sex. Leon Morris says this phrase,

> 'looks like another expression used by the Corinthians. Eating is a natural activity and they apparently held that one bodily function is much like another. Fornication is as natural as eating.'[289]

---

[285] Stern, *JNTC*, p. 451 says that it 'was not a central principle' of Paul 'but a saying in use among a group of Corinthians who would later have been called gnostic libertines.' On the other hand, Morris, *1 Corinthians*, p. 95 states, 'It looks like a catch-phrase the Corinthians used to justify their actions, possibly one they would have derived from Paul's teaching.' Either way, some Corinthian believers were using this to philosophically justify their unrestrained sexual lust.

[286] Today being free in Christ means that many Christians walk as the world and don't even realize it. Many Christian women, following Hollywood, dress much more sensually than the ancient cult harlots of Corinth ever did. These Christian women don't understand that their immodestly and ungodliness cause men to stumble. The same holds true for many Christian men.

[287] Stern, *JNTC*, p. 451.

[288] Or 'Food for the belly and the belly for food'; 'meat' being a KJV word for 'food.' It's quite likely this also spoke of their gluttonous eating or feasting at the pagan shrines where cult harlotry took place.

Without an understanding of Torah (God's will), there wasn't any sexual restraints for them. If it's good to feed the body with food, a natural function, why would it be bad to have sex with a prostitute? The sexual desire is as natural as eating so there shouldn't be any need for sexual restraint. Pagan thinking wasn't illogical, it was just ungodly. *Wycliffe* states,

> 'the moral laxity that polluted the church, apparently' (was) 'caused by the application of the truth of Christian liberty to the sexual realm. The question is: If there are no restrictions in food, one appetite of the body, why must there be in sexual things, another physical desire?'[290]

Paul countered the libertine philosophy that stressed one's freedom to do however they sexually pleased with what was profitable for them. He also pointed them to Judgment Day by saying that one day, the body and food for it would come to an end (v. 13). In all this, nothing was said about the Law of Moses or it being done away with.

In relation to fornication and harlots mentioned in the passage, Paul links his argument to idol worship (and therefore cult harlotry) by contrasting true worship with pagan worship. He says the body is 'for the Lord; and the Lord for the body' (v. 14), and building on this he says their bodies were members of Messiah (v. 15). The spiritual parallel between being members of Messiah or members of a harlot are equal only if the harlot is a cult harlot.

Paul then says in v. 15, 'Shall I then take the members of Christ and make them the members of an harlot? God forbid!' The Greek for 'take' is 'take away.'[291] People who believe in Jesus would be 'taken away' and made members with this harlot. Something that is missing if this was just a common harlot is that Yeshua is God the Son. For the parallel to be complete, for them to be 'taken away' and given to another, he would have to be speaking of union with a harlot that could offer union with another god.

Leon Morris sees this and presents the possibility that Paul is writing about temple prostitution. He first speaks of the common understanding of 'union with a prostitute' being 'a horrible profanation of that which should be used only for Christ' and goes on to say,

> '*This would be even more so* if the Corinthian prostitute *was connected with the temple*, for then the act would

---

[289] Morris, *1 Corinthians*, p. 96.

[290] Pfeiffer, *WBC*, p. 1238.

[291] Morris, *1 Corinthians*, p. 97.

form a link with the deity.'[292]

Morris realized that the words for harlot and harlotry could also mean cult harlot and cult harlotry. And with ancient Corinth infested with cult prostitution, it would specifically point to this.

In vv. 16-17 Paul uses the word 'joined' twice:

> 16. 'What? Know ye not that he which is *joined* to an harlot is one body? For two, saith he, shall be one flesh. 17. But he that is *joined* unto the Lord is one spirit.'

The Greek word that is translated *joined* is conceptually the same as its Hebrew counterpart in the idolatrous Baal Peor affair in which cult harlotry played a major role. The Greek word is κολλαω (kol-lah-oh) and means to 'join oneself to, join, cling to, associate with.'[293] It also means to 'cleave to, to unite with'[294] and 'to attach one's self to'.[295]

Morris writes that Paul uses it to express the 'physical bond with the harlot.'[296] But there's more here than just a physical bond. The Apostle spoke of the spiritual bond the Corinthians had with Messiah in v. 17. He used the same word for joined in both instances. The parallel is strongest if this harlot were cultic. And there's nothing within the context to negate this, but on the contrary, many things that point to cult harlotry. Why can't this be happening in pagan Corinth? Why wouldn't the Gentile believer, steeped in pagan harlotry, be doing what the Hebrews did when they came out of Egypt?

In v. 18 Paul cries out, 'Flee fornication!' What kind of prostitution is Paul addressing? It could certainly be both as the word conveys both types. If he meant adultery or homosexuality there are Greek words that he could have and would have used to get his point across. That none of those words are mentioned means the Apostle had harlotry in mind. Harlotry is further seen from the noun which comes from pornay'ah. Pornay (vv. 15-16) can only mean a harlot or prostitute (common or cultic) not an adulteress.

Paul states their Christian bodies were for the Lord and that the Lord owned them (v. 14). Then he adds their bodies were members of Christ (v. 15). And now he tells them their bodies are the temple or dwelling place

---

[292] Ibid., pp. 97-98.

[293] Bauer, *GELNT*, p. 441.

[294] Friberg, *ALGNT*, p. 234.

[295] Perschbacher, *NAGL*, p. 243.

[296] Morris, *1 Corinthians*, p. 98.

of God. It's here that the parallel draws closest to understanding that Paul was speaking of temple prostitution:

> 18. 'Flee fornication! Every sin that a man doeth is without the body; but he that committeth fornication sinneth against his own body. 19. What? Know ye not that your *body is the temple of the Holy Ghost which is in you,* which ye have of God, and ye are not your own?' (KJV)

Paul's use of the Greek word for temple ναος (nah-ohs, v. 19) is defined as the place where the deity dwelt, in the inner sanctuary as opposed to the outer courtyard.[297] Paul is saying that the believer's body is the dwelling place of God the Holy Spirit. By implication, believers *should not go* to *another* temple where *another god dwells* and *join themselves* to that god through cult harlotry.

Cult prostitution is further seen in the phrase that the body is 'the temple of the living God' in 2nd Cor. 6:14-16 which is synonymous with Paul's use of 'the temple of the Holy Ghost' in 1st Cor. 6:19 above. In 2nd Cor. 6:14-16 though, it's absolutely clear that he's speaking of cult prostitution and this, to the same group of Corinthians:

> 2nd Cor. 6:14: 'Be ye not unequally yoked together with unbelievers: for what fellowship hath righteousness with unrighteousness? And what communion hath light with darkness?'
>
> 2nd Cor. 6:15: 'And what concord hath *Christ with Belial*? Or what part hath he that believeth with an *infidel*?'
>
> 2nd Cor. 6:16: 'And what agreement hath the temple of God *with idols*? For ye are the *temple of the living God*; as God hath said, "I will dwell in them, and walk in (among) them; and I will be their God, and they shall be my people."' (KJV)

The Apostle contrasts 'Christ with Belial' (v. 15), warning the Corinthian Christians not to be unequally yoked (v. 14), or joined to a cult prostitute who belonged to an idolatrous shrine.[298] He wouldn't use this if it were just a common prostitute *as no religious significance* (Belial), attaches to that kind of harlotry. Also, the use of the word 'infidel' (v. 15) is always

---

[297] Ibid., p. 99.

[298] Most today take this unequal yoking to mean that a Christian shouldn't marry a non-Christian. As correct as the concept is, the text is primarily warning Christians not to have intercourse with cult harlots.

seen in a religious context.

In 2nd Cor. 6:16 Paul speaks of the 'temple of God' and idols. This can only be a contrast between the Lord and cult prostitution. The correlation with 1st Cor. 6 is seen in his use of the concept that God dwells in believers and that believers are the temple of God (1st Cor. 6:19; 2nd Cor. 6:16). It can also be applied to believers not being unequally yoked with unbelievers (1st Cor. 6:15-16; 2nd Cor. 6:14).

In 1st Cor. 6:19 Paul states that they should glorify (worship) God through their body, the temple of God (v. 20), and not 'worship' another with their body. From this context and the parallel to 2nd Cor. 6:16, it speaks of cult harlotry. True worship is within the believer's body, the temple or dwelling place of God. On the other hand, one goes to a pagan temple and gives their body to a temple harlot there, 'to worship' the goddess. The wording of Paul is quite striking. Everything in the text points to this identification with temple harlotry and not common harlotry.

Paul speaks many times of the Holy Spirit dwelling in believers without mentioning they were the temple of the Holy Spirit.[299] Yet here, when speaking of pornay'ah (1st Cor. 6:13, 18 twice), which has to be either common or cult harlotry, and having used the word for harlot (pornay) twice (in vv. 15, 16), he chooses to employ the concept that believers are the dwelling place or Temple of the Living God. This parallels the idea that those who use the harlot are going to the temple or dwelling place of another god. Paul's use of pornay'ah (harlotry) and pornay (harlot) then, in this context, should be seen as cult harlotry and cult harlots.

What most scholars say about this passage in reference to it being common harlotry, or that it was primarily about the common harlot is not acceptable. The parallels are strongest when the passage is taken first and foremost as an admonishment against cult harlotry, especially in a city noted for it throughout the ancient world.

Paul was speaking about cult prostitution to the Corinthian assembly in chapter six. Here are six reasons that support this position:

1. The ancient city of Corinth in northern Greece was known the world over for its temple prostitutes: In Corinth, 'the temple of Aphrodite with its 1,000 hierodules[300] was famous'.[301]

---

[299] 2nd Tim. 1:14. See also Rom. 14:17; 15:13, 16; 2nd Cor. 13:14; Eph. 1:13; 4:30; 1st Thess. 1:6; 4:8; Titus 3:5.

[300] Colin G. Kruse, B.D., M.Phil., Ph.D., Author; The Rev. Canon Leon Morris, M.Sc., M.Th., Ph.D., General Editor, *Tyndale New Testament Commentaries: 2 Corinthians* (Leicester, England: Inter-Varsity Press, 2000), pp. 15-16.

2. The Greek words for harlot and harlotry equally mean cult harlot and cult harlotry. To say that it was only or primarily common harlotry that Paul addressed and not cult prostitution would have meant that Paul was blind to a reality that pervaded the entire city.

3. Paul's use of the phrases, the body is the Lord's, members of Christ

---

Kruse contests this figure of one thousand cult prostitutes in Paul's day. He writes that Strabo's statement (where the thousand cult prostitutes comes from) refers to the city of Corinth before the Romans destroyed it in 146 B.C. The Romans rebuilt it one hundred years later in 44 B.C. (pp. 14-15). It's very possible though that Corinth in Paul's day had the same number of cult prostitutes to Aphrodite. In the Apostle's day it was about a hundred years old and the 'capital for the Roman province of Achaia' (Kruse, p. 16). It was also a chief city of commerce in the Roman world because of its location. Kruse admits there 'is no doubt that Corinth was regaining its wealth and prestige in Paul's time' (p. 16).

He also says that the Corinth of Paul's day was infested with pagan worship and Aphrodite was still the chief goddess. He states the 'new Corinth became a centre for the worship of many of the old Graeco-Roman gods. He' (Kruse speaking of the ancient writer Pausanias, 174 A.D.) 'refers to temples or altars dedicated to Poseidon, Palaemon, Aphrodite, Artemis, Dionysus, Helius, Hermes, Apollo, Zeus, Isis, Eros and others. Strabo records that in his time there was a small temple to Aphrodite on the summit of Acrocorinth, while' by the time of Pausanias, 'the ascent to the Acrocorinth was punctuated by places of worship dedicated to various deities including Isis, Helius, Demeter and Pelagian. On the summit there was still found the temple of Aphrodite with images of Helius, Eros and Aphrodite herself. Clearly then,' Kruse continues, 'the new Corinth of Paul's day was still a center for the worship of Aphrodite, *as the old city had been prior to its destruction* in 146 BC' (p. 15).

Even if the new Corinth couldn't rival the old for its thousand cult prostitutes to Aphrodite, how many less did it have in Paul's day? Aphrodite was the chief goddess, as attested by her temple being on the highest point of the city and Corinth was the fourth largest city in the Roman world at that time (Findlay, *St. Paul's First Epistle to the Corinthians*, p. 730). Morris (*1 Corinthians*, p. 18) writes, the 'new Corinth' would have 'an equally unsavory reputation'. There were probably a thousand or more cult prostitutes for Aphrodite in Paul's day. Whatever their number, Paul and the Corinthian believers would still have to deal with them and *all the cult harlots* of the *other* gods and goddesses in Corinth. Whether Aphrodite had a thousand or just five, cult harlotry among the Corinthian believers was a major problem for Paul and also for the average sailor. Most likely what Strabo wrote of Corinth in his day (63 B.C. to 22 A.D.) still pertained to Corinth in Paul's day: 'Many sea captains squandered their money paying for the services of these cult harlots, so that the proverb, "Not for every man is the voyage to Corinth," was in use among them' (Kruse, p. 14).

[301] Kittel, *TDNT*, vol. VI, p. 582.

and the temple of God, imply a direct connection to idolatry. These, along with his use of *joined* which conceptually links it to the Baal Peor fiasco, lend themselves to seeing the passage as a contrast between Yeshua and other gods, not just a common prostitute. And Paul will speak of the Baal Peor affair in chapter ten which specifically deals with cult prostitution.

4. Paul's use of the phrase 'All things are lawful to me' is also repeated in 1st Cor. 10:23 where cult prostitution and sacrificial idolatry are specifically referred to. This lends itself to chapter six dealing with the same problem that chapter ten deals with. Chapter ten is a further teaching and admonition to the Corinthian Christians that begins in chapters five and six.

5. In an almost identical rebuke in *2nd* Cor. 6:14-17, Paul speaks against cult prostitution. In 1st Cor. 6:19 he writes of the believer's body being the temple of the Holy Spirit and the dwelling place of God. This he reiterates in 2nd Cor. 6:15-16 with the words 'Belial' and 'idols.' Paul addresses against cult prostitution in 2nd Cor. 6. The parallel to 1st Cor. 6 seems obvious.

6. As R. J. Knowling stated[302] and as the section on *Cult Prostitution in the New Testament* will point out, the use of pornay'ah in the New Testament speaks first and foremost of cult prostitution, not common prostitution. For anyone to suggest common harlotry over cult harlotry, they would have to prove it but this isn't possible.

These six reasons uphold that the prostitution the Apostle spoke of in 1st Cor. 6 was temple prostitution and not common prostitution.

In relation to Torah, Paul is not doing anything in this passage that conflicts with the Law of Moses. He's not suggesting that one can break any of the laws of Moses even with his use of the phrase 'All things are lawful unto me.' On the contrary, he's calling the Corinthians to accountability in the area that Torah is most adamant about, even though they are free in Christ and under Grace.

The use of pornay'ah (cult harlotry) in 1st Cor. 6 is exactly what James speaks about in his Decree of Acts 15:20. Conversely, Paul's admonition to the assembly at Corinth supports the understanding that pornay'ah in Acts 15:20 means cult harlotry.

---

[302] See p. 82 above. Knowling, *The Acts of the Apostles*, p. 324. Witherington, *The Acts of the Apostles*, p. 463. Witherington says of pornay'ah in Acts 15:20 that its 'most basic meaning refers to prostitution, *including* so-called sacred prostitution'.

More Cult Prostitution in Corinth: 1st Cor. 10

Paul begins chapter ten by speaking of the real danger of walking in idolatry and how it can sever one from God. Ancient Israel in the Wilderness had much in the way of God's divine Hand upon them but failed to walk in faith when God tested them (Dt. 8:1-3). Paul cautioned the Corinthians against such things, specifically writing against cult prostitution in v. 8. The first four verses express the *conceptual unity between ancient Israel and the Gentile Corinthian believers*. Paul shows them that the Fathers of Israel were their Fathers too:

> 'For I do not want you to be unaware, brethren, that our Fathers were all under the Cloud and all passed through the Sea and all were baptized into Moses in the Cloud and in the Sea. And all ate the same spiritual food and all drank the same spiritual drink for they were drinking from a spiritual Rock which followed them[303] and the Rock was Christ.' (1st Cor. 10:1-4)

The Apostle wanted the Corinthians to understand that Israel too was in covenant with Yahveh and that the 'Body of Moses' preceded, and was a picture of, the Body of Messiah. Both were chosen of God. Both had God's gracious Hand upon them. But people in both could be severed. Morris sees this parallel and writes,

> 'the Israelites, without exception, received the tokens of God's good hand on them. The fact that most perished (v. 5) comes accordingly with greater force. The cloud was the means of divine guidance at the time of the Exodus (Ex. 13:21-22), when the people passed through the sea (Ex. 14:21-22).' Their 'participation in the great events of the Exodus brought the Israelites under the leadership of Moses'. They 'were united to him' in a similar way that we are to Messiah. They were all likewise sustained by

---

[303] Paul's Pharisaic training comes to the forefront in the Rock that followed them. It's not found in the Bible, but the Rabbis taught that a literal rock actually followed Israel. Conceptually we see a similar thing with Jude saying the Devil contended for the body of Moses (Jude 1:9; see Dt. 34:5-6). Nowhere in Scripture is that spoken of. Jude most likely got this from an apocryphal book of the first century B.C. called the Assumption of Moses. These are two instances of 'understanding' from the first century when Paul and Judah (Jude, a half brother of Yeshua) lived. They come into the New Testament as fact but in reality are only rabbinic traditions. (See also 2nd Tim. 3:8)

the manna (Ex. 16:4, 13f.)' 'and spiritual drink' 'which refers to Christ and sees him as following the Israelites and continually giving them drink.' 'Nevertheless' 'although God had given them such signal manifestations of his power and goodness, the majority failed to enter the Promised Land' and that Paul's warning now 'against idolatry is very relevant to conditions in Corinth.'[304]

Paul will link the idolatry of the Corinthians with the debacle of the Gold Calf orgy, and the 'craving for food' that killed many in the Wilderness (Num. 11:4-34). He'll reference Israel at Baal Peor and use it as a springboard to declare cult prostitution 'off limits' for the Corinthians. The Apostle will then bring the identification to a point, warning the Gentiles that membership in the Body of Messiah is not a guarantee of never falling from Grace. He writes,

'Nevertheless, with most of them God was not well pleased for they were laid low in the Wilderness. Now these things happened as examples for us, so that we would not crave evil things as they also craved.' (1st Cor. 10:5-6)

'Do not be idolaters, as some of them were; as it is written, "The people sat down to eat and drink, and stood up to play." Nor let us act immorally, as some of them did' (lit. 'Neither let us commit fornication as some of them committed fornication')[305] 'and twenty-three thousand fell in one day.'[306] (1st Cor. 10:7-8)

The reference to the people sitting down to eat and...to play (the harlot) is a direct reference to the Gold Calf (Ex. 32:6). Here cult harlotry was practiced in the Name of Yahveh, the Calf being given the name Yahveh (Ex. 32:4-5, 8). 'To play' speaks of sexual misconduct. It's another way of

---

[304] Morris, *1 Corinthians*, pp. 139-140.

[305] Brown, *NGEINT*, p. 601.

[306] This is a reference to Num. 25. Even though Paul seems to be 'off' by 1,000, Keil, *The Pentateuch*, p. 792 states, 'The Apostle Paul deviates from this statement in 1st Cor. 10:8 and gives the number of those that fell as twenty-three thousand, probably from a traditional interpretation of the schools of the scribes, according to which a thousand were deducted from the twenty-four thousand who perished, as being the number of those who were hanged by the judges' (i.e. at the command of Yahveh; Num. 25:4-5), 'so that only twenty-three thousand would be killed by the plague; and it is to these alone that Paul refers.'

translating the Hebrew verb zanah (to prostitute; to play the harlot). Israel sacrificed to and worshiped the god of gold indulging in idolatrous sex, in the Name of Yahveh.

Paul's second reference to those that fell in one day ('Neither let us commit fornication...23,000 fell in one day' v. 8), is rightly seen by Stern, Morris, Findlay and *Wycliffe* as the Baal Peor affair. Obviously fornication here must mean cult harlotry (and sacrificial idolatry). There'd be no reason to give these sexually idolatrous warnings if some Corinthian believers weren't engaged in cult prostitution. Paul writes,

> 'Now these things happened to them as an example, and they were written for our instruction, upon whom the ends of the ages have come. Therefore let him who thinks he stands take heed that he does not fall. No temptation has overtaken you but such as is common to man; and God is faithful, who will not allow you to be tempted beyond what you are able but with the temptation will provide the way of escape also, so that you will be able to endure it. Therefore my beloved, *flee* from idolatry!' (1st Corin. 10:11-14)

The idolatry that Paul warned the Corinthians to flee from was sexual in nature. It was cult prostitution. The phrase 'No temptation has overtaken you but such as is common to man' speaks of temple harlotry (v. 8), not just any temptations; idolatry (vv. 7, 14); tempting Messiah (v. 9, which involves disbelief and complaining about one's situation, as the fiery serpents sent among them spoke of Israel's belligerence over not having the food and water they wanted; Num. 20:5-9); and carnal lust for meat (v. 6). Paul told them that he realized cult harlotry was a great temptation (craving or lust).[307] He was warning them too. He pointed out that as those Israelis fell, so would the Gentile believers who continued in sacrificial-sexual idolatry. Cult harlotry and belief in Yeshua were incompatible.

Not all idol worship involves prostitution. In some instances idol worship or idolatry is the burning of incense to a statue or ancestor worship, astrology or magic, etc. Israel entered into cult prostitution through idolatrous

---

[307] Believers are continually bombarded today by the spirit of harlotry (Hos. 5:11; Rev. 17:1-6). Newspapers, billboards, television and movies are filled with men and women seductively tempting all who happen to look their way. One can even find men wearing underwear and women in bras and panties or less. Pornography (a word from pornay'ah; prostitution), is all around and many believers are ignorantly emulating these shameful and corrupt living idols. It'd be enough to make the ancient bold-faced harlots of Israel blush.

sacrifices and orgies (Ex. 32:1-6f; Num. 25:1-13). Cult prostitution falls under the general heading of idolatry. It's the *sexual* expression of idolatry. By telling the Corinthian believers to flee from cult prostitution in 10:14, Paul was reinforcing what he had written in 6:18.

Paul admonishes the Corinthians not to commit this abomination against God. The Greek word for fornication is pornay'ah (10:8). It's also used in 1st Cor. 5:1 (twice), 6:13 (once), 6:15-16 (twice pornay; prostitute) and 6:18 (twice; fornication and fornicating). Why would pornay'ah be *cult* prostitution in chapter ten and only common harlotry (or 'sexual immorality') in chapter six? Was Paul addressing two different groups of Christians within the assembly at Corinth; one for chapter six and the other for chapter ten? This could hardly be the case as he doesn't mention leaving off from one group to write to the other but continually addresses them as one body in the midst of their cliques (1st Cor. 1:12-13; 3:1-4, 21; 10:17).

Chapter ten is the follow-up to chapters five and six. It's dealing with the same problem and the same people but from a different angle. In chapter five, Paul dealt with the specifics of the man involved in incestuous cult harlotry. In chapter six he resorted to a philosophical-religious approach ('All things are lawful' and the believer is 'the temple of God,' etc.). In chapter ten the Apostle spoke of the history of Israel and how the Corinthians were part of the Body of Israel and should learn from them ('examples for us' v. 6 and 'for our instruction' v. 11).

In chapter seven, Paul told them to get married if they couldn't abstain (stating in v. 2 to avoid fornication by having a spouse). In chapter eight he spoke of the eating of idolatrous sacrifices and in nine he declared that he had every right to be paid by the Corinthians for the spiritual services he rendered. But he said he wouldn't take that right as it might interfere with the Great News (Gospel). Then he continued his thoughts from chapters five, six (and eight), concerning fornication, into chapter ten.

Why didn't Paul write chapter ten immediately after chapters five and six (and include eight in the middle)? There's really no problem with Paul's discourse except that we see it in different chapters, but he didn't insert chapter and verse. Perhaps if he had a computer he could have tidied it up a bit more. That it may not be the most logical sequence for some people doesn't allow Paul to be a human being writing a letter nearly 2,000 years ago. Most likely he was dictating his thoughts as they came to him (1st Cor. 16:21). It's not uncommon for Paul to wander off in another direction and then return to a previous thought and expound upon it. But even here those who would discredit the Apostle concerning chapters five to ten don't do him justice. The chapters indeed reveal a development along the theme of Corinthian behavior in relation to cult prostitution, pagan sacrifices, and their attitude toward one another.

Leon Morris relates that chapter ten is not a fresh thought for Paul but a continuation of the Apostle's thoughts on cult prostitution:

> 'This is not a new subject, for *fornication*' 'formed a part of much *idol worship*. Sacred prostitutes were found at many shrines and Corinth had an unenviable notoriety in this respect. But Paul's *primary* reference is to the incident in which 'Israel began to indulge in' cult harlotry 'with Moabite women' and '*joined in worshipping* the Baal of Peor'.[308]

Morris sees fornication here as cult prostitution ('idol worship', 'Sacred prostitutes' and 'many shrines'), and this wasn't the first time in the letter that Paul spoke about it ('not a new subject'). Paul was further addressing the problem from chapters five, six and eight as the Spirit led him. And this wasn't the first (or last) time that Paul would address cult prostitution among his Gentile believers.

Witherington finds in Paul's first letter, the Apostle addressing pornay'ah in First Thessalonians (50 A.D.), written about a year after the Council of Acts 15 (48–49 A.D.). He notes the similarity between James speaking about the Gentiles *turning to God* (Acts 15:19, and therefore needing to give up idolatry), and Paul saying the Thessalonians had 'turned to God from idols' to serve 'a living and true God (1 Thess. 1:9).'[309] Paul addresses pornay'ah in 1st Thess. 4:1-9 but Witherington says the,

> 'fuller discussion of Paul's understanding of the decree comes however, in 1 Corinthians, especially chapters 5-10, where' (in 1st Cor. 10:7) 'ειδωλοθυτον' (ae-doe-lo-thu-tone) 'refers to meat sacrificed and eaten in the presence of idols.'[310]

Corinth wasn't an isolated incident.[311] A translation that would vastly im-

---

[308] Morris, *1 Corinthians*, p. 142.

[309] Witherington, *The Acts of the Apostles*, p. 465. See also further on in the letter where Paul seems to hearken back to both 1st Thess. 1:9 and Acts 15:20 when he speaks of the commandments he gave the Thessalonians (4:2), his use of pornay'ah (sacrificial-sexual idolatry) and sanctification (4:3), the passion and lust of the Gentiles (4:5), uncleanness (4:7), and the Holy Spirit (4:8). All these point to the theme of Acts 15:20.

[310] Ibid., p. 466.

[311] Paul also writes of it in Gal. 5:19; Eph. 5:3 and Col. 3:5.

117

prove understanding for 1st Cor. 6:15-16 would use 'temple harlot' or 'cult prostitute' instead of just 'harlot' or 'prostitute.' Without this the translation gives the impression that the fornication Paul was telling them to flee from was common harlotry (6:18).

Obviously cult prostitution is sexually immoral. But who would be able to decipher 'sexual immorality' either in 1st Corinthians (52 A.D.), or Acts 15:20 (48–49 A.D.), to understand that it was cult prostitution?

Some questions that might be asked are, 'Why didn't Paul appeal directly to the Law of Moses if the Law was still in effect? And why didn't he just include the four rules from James?'

Paul appeals to the Law in chapter ten, relating that ancient Hebrew history was written *for Gentile Corinthian example and instruction* too. He's giving the consequences of breaking the Law to impress upon them what could happen to them also.[312]

Paul also dealt with the Corinthians in chapters six and ten, using their own terms and philosophy, and the historical-spiritual reality of ancient Israel. Perhaps he saw this as a more powerful way to deal with them then to put forward the rules of James which they most likely already knew (Acts 16:4) but hadn't been obeying. Findlay writes,

> 'To draw a hard and fast line in such questions and to forbid all participation in idolothyta, after the precedent of Acts 15, would have been the simplest course to take; but Paul feels it necessary to round the matter on fundamental principles.'[313]

Paul was dealing with a people steeped in cult prostitution and diabolical philosophy. As a shepherd he was dealing with it in the way the Spirit was leading him, given the people and the situation. He was teaching them from different concepts, the reasons for the rules and why they shouldn't be involved in cult prostitution. Knowling sees this and adds that just because Paul doesn't mention the Decree, one shouldn't put forth that it never happened or that Paul didn't recognize it:

> 'St. Paul's language in 1 Cor. 8:1-13; 10:14-22; Rom. 14, may be fairly said to possess the spirit of the Decree, and to mark the discriminating wisdom of one eager to lead his disciples behind the rule to the principle; and there is

---

[312] See p. 99 note 263 above, for places where Paul uses the Law in 1st Corinthians to validate his points.

[313] Findlay, *St. Paul's First Epistle to the Corinthians*, pp. 731-732.

no more reason to doubt the historical truth of the com-
pact made in the Jerusalem Decree, because St. Paul never expressly refers to it, than there is to throw doubt upon
his statement in Gal. 2:10, because he does not expressly
refer to it as an additional motive for urging the Corinthians to join in the collection for the poor saints, 2 Cor
8:9.'[314]

Paul addressed them in ways that we'd like to be addressed if we were
walking in darkness and thinking it was Light. His not mentioning the Decree of Acts 15 doesn't mean that it didn't happen, or that Paul rejected it,
or that he never gave it to the Corinthians.

The Law was valid for the Apostle (Rom. 3:31; 7:12, 14; 1st Cor. 5:6-8;
7:19, etc.). In First Corinthians Paul uses a specific commandment in the
Law of Moses to establish his authority and right to collect funds from
them. He relates in 9:8-9 (and 1st Tim. 5:18), that the ox treading out the
corn was not to be muzzled (a commandment of the Law; Dt. 25:4). He
then goes on to draw the analogy between spreading the Gospel and re-
ceiving money from those who benefited from it. The Apostle gives analo-
gies from various forms of work (soldier, farmer, etc.) and then turns to
the Law *to cement his legal basis for this right.* As Morris states, Paul's
use of the commandment is *authoritative* as the Law settled the issue of
Paul's right to funds:

> 'Paul rejects the thought that the principle he is enunciat-
> ing and illustrating from various fields of human endeavor
> rests simply on human wisdom (it is not a human point of
> view). He can show it in the *Law*' which 'is *always re-
> garded as authoritative.*'[315]

Paul used the Law to support his argument that he was entitled to financial
support from the Corinthians. If the Law wasn't for Christians, Paul
couldn't have used it.

The concern that James had in Acts 15:20, about cult prostitution in the
Gentile community, was a stark reality that Paul faced among the Corinthian believers. That believers would do this, *thinking that it was alright*
shows us their spiritual condition. The Blood of Yeshua forgives things
that could not be forgiven under Mosaic Law, like murder and adultery
(Acts 13:38-39; see also Joel 3:20-21). This, and the fact that the Gentiles
were just learning to walk in Christ, enabled Paul not to sever them imme-

---

[314] Knowling, *The Acts of the Apostles*, p. 336.

[315] Morris, *1 Corinthians*, p. 132. Italics are those of Morris.

diately from the believing community for their sacrificial-sexual idolatry (although he did act decisively with the Christian in 1st Cor. 5:1-5). But is there anyone who would suggest that if those Corinthians continued in temple prostitution, that Grace would cover them forever (Gal. 5:19-21)?

Presenting the significant places in First Corinthians where pornay'ah appeared[316] revealed that cult harlotry was specifically meant when Paul used pornay'ah (fornication KJV). Cult prostitution was primarily what Paul had in mind when he wrote chapters five, six and ten.

First Corinthians provides biblical and historical support for how Yakov used the word, even if his context wasn't seen as sacrificial idolatry. Being listed with three other rules on idolatry only strengthens the position that Yakov was warning the Gentiles not to engage in sacrificial-sexual idolatry. It had nothing to do with table fellowship and cannot be used to prove that the four rules were the only rules for the Gentile.

In the days of Paul, going to pagan temples and cult harlots was as acceptable and honorable to the Gentiles as going to church is to Christians today. There was no social or moral stigma attached to it. Aside from Israel when she was faithful, that's the kind of darkness *the whole world was in.*

Yakov instituted the four rules as a filter for Gentiles entering into the Kingdom who wouldn't have a proper understanding that temple harlotry and the worship of other gods was wrong. These four rules were the most important rules for the Gentile to know immediately, but obviously not the only rules.

These four rules actually prove that Torah is for every believer today. Specific laws from Torah were given to the Gentiles outside of the traditional moral laws that the Church affirms. Grace must always be tempered with Law or people will do what they think is right in their own eyes. Many times, like we find in Corinth, this is sin in God's eyes (Dt. 12:8; Judges 17:6; 21:25).

The Corinthians had other problems that revolved around sacrificial idolatry that needed to be addressed. The next two sections deal with the idolatrous practice of drinking blood, and the eating of the meat sacrificed to the idols. The first is obviously idolatrous and part of the four rules. The second is problematic to some, with questions arising as how Paul and James can be reconciled at this point.

---

[316] The reference in 1st Cor. 7:2, where the Apostle offers marriage as a viable option to fornication, can mean either cult or common prostitution.

Fellowship with Devils: 1st Cor. 10:16-22

In looking at another aspect of pagan worship from Acts 15:20, the drinking of blood (or a symbolic representation of the blood)[317] the Apostle Paul strongly rebukes some of the Corinthians for partaking of the cup of demons![318] Can this really be?! Christians drinking blood to demons and thinking that it's alright? Paul speaks of how it would make Yeshua feel (jealous), and what it would mean to them (they'd be severed or cut off from Messiah). Both concepts recall ancient Israel. Paul writes,

> 'Is not the cup of blessing which we bless, a sharing in the Blood of Christ? Is not the bread which we break a sharing in the Body of Christ? Since there is one bread, we who are many are one body; for we all partake of the one Bread. Look at the nation of Israel. Are not those who eat the sacrifices sharers in the Altar? What do I mean then? That a thing *sacrificed to idols* is anything or that an idol is anything? No, but I say that the things which the Gentiles sacrifice, they sacrifice to demons and not to God and I do not want you to become sharers in (partners with)[319] demons.' (KJV: 'and I would not that ye should have fellowship with devils.')

> 'You cannot drink the Cup of the Lord and the cup of demons! You cannot partake of the Table of the Lord and the table of demons! Or do we provoke the Lord *to jealousy*?! We are not stronger than He, are we?' (1st Cor. 10:16-22)

It's not a minor problem that Paul is addressing. His reference to idols and jealousy speak of how Yahveh felt in the Baal Peor affair (Num. 25:11, 13). It means that Yeshua would cut them off just as Yahveh cut off those Israelis who sacrificed to Baal Peor. What God had done to His people Israel, He was capable of doing to His people Israel who were Gentiles.

---

[317] Hislop, *The Two Babylons*, p. 5. An alternative drink could be made of 'wine, honey, water, and flour' as an intoxicant to dull the senses, arouse the passions and lead the pagan further on. Flour would make the mixture thicken so it would resemble blood all the more.

[318] 1st Cor. 10:16-22. The whole congregation wasn't doing this but obviously some (many?) were. This is an example where, if they had been raised in the Law of Moses they'd never have even considered this.

[319] Brown, *NGEINT*, p. 472.

It seems some Gentile believers were drinking the cup of demons and didn't realize that it was wrong! Their religious culture permitted them to include the worship of Jesus with the practices of their other gods. Paul told them they couldn't mix their gods with worship of Yeshua (the cup and table of demons). The history of Israel was to be their example. He didn't want them unaware or ignorant of their responsibility and what could happen to them.

Those Corinthian believers drank the blood of the sacrifice as part of the ritual of sacrificial-sexual idolatry. As to the seriousness of the matter, Findlay states,

> 'where the feast is held under the auspices of a heathen god and as a sequel to his sacrifice...participation under these circumstances *becomes an act of apostasy*, and the *feaster identifies himself with the idol* as distinctly as in the Lord's Supper he identifies himself with Christ'.[320]

The reference to the table of demons is the first rule of James: don't eat meat sacrificed to an idol at the time and place of the sacrifice. Three of the four rules of James are expressly pointed out by Paul in First Corinthians (cult harlotry, sacrificial blood and sacrificial meat). Also, this section is Paul's closure for chapter eight where some might think he was condoning the eating of meat sacrificed to an idol in the temple; 8:1-13.

T. R. Schreiner in his article on *Sacrifices and Offerings in the NT* affirms that Paul was dealing with some incredibly perverse concepts of what it meant 'to believe in Jesus.' He writes,

> 'how can they sit at the Lord's table and participate in the benefits of the Lord's death and at the same time sit down in an idol's temple and participate in the benefits of that which was sacrificed to idols? Obviously, such behavior is completely incongruous and inappropriate. One cannot have it both ways, gaining the benefits of Christ's death and at the same time expose oneself to demonic influences (1 Cor. 10:20-22).'[321]

This is why, and what James meant, when he used *pollutions of idols* and *blood* in Acts 15:20. What's plain for all to see today was a mystery to many lawless Gentiles in Corinth. The need for the four rules and the Torah was very necessary in Corinth.

---

[320] Findlay, *St. Paul's First Epistle to the Corinthians*, p. 732.

[321] Bromiley, *ISBE*, vol. four, p. 277.

Beef in the Market: 1st Cor. 10:23-28

The buying and the eating of meat in the marketplace for common consumption is a corollary to what Paul's been addressing. In 1st Cor. 8, Paul seems to allow the believer to enter the pagan shrine and eat the sacrificial meat. His reasoning? The 'idol is nothing.' This would seem to contradict James. But Morris rightly points out that chapter eight wasn't Paul's final word on the subject. It only brings out his thoughts that an idol is nothing. Morris writes that Paul,

> 'is certainly not giving his own full idea on the matter, for he later says that what is sacrificed to idols is actually sacrificed to devils (10:20). There are spiritual beings behind the idols, though not the ones their worshippers thought. But here this is not the point. Paul is prepared to agree that the gods the heathen worship are no gods.'[322]

The Apostle also speaks of not making one's brother stumble if he saw the Christian in the pagan temple (1st Cor. 8:7-13). By dealing with the issue of temple attendance this way, Paul is saying that the believer shouldn't be seen in the temple even though the idol is nothing. This is his way of prohibiting the believer who thinks that there's nothing wrong with eating the meat at the temple.

When Paul speaks of the sacrificial meat ('table of demons') in 10:21 he reveals his fuller thoughts on the subject by declaring that they weren't to do that. With meat in the market, the main difference is that the believer is *not a participant in the temple sacrifice*. This is an important distinction. In 1st Cor. 10:23-28 Paul writes,

> 'All things are lawful, but not all things are profitable. All things are lawful but not all things edify. Let no one seek his own good but that of his neighbor. Eat anything that is sold in the meat market without asking questions for conscience sake, for the Earth is the Lord's and all it contains.'

> 'If one of the unbelievers invites you and you want to go, eat anything that is set before you without asking questions for conscience sake. But if anyone says to you, 'This is meat sacrificed to idols,' do not eat it for the sake of the

---

[322] Morris, *1 Corinthians*, p. 122.

one who informed you, and for conscience sake'.

In chapter six the understanding that all things were lawful for Paul meant that theoretically, he too was able to do anything he wanted within Roman jurisprudence. For Paul, the phrase 'eating anything' would fall within the boundaries of 'anything' that God declared to be clean. He wouldn't eat a ham sandwich because he knew that it was a sin for him and for others.[323] The text is not speaking about clean vs. unclean meat but meat sacrificed to idols. Paul isn't authorizing the eating of unclean meat. He's saying it's alright to eat meat bought at the market (or meat given for dinner in another's home which had been sacrificed and then sold at the market), as long as one didn't know it had been sacrificed.

From two very important passages of Scripture (Acts 15:20; Rev. 2:20) it has seemed to some that Paul is contradicting both Jesus and James in allowing believers to eat meat offered or sacrificed to idols. But James admonished the Gentile believers not to eat meat that was literally just sacrificed on the altar, specifically referring to it in Acts 15:20 as 'the pollutions of idols.' In 1st Cor. 10, Paul forbid the same thing. Eating from the table of demons spoke of eating the just sacrificed animal, the person actually participating in the sacrifice and worship of another god. (The same would apply to the drinking of its blood.)

In Rev. 2:20-21 Messiah Yeshua comes against the eating of the meat at the time of the sacrifice (and cult prostitution; fornication),

> 'Notwithstanding I have a few things against thee, because thou sufferest that woman Jezebel, which calleth herself a prophetess, to teach and to seduce my servants to commit *fornication* and *to eat things sacrificed unto idols.* And I gave her space to repent of her fornication; and she repented not.' (Rev. 2:20-21 KJV)

These Gentile Christians at Thyatira were indulging in temple prostitution and eating the animal sacrificed to the idol within the framework of a pagan ceremony. Yeshua declared it was wrong to eat that meat, and of course, to have sex with the cult harlots. He said Jezebel was teaching and seducing those believers into doing just that...offering 'worship' to another god as a Christian. In other words she taught this was an acceptable Christian practice.

---

[323] See 1st Tim. 4:4-5 and note the two qualifications for what makes food acceptable to eat; prayer *and* the Word of God (i.e. the Scriptures, specifically Lev. 11), not just prayer. See *Law 102* at www.seedofabraham.net for why the Church's position on the Law in the New Testament is not biblical.

Paul allows believers to eat of sacrificial meat (1st Cor. 10:23-28) but not at the sacrifice to the god. It pertains to the Gentile in the marketplace seeking to buy some meat. They're told by Paul not to ask if it had been sacrificed, which means that all meat sold in the market didn't come from pagan sacrifices. This is how Paul could say what he does and not be coming against Jesus or James. Paul allows the Gentile to eat this meat because 'idols are nothing' (1st Cor. 8:4, 7, 10), and the Earth is the Lord's and everything in it (1st Cor. 10:28; Ex. 9:29; Ps. 24:1).

Some of the meat in the marketplace would come from a pagan sacrifice, the pagan priests selling the excess to the vendors in the market. This was common. Morris states, 'The priests customarily sold what they could not use.'[324]

Other meat might be 'blessed' by a pagan priest and then slaughtered in the marketplace by the 'butcher' (but not literally sacrificed on the pagan altar). With the blessing of the pagan priest the meat would be seen as 'fit for consumption' having received the pagan 'seal of approval.' But it might concern some believers even though it hadn't been part of a sacrificial ceremony.[325] This is why Paul can tell them they can eat the meat in the market. Just don't ask if it was sacrificed.

Why Paul told them not to eat the meat if the unbeliever said it was from a pagan sacrifice rests on not confusing the unbeliever in terms of being able to present the Great News to them. What he's not saying ('don't ask') is that if someone puts pork chops in front of you, you can eat it. No, Paul is addressing the problem of meat bought at the market or eaten at an unbeliever's home that may have been used in a pagan sacrifice, not which meat to eat (clean vs. unclean). In the year and a half that Paul taught the believers at Corinth (Acts 18:11), he most likely would have had a few classes on the dietary laws (Lev. 3:17; 11:1-47; Dt. 12:16, 23; 14:1-21).

Witherington notes the difference in the Greek words for food eaten at the temple and sacrificial food eaten at home. He states,

'It was okay to eat food sacrificed in a pagan temple at

---

[324] Morris, *1 Corinthians*, p. 120.

[325] This is what Paul addressed in Rom. 14, not clean vs. unclean meats. This also happens in South Africa today where Moslem 'priests' offer their blessing to Allah before the animals are slaughtered for market. When one goes to the grocery store to buy meat, this is the only meat offered. It has the Moslem religious seal on the wrapper declaring that the meat was offered to Allah and is 'fit to eat.' A number of believers in South Africa voluntarily refuse to buy meat as a witness to others that Allah is not God.

home. Paul specifically chooses a different term to refer
to food that comes from the temple and is eaten elsewhere—ειποθυτον' (ae-po-thu-tone) '(1 Cor. 10:28). In
short, Paul, like James, insists that pagans flee idolatry'
and cult prostitution 'and the temple context where such
things' were 'prevalent.'[326]

Paul wasn't rebelling against James in his allowing the Corinthians to eat
meat from the market even if it had been part of a sacrificial rite. His
teaching complements what James wrote, addressing the issue of sacrificial meat in the market.

First Corinthians ten deals with cult harlotry and some Corinthian believers engaging in it, along with the eating of sacrificial meat from the pagan
altar and the drinking of the blood from the sacrifice. Paul warns them to
flee from it, presenting the Baal Peor affair to show the Corinthians that
their salvation would be nullified if they continued in sacrificial and sexually idolatrous practices.

Yakov's rules were certainly needed in the Corinthian congregation. This
only emphasizes the need for the Law of Moses, so the believer can be
'fully equipped for every good work.' The Corinthian assembly fell behind none of the other assemblies in the Gifts of the Spirit (1st Cor. 1:4-7)
yet their need for *instruction* in the laws of righteousness (2nd Tim.
3:16-17) was all too evident.

A number of places in First Corinthians that seemed to deal with common
harlotry actually spoke of cult harlotry. It wasn't an isolated incident
among Gentile believers as Revelation (2:20-21) brought out. Corinth was
in Achaia (northern Greece). Thyatira was in (modern day) western Turkey but both were firmly rooted in ancient pagan ways.

---

[326] Witherington, *The Acts of the Apostles*, p. 466.

CULT PROSTITUTION IN REVELATION

There are many places in the New Covenant that use πορνεια (pornay'ah; fornication: cult or common prostitution) but none present as clear a picture of its cultic use, as well as its symbolic use, as does the Book of Revelation. In Rev. 2:20-21 and 2:14, in both Thyatira and Pergamos, Yeshua Himself rebukes Christians for cult prostitution and the eating of meat sacrificed to idols at the pagan sacrifice. In the first passage, it was a prophetess within the congregation who was authorizing this in the Name of Jesus. To the assembly at Thyatira Yeshua said,

> 'Notwithstanding I have a few things against thee, because thou sufferest that woman Jezebel, which calleth herself a prophetess, to teach and to seduce my servants to commit *fornication* and *to eat things sacrificed unto idols*. And I gave her space to repent of her fornication; and she repented not.' (Rev. 2:20-21 KJV)

Of course it's hard to imagine that Christians would continue in this practice so many years after Acts 15, and Paul's letters to Corinth, etc. And this, in the very area of western Turkey that Paul had evangelized. More than forty years later Jesus revealed to the Apostle John that Christians were still practicing cult prostitution and eating pagan sacrifices.

The phrase eating 'things sacrificed to idols' immediately following 'fornication' implies they were part of the same pagan ceremony. One complemented the other, the nature of which was union with the god (or goddess). Part of the problem at Thyatira was that Christians were being taught to fornicate *in the Name of Jesus*. Was this the New Testament version of the Gold Calf? Were they practicing sexual idolatry in the congregation to an image of Jesus and Mary? More subtle than all the beasts of the field is the Serpent. The Gentile Christians didn't see themselves as committing sin but performing their religious duty.

Yeshua, calling this prophetess in Thyatira Jezebel, was no light matter. A daughter of the King of Sidon, Jezebel became the wife of King Ahab who ruled the northern kingdom of Israel for 22 years (1st Kings 16:29), from 876–853 B.C. She led Ahab and Israel astray by bringing in her god Baal (1st Kgs. 16:31-33) and cult harlotry. Sacrifice to Baal also meant infant sacrifice. Jezebel murdered the true prophets of Yahveh (1st Kgs. 18:1-4) and wanted to murder Elijah as well (1st Kgs. 19:1-3; see also 1st Kgs. 17:29-33; 21:1-29; 2nd Kgs. 9:1-17). Everyone who knew Scripture would know what He thought of her. He gave this Jezebel time to repent. In 1st Cor. 10 Paul did the same thing for the Corinthians didn't understand that Yeshua wasn't like Zeus and Aphrodite. The Gentiles hadn't been at Mt. Sinai or Baal Peor or taken into captivity to Babylon because of cult harlotry. But this time of grace has an end too (2nd Corinthians 12:21-13:6; Rev. 2:20-23).

Some might say, 'Well that's a lot different from when God immediately destroyed 24,000 of them.' That's true but looking at the whole picture of Israel, Yahveh also strove with Israel *many centuries* concerning cult harlotry, sending His prophets to warn them (2nd Kgs. 17:1-23; Jer. 7:25; 35:15). *That* Israel hadn't crossed the Red Sea. *That* Israel hadn't heard the Voice and seen the Fire on the Mountain (Ex. 19:16f).

Also, Yahveh's literal Presence was with Israel in the Wilderness at the Baal Peor affair. And the reality of Yahveh's Presence existed after the Resurrection for the Jerusalem body. All the Jewish believers heard about the untimely deaths of Ananias and Sapphira (Acts 5:1-11). The two of them only lied to Peter about how much money they actually got from the sale of their property but the Holy Spirit killed them. The Spirit would not do so in Jeremiah's day, or at Corinth in Paul's day. Some Corinthians and Thyatirians didn't seem to grasp the idolatrous significance. The main difference was the manifestation of the Lord or the lack of it, which determined whether the punishment would be carried out immediately or not (with time given to repent).

That the Holy Spirit wasn't manifesting in the same way for Paul is evident from all the problems that he had with the Corinthians. Many times he had to threaten them, particularly the ones who said that he was a powerful letter writer, but in person he was 'weak and nothing' (2nd Cor. 10:8-11; see also 1:23; 12:20f.). Can you imagine any Christian saying that about the Apostle Paul? If lying to Peter was enough for Ananias and Sapphira to be instantly killed by God, how much more those in Corinth who rebelled against Paul's authority and/or frequented temple harlots?

Yeshua also warned the congregation at Pergamos (another congregation in western Turkey). They were doing the same things as Thyatira. Here though the Lord points them *back to Balaam* and Israel in the Wilderness. Balaam taught the daughters of Moab to seduce the Sons of Israel in the wickedness at Baal Peor. Yeshua said to the Pergamos Christians,

> 'I know thy works and where thou dwellest, even where Satan's throne is, and thou holdest fast my name, and hast not denied my faith, even in those days wherein Antipas was my faithful martyr, who was slain among you where Satan dwelleth.'[327]

> 'But I have a few things against thee, because thou hast
> there them that hold the *doctrine of Balaam*, who taught
> Balak to cast a stumbling block before the Sons of Israel,
> *to eat things sacrificed unto idols* and *to commit fornica-*
> *tion.*' πορνευσαι (por-nu-sai) (Rev. 2:13-14 KJV)

With the mention of Balaam, the fornication spoken of has to be cult harlotry, not common harlotry. The Baal Peor disaster is attributed to him via
Balak (Num. 22–24), and in Num. 31:16 it says Balaam caused Israel to
sin at Baal Peor (and Joshua killed him for what he did; Josh. 13:22).

Pergamos was *especially* noted for sacrificial-sexual idolatry. The fornication spoken of there would have to be linked to cult harlotry even if the
Lord only mentioned fornication in and of itself. The fact they were eating
things sacrificed unto idols clearly shows it was sacrificial-sexual idolatry.

Wycliffe states the city was 'given to idolatry *more than all Asia.*' And,

> the 'hill behind it was adorned with numerous temples,
> among which was the great temple to Zeus, who was
> called Soter Theos, the Savior God.'[328]

Morris says that the eating of food sacrificed to idols and harlotry,

> 'refer to idolatrous practices. Feasting on sacrificial meat
> and licentious conduct *were usual accompaniments of the*
> *worship of idols, both in Old and New Testament*
> times.'[329]

Stern confirms that the problem at Pergamos wasn't the same problem that
Paul dealt with in Corinth when sacrificial meat was sold at the marketplace. He says the,

> 'issue here is not eating meat used in pagan rituals...but
> actually participating in idolatrous feasts and sexual sin,

---

[327] Hislop, *The Two Babylons*, pp. 240-241. Yeshua was literally declaring Pergamos to be the place where Satan established his headquarters (throne). Just as
Jerusalem is the home of Yahveh (Ps. 48:2), so ancient Babylon was the
Throne of Satan. When Babylon was destroyed, Satan transferred his headquarters to Nineveh and after that, to Pergamos. It was in Pergamos with the
'worship of Aesculapius, *under the form of the serpent*' that 'frantic orgies
and excesses' were practiced 'that elsewhere were kept under some measure
of restraint.' After Pergamos it was transferred to Rome.

[328] Pfeiffer, *WBC*, p. 1504.

[329] Leon Morris, The Rev. Canon, M.Sc., M.Th., Ph.D., *Tyndale New Testament*
Commentaries: Revelation (Leicester, England: Inter-Varsity Press, 2000), p.
67.

thus violating the mitzvot laid down for Gentile believers
at' Acts '15:28-29.'[330]

These two Christian assemblies in southwest Turkey, Thyatira and Pergamos, were accused by Yeshua around 95 A.D. They were walking in the
same sins that Israel had walked in at Baal Peor 1,500 years earlier. Not
much had changed in paganism in all that time. *TDNT* confirms this:

> 'For the author, the OT model for this is the doctrine of
> Balaam who led Israel astray in the same fashion, Num.
> 25:1ff; 31:16. Along the same lines the church of Thyatira
> is charged with tolerating a prophetess who teaches the
> same practices, 2:20f; the name of Jezebel is the OT refer-
> ence in this instance, 2nd Kings 9:7, 22.'[331]

More than forty years after Yakov made his ruling, Yeshua had to speak
against these idolatrous practices at two Christian assemblies in Asia Minor. It wasn't without foresight that Yakov gave those four rules under divine inspiration of the Holy Spirit (2nd Tim. 3:16-17; 2nd Pet. 3:15-18).

The diabolical scheme of Satan has been to beguile the whole world into
worshipping him instead of Yahveh. And this, even and especially in Israel among His own people. (There's a strong message to the Church here
about her pagan practices. She's not immune to false ways and must forsake them.) The core of that worship was cult harlotry. This came from
Babylon, the great seducer of Man's heart.

Babylon is the seducer of all the nations, causing the peoples to worship
Satan, getting the Gentile and Jewish peoples to think they were worshiping the True God when in fact they were worshiping Satan in one of his
many different guises. The Great Harlot is mentioned in nearly three
identical passages (Rev. 14:8, 17:2 and 18:3), relating to what she has giv-
en Mankind to drink; the wine of her harlotry:

> Rev. 14:8: 'And there followed another angel, saying,
> Babylon is fallen, is fallen, that great city, because she
> made all nations drink of the wine of the wrath of her *for-
> nication.*' πορνειας (pornay'ahs) (KJV)

> Rev. 17:2: 'With whom the kings of the Earth have com-

---

[330] Stern, *JNTC*, p. 796. The Hebrew term 'mitzvot' means 'commandments' referring to those given by God or His authorized agents (e.g. Moses, Paul and
Yakov, etc.). Stern writes that the rules the Gentiles in Pergamos were 'violating' came from Acts 15:28-29, the actual recording of the letter sent to the
Jewish and Gentile community of Antioch.

[331] Kittel, *TDNT*, vol. VI, p. 594.

mitted *fornication* επορνειας (eh-por-nay-ahs), and the inhabitants of the Earth have been made drunk with the wine of her *fornication*.' πορνειας (pornay'ahs) (KJV)

Rev. 18:3: 'For all nations have drunk of the wine of the wrath of her *fornication* πορνειας (pornay'ahs) and the kings of the Earth have committed *fornication* επορνευσαν (eh-por-nu-sahn) with her, and the merchants of the Earth are waxed rich through the abundance of her delicacies.' (KJV)[332]

All nations, Jewish and Gentile, have drunk of the fornication of the Harlot of Babylon. That the term fornication here means more than cult harlotry is obvious. It should be just as obvious that it includes it. Fornication here takes in all spheres where one can prostitute their soul; from sacrificial-sexual 'worship' to financial greed, physical lust, political and even satanic power.

Babylon is the diabolical opposite of the heavenly Jerusalem where the True God is worshiped. *TDNT* speaks of Babylon and the Harlot as the antithesis of Jerusalem and God. The Harlot's fornication is also cultic:

'In the description of the world power and metropolis of Rome, the counterpart of ungodly Babylon...πορνη' (pornay; harlot), 'and πορνευω' (por-nu-oh; harlotry), 'are used as comprehensive terms for its utter degeneracy. Like the city harlots of the day it bears its name on a golden headband, and this name declares its nature: Rev. 17:5'.[333] 'And upon her forehead was a name written, Mystery, Babylon the Great, the Mother of harlots and abominations of the Earth.'

'It is the leading harlot of the world, the great seducer of the nations and their kings.' 'They seek its favors politically and economically. But the word embraces more than this. The nations ape the customs of the metropolis *even to whoredom in the literal sense.* Above all, the capital is called πορνη' (pornay; harlot) 'as the *center of paganism* with its harlot-like apostasy from the true God.'[334]

---

[332] Both the Textus Receptus and the United Bible Societies' Greek New Testament are identical in their usage of the Greek words concerning fornication and adultery in all these cites for Revelation. The KJV translation is used here as it has the English term fornication.

[333] Kittel, *TDNT*, vol. VI, p. 594.

From the Book of Revelation, whether looking at Thyatira, Pergamos or the Great Whore, the worship of another god or goddess through sex (cult prostitution), was a major part of what has shackled Mankind to Hell. The Gentiles never had a Father Abraham who worshiped the Living God or a Moses who led the Sons of Israel out of Egyptian slavery under the mighty outstretched Arm of Yahveh. The Gentiles had no divine Lawgiver like Moses. They had no godly boundaries to restrain their perverse worship. With no Torah, their lusts were directed by Satan and fueled by their carnal nature.

All the Gentile lands and peoples were steeped in sacrificial-sexual idolatry. It permeated their thinking and their way of life. Part and parcel with this was the belief that one could have as many gods as they wanted. It would be very natural for them to *add* Jesus into their pantheon. Both First Corinthians and Revelation attest to the seriousness of the problem, and how widespread it was among professing Christians.

Of course, not all Gentile believers would do this for there would be some 'God-fearers' like Cornelius who would have been taught to stop practicing idolatry before they came to Yeshua. And there would be others who would immediately stop when they found out what Yeshua required of them in that area; from the Decree of James, the letters of Paul and their learning of Torah every Shabat.

Many of them though would do it in ignorance, while others would do it in their prideful and self-indulgent 'freedom in Christ' philosophy. This is what the Apostle Paul dealt with at Corinth, and this is why Yakov gave the four rules. The four rules had nothing to do with table fellowship but with the placing of these important godly boundaries before the Gentiles.

James would not only tell the Gentile what he needed to do in order to be saved, but also what would sever him from his Savior. It was because of Gentile need to understand this, that they couldn't worship Yeshua and their former gods in sacrificial-sexual idolatry, that the four rules were issued. This is a unique glimpse into the religious world at the time of the Apostles. It was a world that was neck deep in satanic quicksand and thinking nothing of it. The great power of sin is its ability to deceive.

What compassion the God of Israel has for all peoples in sending His Son. He's displayed a love that is infinitely beyond our ability to comprehend.

---

[334] Ibid.

CULT PROSTITUTION
IN THE NEW TESTAMENT

All the places in the New Testament where the word pornay'ah (fornication), and its noun derivatives occur, will be listed in order to get a sense of *how* the words are used. Fornication itself is mentioned 32 times in the New Testament and the overwhelming majority of those times (26) clearly speak primarily of cult prostitution. A few times it's found in lists with other sins, and with no context given it, it can't be certain if cult or common harlotry is primarily meant. And in Revelation it's used both symbolically as well as literally as Rev. 14, 17 and 18 spoke of.

Fornication: Cult Prostitution

1. Matt. 5:32: 'But I say unto you, that whosoever shall put away his wife, saving for the cause of *fornication*, causeth her to commit adultery. And whosoever shall marry her that is divorced committeth adultery.'

2. Matt. 19:9: 'And I say unto you, whosoever shall put away his wife, except it be for *fornication*, and shall marry another, committeth adultery. And whoso marrieth her which is put away doth commit adultery.'

Mt. 5:32 can't be common harlotry as only cult harlotry is unforgivable. The sexual worship of another god is biblical grounds for severing a marriage between two believers. (Mt. 19:9 declares the same thing.)

3. John 8:41: "'Ye do the deeds of your father.' Then said they to him, 'We be not born of *fornication*; we have one Father, even God.'"

The context speaks of those whom Yeshua said were the offspring of another god and v. 44 specifically has Yeshua saying they're of the Devil. The Pharisees didn't answer and say their earthly father wasn't involved in common prostitution or adultery, etc. Their speaking of *God* as their Father means that fornication here is to be understood as cult harlotry.

4. Acts 15:20: 'But that we write unto them, that they abstain from pollutions of idols, and from fornication, and from things strangled, and from blood.'

The text speaks of cult harlotry. Its biblical usage, Hebrew and Greek word definitions, and its listing in the passage immediately after eating the meat of a pagan sacrifice at the sacrifice, confirm this. The next two passages are references to this one:

5. Acts 15:29: 'That ye abstain from meats offered to idols, and from blood, and from things strangled, and from *fornication*: from which if ye keep yourselves, ye shall do well. Fare ye well.'

6. Acts 21:25: 'As touching the Gentiles which believe, we have written and concluded that they observe no such thing, save only that they keep themselves from things offered to idols, and from blood, and from strangled, and from *fornication*.'

7. 1st Cor. 5:1: 'It's reported commonly that there is *fornication* among you, and such fornication as is not so much as named among the Gentiles; that one should have his father's wife.'

1st Cor. 5:1 was incestuous cult harlotry. This astonished even Paul. In the next two verses the parallels to religious harlotry speak primarily of cult prostitution over common prostitution:

8. 1st Cor. 6:13: 'Meats for the belly, and the belly for meats but God shall destroy both it and them. Now the body is not for *fornication* but for the Lord and the Lord for the body.'

9. 1st Cor. 6:18: 'Flee *fornication*! Every sin that a man doeth is without the body; but he that committeth *fornication* sinneth against his own body.'

The next verse falls between chapters five and ten of First Corinthians, an area which spoke of cult harlotry, although common harlotry would certainly be included in this admonition:

10. 1st Cor. 7:2: 'Nevertheless, to avoid *fornication*, let every man have his own wife, and let every woman have her own husband.'

The next cite refers to the Baal Peor affair (Num. 25), and certainly speaks of cult prostitution:

11. 1st Cor. 10:8: 'Neither let us commit *fornication*, as some of them committed, and fell in one day three and twenty thousand.'

This next verse includes the main theme that Paul addressed to the Corinthians in his previous letter. Cult harlotry is obviously meant:

12. 2nd Cor. 12:21: 'And lest when I come again, my God will humble me among you and that I shall bewail many which have sinned already and have not repented of the uncleanness and *fornication* and lasciviousness which they have committed.'

The problem of cult harlotry among believers wasn't easily remedied.

Now, passages in Revelation that speak of cult prostitution:

13. Rev. 2:14: 'But I have a few things against thee, because thou hast there them that hold the doctrine of Balaam, who taught Balak to cast a stumbling block before the children of Israel, to eat things sacrificed unto idols, and to commit *fornication*.'

14. Rev. 2:20: 'Notwithstanding I have a few things against thee, because thou sufferest that woman Jezebel, which calleth herself a prophetess, to teach and to seduce my servants to commit *fornication*, and to eat things sacrificed unto idols.'

15. Rev. 2:21: 'And I gave her space to repent of her *fornication*; and she repented not.'

16. Rev. 14:8: 'And there followed another angel, saying, Babylon is fallen, is fallen, that great city, because she made all nations drink of the wine of the wrath of her *fornication*.'

17. Rev. 17:2: 'With whom the kings of the Earth have committed fornication, and the inhabitants of the Earth have been made drunk with the wine of her *fornication*.'

18. Rev. 17:4: 'And the woman was arrayed in purple and scarlet colour, and decked with gold and precious stones and pearls, having a golden cup in her hand full of abominations and filthiness of her *fornication*:'

19. Rev. 18:3: 'For all nations have drunk of the wine of the wrath of her *fornication*, and the kings of the Earth have committed *fornication* with her, and the merchants of the Earth are waxed rich through the abundance of her delicacies.'

20. Rev. 18:9: 'And the kings of the Earth, who have committed *fornication* and lived deliciously with her, shall bewail her, and lament for her, when they shall see the smoke of her burning'.

21. Rev. 19:2: 'For true and righteous are his judgments: for he hath judged the great whore, which did corrupt the Earth with her *fornication*, and hath avenged the blood of his servants at her hand.'

The first three texts (Rev. 2:14, 20-21) explicitly speak of cult harlotry and all the other texts can't be said to exclude it.

In the next verse, Judah (Jude) certainly speaks of homosexuality when he writes of fornication in his letter. It refers to the ancient city of Sodom in the Old Testament that God overthrew because of its wickedness (Gen. 18–19). But was this *fornication* only *common* homosexuality?

22. Jude 1:7: 'Even as Sodom and Gomorrah, and the cities about them in like manner, giving themselves over to *fornication*, and going after strange flesh, are set forth for an example, suffering the vengeance of eternal fire.'

Going 'after strange flesh' is a euphemism for homosexuality but was Judah excluding *cult* homosexuality? Homosexuality was certainly part of the perversion that plagued the cities of Sodom (Gen. 19:5) and Gomorrah and would be practiced at their cult temples. Here is homosexual cult harlotry, men with men (although men with women weren't excluded from this either).

This homosexual cult harlotry would be practiced by the Hebrews when they entered the Land.[335] Canaan was a land that 'outdid' all the ancient lands in its perversion and was noted for its homosexual cult harlotry.[336] It's not unreasonable to assume that Judah is speaking of cult homosexuality when he writes of fornication.

The next six verses that use pornay'ah appear in lists and don't lend themselves to a specific form of harlotry (cult or common). Of course cult harlotry should be given primary consideration whenever pornay'ah is used. Cult prostitution was what the writers of the New Testament overwhelmingly addressed even though common harlotry might be included.

Pagan worship with its cult harlots was practiced throughout the Roman Empire. Both Paul and John, who wrote these next six verses, certainly saw this as a serious problem. If they were addressing something other than harlotry (e.g. adultery), they would have chosen to include those specific Greek words. In Gal. 5:19 (#24), Paul does just that. The Textus Receptus has both adultery (moi-kay-ah), and prostitution (pornay'ah):

23. Romans 1:29: 'Being filled with all unrighteousness, *fornication*, wickedness, covetousness, maliciousness; full of envy, murder, debate, deceit, malignity; whisperers'.

24. Gal. 5:19: 'Now the works of the flesh are manifest, which are these; Adultery, *fornication*, uncleanness, lasciviousness'.

25. Eph. 5:3: 'But *fornication* and all uncleanness or covetousness, let it not be once named among you, as becometh holy ones'. (Hebrew kadosh, holy ones; Greek hagios, holy ones.)

26. Col. 3:5: 'Mortify therefore your members which are upon the

---

[335] See pp. 47-50 above.

[336] See pp. 61-62 above.

Earth; *fornication*, uncleanness, inordinate affection, evil concupiscence and covetousness which is idolatry'.

27. 1st Thess. 4:3: 'For this is the will of God, even your sanctification, that ye should abstain from *fornication*'.

28. Rev. 9:21: 'Neither repented they of their murders, nor of their sorceries, nor of their *fornication*, nor of their thefts.'

Three of the texts above (23, 24 and 26) are most likely speaking of fornication as cult harlotry, but common harlotry and possibly a general spirit of whoredom (promiscuity), might have been meant too. The latter deals not with idols or the taking of money, but with carnal sexual indulgence. This is prevalent in Western society today.

Numbers 25 and 27 appear to speak primarily of cult prostitution. And 28 can be said to also include it.

In the New Testament the term fornication is used 32 times (in the 28 verses above). The overwhelming majority of its usage (26 times), clearly speaks of cult prostitution. And the rest can certainly be said to include it. To translate pornay'ah in Acts 15:20 as 'sexual immorality' or unchastity is a serious linguistic error just from its word usage in the New Testament. It's also a grave theological disservice to those who desire to know what God's Word is saying to them.

Fornications

Only twice in the New Testament is the plural of fornication used. Both times relate to the same teaching and can be seen as encompassing both cult and common prostitution (but not adultery as it's mentioned in both instances).

1. Matt. 15:19: 'For out of the heart proceed evil thoughts, murders, adulteries, *fornications*, thefts, false witness, blasphemies.'

2. Mark 7:21: For from within, out of the heart of men, proceed evil thoughts, adulteries, *fornications*, murders'.

The plural of fornication is a way of emphasizing the number of times it occurs in the heart. This is seen with murders and adulteries, etc.

The noun fornicator appears twice in the next section. The first instance speaks of incestuous cult harlotry as the man slept with his father's cult harlot wife (1st Cor. 5:1-5). The second verse could speak of both common and cult harlotry.

Fornicator

1. 1st Cor. 5:11: 'But now I have written unto you not to keep company, if any man that is called a brother be a *fornicator*, or covetous, or an idolater, or a railer, or a drunkard, or an extortioner; with such an one no not to eat.'

2. Heb. 12:16: 'Lest there be any *fornicator*, or profane person as Esau, who for one morsel of meat sold his birthright.'

Fornicators

The plural of fornicator is mentioned three times. All of them occur in First Corinthians within 14 verses. They relate to those who frequent temple prostitutes. This is one of Paul's themes in the letter and must have been a theme in his previous letter also (1st Cor. 5:9):

1. 1st Cor. 5:9: 'I wrote unto you in an epistle not to company with *fornicators*:'

2. 1st Cor. 5:10: 'Yet not altogether with the *fornicators* of this world, or with the covetous, or extortioners, or with idolaters; for then must ye needs go out of the world.'

3. 1st Cor. 6:9: 'Know ye not that the unrighteous shall not inherit the Kingdom of God? Be not deceived: neither *fornicators*, nor idolaters, nor adulterers, nor effeminate, nor abusers of themselves with mankind,'

The first two cites refer to incestuous cult harlotry. Paul's *fornicators* of 1st Cor. 6:9 speak primarily of those who use cult harlots as it not only comes right on the heels of chapter five, but only three verses later, in 1st Cor. 6:12-20, Paul begins to speak of temple harlots and the Temple of the Living God.

From this survey of all the places where fornication, etc., has been used in the King James New Testament, fornication speaks primarily of cult prostitution. From just this perspective on how pornay'ah is used in the New Testament there should be no question as how to translate the second rule of Acts 15:20. Yakov spoke of cult prostitution when he issued the Decree, not sexual immorality, prohibited marriages, common homosexuality or even common prostitution.

THE THIRD RULE: THINGS STRANGLED

The third rule in Acts 15:20 is, things 'strangled' but some think Yakov never said it. The *Interlinear* has a footnote to the verse, 'Other ancient authorities lack, "and from whatever has been strangled."'[337] Marshall explains why some manuscripts don't have the third rule and why Yakov did indeed give it:

> 'As the RSV mg. indicates, later scribes re-worded the list of forbidden things; the omission of 'things strangled' leaves three words which can be understood in a moral sense—idolatry, unchastity and murder ('blood'). This alteration was probably made by scribes who no longer understood the first century situation; in course of time the need for the prescriptions about food acceptable to Jewish Christian consciences disappeared.'[338]

With 'later scribes' re-wording the text, it appears that Yakov gave the rule. Marshall's explanation, that some scribes saw the three rules as 'a moral package deal' is interesting. This is because those Christian scribes not only hid a rule of James (strangled), but erroneously present blood as murder, and unchastity as the meaning of fornication. The next section will reveal why blood in Acts 15:20 cannot be equated with murder. As noble as this moral lesson sounds, it wasn't what Yakov addressed.

Wesley Perschbacher says that strangled means 'strangled' or 'suffocated' and that it's,

> 'the flesh of animals killed by strangulation or suffocation, Acts 15:20, 29; 21:25'.[339]

Friberg agrees and speaks of *the blood not being drained*:

> 'choked; of animals killed by strangling so that the blood is not drained from them'.[340]

Bauer states that the word strangled wasn't found,

> 'in the Septuagint nor in Hellenistic Jewish writings' but in Acts 'it plainly means strangled, choked to death' 'of

---

[337] Brown, *NGEINT*, p. 473. It states this for every passage where the four rules are mentioned (Acts 15:20, 29; 21:25). The NRSV has it but says that 'some ancient authorities' lack it.

[338] Marshall, *Acts*, pp. 253-254 note 1.

[339] Perschbacher, *NAGL*, p. 334.

[340] Friberg, *ALGNT*, p. 319.

animals killed without having the blood drained from
them whose flesh' (meat) 'the Jews were forbidden to eat'
'Lev. 17:13f.'[341]

It's true that Yahveh didn't want His people Israel to eat meat with the
blood in it (Lev. 19:26; Ezk. 24:1-24). To allow the blood to remain within the animal corrupts the meat by its very presence as many toxins or poi-
sons are carried by the blood and remain in the meat if not properly
drained. Most hunters know this and upon killing an animal, hang it up
and slit its throat as soon as possible so the blood drains out. It seems the
Greeks knew this too. Bauer states,

> 'the Pythagorean dietary laws forbid' meat from 'animals
> that have not been properly slaughtered'.[342]

Ancient man knew to take the blood out of the animal in order to eat it. In
other words, it may not have been a *common* practice to sell meat in the
marketplace that hadn't been properly slaughtered. But even if some meat
wasn't properly drained of blood, is that what Yakov addressed?

Howard Marshall logically lumps together the third rule (strangled) with
the fourth (blood) and says that strangling the animal,

> 'meant that the blood remained in the meat, and the fourth
> item was blood itself.' These 'food regulations resemble
> those in Lev. 17:8-13.'[343]

Wycliffe too believes it pertains to 'Meats from which the blood had not
been properly removed.'[344] Bruce thinks that the,

> "prohibition against eating flesh with the blood still in it
> (including the flesh of strangled animals) was based on
> the 'Noachian decree of Gen. 9:4.'"[345]

Stern says it meant 'meat from animals not slaughtered in a way that allows the blood to flow out.'[346] Knowling writes that a prohibition against
strangling can't be found in the Law of Moses but agrees that eating meat
with blood in it would be offensive to a Jew. He writes that the rule pertains to,

---

[341] Bauer, *GELNT*, p. 680.

[342] Ibid.

[343] Marshall, *Acts*, p. 253.

[344] Pfeiffer, *WBC*, p. 1152.

[345] Bruce, *The Book of the Acts*, p. 296.

[346] Stern, *JNTC*, p. 277.

'beasts as had been killed through strangling, and whose blood had not been let out when they were killed. For this prohibition reference is usually made to Lev. 17:13; Dt. 12:16, 23'. 'But on the other hand, Dr. Hort contends that all attempts to find the prohibition in the Pentateuch quite fail, although he considers it perfectly conceivable that the flesh of animals strangled in such a way as not to allow of the letting out of blood would be counted as unlawful food by the Jews'.[347]

David Williams also believes that strangling means one shouldn't eat meat with blood in it.[348] Most Christian scholarship believes that the rule *strangled* means not to eat meat with blood in it. One can only begin to wonder that if Christian scholars believe this, why doesn't the Church practice this today? Why is there no teaching from the pulpit that one shouldn't eat meat with blood in it? Some scholars have connected *strangling* with the fourth rule, blood. Although this may seem logical, it's not what Yakov meant.

Although these rules might resemble food regulations, as Marshall wrote, one would be hard pressed to understand why James didn't include *which animals* could be eaten when properly slaughtered, so as *not to offend the Jews*. If James was going to caution against not eating animals that had been strangled, and therefore had blood in the meat, he failed to tell the Gentiles *which animals God forbid to eat* (Lev. 11; Dt. 14). Could such a major part of the rule have escaped his attention? Perhaps at the time of the ruling (Acts 15:20), but certainly not till the end of the book of Acts, and *nothing is said anywhere else in the New Testament* that *strangled* pertains to a food regulation, or that it's part of the fourth rule on *blood*. No, the rule doesn't concern a dietary regulation even though it speaks of strangled animals.

Only Ben Witherington and Tim Hegg rightly understand that strangled relates to sacrificial idolatry.[349] This rule falls within the context of an animal being sacrificed to a god by strangling.[350] The rule's function has

---

[347] Knowling, *The Acts of the Apostles*, pp. 324-325.

[348] Williams, *Acts*, p. 266.

[349] Witherington, *The Acts of the Apostles*, p. 464. Hegg, *The Letter Writer*, p. 277. Unfortunately, Hegg wrongly thinks it's also a dietary regulation: no *strangled* meat because of blood being in it.

[350] Strangling is defined as suffocation or choking. The concept includes the wringing of the neck of a bird and the breaking of the neck of a larger animal through twisting it.

nothing to do with blood remaining within the victim for the general public to eat but as a sacrifice to a god. The 'animal' in this case would most likely be a bird. Doves and pigeons, etc., were often used as a sacrifice, not only to the God of Israel (Lev. 1:14-17; 5:7-10; 14:5; Luke 2:24, etc.) but to other gods as well.[351] Birds were very plentiful, inexpensive (Lk. 12:6), and a 'perfect' sacrifice for the common people to bring.

Strangling wasn't necessarily limited to birds though. In Isaiah 66:3 the prophet speaks of an Israeli who sacrifices a lamb being like one who breaks a dog's neck, something very similar or identical to strangling. The *Theological Dictionary of the Old Testament* says the polemic of the prophet attacks the '*simultaneous engagement* in both legitimate and pagan cults'.[352]

Isaiah's speaking on the dual attitude of the Hebrews, sacrificing the required sacrifice to Yahveh (the lamb), but also sacrificing an unclean dog to a pagan god. The relevant point is that the breaking of a dog's neck was part of a pagan sacrificial rite in the days of Isaiah, 700 years before James gave the four rules. Would it be unreasonable to assume that pagans continued this practice of strangling into the time of Yakov, and that it too may have been a fairly common pagan rite, along with bird sacrifice by strangling?

It's well attested in ancient literature that Gentiles sacrificed dogs to their gods.[353] There were dog cults in ancient Egypt and Mesopotamia.[354] Gula, the goddess of healing in Mesopotamia, had dogs sacrificed to her. *TDOT* states that 'dogs were sacrificed to the goddess' and there's 'evidence of buried dog skeletons'.[355]

---

[351] The priests of Yahveh wrung the neck off the bird and didn't leave the blood within it, draining it at the Altar. The priests didn't eat the dedication sacrifice (whole burnt offering; Lev. 1:14-17) but did eat the birds of the sin sacrifice (Lev. 5:1-10; 6:24-26). See Lev. 6:9-11; 12:6-8; 14:1-8, 22-32, 48-53; 15:13-15, 28-30 for other places where God required birds for sacrifice.

[352] Botterweck, *TDOT*, vol. VII, p. 155.

[353] Howard F. Vos, *Nelson's New Illustrated Bible Manners and Customs* (Nashville, TN: Thomas Nelson Publishers, 1999), p. 611 speaks of Rome's Lupercalia on Feb. 15th (now known as St. Valentine's Day). It was a 'purification and fertility' feast with much sexual revelry. The priests, 'called luperci sacrificed goats and a dog on the Palatine Hill.' 'Because of this festival's popularity, the church absorbed it instead of abolishing it. Pope Galesius V in 494 made it the Festival of the Purification of the Virgin Mary.'

[354] Botterweck, *TDOT*, vol. VII, pp. 148-149.

[355] Ibid., p. 150.

The God of Israel also commanded that larger animals would have their necks broken (twisted or strangled). In response to refusing to redeem a donkey with a lamb,[356] the neck of the donkey would be broken. And in the ritual attached to the unsolved murder in the open field in the land of Israel, an animal as large as a heifer had its neck broken (Dt. 21:1-9).[357]

Philo (20 B.C. to 50 A.D.), a Jewish philosopher born in Alexandria, Egypt, lived during the time of Messiah Yeshua. He confirms in his day 'that pagans were sacrificing animals by means of strangulation.'[358] And Witherington states there's,

> 'evidence that the choking of the sacrifice, strangling it'
> 'transpired in pagan temples.'[359]

Citing the *Magical Papyri*, Witherington writes that with the strangling of the animal, the pagans believed that the 'life breath or spiritual vitality *went into the idol*'.[360] Both this concept, and strangling of a pagan sacrifice are seen in the *Magical Papyri* as the pagan priest is instructed:

> 'Take also on the first day seven living creatures and *strangle them*; one cock, a partridge, a wren...Do not

---

[356] Ex. 13:13: 'But every first offspring of a donkey you must redeem with a lamb but if you do not redeem it then you shall break its neck. And every first-born of man among your sons you shall redeem.'

[357] Dt. 21:4: 'and the Elders of that city shall bring the heifer down to a valley with running water, which has not been plowed or sown, and shall break the heifer's neck there in the valley.'

[358] Hegg, *The Letter Writer*, p. 277 note 588: Philo, *The Special Laws*, iv: xiii. 122. Unfortunately Hegg also thinks that *strangled* also refers to 'blood within the meat' (of meat from the pagan temples) p. 277. If that were the case Yakov would have had to include the dietary laws from Lev. 11 and Dt. 14, etc., as part of his rules. Even if a Gentile properly slaughtered and hadn't strangled his animal he'd have to know which meats couldn't be eaten (i.e. which were clean and which were unclean, and not to eat any fat, etc.). Yakov never addressed this and so strangled cannot relate to blood in meat (as a dietary prohibition) but only to that part of the idolatrous sacrifice where the strangling of an animal or bird actually happened.

Hegg does present the four rules as a 'prohibition of idol worship in the pagan temples' (p. 269) but also interprets strangled to mean, 'not to eat meat with blood in it.' This takes it out of the realm of sacrificial idolatry and into the realm of the dietary laws. The third rule of James cannot pertain to a dietary regulation, as important as that is.

[359] Witherington, *The Acts of the Apostles*, p. 464.

[360] Ibid. The demons 'in back of the idol' might animate it (1st Cor. 10:20), giving it the impression that the life of the sacrifice had indeed gone into the idol.

make a burnt offering of any of these; instead, taking them in your hand, *strangle them*, while holding them up to your Eros[361] until each of the creatures is suffocated and *their breath enter him*. After that, place the strangled creatures on the altar together with aromatic plants of every variety.'[362]

The third rule, *if taken on its own*, would be impossible to definitively place within the category of sacrificial idolatry because of the scant information given in the text. *Strangled* can obviously be *interpreted* to mean the abstention from meat that has been strangled. But coming on the heels of two rules pertaining to sacrificial-sexual idolatry, it lends itself to being part of that concept. And devoid of which animals couldn't be eaten, *can only point to a pagan ritual.*

The third rule isn't a prohibition against eating meat with blood in it that had been slaughtered by strangling, as sinful as that is. It has to do with an idolatrous ceremony where a bird (or animal) is strangled. James most likely included it among the rules because it must have been a prolific pagan sacrificial practice in his day.

Most Christian scholars never thought of the possibility that strangled could relate to a pagan sacrifice. This points to a greater problem of interpreting Scripture from one's *already formed* 'theological grid.' Their perception of the rule, having to fall within only a certain category, food regulations for table fellowship (whether the prohibition against eating blood from Lev. 17 or the Noahide Laws), is seen in the light of their false concept that the Law of Moses 'is done away with.' If scholars could see outside of their box as Witherington and Hegg have, they'd have been able to postulate that if the first two rules spoke of sacrificial idolatry, perhaps strangled did also.

Things strangled has nothing to do with Jewish dietary regulations or table fellowship. It was a prohibition against participating in an idolatrous pagan ceremony that strangled birds and/or animals.

---

[361] *Encyclopedia Mythical* at http://www.pantheon.org/articles/e/eros.html. Eros is the Greek counterpart to the Roman Cupid. Cupid's arrows speak of him representing Nimrod, the first 'mighty hunter' (Gen. 10:9). See Hislop, *The Two Babylons*, pp. 19-40, 187-191, for why Cupid is not as innocent as he appears.

[362] Witherington, *The Acts of the Apostles*, p. 464 note 423. *Magical Papyri* PGM XII. 14-95.

THE FOURTH RULE: BLOOD

The Greek word for blood, the fourth rule in Acts 15:20 is 'αιματος (hai-mah-tos).[363] Perschbacher says it means, 'blood; of the color of blood; bloodshed; blood-guiltiness; natural descent.'[364] Bauer states,

> 'of human blood' 'of the blood of animals'. 'Its use as
> food is forbidden (compare Lev. 3:17; 7:26; 17:10) in the
> apostolic decree' Acts '15:20, 29; 21:25'. Some 'interpret
> this passage as 'a command not to shed blood'. Figura-
> tively 'as the seat of life' 'blood and life as an expiatory
> sacrifice' 'especially of the blood of Jesus as a means of
> expiation' and, 'of the (apocalyptic) red color, whose ap-
> pearance in heaven indicates disaster'.[365]

Friberg follows a similar line of thinking. He states that the word means,

> 'blood' 'human blood' 'by metonymy, human nature,
> physical descent' 'of sacrificial animals, blood' 'literally
> pour out blood, i.e. kill' 'menstrual flow, hemorrhage'
> 'literally fountain of blood, i.e. bleeding (Mk. 5:29);' 'by
> metonymy, of another's murder' 'of Christ's atoning sac-
> rifice' (death) and 'in apocalyptic language, the red color
> of blood as symbolizing disaster'.[366]

There are a number of ways one can interpret blood in Acts 15:20. It can literally mean blood from an animal sacrifice, or blood in 'food' (meat) being 'forbidden' in the Apostolic Decree as Bauer suggests, or sin (mur-der; bloodshed). It can also be the guilt of murder or one's lineage or even an apocalyptic disaster. How should it be interpreted?

Marshall interprets blood in Acts 15:20 as a food regulation; blood within the meat.[367] *Wycliffe* states that it,

> 'refers to the pagan custom of using blood as a food. The
> last two requirements' (of Acts 15:20) 'involved the same
> offense, for the Jew who believed that the life is in the
> blood' (Lev. 17:11) regarded the eating of any blood par-
> ticularly offensive. This decree was issued to the Gentile

---

[363] Brown, *NGEINT*, p. 473.

[364] Perschbacher, *NAGL*, p. 8.

[365] Bauer, *GELNT*, p. 22.

[366] Friberg, *ALGNT*, p. 37.

[367] Marshall, *Acts*, pp. 243, 253.

churches not as a means of salvation but as *a basis for fel-lowship*, in the spirit of Paul's exhortation that those who were strong in faith should be willing to restrict their liberty in such matters rather than offend the *weaker* brother (Rom. 14:1 ff.; 1st Cor. 8:1 ff.).'[368]

It seems strange that James would make two rules (strangled and blood), for the same offense when only one was needed (e.g. 'blood' i.e. don't eat meat with blood in it). *Wycliffe* sees the rule for the weaker brother, the Jewish believer. It seems they think the eating of meat with blood in it is alright but only for strong Gentile Christians.

Stern presents three possible meanings for blood. It could be literal,

referring to *drinking animals' blood*, or failing to remove it from meat, or figurative, a metaphor for murder.'[369]

Stern acknowledges that blood can be referring to the actual drinking of it from a pagan sacrifice but doesn't understand it as such by offering three to chose from without saying what James meant. But at least the idea of drinking sacrificial blood is brought into the arena of possibilities.

Stern also offers a Jewish twist on what Marshall wrote. If strangled *wasn't* originally part of the text,

'then one is left with the three things that the Rabbis say that a Jew was to die for, rather then transgress. A Jew could transgress all the Commandments in order to save life, but not idolatry, fornication or murder' (San. 74a).[370]

This is the 'Jewish side' to the Gentile scribes' interpretation of the three rules 'on morality.' Unfortunately blood would have to be equated with murder in both cases. This isn't possible for Acts 15:20.

Bruce too believes the rule reflects the prohibition against eating blood in the meat. He sees this as coming from the Noahide Laws and believes it has to do with table fellowship between Jewish and Gentile believers.[371]

Williams says the rule means 'not to eat any blood itself.' This must mean for him that it's blood in the meat as he fails to say that the practice of eating (or rather drinking) blood was part of pagan sacrifices.[372]

---

[368] Pfeiffer, *WBC*, p. 1152.

[369] Stern, *JNTC*, p. 277.

[370] Ibid., p. 278. Fornication for Stern is 'any form of sexual immorality' including temple prostitution and other improper practices. See p. 82 above.

[371] Bruce, *The Book of the Acts*, pp. 295-296.

Knowling also believes it was blood from meat but suggests that the reason *behind* the rule had to do with the ancient fascination of what blood symbolized. He writes that it was,

> 'specially forbidden by the Jewish law, Lev. 17:10' 'and we may refer the prohibition' 'to the feeling of *mystery* entertained by various nations of antiquity with regard to blood, so that the feeling is not exclusively Jewish, although the Jewish law had given it such express and divine sanction.' 'Nothing could override the command first given to Noah, Gen. 9:4, together with the permission to eat animal food, and renewed in the law.'[373]

Knowling brings out the reverence that the ancients had for blood (mystery) and says it was universal; not just among the Jews. This accounts for pagan sacrifice as well as Hebrew sacrifice in that blood was seen to contain the life of the animal or person.

Knowling further comments about blood not being able to be equated with murder in Acts 15:20 because of,

> 'the collocation[374] with πνικτου' (nik-too: *strangled*) being 'against any such interpretation.'[375]

He cites Cyprian and Tertullian as first recognizing this. This supposes that *strangled* and *blood*, because of their being one right after the other in the rules, are part of the same theme (i.e. not eating meat containing blood in it from strangled animals). This would rule out blood being equated with murder for him but unfortunately fails to answer why Yakov didn't tell the Gentiles what animals were acceptable to eat.

Witherington says that Gentiles drank (and tasted) blood at their pagan temples.[376] But he errs in thinking that it could also double as murder. Hegg too sees blood as 'something not uncommon in idol rituals' but unfortunately thinks strangling can speak of eating meat with blood in it.[377]

The fourth rule is blood. Much of Christian scholarship says it means not

---

[372] Williams, *Acts*, p. 266.

[373] Knowling, *The Acts of the Apostles*, p. 325.

[374] Sinclair, *CED*, p. 316. Collocation means, 'a grouping together of things in a certain order, as of the words in a sentence.'

[375] Knowling, *The Acts of the Apostles*, p. 325.

[376] Witherington, *The Acts of the Apostles*, p. 464.

[377] Hegg, *The Letter Writer*, p. 276-277.

to eat meat that has blood in it. Stern and Williams suggested that it could be blood that was drunk but weren't sure about it. Only Witherington and Hegg thought it related to a pagan sacrifice in which the blood was drunk. Stern and Witherington brought up that it could possibly refer to murder, and Hegg believed blood wasn't to be eaten in strangled meat.

The proper slaughtering and roasting (or cooking) of the animal, so there wouldn't be any blood left in the meat is a biblical reality.[378] Although both of these, murder, and the eating of blood within the meat, are considered sin by God, there's no evidence for either of them being what James meant when he spoke of blood in Acts 15:20.

It can't be determined from the word itself what Yakov meant, as the different authorities display. This is where common sense and context come in. Common sense tells us that murder has to be ruled out because murder was a very serious crime in the Roman Empire and everyone knew it. The need for a Jewish man in Jerusalem to make a ruling on murder wasn't necessary. After all, how many Gentiles were running around murdering people and *thinking it was alright*?

Another obvious point is that there's no mention of what meats *could* be eaten. The same reason that *things strangled* couldn't be a food regulation applies to *blood*. If James meant that Gentiles couldn't eat blood in meat, so as not to offend Jewish sensitivities, he never once addresses which animals weren't to be eaten (e.g. pigs, dogs, cats, etc., Lev. 11; Dt. 14).

Theoretically one could slaughter a pig properly so that the blood was removed and cooked till it was 'well done.' But sitting down with a Jewish believer and offering him some hot pork chops would definitely offend his Jewish sensibilities.

This also torpedoes the traditional interpretation of the rules dealing with 'fellowship toward the weaker brother.' Yakov, in not indicating which animals weren't to be eaten, renders the interpretation of table fellowship impossible. Scholars should know that eating bacon, even 'well done,' next to a Jewish believer would certainly offend him. *All* the Jewish believers continued to keep the Law of Moses *after* the Resurrection (Acts 21:20, 24; 22:12; 24:14; 25:8; Rom. 3:31; 1st Jn. 5:1-3; Rev. 14:12, etc.).

On the other hand, the need to prohibit the Gentile from not drinking the blood from sacrifices offered to idols was necessary. The eating of the flesh of the sacrifice and the drinking of its blood were major themes of idolatry. This is the pagan counterfeit to eating the Flesh and drinking the Blood of Messiah Yeshua. Pagans believed that the eating of the flesh of

---

[378] Lev. 3:17; 7:26-27; 19:26; Ezk. 33:25.

the sacrificial victim and the drinking of its blood gave them the life of the victim. *The International Standard Bible Encyclopedia* says it's,

> 'significant that eating blood was prohibited in earliest Bible times (Gen. 9:4). The custom' *'prevailed among heathen nations as a religious rite'*.[379]

The custom they are referring to of course is the drinking of fresh blood from an animal sacrifice. That it's not the eating of meat with blood in it is seen from their use of the phrase that it was 'a religious rite.' There are no pagan religious rites that deal with eating blood in rare roast beef. Paul warned the Gentile Corinthian believers against *drinking* the cup of demons (1st Cor. 10:21).[380] Obviously the need to speak against the drinking of blood at a pagan sacrifice was very necessary for Gentile converts to the God of Israel.

The *Theological Dictionary of the Old Testament* states that the concept of blood among the pagan nations was very powerful. Blood,

> 'is thus understood as the *essence* of the personal powers that are at work in man and beast'.[381]

This *essence* is what motivated the pagans to drink the blood, for in so doing they were desiring the essence or power of the creature whose blood they were drinking. And as animals were a representation of the god they were worshiping, the psychological power derived from such a sacrifice took on enormous value for them, just as drinking Yeshua's Blood does for believers. The pagans weren't wrong in their understanding of the life properties within blood. They were just deceived as to Whose Blood they needed.

James Freeman writes,

> 'Hindoo devotees drink the reeking blood from newly killed buffaloes and fowls.'[382]

The Hindoos that Freeman describes are not the ancient temple worshippers of Zeus, Adonis or Baal in Greece or Canaan. But they do present the

---

[379] Bromiley, *ISBE*, vol. one, p. 526. See also Psalm 16:4.

[380] The Jewish believers at Corinth weren't drinking blood. They were raised in the Law and knew how offensive it was to Yahveh. Their coming into the Kingdom of Yeshua would only heighten their understanding.

[381] Botterweck, *TDOT*, vol. III, p. 237.

[382] Rev. James M. Freeman, *Manners and Customs of the Bible* (Plainfield, NJ: Logos International, 1972; originally written around 1874), pp. 106-107 section 192.

fact that the drinking of blood in Freeman's day (the 1870's) was still part of paganism.

Alexander Hislop reveals that the religion of the Hindoos originally came from Babylon. The Hindoo practice was a reflection of many ancient pagan religions.[383] *The International Standard Bible Encyclopedia* states that blood was used in other ways also:

> a 'blood friendship is established by African tribes by the mutual shedding of blood and either drinking it or rubbing it on one another's bodies.'[384]

In ancient Egypt the gods drank the blood of the sacrificial animals.[385] Could the priest and the people be far behind?

As King Solomon once said, 'There's nothing new under the sun' (Eccl. 1:9). Paganism takes many of its principles from the God of Israel and His Kingdom and perverts them. Thus it's seen that in idolatrous sacrifices the drinking of blood can 'be commanded ritually' and that one could be initiated into a pagan cult with 'a baptism of blood.'[386]

TDOT speaks of this baptism being done by having the initiate in a dugout section of earth while the sacrificial victim was positioned above him. The priest would slit the throat of an animal as large as an ox and the blood would come cascading down upon the initiate(s) below, thus 'baptizing' him in the animal's blood.

This was Man's way via Satan of dealing with issues like sin, justification and eternal life. Conceptually it's similar to the way Israel was baptized into the Covenant at Sinai. In Ex. 24:6-8 Moses,

> 'sent young men of the Sons of Israel and they offered burnt offerings and sacrificed young bulls as peace offerings to Yahveh. Moses took half of the blood and put it in basins and the other half of the blood he sprinkled on the altar. Then he took the Book of the Covenant and read it in the hearing of the people and they said, 'All that

---

[383] Hislop, *The Two Babylons*, p. 96. 'Hindoo Mythology' 'is admitted to be essentially Babylonian'. (See also pp. 15-16, 27, 36-37, 60-61, 65, 70-71, 101, 159, 187, 230, 243-244, 272, 282, 319, etc.) See *Hislop Under Attack* at http://www.seedofabraham.net/2babreb.htm for anyone concerned about R. Woodrow's critique of Hislop.

[384] Bromiley, *ISBE*, vol. one, p. 526.

[385] Ibid., vol. 3, pp. 237-238.

[386] Ibid., p. 237.

Yahveh has spoken we will do and we will obey!' So Moses took the blood and sprinkled it on the people and said, 'Behold the Blood of the Covenant which Yahveh has made with you in accordance with all these words.'

There's something extremely powerful about blood in the spiritual realm. The reality behind the Mosaic sacrificial system was the sacrifice of Yeshua. This ultimately gives much power and authority to blood. In Lev. 17:11 it states,

'For the life of the flesh is in the blood and I have given it to you upon the Altar to make atonement for your souls. For it's the blood by reason of the life that makes atonement.'

Substituting 'His' in certain places of the verse, the tremendous significance of Yeshua's Sacrifice is seen:

'For the Life of His flesh was in His Blood and I have given It to you upon the Altar to make atonement for your souls. For it's His Blood by reason of His Life that makes atonement' (for you).

This is how the Blood of Messiah Yeshua deals with sin *and* sin nature. And how believers will be glorified and become exactly like He is now (except that He was always God the Son while believers will be created to be like Him). This is the New Creation, the New Jerusalem coming down from the Heavens; the Bride of Messiah Yeshua (Eph. 5:32; Rev. 19:7; 21:1-2, 9, etc.), which makes the first Creation pale in splendor.

The eternal life and character that *is* Yeshua is in His Blood. His Blood makes *new creatures* of Adam's descendants. *Everything* that *is* Yeshua is in His Blood (and Body) and we are given access to this because of His crucifixion (Gal. 3:13-14). This is what He meant when He said,

'I tell you the truth. It's for your good that I go. Unless I go away, the Comforter won't come. But if I go, I will send the' Spirit to you. (Jn. 16:7)

It's also written that 'the blood is the life' and 'the life of every creature is the blood of it' (Dt. 12:23; Lev. 17:14). The ancient peoples understood the connection of the blood and the life being interwoven. That's why they ate the animal flesh and drank it's blood in their pagan ceremonies.[387]

God warned Israel many times not to eat the blood of a sacrifice.[388] And

---

[387] Ibid., pp. 234-250.

that's why many Jews left Jesus that day in Capernaum when He said,

> 'Truly I tell you, unless you eat the Flesh of the Son of
> Man and drink His Blood, you have no life in you. Those
> who eat My Flesh and drink My Blood have eternal life
> and I will raise them up on the Last Day.' (John 6:53-54)

In Dt. 12:16 it states,

> 'you must not eat the blood! You are to pour it out on the
> ground like water.'

This pertains to the drinking of fresh blood from a slaughtered (or sacrificed) animal. It's different from eating blood in strangled or 'rare meat'
(e.g. Lev. 19:26). They're both sins but only one is idolatrous.

The pagans had the right idea but were applying it to the wrong reality.
For even when Yeshua said what He did about eating His Flesh and drinking His Blood, He wasn't looking for Jews to begin chomping on His
arms and legs. It's a spiritual reality that comes through the Holy Spirit
and prayer.

The reason the fourth rule was given was to stop the Gentile believer from
drinking the blood of a pagan sacrifice. It has nothing to do with blood
equaling murder and thus nullifies the tampering with the text (the
removal of 'strangled') that some Gentile scribes did to Acts 15:20 to
present their moral catechism. And of course it doesn't speak of the three
sins that a Jew should die for in resisting idolatry, fornication or murder.

It's also evident that it doesn't mean 'blood within the meat.' Yakov never
spoke of which meats would be considered unclean from a biblical perspective. If 'Jewish sensitivities' were supposed to be the reason for the
rule, a Gentile eating unclean meat in the presence of a Jew, even if it had
been properly slaughtered and drained of its blood, would certainly fail
the criteria of the scholars for not 'offending the Jew.' How could they not
have seen that?

Blood centers around how Yakov perceived the need. Drinking blood as
part of a pagan sacrifice was not a crime against Rome but it was a gross
idolatrous sin against the God of Israel. Yakov ruled that the drinking of
sacrificial blood was forbidden. This rule obviously falls under the category of sacrificial idolatry and cements the four rules of Acts 15:20 as a conceptual unit on sacrificial-sexual idolatry. Now the way is paved for Acts
15:21 to be properly understood and implemented. But before that *Some
Concerns.*

---

[388] Lev. 3:17; 7:26-27; 17:12, 14; Dt. 12:16, 23; 15:23, etc.

ACTS 15: SOME CONCERNS

Before expressing *Yakov's Concern* there are six subjects to cover that directly relate to Acts 15:20. The six are found in Acts 15:10, 19, 21 and 21:25, and the fact that the rules don't appear in the same order the second and third time they're recorded (Acts 15:29; 21:25). Most interpret three of these cites (15:10, 19; 21:25) as proof that the Law is not for believers today.

The first one (15:10) has to do with the 'yoke' that Peter speaks of that neither he nor his Fathers could bear. The second (15:19) is Yakov's statement about 'not troubling the Gentiles.' The third and fourth (15:21) have Yakov declaring that Moses is taught in all the synagogues, and also speaks of those who preach Moses. The fifth deals with Yakov's admonition that the Gentiles 'observe no such thing' (Acts 21:25). And the sixth looks at the rules not being written in the same order (Acts 15:20, 29, 21:25) and why Yakov might have done this.

Acts 15:10—The Yoke

The yoke that Peter speaks of in Acts 15:10 is the Law.[389] Many see the Law as the yoke in and of itself but that's not what Peter meant. Here's what he said:

> 'Now therefore why do you put God to the test by placing
> upon the neck of the disciples, a yoke which neither our
> Fathers nor we were able to bear?'

Bruce says 'a proselyte, by undertaking to keep the law of Moses' was said to 'take up the yoke of the kingdom of heaven.'[390] And that the Law was the burden the Fathers 'found too heavy.'[391] Obviously he wasn't thinking of Father David[392] otherwise known as the greatest king the world

---

[389] Knowling, *The Acts of the Apostles*, p. 320. It's a 'metaphor common among the Rabbis, and also in classical literature,' cf. Jer. 5:5; Lam. 3:27; Ecclus. 51:26 (Zeph. 3:9) and Matt. 11:29 (Luke 11:46) Gal. 5:1. 'Possibly in' Jer. 5:5 'reference is made to the yoke of the law, but *Psalms of Solomon*' 7:8 cf. 27:32 'present undoubted instances of the metaphorical use of the term "the yoke" for the service of Jehovah. In *Sayings of the Jewish Fathers*' 3:8 '(Taylor, second edition, p. 46), we have a definite and twice repeated reference to the yoke of Thorah'. 'It would seem therefore that St. Peter uses an almost technical word' for the Law of Moses.

[390] Bruce, *The Book of the Acts*, p. 290.

[391] Ibid.

has ever seen, outside of his Son Yeshua. David said many things about the Law, none of which seem to correspond with what Bruce thought of it. Here's a sample of what David thought:

> 'The Law of Yahveh is *perfect*, restoring the soul. The testimony of Yahveh is sure, making wise the simple. The precepts of Yahveh are right, rejoicing the heart. The commandment of Yahveh is pure, enlightening the eyes. The fear of Yahveh is clean, enduring forever. The judgments of Yahveh are true, they are righteous altogether. They are more desirable than gold, yes, than much fine gold. Sweeter also than honey and the drippings of the honeycomb. Moreover by them Your servant is *warned*. In keeping them there is great reward.' (Psalm 19:7-11)

David clearly extols the Law as something that is good and beneficial to him. His different ways of speaking of the Law (e.g. its precepts and judgments, etc.) are very Hebraic and found within the Law as describing its commandments.[393] David sings much of the praise of Yahveh's Torah (Ps. 1:2; 37:31; 40:8; 119:1, 77, etc.) because he knew the wisdom and understanding that were inherent in it (Dt. 4:5-8; 30:15, 19, 20; 32:47, etc.).

If the laws of God were holy and righteous for Moses, David, Isaiah and Jesus, why wouldn't they matter after the Resurrection? Why would they be any less holy for the Gentile believer who has been grafted into the Family (Israel) of God (Rom. 11:13-12:5; Eph. 2:1-22; Gal. 6:16)?

Yeshua kept the Law all His life. And all the Jewish believers, many years after the Resurrection, kept the Law too (Acts 21:20, 24; 24:18; 25:8). Perhaps the Apostles didn't understand 'the yoke' as Bruce presents it? Bruce errs because of his 'law-free gospel.'[394]

The Wycliffe Bible Commentary states that the term *yoke* is not necessarily a negative word:

---

[392] David is called πατριαρχου (Patriarch; Father) in Mk. 11:10 and Acts 2:20.

[393] Words like judgments and statutes, etc., are synonymous with God's Law and speak of His holy Instruction or Teaching (Torah) to Israel (Dt. 4:44-45; 5:1-22; 7:11, etc.). For testimony see: Ps. 78:5; 119:88; 132:12; Is. 8:20, etc. For testimonies: Dt. 4:45; 6:17, 20; Ps. 25:10; 78:56; 99:7, etc. For judgments: Lev. 18:4, 5, 26; 25:18; Dt. 4:1, 5, 8; 5:31, etc. For ordinances: Ex. 21:1; 24:3; Lev. 19:37; 20:22; 26:15; Num. 9:3, etc. For statutes: Ex. 18:20; Lev. 10:11; 18:4, 5, 26; 19:19; 20:8; Dt. 6:1, etc. For commandments: Ex. 15:26; 16:28; Lev. 22:31; Num. 15:22; Dt. 6:17, etc. For fear of Yahveh: Ex. 9:30; 18:21; 20:20; Lev. 25:17; Dt. 4:10; 5:29; 6:2, 13, 24; Mt. 10:28, etc.

[394] Bruce, *The Book of the Acts*, p. 285.

'a yoke in Jewish thought does not necessarily mean a burden but designates an obligation.'[395]

The yoke Peter spoke of was the Law of Moses but if it wasn't the burden then what was? *Wycliffe* lumps both the Law of Moses and legalism together, declaring the Law a burden in spite of what they just said:

'Peter asserts that Jewish legalism was an obligation and a burden that the Jews were unable to bear. In contrast to the burdensomeness of the Law, salvation is through grace'.[396]

In making the Law a burden, Bruce, *Wycliffe* and all those who espouse such, make the God of Israel who gave it a very hard taskmaster. The Jews were saved out of Egypt, not by the Law but by God's Grace. Did God save them out of Egyptian slavery only to place a different type of slavery and legalistic burden upon them at Mt. Sinai?

Williams too misses the point when he states that 'any attempt to revert to a religion of law was to try to test God'.[397] Stern also stumbles but rightly comes against the verse being used to disparage the Law of Moses:

'Much Christian teaching contrasts the *supposedly* onerous and oppressive 'yoke of the Law' with the words of Yeshua, 'My yoke is easy and my burden is light.'[398]

Stern makes two points about the Law. One, if a person thinks something is *pleasant* then one cannot project onto him that it's not. But this can't be used in defense of the Law or the yoke because it's very subjective. Most Christians see the Law as a burden and if *subjectivity* is the criteria for judging, the Law is very oppressive. But the criteria is not how we think or feel about the Law but what God says about it (Dt. 4:1-8; 12:8; 29:29) specifically in the New Testament (Mt. 5:17-19; Rom. 3:31; 7:12, etc.).

For his second point Stern says the commandments are not oppressive. Although he's right, Peter called *something* unbearable. Stern says the commandments are not 'an oppressive burden any more than Yeshua's yoke is.' He correctly states the yoke of the Law is 'acknowledging God's sovereignty and his right to direct our lives' and that if God has given commandments 'we should obey them.'[399] This is all very true. The Law is not

---

[395] Pfeiffer, *WBC*, p. 1151.

[396] Ibid.

[397] Williams, *Acts*, p. 264.

[398] Stern, *JNTC*, p. 276.

a burden, God is sovereign and He does have the right to direct the lives of believers in Yeshua by His commandments. But Stern believes Peter's yoke was *legalism*, the 'detailed mechanical rule-keeping, regardless of heart attitude, that some' Pharisees had. He states that it was this 'yoke of legalism' that was indeed 'unbearable.'[400] No flesh shall be justified by legalism? As true as that is, what is biblically true is, 'No flesh shall be justified by doing the *works* of the Law' (Gal. 2:16). One can't be Born Again by doing good deeds (and that's Paul's point). No amount of good works will transform one's nature into that of the Son of God (Gal. 4:21).

Witherington also believes the yoke was the Law. He states that Peter, as 'a Galilean fisherman' may not have liked parts of the Law that would have been a burden to him, such as going to Jerusalem three times a year for the annual Feasts (Ex. 23:17). This would have meant he couldn't work to support his family.[401]

As logical as this may seem it totally misses the mindset of a Jew who was all too happy to leave work for a week or so on God's ordained 'holy vacations' to go to Jerusalem and worship Yahveh in the midst of all his brethren. After all it was Yahveh who made him a fisherman and ultimately provided for him and his family. And this every Jew knew but Witherington, in failing to understand the divine place of the Law and the joy of celebrating the Feasts, stumbles. He also adds that the Gentile was being required to become a proselyte to Judaism.[402] This was true but neither Peter nor his Fathers were proselytes so that can't be the burden either.

Hegg believes the yoke was the Gentile becoming a proselyte also, with the traditional interpretation of Torah and the cumbersome man-made rules of the Pharisees attached to God's commandments (Stern). The Gentile would have to be circumcised, become a proselyte and comply with all these in order to become part of Israel (to 'get in' to the 'saved Jewish community' as E. P. Sanders speaks of). In this, *being part of Israel*, the Gentile would be saved. He writes,

> the "yoke they are unwilling to place upon the backs of

---

[399] Ibid.

[400] Ibid.

[401] Witherington, *The Acts of the Apostles*, p. 454.

[402] Ibid., pp. 453-454. He also speaks of the possibility that Peter spoke of the 'priestly requirements of the Law' that the 'Pharisees and the Qumranites' were wanting all Jews to walk in as well as suggesting that Jesus may have thought the Law to be heavy (Mt. 11:30). It wasn't the glorious Law that Yahveh had given to Israel (Dt. 4:5-8; Rom. 7:12) that Yeshua spoke of as heavy, but the weight of sin and guilt upon each person (Rom. 7:7).

the Gentile believers is the yoke of man-made rules and laws that required a ceremony to 'get in' and submission to untold number of intricate *halachah*."[403] (italics his)

Those Pharisaic believers who wanted the Gentiles circumcised (Acts 15:1, 5) were looking for them to become Jews (proselytes). That a proselyte was a Jew, part of the Jewish people, is seen in Nicolas being counted

---

[403] Hegg, *The Letter Writer*, pp. 265; 280-281f. Halachah means 'the way to walk' and is used by the Rabbis to describe their rules for living in this world.

Hegg is quite mistaken on the ability of a Gentile to be circumcised. He teaches that Timothy was a Gentile (pp. 113, 285), and because he realized that his faith saved him, he could be circumcised. This is pure conjecture but Hegg uses his view to build a theological position that Gentiles can be circumcised, for the right reasons (p. 114). But why would Paul circumcise Timothy if he taught against it (Acts 16:4; 1st Cor. 7:17-19, 24; Gal. 2:3; 5:2)?

Timothy is *not* an example of Gentile circumcision. He didn't ask to be circumcised (and there's not a hint of Gentile circumcision in the N.T. either). Paul circumcised Timothy because he wanted Timothy to go with him. Timothy was seen as a Jew. Acts 16:3 states, 'Paul wanted this man to go with him and he took him and circumcised him *because of the Jews* who were in those parts, for they all knew that his father was a Greek.' Why would Jews care if a Gentile boy was circumcised? The verse only makes sense if Timothy was seen as a Jew by those Jews (and Paul), and hadn't been circumcised when he should have been (at eight days old; Gen. 17:10-14). His mother was Jewish (Acts 16:1), and this seems to be the criteria that Paul went by (despite some information from the Mishna to the contrary that Hegg presents; p. 113, notes 232-233). In Orthodox Judaism, if the mother is Jewish, the child is too.

There's no place in the New Testament that even hints that a Gentile (or his new born son), should receive circumcision if he understood that he wasn't doing it in order to be saved. The New Testament never speaks of it or authorizes it. On the contrary, a number of places in the N.T. explicitly state (or imply), that the Gentile *isn't* to be circumcised (Acts 15:1-21; Rom. 3:30; 4:7-12, 16; 1st Cor. 7:17-19, 24; Gal. 2:3; 5:2). But didn't God realize what He said to Abraham and Moses about circumcision (Gen. 17:14; Ex. 12:48)? It seems that the 'circumcision made without hands' by Messiah Yeshua (Col. 2:11; Phil. 3:3), pictured in Dt. 30:6, has superseded physical circumcision *for the Gentile,* and places every believer in the New Jerusalem (Gal. 6:16), where Yeshua is King. (See also Rom. 2:26-29; 4:9-12.)

With Timothy being circumcised, boys born to a Jewish woman should be considered Jewish. And even if 'only' the father is Jewish, the child should still be circumcised. This transcends rabbinic tradition (i.e. only the mother 'makes' the child Jewish). But Tamar wasn't a Jewess, yet who would say that Perez wasn't a Hebrew (Gen. 38:29; 46:12)? And Asenath was an Egyptian (Gen. 41:50f.), but both her sons, Efraim and Manasa, literally become two of the Tribes of Israel (Gen. 48:1-5; Num. 1:10). Therefore sons born to a Jewish parent should be seen as Jews and circumcised on the eighth day.

as such (Acts 6:5), and in Yeshua speaking of them (Mt. 23:15). Alfred
Edersheim says that the children of a proselyte were 'regarded as Jews'.[404]
He states that once the proselytes 'were circumcised, immersed in water
and offered a sacrifice' they became,

> 'children of the covenant' 'perfect Israelites' 'Israelites in
> every respect, both as regarded duties and privileges.'[405]

Herbert Loewe (1882–1940) in *A Rabbinic Anthology* adds that a 'proselyte can say "God of our Fathers" because he is a full Jew'.[406]

The *yoke* though isn't about becoming a proselyte with its 'man-made
rules' and keeping the Law (symbolized in circumcision). Peter wasn't a
proselyte and he didn't keep 'man-made rules' (Mt.15:2 by inference).
This isn't the burden he spoke of.

The yoke that neither Peter nor his Fathers could bear was the keeping of
the Law...for Eternal Life (salvation; justification before God). *This* is
what circumcision ultimately implied despite objections to the contrary.
And this is what the Council struck down: *the false teaching that the Law
was a vehicle for salvation*[407] (as well as the thought that Gentiles needed
to become Jews in order to be saved). The yoke has nothing to do with 'legalism' or 'intricate halachah' or 'mechanically' keeping the Law. Stern,
Hegg and much of Christianity miss it at this point.

Marshall adroitly perceives that the yoke Peter spoke of was the Law used
for justification:

> '*The point here* is not the burdensomeness or oppressive-
> ness of the law, but rather the inability of the Jews to gain
> salvation through it, and hence its irrelevance *as far as
> salvation is concerned.*[408]

Exactly! But this is how Jews thought one earned eternal life despite the
New Perspective presenting Judaism as a *faith based* religion that didn't
look to the Law for salvation. Before Sanders, Judaism espoused the 'joy

---

[404] Alfred Edersheim, *The Life and Times of Jesus The Messiah* (Peabody, MA:
Hendrickson Publishers, 2000), p. 1015.

[405] Ibid., p. 1014.

[406] C. G. Montefiore and H. Loewe, *A Rabbinic Anthology* (New York: Shocken
Books, 1974), p. lxxxv.

[407] Marshall, Acts, p. 250. 'What the legalists were trying to do was to place the
yoke of the law on the Gentiles, a yoke which the Jews themselves had never
been able to bear successfully' 'as far as salvation is concerned.'

[408] Ibid.

of the commandment' as an idea stressed by the Rabbis.[409] And that 'the Law must be fulfilled for its own sake and for the love of God and *not* for reward.'[410] In other words, one kept the Law because one was *already saved,* responding to it from a sense of gratitude, not works of righteousness (doing the Law to be saved).

The New Perspective on Judaism, brought into Christianity by Sanders, Dunn and Wright, follows that line of thinking, believing that the Jew wasn't concerned about salvation because he was part of the Chosen People, which guaranteed his salvation. So the Jew didn't have to keep the Law for salvation. He just walked out his faith in gratitude, believing he'd be given eternal life. But this was an ideal never achieved.

Scot McKnight, summarizing this 'new perspective' on Judaism states,

> 'Israel was elected by God, brought into the covenant and given the law to regulate how covenant people live.'[411]

And James Dunn, speaking of Sanders says,

> 'the commandments are not a way of earning God's favor but a way of showing how the people of God should live. That's the basic point that had to be made in terms of the new perspective.'[412]

The Christian New Perspective thinking on Judaism is 'off base' at these points. Theoretically, the Law of Moses is 'faith based' with belief in God and that He would do His part and bless Israel (Lev. 27; Dt. 28–20) as they walked in His Commandments. By the days of the Rabbis though, it had come to be the vehicle for Paradise. Using the Law as a vehicle for salvation was never what God intended. The Rabbis were wrong.

The idea of the Rabbis, that eternal life was given if one was part of the Chosen People, was also wrong. There's no Scripture to validate it. And it's not what was *practiced* in Judaism. Loewe states that Judaism,

> 'like Hellenism or Islam, can be expounded and understood *without being followed in practice.*'[413]

Rabbi Akiva (50–135 A.D.) whom Judaism revers, lived a generation after

---

[409] Montefiore, *ARA*, p. 202.

[410] Ibid., p. xxxvi. Italics are Montefiore's.

[411] McKnight: http://www.jesuscreed.org/?p=2690. Aug. 9th, 2007.

[412] Wright: *The Paul Page*, http://www.thepaulpage.com/Conversation.html, p. 2. Oct. 25th, 2004.

[413] Montefiore, *ARA*, p. lvii.

Yeshua. He knew the inherent dangers of relying on 'being a covenant member' to automatically garner Paradise. It's written of him that he,

> 'seemed to hold that the future life is a privilege to be gained through positive upright living, *rather than an inherent right which can only be forfeited as a penalty.* Sometimes he asserted God's mercy to be such that a single meritorious act will win a man admission to the future world.'[414]

Meritorious acts or good deeds (of the Law) were seen as *necessary* for eternal life even if one were 'in covenant.' In the New Perspective on Judaism and Paul 'works of the Law' has taken on the connotation of being specific Jewish works such as keeping the Sabbath and circumcision, etc. The *works of the Law* for Dunn are 'sociological markers' of the Jewish community so that 'works of the Torah' were not 'merit-seeking works' but 'boundary-marking works' (things like the Sabbath and circumcision, etc.)[415] N. T. Wright says that Dunn is 'exactly right.' For Wright the 'works of the Law' *aren't* the,

> 'moral works though which one gains merit but the works through which the Jew is defined over against the pagan.'[416]

He adds that the works of the Spirit are those things that show that one is 'in Christ.' This would be things like bringing people into the Kingdom.[417]

Contrary to this pristine myopic evaluation of first century Judaism, 'works of the Law' are *all* the good works (good deeds) that stem from doing the Law. It's equally Sabbath observance as well as feeding the poor and caring for the widow and the orphan (compassion, justice and love of neighbor; Lev. 19:18; Mt. 5:16; Gal. 2:10; 1st Tim. 5:10; 6:17-19; Titus 2:11-14; 3:8, 14; Rev. 19:8), *and* the mighty works or miracles that Yeshua did (Mt. 11:2; Jn. 5:36; 15:24, etc.). *All* these stem from the Law's commandments and the physical and spiritual *freedom* found in the Law and the Jubilee Year (Lev. 25:8-10; Is. 61:1-2; Lk. 4:18-19).

Yahveh says of Yeshua, 'You are My Servant *Israel* in whom I will be glorified (Is. 49:3).'[418] Yeshua is the quintessential Israeli. He is the Exam-

---

[414] Montefiore, *ARA*, p. 664 note 13.

[415] McKnight: http://www.jesuscreed.org/?p=2688. Aug. 7th, 2007.

[416] N. T. Wright: *New Perspectives on Paul* at http://www.ntwrightpage.com/ Wright_New_Perspectives.htm, p. 4, Aug. 26th, 2003.

[417] Ibid., p. 11, Aug. 26th, 2003.

ple par excellence of one who is fully given over to God and walking in His ways (the Law). Torah is the verbal expression of Yahveh; Who He is, what's He's done for Israel, and His will for Israel. Yahveh has magnified and glorified His Law through Yeshua. Isaiah said,

> 'Yahveh was pleased for the sake of His righteousness to *magnify His Law and make it glorious.*' (Is 42:21)

Yeshua was like a prism through which the Law and the Holy Spirit were seen. He is the Living Torah, the Word of God (Rev. 19:13). The good and mighty healings Yeshua did sprang from the Law and Spirit within.[419]

The Holy Spirit is able to empower believers so they can do all the works of the Law as Yeshua did.[420] These works all stem from the Power and Fruit of the Spirit (Gal. 5:22-24). Torah forms the internal grid-work for one to be '*fully* equipped for every good work' (2nd Tim. 3:16-17).

Claude Montefiore (1858–1938) sums up Judaism's concept of righteousness and therefore eternal life. He states,

> 'There is no rigid or worked-out doctrine about Works and Faith. On the whole, the theory of *justification by works* is *strongly pressed.*'[421]

Montefiore also speaks of the individual being regarded as a,

> 'bundle of deeds. If he has done 720 good deeds and 719 bad ones, he is more righteous than wicked (with due consequences as regards divine punishment and reward)'.[422]

> 'At the judgment in the world to come, paradise or hell is given *according to the majority of good deeds or evil*'.[423]

Is this a concept of Judaism that wasn't there in the days of Yeshua and Paul? Has Judaism 'gone backward' in it's thinking? Once they were saved by just being in covenant but today it takes the works of the Law?

Jewish thought in the days of Yeshua and the Apostles wasn't like the monolithic religion of Roman Catholicism a thousand years ago. There were more than twenty different sects of what constituted 'the proper way'

---

[418] Jn. 14:10-12; 12:28; 16:14; 17:1, 5; 21:19.

[419] Mt. 11:4-6; 23:23; Jn. 5:36; 9:3-4, etc.

[420] Mt. 5:16; Jn. 14:12; Acts 4:8; 8:6-7, etc.

[421] Montefiore, *ARA*, p. xxxv.

[422] Ibid., p. xxxv.

[423] Ibid., p. 596.

(e.g. Pharisee, Essene, Sadducee, Herodian, Zealot, etc.). But what was Peter calling a yoke? And is it possible to understand some kind of official Jewish thought about eternal life from the New Testament?

The Council met to see if the Gentile needed to become a Jew and to keep the Law of Moses, symbolized in circumcision, for eternal life, *along with faith in Jesus*. The Torah was being used or rather abused as a means of salvation by the Pharisees and Rabbis, etc. This was the common *and* official understanding for eternal life among the Jewish people in the days of Peter and Paul (Rom. 9:30-32), as well today.

Moses hadn't placed this yoke upon the necks of the Fathers; the Pharisees had. God never intended this perverse use of His Law. This is what Peter and his Fathers (his genealogical fathers as well as the Elders of Israel), had been *deceived* into believing: that God would give them Eternal Life if they kept the Law. ***This is the yoke*** that no one could bear (Rom. 3:20, 28; Gal. 2:16-17). And this is exactly what Yeshua brings out when He speaks to the Jewish authorities (Jn. 5:10) and the Jewish people who looked for salvation *from the doing of the Law*. Yeshua said in John 5:39,

> 'You search the Scriptures because you *think that in them you have eternal life*, but it is they that testify of Me.'

Yeshua Himself, the highest authority in any matter, speaks of Jewish expectation for eternal life residing within the Torah. This is also brought out in John (7:43-49). The Pharisaic leaders and chief priests in the Sanhedrin said the common Jewish people were cursed because *they didn't know the Law* ('this multitude which doesn't know the Law is accursed!' v. 49).

All those 'cursed' folks were Jews 'in covenant' but Jews that didn't know the Law the way the Pharisees, scribes and Sadducees did and so were obviously not candidates for Heaven, at least in their minds. This is a biblical insight into how the highest Jewish authorities at that time thought about blessings from God and eternal life. Obedience to the Law *was* righteousness as the Law and Paul state (Dt. 6:25; 24:13; Rom. 10:5). But extending it to eternal life wasn't God's way for eternal life.

This same Sanhedrin despised the man born blind whom Yeshua gave sight to. They said to the former blind man,

> 'You were completely born in sins and are you teaching us?! And they cast him out.' (Jn. 9:34)

The Sanhedrin, the highest religious authority in the days of Yeshua, reveals *official* Jewish understanding of which Jews would attain Heaven and which Jews wouldn't (sinners). The man 'born in sin' even though he was obviously a Jew, circumcised on the 8th day, and part of the Chosen People, didn't qualify even though his answers to them were excellent and exceptionally perceptive (Jn. 9:13-34).[424] Their thinking on this subject is of greater value than what some Rabbis may have written in trying to idealize their religion. It also outweighs New Perspective Christian thinking about how the Jews perceived salvation for themselves. The truth was that one needed to keep the Law for Paradise.

The Rabbis knew better than to think that all Israel would be saved, even though Yahveh had saved them from Egyptian slavery and brought them into covenant. They knew Israel's history was permeated with wicked Israelis whom Yahveh destroyed or whom the Scriptures speak of as evil.[425] The Rabbis knew this side of Israel too and believed that obedience to the Torah was the key to inheriting eternal life in paradise, as Yeshua pointed out to their spiritual ancestors (Jn. 5:39; see also Rev. 20:12-13).

The mainstream rabbinic position was that those who kept the Law would inherit Life in the world to come. A rabbinic story reveals the problem the Rabbis faced with this concept. A great rabbi lay dying on his deathbed. All his students gathered around him and noticed that he was very sad. They asked him about his sorrow. He said,

> 'I am soon going to be before the Holy One and *I don't know if I will be accepted.*' They said, 'But you are a great rabbi! You have taught us how to walk in Torah and

---

[424] The Sanhedrin was confronted with the Messiah and they knew it. That's why they made doubly sure that the man had been born blind (by asking his parents to come; Jn. 9:18-23). There was a legend at that time that a righteous man could open the eyes of a blind man, but *only the Messiah* could open the eyes of one *born* blind. And here was this man who had been born blind looking right at them as they tried to discredit Yeshua. It shouldn't be overlooked though that some members of the Sanhedrin (like Nicodemus and Joseph of Arimathea, etc.) voiced their opinions. It states that even though it was the Sabbath when the miracle had been done, because the miracle was so incredible, they questioned the party line that Yeshua was a sinner (Jn. 9:16).

[425] Ex. 32:1-35 is the sin of the Gold Calf; Num. 16:1-40 esp. v. 26 is the sin of Korah; Num. 16:44-45 is the sin of Israel in wanting to stone Moses and Aaron saying that they had murdered Korah. Num. 13:1-14:45 esp. 14:26-38 is the sin of the entire Camp in believing the ten spies and turning Israel against Yahveh and His promise to bring them into the land of Canaan for which they wandered in the Wilderness for 40 years (see also Num. 17:5, 10; 18:5). The sins of all the kings of the northern kingdom of Israel, for which Yahveh finally annihilated it through the king of Assyria in 721 B.C. And the sins of most of the kings of the southern kingdom of Judah, with many being destroyed and a tiny remnant being led away into Babylon captivity.

have kept Torah all your life!' Whereupon he answered
them, 'To you I am great but in the eyes of the Holy One,
every wicked thing is seen.'

This reveals the problem with trying to use the Law as a gauge to determine one's fitness to stand in God's presence on Judgment Day. There's
no amount of walking in, or doing of the Torah, or the doing of good
deeds (works of the Law) that can give one eternal life or the assurance
thereof.

It also brings out that just being 'part of Israel' wasn't enough, even for a
great rabbi. The *Gentile* 'getting into' the 'covenant-saved people' would
still be expected to keep the Law *for eternal life* (Rom. 2:17, 25; Gal. 5:4).
This was the burden that neither Peter nor his Fathers could bear. After
Peter spoke of the yoke, his next words (Acts 15:11) declared that the
Gentile was saved *just as he had been*:

'But we believe that they' (i.e. the Gentiles) 'are saved
just as we are, *by the Grace* of the Lord Jesus.'

In other words Peter could have also said,

'We used to think that keeping the Law entitled us to
Heaven (Jn. 5:39) but we've come to see that this was a
perverse concept the Pharisees gave to God's holy Law.'

The Council met because some believing Pharisees wanted to make Jews
of the Gentiles *and attach the Law to faith in Yeshua* through circumcision
(Acts 15:1, 5). In other words, they would say that salvation or entry into
the Kingdom of Yeshua consisted of faith in Yeshua plus the keeping of
the Law (symbolized in circumcision). And of course they would have
thought that for themselves too. They hadn't fully realized what the Blood
of the Lamb was all about concerning entry into, and maintenance within,
the Kingdom of the Son. This is what Peter is addressing. He's not speaking against the Law. He's coming against the Law being attached to faith
in Jesus for salvation.

This was a new concept for those believing Pharisees and most everyone
else. That's what the Council was all about. The congregation in Antioch
wanted to know what was required for Gentile salvation. In a very real
sense it was logical for the believing Pharisees to think that way. This is
how Gentiles became part of Israel before Messiah Yeshua, by being circumcised (Ex. 12:48) and keeping the Law (Ex. 12:49; Lev. 19:34; 24:22,
etc.). But this was a new Kingdom and a new way of entering it.

Only after much debate in Jerusalem (Acts 15:7) did the outcome prevail
that we read of. It most likely took several hours. Then Peter stood up and

declared the council of God. It seems that Paul and Barnabas already understood this (Acts 15:1-2). But it wasn't 'a given.'

Yes, the Law had also become enmeshed with the Traditions of the Elders but the main point that Peter is making is that the Law cannot be attached to Jesus for salvation. Peter and the other Apostles only came to see this after they realized how God had given them eternal life: through faith in His Son *plus nothing else*. This was the entry point, the middle point and the end point, although led of the Spirit, good works are a spiritual by-product of faith in Yeshua.[426]

Now, once in the Kingdom, does it matter if one sins against God or not? Here is where the Law comes to the forefront. It declares what is right and holy, sin and abomination in Yahveh's eyes for Jew and Gentile.

Before Peter and Paul had known Yeshua, they too had been deceived into thinking that the keeping of the Law would merit them eternal life with God. But now in Acts 15:10 Peter was setting the record straight, something that Paul would do in Rom. 3:31 where he writes of establishing (the place of) the Law in the life of every believer.

Paul's saying that the place of the Law is not for eternal life as he had previously thought, unregenerate Pharisee that he was. But now, it was the criteria for knowing God's view on what is sin and what is right living (Rom. 7:7, 12, 14; 1st Cor. 7:19, etc.) even and especially when a person enters the Kingdom by faith in Yeshua. Was Paul writing to the Sanhedrin, or to believers in Rome and Corinth?

Religious traditions that nullify God's Word are very hard to perceive when one grows up in them. This is true for those Jewish believers back then and for so many in the Church today. Tradition blinds people into thinking that it's of God. When one looks at the Pharisees, locked in mortal combat with the Son of God, one sees how tradition can bring one to fight against the Living God Himself. Only the Holy Spirit can bring Light that reveals the deception, and desire to motivate for change.

Paul fought this false teaching on salvation (of combining circumcision with faith in Jesus) in his letter to the Galatians. He now understood the difference of using the Law for salvation, and the Law as a means for divine living. Here is his conclusion of the matter, on using the good deeds of the Law (symbolized in circumcision) for justification in Gal. 5:4:

'You have been severed from Christ, you who are *seeking*

---

[426] Mt. 25:31-46; Rom. 2:5-8, 13; Eph. 2:10; 1st Tim. 2:10; 5:9-10; 6:18; 2nd Tim. 2:21; 3:14-17; Titus 1:16; 2:6, 13-14; 3:1, 8, 14; James 2:14-26; Rev. 2:2-5, 9; 13:13.

to be justified by Law! You have fallen from Grace!'

Some of the Galatians were seeking to be justified by faith in Messiah *and* the Law. Anything attached to, or added to Yeshua denies the sufficiency of Who He is and What He did. But once in the Kingdom, does it matter if we obey the King? His laws are meant to be for our *lifestyle* in His Kingdom just as they were for Him, and to set us apart (i.e. make us holy and distinct) from the world of darkness just as they did with Him. They're for our protection and blessing (Lev. 26; Dt. 28–30). God didn't give the Law to Israel because He hated her or wanted to enslave her. He was sharing His wisdom and character with her. He'd like to do that with us too.

Yahveh never intended that the Law would be a means of eternal life. Nowhere within the Law does God say that if it's obeyed, the reward will be eternal life. No one can be 'justified' or 'Born Again' by the keeping of the Law. The Law was never intended as such. The Law gave Israel the holy rules for covenant relationship with Yahveh and with their fellow Hebrews after they were delivered or saved from Egyptian slavery. Once delivered and saved from Satan's Kingdom of slavery to him, sin and death, the Law is the holy guideline for the Gentile too.

The yoke that neither Peter nor his Fathers could bear wasn't the Law. The Law is a holy Gift from Above (Lev. 18:5; Dt. 4:5-8; Rom. 7:12). It wasn't circumcision. Peter was circumcised and neither he nor his Fathers found that unbearable. It wasn't being or becoming a Jew. Peter and his Fathers were Jews. They realized that God had been very gracious to them and had chosen them out of all the peoples on the face of the Earth.[427]

The yoke that neither Peter nor his Fathers could bear was the keeping of the Law for salvation symbolized in circumcision. This is a tremendous burden (Mt. 11:28-30), as the story of the great rabbi illustrated. And works righteousness nullifies the Person and Work of Yeshua.

Acts 15:10 cannot be used to prove that the Law is the yoke that Peter spoke of and therefore 'not for the Gentiles.' It's a verse that reveals the bankruptcy of trying to keep the Law for salvation (Rom. 9:30-32). The New Testament doesn't negate Mosaic Law (Mt. 5:17-19; Rom. 3:31; 7:7). Peter wasn't doing away with the Law either. He said the keeping of the Law for salvation was a yoke that neither he nor his Fathers could bear. He had found the True Yoke (Mt. 11:28-30).

---

[427] Ex. 14:4-30; 19:5; 33:12-17; 34:8-11; Lev. 20:24, 26; Num. 33:50-56; Dt. 4:5-37; 14:2; 26:18-19; 1st Kgs. 8:53; 2nd Kgs. 21:7-8; Ps. 132:13-18; 135:4; 144:15; Isaiah 27:2-6; 41:8-9; 42:1; 43:3, 4, 15, 20, 21; 44:21, 22; 45:4, 17, 19, 25; 46:3, 4, 13; 49:14-16; 52:8:18; Jer. 46:27-28; 50:11, 18-20, 33-34; 51:19, 24, 45, 49; Ezk. 20:6; Zech. 2:8; 8:2-8; Rom. 9–11; Rev. 21, etc.

Acts 15:19—Don't Trouble Them!

In Acts 15:19 Yakov says not to 'trouble those who are turning to God from among the Gentiles'. Many take this phrase to mean that the Jews shouldn't trouble the Gentiles with the Law.

Williams states that 'nothing more than faith should be asked of them as necessary for salvation.'[428] This is true because salvation isn't based on doing the Law but he goes on to say that 'once in the kingdom *certain things* could fairly be asked of them.'[429] He's speaking of the four rules of Yakov in relation to his understanding of table fellowship.

Bruce and Witherington see the 'troubling' Yakov speaks of was aimed at those who wanted the Gentiles to be circumcised.[430] *Wycliffe* says they,

> 'should no longer trouble the Gentiles by demanding that
> they accept circumcision and the law of Moses.'[431]

Hegg thinks the troubling of the Gentiles has to do with not giving them all the rabbinic traditions, just the four rules, which he believes come from the Rabbis.[432] Of course the rabbinic concept of the Law included all the rabbinic traditions but that's not the point. The four rules weren't given to the Gentiles as a trade-off in lieu of all the rabbinic traditions. They were the first of many rules of God that the Gentile needed to walk in.

The three major rules come directly from the Law. In Ex. 34:12 Yahveh warns Israel not to make any covenants with the inhabitants of the land that He was giving them. In v. 14 He says that He won't tolerate worship of Him with another god. And in vv. 15-16 He specifically warns them not to play the harlot, worshiping other gods through *cult prostitution*, and not to eat of the sacrifice (which would include the *eating of the meat* and the *drinking of the blood*).

In the Ten Commandments (Ex. 20:5) Yahveh forbids Israel to worship (which is synonymous with sacrifice; Ex. 10:25-26), another god. In Lev. 17 Israel was told they *weren't to sacrifice to demons* and *play the harlot* (v. 7), *nor to drink the blood* of the sacrifice (vv. 10, 12-14). In the Baal Peor debacle (Num. 25) Israel sacrificed to Baal, *ate of the sacrifice* and *played the harlot*. With just these cites, the three major rules of Yakov are seen (not to eat meat sacrificed to idols at the sacrifice, not to drink the

---

[428] Williams, *Acts*, p. 266.

[429] Ibid.

[430] Bruce, *The Book of the Acts*, p. 295. Witherington, *The Acts of the Apostles*, p. 441.

[431] Pfeiffer, *WBC*, p. 1152.

[432] Hegg, *The Letter Writer*, pp. 281; 275-282.

sacrificial blood and not to lay with the cult harlots).[433]

The strangling of birds for pagan sacrifices in Yakov's day may very well have been prolific and led him to include this rule. Something like this is reasonably deduced from the Torah because pagan sacrifice was off limits whether it was a bull or a bird.

James didn't need to explain what he meant. Everyone understood.[434] And he didn't have to go to the Rabbis to formulate his rules. He knew about sacrificial-sexual idolatry from his own Family history Book (the Hebrew Bible) and the state of pagan affairs. The four rules concretely spelled it out for the Gentile.

The troubling that James spoke of had to do with those Jewish believers who had previously gone to Antioch and stirred up the theological debate. They weren't officially sent from James but were part of the believers in Jerusalem (Acts 15:1, 24). They told the Gentiles they needed to be circumcised (i.e. keep the Law) for salvation along with faith in Yeshua (15:1, 5). This *troubling* can be seen to relate to both the human trouble-makers and their troublesome teaching.

Yakov told everyone the arguing was over (v. 19). He had judged the issue and come to a ruling. Many acknowledge his authority to do this. R. J. Knowling says Yakov was the 'president' of the meeting and that this was known in the days of Chrysostom (347–407 A.D.).[435] That Yakov was *the* authority is also evident from his use of the emphatic 'I' (εγω; eh-go) in 'I judge'.[436] Witherington says the Greek construction for 'I judge,'

> 'makes the ruling more emphatically one of James's in particular—"I myself judge/rule."'[437] 'This way of putting it is equivalent to the familiar Latin phrase ego censeo used by Roman rulers and judges.'[438]

Witherington negates Bruce's perspective on what James was doing by saying,

---

[433] The commandment not to worship other gods (Ex. 20:5; 23:24; Dt. 4:19, etc.) covers all four rules. Strangling is not literally found in Torah but the point is that Gentiles were given laws from Torah that the Church would say were ceremonial, hence Torah was valid for the Gentile.

[434] See Witherington and Hegg on p. 48 and notes 135-136 above.

[435] Knowling, *The Acts of the Apostles*, p. 323.

[436] The KJV has 'my sentence' and the NASB 'my judgment'.

[437] Witherington, *The Acts of the Apostles*, p. 467.

[438] Ibid., note 437.

'Bruce is quite wrong that James is putting forward a 'motion' to the assembly. Various parties have spoken and conferred, and now James will conclude the matter. We are indeed dealing with a decree or ruling from a recognized authority.'[439]

Witherington goes on to say that verse 22,

'is about the decision to send representatives of the Jerusalem church with Paul and Barnabas with the decree. It is not about confirming the decree by the assembly's consent.'[440] 'In other words, James is portrayed as more than just another rhetor; he is...a judge or authority figure who can give a ruling that settles a matter.'[441]

Yakov's authority is also seen by the way Paul speaks of him along with the two chief Apostles Peter and John in Gal. 2:9. And also by the way Luke writes about him.[442] Yakov, because he was the oldest half-brother of Yeshua, commanded an authority that was second to none, not even the Apostles. B. Bagatti writes,

'James...was superior to Peter and Paul, because he was a descendant of David, of the same blood as Jesus, and therefore the legitimate representative of the sacerdotal race'. No 'apostle could claim such prerogatives.'[443]

Yakov must have been the second son of Yosef (Joseph) and Miryam (Mary).[444] This would have made him the heir to the Throne of Israel now that his elder brother Yeshua was not physically in Israel as he was 'next in line' among his brothers (Mt. 13:55; James, Joseph, Simon and Judah). This is why Yakov was the Nasi or Prince (President) over all the Jews

---

[439] Ibid., p. 467.

[440] Ibid., p. 451.

[441] Ibid.

[442] Ibid., see Acts 12:17; 21:18. Also 1st Cor. 15:7; Gal. 1:19; 2:9, 12.

[443] Dr. Samuele Bacchiocchi, *From Sabbath To Sunday* (Rome, Italy: The Pontifical Gregorian University Press, 1977), p. 145, quoting B. Bagatti, *The Church from the Circumcision*, 1971, p. 70.

[444] Yeshua had four younger brothers (Mt. 13:55; Mk. 6:3) and two of them, Yakov (James or rather Jacob) and Yehuda (Jude or rather Judah) wrote letters that are considered authoritative (i.e. Scripture). As Yakov is mentioned first in both passages (Mt. 13:55; Mk. 6:3), and he's the head of the Council in Acts 15 and 21, it's reasonable to assume that he was the first son born after Yeshua. Also, Paul mentions Yakov as Yeshua's brother (Gal. 1:19).

that believed in Yeshua including the Apostles.[445]

The debate about what a Gentile needed to do in order to be saved had ended. Yakov had come to a decision and would not have the Gentiles attacked or troubled by a perverted teaching and perverted teachers. Verse 19 also ended the believing Pharisaic desire for the Gentile to become a Jew (by circumcision) and keep the Law along with faith in Jesus for eternal life.

The judgment of Yakov assured the Gentile full partnership with the Jewish believers without having to become a Jew. This is seen from what both Peter and Yakov say in vv. 7-18. And none of this negates the Law of Moses as a way of life for the Gentile once he's in the Kingdom.

The next verse (v. 20) laid down the litmus test. Yakov gave his four authoritative rules for the Gentiles. If the Holy Spirit was directing him, and there's no reason to assume otherwise, then these rules can rightly be called commandments from Jesus to the Gentile believers through the head of the 'mother Church' in Jerusalem.[446]

These rules were the filter which every Gentile had to pass through in order for his faith in Yeshua to be seen as biblically genuine. And then Yakov said something that hasn't been correctly understood for almost two thousand years.

---

[445] See Acts 12:17; 21:18; 1st Cor. 15:7; Gal. 2:9; Jude 1:1-25, etc.

[446] See Acts 16:4; also 1 Cor. 14:37; 2nd Cor. 8:8 (by inference); 1st Tim. 6:14 2nd Peter 3:2, 14-16.

Acts 15:21 — Go to the Synagogue?!

Acts 15:21 is another example of scriptural misinterpretation by theologians due to their bias against the Law of Moses. The verse is not understood by Christian scholars and some are honest enough to present it as an enigma. In an anti-Law environment this verse just doesn't make any sense. Marshall realizes this and writes, 'James's concluding statement is puzzling.'[447] The verse reads,

> 'For Moses from ancient generations has in every city those who preach him, being read in the synagogues every Sabbath' day.

Why did James end his decision with that? Marshall posits two possibilities as to what James meant. For the first he proposes,

> 'since there are Jews everywhere who regularly hear the law of Moses being read in the synagogues, Christian Gentiles ought to respect their scruples, and so avoid bringing the church into disrepute with them.'[448]

On the surface, respect for one another is a godly ideal but it has nothing to do with the verse. First of all Marshall seems to be speaking about Jews who didn't believe in Jesus ('Jews everywhere'). *Those* Jews could care less about what some Gentiles were doing believing in a crucified Jewish man.

If he meant the believing Jews, Yakov didn't give enough rules for there to be no dispute among the two groups. A Jewish believer would be very offended by a Gentile believer who did not keep the Sabbath day holy, a rule not mentioned by James but obviously kept by the Apostles and all the Jewish believers.[449] They would also be offended by a Gentile believer eating pork, another rule not mentioned by James. Jewish believing scruples cannot possibly be the reason for this verse.

In his second stab at an explanation, Marshall says something very ironic. He writes,

> 'if Christian Gentiles want to find out any more about the Jewish law, they have plenty of opportunity in the local synagogues, and there is no need for the Jerusalem church

---

[447] Marshall, *Acts*, p. 254.

[448] Ibid.

[449] It's obvious that the 7th day Sabbath was still considered holy by all the Jewish believers. James speaks of it in this very verse (v. 21) as the day when Moses is read (and all assemble to hear him). And as all the Jewish believers kept the Law (Acts 21:20), this would certainly include the Sabbath.

to do anything about the matter.'[450]

Why would any Gentile Christian want to find out more about the 'anti-quated Law' if it only placed men in bondage, and Christ came 'to do away with it'? If James was offering this bit of information to the Assembly, with the understanding that the Gentile could, if he so chose, go to the synagogue to learn of Moses, it can only be seen as one going to a prehistoric museum where the fossils of dinosaurs are, to look at what was in the past but was now no more. The Gentiles would come to the synagogue to gape at how all the Jews (believers included), were still following a way that held no relevance for the Gentile believers.

This is theological groping in the dark. To throw out the Law on one hand, and then to say if anyone wanted to find out more about it on the other, is very strange thinking. It shows the futility of Christian scholarship in its attempt to give the verse meaning, devoid of the Law.

Marshall realizes that 'Jewish Christians...continued to live by the Jewish law'.[451] And that according 'to Luke, many Jewish Christians continued to keep the law'.[452] And also that James, 'In later literature...was typified as a law-abiding Jewish Christian'.[453] With this information and the fact that the whole Jewish believing community was keeping Torah (Acts 21:20), Marshall isn't able to see past his theological *tradition* that wrongly nullifies the Law (Mt. 15:9).

What comes to the forefront is certainly a slap in God's face. It's believed by the Church that the Apostles and all the Jewish believers didn't understand that the Law was done away with. Did God forget to tell them? As far as the Book of Acts is concerned they never seemed to grasp this 'truth,' not even Paul (Acts 28:17, 23-24; Rom. 3:31; 1st Cor. 7:19).

Samuele Bacchiocchi, who wrote a masterful work on why the Sabbath is still holy (and for believers today), also fails to understand the significance of it. He states the *old ways* of the Jews were just too hard for Jewish believers to let go of. The,

> 'attachment of the Jerusalem Church to Jewish religious customs may perhaps perplex the Christian who regards the Mother Church of Christendom as the ideal model of his religious life. One must not forget, however, that

---

[450] Marshall, *Acts*, p. 254.

[451] Ibid., p. 243.

[452] Ibid., p. 250.

[453] Ibid., p. 251.

Christianity sprang up out of the roots and trunk of Judaism. The early Jewish converts viewed the acceptance of Christ not as the destruction of their religious framework, but as the *fulfillment of their Messianic expectations* which enhanced their religious life with a new dimension. The process of separating the shadow from the reality, the transitory from the permanent, was gradual and not without difficulty.'[454]

While Bacchiocchi recognizes that all Jewish believers followed the Law, and that Jerusalem was 'the Mother Church' (and the ideal model of religious life), he fails to appropriate the full impact of what he's written. If it was good for all of them, if they could believe in Jesus and keep the Law, then why wouldn't it be appropriate for the Gentile? Why would it have to 'give way' to 'no Law'? Weren't the Gentiles grafted into Israel? Isn't Jesus, who kept the Law, their Example too (1st Jn. 2:3-6)?

Bacchiocchi says that the Law faded away but 'not without difficulty' yet we never read in Scripture or church history of the Jerusalem congregation or their spiritual descendents ever renouncing the Law as wrong or 'gone.' Just the opposite is true. The ancient Jewish Nazarenes, who were the spiritual descendents of the Jewish believers of apostolic Jerusalem, continued to keep the Law of Moses. Epiphanius, bishop-historian of Salamis and Metropolitan of Cyprus[455] in the *fourth century A.D.* branded them heretics but unjustly so. He wrote,

> 'The Nazarenes do not differ in any essential thing from them (i.e. Jews), since they practice the custom and doctrines prescribed by the Jewish law, except that they believe in Christ.' 'They preach that God is one and that Jesus Christ is his Son.' They 'differ both from the Jews and from the Christians'; 'from the former, because they believe in Christ; from the true Christians because they fulfill till now Jewish rites as the circumcision, the Sabbath and others.'[456]

As Bacchiocchi rightly points out, the picture of the Nazarenes 'matches very well that of the Jerusalem Church' of the first century (i.e. of the Law

---

[454] Bacchiocchi, *From Sabbath To Sunday*, pp. 149-150.

[455] E. A. Livingstone, *The Concise Oxford Dictionary of the Christian Church* (Oxford, England: Oxford University Press, 2000), p. 193. Epiphanius lived from 315–403 A.D. Salamis is an island near Greece.

[456] Bacchiocchi, *From Sabbath To Sunday*, p. 157. Epiphanius, *Adversus haereses* 29, 7, PG 41, 402.

keeping Apostles in the New Testament). He goes on to say,

> 'The possibility exists therefore that the Nazarenes repre-
> sent the survival of both the ethnic *and theological* legacy
> of' the apostolic community.[457]

Exactly! They were following in the theological footsteps of all the Apostles and Jewish believers before them. If the Law was still valid and oper-
ative for all Jewish believers throughout the Book of Acts and centuries
thereafter, isn't it possible that *this is the correct understanding* of the
Law for both Jew and Gentile who have faith in Yeshua today?

Many, not being able to say much about why all the Apostles and all the
Jews still continued to walk in Torah so long after the Resurrection, have
the audacity to say the Apostles didn't have the full understanding of what
Yeshua's atoning death meant. Is that *possible*? God didn't tell the *Apostles* they were wrong in such a monumental area as their perspective on
the Law? Not at Acts 15, and not at Acts 21:20, 24. Did Paul differ from
them? They can't prove that from Paul in Acts but they go to some of his
letters where they think that Paul is doing away with the Law. Could it be
they have misinterpreted the Apostle to the Gentiles also?

ISBE says that Paul's Gospel was *essentially the same* as Peter's (Gal.
2:9), and there's no hint in Acts 21:20 of a different Gospel. Paul's anath-
ema on those who preached a different Gospel (Gal. 1:8f.), is never pro-
nounced upon the Jewish Apostles of Jerusalem.[458] And Peter, about 64
A.D. affirms Paul as 'a beloved brother' who although writes some things
that are 'hard to understand' nevertheless speaks of it as Scripture (2nd
Pet. 3:15-16; see also Paul on Peter; 1st Cor. 3:21-22; 9:1-6; Gal. 2:1-10).

The Church takes its position on the Law from *only some* of Paul's letters.
But please note, it's only the Apostle Paul that they can go to for their
doctrine. It's *not any of the other Apostles* that have written Scripture for
the New Testament and certainly not the words of Jesus or the Book of
Acts. Under careful examination of those Pauline texts that the Church
holds up as proof of the Law's demise, their interpretation will be found to
be unbiblical, just as their understanding of Acts 15:20 has proven.

F. F. Bruce believes that James spoke v. 21 to appease those Pharisees

---

[457] Ibid. Bacchiocchi also notes, 'The fact that they retained Sabbath keeping as
one of their distinguishing marks shows persuasively that this was the original
day of worship of the Jerusalem Church and that no change from Sabbath to
Sunday occurred among' the Jewish believers even after the destruction of the
city in 70 A.D., forty years after the Resurrection.

[458] Bromiley, *ISBE*, vol. three, pp. 699-700.

who 'lost out' on circumcising the Gentiles. He says that James really didn't mean that the Gentiles should go to the synagogue to learn about Moses, because the Gentiles weren't the disciples of Moses. He quotes R. B. Rackham to sum up his own position:

> 'Moses, so to speak, would suffer no loss, in failing to obtain the allegiance of those who had never been his.'[459]

Yakov's implication that Gentiles go to the synagogue really meant that he *didn't* want them to go? He only said it 'to throw a bone' to some disgruntled believing Pharisees?

This kind of theologizing is extremely shallow. First, it makes James out to be a clever politician or a liar, saying something he didn't mean just to pacify the Pharisees. James didn't pacify them when it came to 'Jesus *and* circumcision' (the very ruling of Acts 15!). And there's no need for James to do that here, especially in light of his godly leadership. Why would James want to mislead the Gentiles (and all the other Jewish believers) by saying something he really didn't mean? This doesn't fit with his character, or with Luke writing Acts 15 under the inspiration of the Holy Spirit, or with the text in question.

Second, this saying of Rackham's has James concerned for Gentile disciples of Moses that would *never come to believe in Jesus*. But James wasn't recruiting Gentiles for the Rabbis who didn't believe in Jesus.

Third, it seems to pit Moses against Jesus, as though the two of them were at odds. Didn't Jesus walk in all the laws of Moses that applied to Him? Jesus, in a very real sense, was the greatest 'disciple' that Moses ever had. Aren't believers supposed to *follow* Jesus? To be *like* Him? Or is it just a spiritual following? The Apostle John says that if one wants to be like Jesus, they must keep from sin. How can one know when they *sin*?

> 'Beloved, now we are children of God, and it has not appeared as yet what we will be. We know that when He appears, we will be like Him, because we will see Him just as He is. And everyone who has this hope fixed on Him, purifies himself, just as He is pure. Everyone who practices sin also practices lawlessness; and *sin is lawlessness*.' (1st John 3:2-4, see also 2:1-6)

The Law reveals what sin is (Mt. 5:19; Rom. 7:7). Without Moses, the Church fails to see some basic rules that Jesus wants His Bride to walk in. She sins against Him by breaking His Sabbath day, not keeping Passover

---

[459] Bruce, *The Book of the Acts*, p. 296.

holy, and eating things that aren't meant for the Bride to eat, etc. This isn't the Way of Jesus. Without knowing Moses, one is a handicapped disciple of Jesus. Here's what the Master said about those in His day who had a knowledge of Torah and who would enter His Kingdom:

> 'And Yeshua said to them, 'Therefore every scribe' (of Moses) 'who has become a disciple of the Kingdom of Heaven is like a head of a household who brings out of his treasure things new *and* old.' (Mt. 13:52)

Yeshua is not denigrating the 'old' but acknowledging its place or importance. Did Jesus really come to do away with the Sabbath day or the Law? And if so, where does *He* say that? If the Sabbath and Passover (1st Cor. 5:6-8) are still in effect then the Law of Moses must be too.

Knowling lists three possibilities for consideration for Acts 15:21. One, that Gentiles who had frequented the synagogue before coming to Jesus would more easily accept the rules as they had heard the Law. Two, that unless the Gentiles accepted the restrictions, the 'Jewish Christians' wouldn't fellowship with them. And three, that James was telling the Jews 'not to worry about Moses; he wouldn't be neglected.'[460]

It's true there were Gentiles who had frequented the synagogues before giving their lives to Jesus. But the rules were for all the Gentile believers, not just those who had attended synagogue before coming to Jesus. Many of the Gentiles that came to Messiah Yeshua hadn't been synagogue attendees.

Possibility two seems to stand out as a threat that James was giving to the Gentile believers. But there's nothing in v. 21 that threatens the Gentiles with negation of fellowship. There's a demand by James that the Gentiles cease from pagan sacrificial rites, with the implication that if they don't they'll lose their salvation. This is not based on a threat but on the understanding that the worship of another god along with Yeshua would sever them from the Head and His Body. But that's in v. 20, not v. 21.

Possibility three is similar to Bruce's interpretation. Perhaps this is where Bruce and Rackham picked it up from? There will be plenty of Jews (and Gentiles) who only followed Moses. But it really wasn't a popularity contest between Moses and Messiah.

Williams too glides along the path of least resistance, offering no more than a superficial opinion for v. 21. He says that since the Jewish believers were 'prepared to lay aside their long-standing prejudice against' the Gen-

---

[460] Knowling, *The Acts of the Apostles*, p. 325.

tiles, then the Gentiles should give up something too.[461] This seems to make it more like a children's game than the 'epoch making' drama that was Acts 15.[462] There's nothing in the text to warrant this 'tit for tat' concept.

Williams also says that because the Jews had walked in the Law so long, it was tough for them to 'lay it aside.'[463] He and Bacchiocchi make the Law out to be a nasty social habit that the Jew had picked up, but the Gentile should just put up with it. This view makes the Jew caught in something that he should really give up but the Gentile will go out of his way and perform his Christian duty toward him. Yet the verse in question implies that the Gentile was to go to the synagogue. Why should a Gentile have to go to a Jewish synagogue on the Sabbath day to appease the Jew caught in the web of the Law?

Stern says it's 'a difficult verse.' He presents six options to choose from, saying that 'a good case can be made for any of the first four' while also stating that 'it is hard to choose between' the four.[464] His first possibility was seen before with Marshall: Jewish 'scruples are to be respected.'[465] That is, don't offend the Jews or the Pharisees. How this relates to a Gentile going to the synagogue, especially if they are not to walk in the Law, could only have the opposite effect of disturbing *all* the Jews.

Stern's second view was seen with Knowling and Bruce. Moses won't lose disciples from the Gentiles.[466] This says that there'll always be disciples of Moses from the Gentiles but just not the Christian Gentiles. This view is distorted. It would seem that James would be more interested in Gentiles coming to Jesus than just to Moses. The only people this would make happy would be Jews that didn't believe in Jesus! This is hardly worth considering.

His third view has some Gentile Christians already having been in the synagogue, learning the Law (Knowling) but they didn't choose to convert to Judaism. Don't press them now to do so.[467] How this is supposed to be an interpretation of the verse is beyond understanding. It also doesn't explain what happens to the rest of the Gentiles that never went to syna-

---

[461] Williams, *Acts*, p. 266.

[462] See pp. 1-2 notes 2 and 4.

[463] Williams, *Acts*, p. 267.

[464] Stern, *JNTC*, p. 279.

[465] Ibid.

[466] Ibid.

[467] Ibid.

gogue before they came to Jesus, or why James was sending more there.

Stern's fourth opinion says the Gentile Christians will continue to visit the synagogues to learn how to live a godly, ethical lifestyle. He also states that the Council's view was 'temporal' and only applied to the first century as 'Gentile Christians have long ceased to visit the synagogue in significant numbers.'[468] So Gentiles don't need to learn 'how to live a godly, ethical lifestyle' now? Keeping the Sabbath day holy is more ethical than stealing or lying (consider their punishments),[469] and no one writes that the Decree was temporal. The Law (Moses) was to be learned on the Sabbath day and is 'eternal.'[470] Yeshua said, till this Earth and these Heavens no longer exist (Matt. 5:18; see also Heb. 8:13; Rev. 12:17; 14:12).

Stern's fifth view states that the Gentile Christians going to the synagogue would eventually become Jews'.[471] As he points out, this view is contradicted in the New Testament.

His sixth opinion is that the Gentiles, in going to the synagogues on the Sabbath will keep on hearing the four rules of James 'emphasized over and over and will keep being sensitized to them' (Knowling). Aside from the fact that they wouldn't hear a prohibition against strangling (as it's not literally mentioned in Torah), it stands to reason that they'd hear and be sensitized to other rules too and wonder why they weren't keeping them. Especially as they saw their Jewish brethren who believed in Jesus following the Law. This would certainly make for two different classes of believers, something Yeshua never intended in His Kingdom.

Witherington slips here also. He sees v. 21 as a witness to the Jews in the synagogues that the Gentile believers weren't practicing sacrificial-sexual idolatry any longer.[472] How this can be read into the verse is hard to fathom. Could good Sabbath attendance at the church negate Sunday worship of Diana or Aphrodite? Some Corinthian believers went to church on the Sabbath, and then to the temple prostitutes on Sunday. No, the practice of sacrificial-sexual idolatry could continue even with good synagogue attendance on the Sabbath.

---

[468] Ibid.

[469] The Sabbath's greater moral value is seen in that its punishment for violation is greater than that of stealing or lying, two highly ethical commandments themselves (Ex. 31:12-17; Lev. 6:1-7).

[470] In the New Jerusalem there won't be any need to learn about Moses. Everyone will be a pure reflection of what Moses wrote of, Yeshua (Jn. 5:39).

[471] Stern, *JNTC*, p. 279.

[472] Witherington, *The Acts of the Apostles*, p. 463.

Some others, seeing how shaky these interpretations are, come up with a linguistic twist to try and discredit the plain meaning of v. 21. They say that the only reason Moses is mentioned is because James is telling everyone *where* he got the rules of v. 20 from (i.e. the Law). This particular belief centers around the Greek word (gar) that links v. 20 with v. 21. It states there's nothing binding on the Gentile except the four rules which they see as rules for table fellowship. This is another fruitless attempt to discredit the Law for every believer.

The Greek word that links Acts 15:20 to v. 21 is γαρ (gar; 'for'). Wright sums up its meaning by saying it's always that which explains 'something that has just gone before' it.[473] Friberg defines it as,

> 'a conjunction' (meaning *for* or *because*) 'that basically *introduces an explanation* or an exhortation or a word that expresses cause or reason for, because' or 'an exclamation to point to *a self-evident conclusion*'.[474]

It can also mean that the phrase or sentence written after it is the 'tip of the iceberg' as to the author's thought on the topic;

> 'often the thought to be supported is not expressed, but must be supplied from the context, e.g. (he has truly been born) for we have seen his star'.[475]

The proponents of gar say that Yakov was *only* explaining in v. 21 that he took the rules of v. 20 from the Law. *That's why Moses is mentioned.* To use gar this way seems to defy common sense though. Why? Because there's no mention in their explanation as to why Moses is mentioned 'from ancient generations' 'in every city' having 'those who preach him' 'being read in the synagogues' 'on every Sabbath day.'

Yakov didn't just mention Moses; he was *extremely* specific about him (i.e. the places *where* the Law was read, the *day* it was read on, etc.). This hardly seems to be just a passing reference as to where Yakov may have gotten the four rules from.

Yakov tells everyone that Moses was preached 'from ancient generations.'

---

[473] N. T. Wright: *Paul in Different Perspectives*, http://www.ntwrightpage.com/ Wright_Auburn_Paul.htm, p. 3. Jan. 3rd, 2005; 'the function of gar always being *to explain something that has just gone before*'.

[474] Friberg, *ALGNT*, p. 96. 'γαρ (gar) a conjunction basically introducing an explanation'. Bauer, *GELNT*, p. 151: 'conjunction used to express cause, inference, continuation, or to explain.'

[475] Bauer, *GELNT*, pp. 151-152.

If he was only telling the Assembly where he got the rules from, there'd have been absolutely no need for him to tell the assembly of *Jewish* believers[476] that Moses had those who preached him 'from ancient generations'. All the Jews knew that.

If Yakov was only telling the Assembly where he got the rules from, there'd have been absolutely no need for him to tell the Jewish assembly that Moses was preached 'in every city.' All the Jews knew that too. Why the need to mention where Moses was preached if Yakov was only mentioning Moses as the place where he got his rules from?

'Moses being preached in every city' cannot be used to say that James was just giving Moses honor either, by mentioning him, as some might say. What would be the need for doing that since he, more than any other, was the symbol of the Law which the Gentiles 'didn't need to keep'?

If Yakov was only mentioning 'in every city' for the Jews at the Council, it would seem a little out of place for another reason too. Most of those Jews at the Council, including Yakov, Peter and John, lived in Jerusalem and *didn't go to the synagogue*. They went to the Temple (Acts 2:46; 3:1, 3; 4:1; 5:20-21; 21:26, etc.). The Law wasn't read at the Temple on the Sabbath, only in the synagogues. Yet all the Jewish believers knew and walked in Torah (Acts 21:20; 25:8, etc.). So that phrase and reason can't be intended for the Jews at the Council either.

Yakov saying that Moses was 'in every city' means that he knew that wherever a Gentile lived, he'd be able to learn Torah, the will of God for the Gentile in the Kingdom. This is especially brought out by Luke's use of the Greek word for 'preachers' in this same verse. More in a moment.

If Yakov was only telling the Assembly where he got the rules from, there'd have been absolutely no need for him to tell the Jewish assembly that Moses was 'read in the synagogues'. All the Jews knew that too. Moses 'being read in the synagogues' meant that Yakov assumed the Gentiles would learn the Law as they heard it read. Why go to the synagogue and hear the Law if not to apply it to one's life?

---

[476] If there were any Gentile converts from Antioch at the Council it remains to be seen, as the other members of the congregation that were sent from Antioch with Paul and Barnabas could be believing Jews (15:2). Be that as it may, whether there were believing Gentiles from Antioch at the Council or not, it wouldn't effect the meaning of the verse or that the vast majority of those present were Jews. From Acts 15:22, all the Apostles, Elders and believing Jews were there (while Acts 15:6 states it was at least the Apostles and the Elders that were discussing the matter). But no Gentiles seem to have been there (who might not have understood what Yakov was saying).

The Law being read in the synagogue isn't like a church sermon that might use a few verses of Scripture and then close the Bible. Every Sabbath, three to six chapters of the Torah are read in sequence, verse by verse. From Genesis to the end of Deuteronomy everyone hears all of the Torah and can apply it to their life. A rabbi might give a message on a part of what was read but the synagogue service centered around the Law being read aloud every Sabbath day. Most Jews didn't have Torah scrolls in their homes. To hear and learn the Word of God, one had little choice but *to go to the synagogue on the Sabbath day.* Where else could the Gentile go to learn the Words of the Living God and what was expected of him?

If Yakov was only telling the Assembly where he got the rules from, there would have been absolutely no need for him to tell the Jewish assembly that Moses was 'read in the synagogues on every Sabbath.' All the Jews knew that. Gentiles were welcome in the synagogue. This is well attested. Paul, whenever he went to a synagogue with his Message of Life, always addressed the Gentiles who were there also. They could be God fearers (Acts 17:17; 13:46, 48; 14:1-2) or those that were just attracted to the morality and reality of the God of Israel without taking any official steps.

Yakov's mention of the Sabbath also reveals that the issue of Sabbath vs. Sunday hadn't come up yet. In other words all believers, both Jewish and Gentile, continued to keep the Sabbath day holy until the Church of Rome changed it around 100 A.D.[477]

After all, *if the Gentiles weren't already coming* and being directed to the synagogue to learn Torah, why is James mentioning Sabbath, synagogue, Moses and all the cities in the world? Wouldn't it have been enough for him just to mention Moses? Or not to say it at all, as everyone knew where the rules came from? Yakov could have said,

> 'I've taken the concept of the four rules from Moses and the Gentiles don't have to be concerned with any other commandments except to love God and neighbor.'

But he didn't say that. What some do in using the Greek word gar to project their theological bias against Torah into v. 21 discredits the plain meaning of the text and reveals how desperate they are to distance themselves from the righteous Law of God. Those that use gar this way use it not as a means to an end, to properly interpret the meaning of the verse, but to pervert and *suppress* the divine meaning of God's Word.

The Greek word gar does absolutely nothing to disrupt the understanding

---

[477] Bacchiocchi, *From Sabbath to Sunday*, pp. 165-212.

that James wanted the Gentiles to go to the synagogue on the Sabbath and learn Torah. Actually it's *self-evident* from the text, if one can cast aside anti-Law sentiments and just allow the text to speak for itself. Yakov's statement in v. 21 reinforces and caps his *filter* decision of v. 20, for gar *truly explains* why Yakov *gave only four rules*. Putting the three verses together gives us an overview of the text. It's really just one long sentence:

> 'Therefore I judge that we do not *trouble* those who are turning to God from among the Gentiles but that we write to them that they abstain from the pollutions of idols and from cult prostitution and from what is strangled and from blood, *because* Moses from ancient generations has in every city those who preach him, being read in the synagogues on every Sabbath.' (Acts 15:19-21)

Why *only* four rules now? Because the Gentiles would learn the rest at the synagogues. More in a moment.

There wasn't any need to *trouble* the Gentiles with *circumcision* for salvation. This is also brought out in v. 24, in the letter that's written to Antioch. But the Gentiles did need to be warned against sacrificial-sexual idolatry, the four rules guarding against those spiritually deadly sins. Further explaining Yakov, he could have also said,

> 'I've given these four rules for the Gentiles and no more, as these will validate their belief in Yeshua. *We've all seen that the Gentile believers have been going, and we believe will continue to go, to the synagogue on the Sabbath*, to learn God's holy commandments of the Law. This way they'll grow in the knowledge of their Messiah and walk in the Way of Life alongside their Jewish believing brethren.'

The Gentiles were *already* learning the commandments at the synagogue. And Yakov had every reason to believe that Gentile believers would continue to go to the synagogue to learn the Law of Moses. *Continue* to go to the synagogue?

Verse 21 has Yakov reflecting to the Jewish believers what they and he had already seen in this area of Gentile salvation for at least eight years. Yakov assumed the paradigm would continue. And this is where gar comes to the forefront as it truly *explains* why James gave *only* these four important rules instead of many others like Sabbath and dietary laws. The Gentile believers were already learning Torah at the synagogues.

Yakov had observed for about eight to nine years, from Cornelius in Acts

10, to his Decree in Acts 15[478] that many *traditional* synagogues continued to be a place of assembly and learning for many Jewish and Gentile believers. Cornelius, his family and friends most likely kept going to the traditional Jewish synagogue after they came to faith in the Jewish Messiah. There were probably Jews there who believed too. Cornelius' new faith in Yeshua would only enhance his life of learning at the synagogue. And many of the Jewish and Gentile believers in Israel and Syria, etc., would continue to assemble in traditional synagogues till around 90 A.D.[479]

The Gentile believers who attended the congregation in Antioch would also have been learning Torah. It was originally made up of only Jewish believers (Acts 11:19) and would have been modeled after a traditional synagogue. Later, Gentiles joined them. Would the new Gentile believers change Sabbath to Sunday and Passover to Easter? Who was learning from whom? Who had come into a new religion and a new way of life?

By Acts 15 Paul had gone on only one missionary journey in what is today Cyprus and south-central Turkey, about 47 A.D.[480] His experience of

---

[478] Acts 10 took place about 40 A.D. Acts 15 was about eight years later in 48 A.D. For Acts 10: Witherington, *The Acts of the Apostles*, p. 347; 39–40 A.D. Marshall, *Acts*, p. 183; 'before 41 A.D.' Knowling, *The Acts of the Apostles*, p. 250; 40–44 A.D. For Acts 15: Douglas, *IBD*, Part 1, pp. 281-283; 48 A.D. Unger, *UBD*, pp. 486-488; 48 A.D. Witherington, *The Acts of the Apostles*, p. 444 note 361; 49 A.D. Bromiley, *ISBE*, vol. one, p. 692; 49 A.D.

[479] The cardinal prayer of the synagogue is the Amida, where the congregation stands to recite 18 prayers to God. Around 90 A.D. another 'prayer' was added to ferret out believers who were by this time considered heretics. In 132 A.D. the disastrous bar Kochba rebellion against Rome began. Jewish believers fought alongside their Jewish brethren (who didn't believe in Yeshua). About a year later, Rabbi Akiva proclaimed bar Kosiba, the general of the rebellion, to be the Messiah. Akiva also changed Kosiba's name to bar Kochba (son of the star, a reference to the 'star of Messiah' prophecy in Num. 24:17). Many Jewish believers refused to fight. They were tortured by this 'Messiah' and his followers, and bitter feelings arose against the Jewish believers. This caused further division between them. Rabbi Akiva, in proclaiming a false Messiah, caused much damage to the Jewish people.

After Rome crushed the rebellion and killed Rabbi Akiva and bar Kochba, Rome changed the name of the land to Philistina (Palestine, in derision of the ancient enemies of the Jews), and Jerusalem to Aelia Capitolina (naming it after one of their gods). They barred Jews from living in the city, only being able to enter it one day a year, on the Day of Atonement (Lev. 23:26-32), to mourn the wholesale slaughter of the Jews, the destruction of the Temple and their national homeland. This was meant to further humiliate the Jewish people. In backing the rebellion against Rome and proclaiming bar Kosiba to be the Messiah, Rabbi Akiva caused the Jewish people to be without their own country for more than 1,800 years (from 135 to 1948).

having to leave some (not all) synagogues, wasn't the norm (Acts 9:31). Also, the congregations that Paul established, what many today would call 'house churches' would in fact have been seen by the Apostles as 'house synagogues' (places of assembly) where obviously they'd be teaching Torah. And Paul didn't have a monopoly on establishing assemblies or 'house synagogues' (Acts 11:19 and Gal. 1:22 by inference, etc.).

The word 'synagogue' comes from Greek and can also mean 'a Christian assembly'.[481] Yakov used it in referring to Christian assemblies (James 2:2; see also Acts 9:1-2; 26:11). It would also be used for the assembly of Jewish and Gentile believers at Antioch, and other believing assemblies, as well as a traditional Jewish congregation. In other words, both a synagogue of Jews that didn't believe in Jesus, as well as an assembly like Antioch, made up of only Jewish and Gentile believers, could equally be called a synagogue. This adds to the understanding of what Yakov said in Acts 15:21, about Moses 'being read in the *synagogues* every Sabbath.'

James already knew the Gentiles were going to the synagogues. As a Jew, the antithetical word 'church' wasn't in his or Paul's vocabulary.[482] He as-

---

[480] Acts 13:1-14:26. Unger, *UBD*, pp. 486-488; 45 A.D. Douglas, *IBD*, Part 1; 46–47 A.D. Bromiley, *ISBE*, vol. one, p. 692; 47–48 A.D.

[481] Perschbacher, *NAGL*, p. 388. *Synagogue*: a 'collecting, gathering; a Christian assembly or congregation, *James 2:2*' where James is speaking of a believing assembly ('for if a man comes into your *synagogue* with a gold ring'). Mounce, *ALGNT*, p. 432 has exactly what Perschbacher has. Bauer, *GELNT*, pp. 782-783: a 'place of assembly' 'a *Christian assembly-place* can also be meant' (*James 2:2*). A 'meeting for worship, of the Jews' '*Transferred* to meetings of *Christian congregations*'.

[482] The Greek εκκλησια (eklaysia), translated into English as 'church' literally means 'an assembly' or congregation (i.e. a synagogue), but it also speaks of those 'called out.' Originally it pictured the Greek 'town meetings' of free men, called out of the populace. The spiritual aspect relates to believers being 'called out of darkness into His marvelous Light' (1st Pet. 2:9) and may be one reason why Paul chose to use this word over synagogue. Christians are the 'Called Out Ones,' the Greek equivalent of the Hebraic 'Chosen People.' Where it says, to the *church* at Corinth, it should be, to the assembly or congregation at Corinth. It could also be, to the *called out ones* of Corinth.

Paul's use of eklaysia in no way opposes the Jewish people. The word was used for Israel about 300 years earlier in the Septuagint. It speaks of the Congregation or 'the Church of Israel' at Mt. Sinai (Dt. 4:10; 9:10; 18:16; see also Acts 7:38). This most likely was the reason why Paul used eklaysia over synagogue. The Church (Assembly of those called out), didn't begin on the *Mosaic* holy day of Pentecost (Lev. 23:15-21; the Feast of Weeks, Shavuote in Hebrew). Jewish believers were *filled* with the Holy Spirit on that day (see Acts 2:46-47; 5:11-12, 42 where 'the Church' met in the Temple). Paul's churches were 'house assemblies' (1st Cor. 16:19; Philem. 1:2; see also Rom.

sumed they'd *continue* to go to the synagogues to learn the Law on the Sabbath day. He was making a statement of observation as well as one of expectation. Wherever Gentile believers were, there'd be synagogues they could learn Torah in, whether believing or non-believing synagogues.

Witherington thinks there were many Gentiles like Cornelius, both in the Promised Land and throughout the Roman Empire. He asks,

> 'Has Luke exaggerated the apparent prevalence of people like Cornelius and the importance of their involvement in the synagogues of the Diaspora and the holy Land?'[483] 'Luke is quite careful in the way he presents the progression of things. Cornelius is not a pagan, nor is this a story about a mission to those Gentile lands. Cornelius is seen as significant in that his case raises the questions about preaching to pagans and going not only into their homes but into their lands. In other words, he is cast as a bride figure standing at the boundary between Judaism and paganism, and living in a very Hellenized city full of Gentiles yet in the Holy Land.'[484]

> 'Often overlooked is the fact that Luke suggests that there were such Gentiles as Cornelius not only in the Diaspora but in Israel as well.'[485] 'What is important about these people for Luke is that time and again they are seen as the bridge between Judaism and Christianity, and on various occasions they are seen as the most likely of those who are within or associated with the *synagogue* to' give their lives to Messiah '(see 18:7-8).'[486] 'Luke's obvious interest in folks like a Cornelius or a Titus might be because he himself, and/or Theophilus, had been a "God-fearer" before' coming to Yeshua.[487]

16:5, 10-11, 14-15, 23), which Jews would call 'house synagogues.' It also doesn't seem that Paul began the congregations in Rome (1:13, 15), Ephesus (1:15), or Colosse (1:3-4, 9), even though house churches are mentioned in two of those letters (Rom. 16:5; Col. 4:15). The assemblies in Rome may very well have begun from Roman Jews in Jerusalem at Pentecost (Acts 2:10).

[483] Witherington, *The Acts of the Apostles*, p. 341.

[484] Ibid., p. 340 note 46.

[485] Ibid., p. 341 note 51.

[486] Ibid., p. 344.

[487] Ibid., note 64: Most likely, 'Theophilus had been a prominent Gentile who was a synagogue adherent before his...conversion to' Jesus '(see, e.g. 17:4).'

Yakov was holding up a paradigm that he knew all the Jews at the Council would be able to follow. Moses was proclaimed and taught in all the synagogues in every city on every Sabbath. The Gentile believers were coming and would continue to go to the synagogues to learn how their God wanted them to order their new lives.

Hegg believes the Gentiles would go to the synagogue every Sabbath and learn the rules of Moses so that they could walk in them.[488] This way they'd be on an equal plane with their Jewish believing brethren. And he poignantly asks, where else could the Gentile go to learn about the One True God?[489] There was no other place in all the world.

The Gentile didn't need to become a Jew in order to be saved. But the Gentile needed to be told what would disqualify him from membership in the Kingdom of Yeshua (v. 20). Yakov and every Jew there knew the Gentile was already going to the synagogue to learn of Moses, and Yakov assumed that it would continue (v. 21). In declaring v. 21 to everyone at the Council, Yakov was *specifically* thinking about Torah for the Gentile. With that he speaks to all of us today, saying that Torah should be a part of every believer's life. Yakov affirmed the place of the Law for those who have faith in Jesus (Rom. 3:31). He was presenting Torah as a lifestyle of sanctification for the Gentile, just as it was for the Jewish believer (e.g. Peter and Paul; Acts 21:24; 25:8; 28:17; Rom. 7:7, 12).

The need for the Law has not yet disappeared (Mt. 5:18; Heb. 8:13). Verse 21 is the 'period' at the end of the sentence. It's the logical reason and explanation of v. 20 and why Yakov gave *only* four rules. The Gentiles would learn the rest of the Law in the synagogue. Verse 21 was also given to assure the Jews there, that Torah *would be* a part of Gentile life...just not the salvation part.

In the synagogue the Gentile would learn all the other rules of the Kingdom that pertained to him. Not every law of God pertained or applied to the Gentile, just as every law of God didn't apply to Yeshua. Jesus didn't need to keep the laws pertaining to offering up the daily sacrifice (Ex. 29:38-42) because He wasn't a priest in the Jerusalem Temple (Heb. 8:4). He wasn't of the lineage of Levi and Aaron, but of Judah and David the King (Mt. 1:1-17; Lk. 1:27; 2:4; 3:23-28; Acts 13:22-23; Rom. 1:3; 2nd Tim. 2:8; Heb. 7:13-14; Rev. 5:5; 22:16). Yeshua kept all the laws that applied to Him and if a believer wants to be like Him, shouldn't they also?

---

[488] Hegg, *The Letter Writer*, pp. 73, 17-22.

[489] Ibid., p. 73. Gordon Tessler in *The Genesis Diet* (1996, p. 116) briefly speaks of this, as well as cult harlots and drinking blood. He predates Hegg (2002).

Acts 15:21—The Preachers of Moses

Some try and connect the phrase in Acts 15:21, 'those who preach him' (i.e. the preachers of Moses), to v. 19 (don't trouble them) 'to explain it.' Their interpretation speaks of the Law's demise. But both the 'connection' and the 'explanation' are poor interpretations of the text.

TDNT presents the connection and interprets it this way:

> 'The verse is probably to the effect that we do not wish to *burden* Gentile Christians with the Law (v. 19). There are enough preachers of Moses. We desire to preach the Gospel.'[490]

TDNT admits that the interpretation of v. 21 is 'much debated.'[491] To use v. 19 their way is contrary to the understanding in the previous section. James wasn't speaking about the Law as trouble, but the Jewish troublemakers who had gone to Antioch and caused strife among the believers with their troubling theology of 'faith in Yeshua *plus* circumcision.'

Furthermore to contrast the preachers of Moses with those who preached the Gospel is also contrary to the meaning of the context and the meaning of the word. The context says that James wasn't contrasting 'Christian preaching' about Jesus with 'Jewish preaching' on the Law. Even with those Pharisaic believers who 'wanted Moses,' it wasn't *just* Moses but Moses (circumcision) *and* faith in Jesus (15:1, 5). It was never 'Moses vs. Jesus' and preaching as to content (Moses or Jesus), never came up. Acts 15 was a theological gathering on what the Gentile needed to do *in order to be saved*, not a pastor's conference on preaching.

The use of the Greek word by Luke, translated as 'those who *preach* him' (v. 21 NASB), and 'them that *preach* him' (KJV), is also very helpful in understanding the verse. The word is κηρυσσοντας (kay-roos-sahn-tahs) and means,

> a 'herald, one who *proclaims public announcements, summons to assemblies*, carries messages, etc.' in the NT one who acts as God's official human messenger, preacher, proclaimer, 1st Tim. 2.7'.[492]

The use of the word is very limited in the New Testament. It only occurs three times.[493] One would expect it to be used much more than that. Al-

---

[490] Kittel, *TDNT*, vol. III, p. 705.

[491] Ibid.

[492] Friberg, *ALGNT*, pp. 229-230.

[493] Kittel, *TDNT*, vol. III, p. 696.

though conceptually it can be linked to 'apostle' (i.e. a 'sent one') or evangelist, *TDNT* tells us the New Testament 'manifestly avoids it.'[494] The reason for this is that the Message or the Proclamation of Yeshua's Person and Work is the central theme of the New Testament, not the earthly messengers (i.e. the preachers) who proclaim (preach) Him. *TDNT* states,

> 'For the true preacher is God or Christ Himself…hence there is little place for the herald.'[495]

Understanding the ancient Jewish preacher will reveal there's another side to what Yakov said. This preacher was very different from the Christian preacher today. He wasn't one who gave the sermon but more like 'the crier who' went 'through the town and' made 'something known.'[496]

Just as the town criers of England 400 years ago would go through the neighborhoods of a city and announce the public news, similarly the Jewish preachers in the days of James. They not only told the daily news as such but announced rabbinic edicts, times of Feasts and *called people to the synagogue* 'to hear Moses.' The preachers would be found on the streets in Jewish neighborhoods, able to tell both visiting Jews and curious Gentiles *where* the nearest synagogue was. In relation to Acts 15:21 it would seem that James was specifically pointing to those Jewish town criers in referring to 'those who preach him'. This is a far cry from just mentioning Moses as where James got the rules from. It reveals that James was specifically expressing that a Gentile wouldn't have any problem finding out where the Law was read, in whatever city he found himself in.[497]

---

[494] Ibid.

[495] Ibid.

[496] Ibid., p. 695.

[497] Ibid., p. 702. The fact that these preachers spoke in the streets about where Moses was read (i.e. the synagogue), is further brought out by *TDNT* in a passage that has a rabbi drawing a crowd to him and then directing them to the Law (to the synagogue), to find out about life.

Rabbi Alexander said, 'Who desires Life?! Who desires Life?!' Then the whole world gathered round him and said, 'Give us life!' Then he spoke to them Psalm 34:12: 'Who is the man who desires life…? Keep your tongue from evil, etc., avoid evil and do good, etc. Perhaps someone will say, I have kept my tongue from evil and my lips from deceitful speech, I will now give myself to sleep, but it then says, 'Avoid evil and do good' and by good is meant the knowledge of the Law, for it is said in Prov. 4:2, 'For I gave you good doctrine, do not disregard My direction' (instruction; Law). In other words, he was directing them to the synagogues to learn the Law, just as James was doing.

The Preachers of Moses were those Jewish officials who publicly went about declaring the news of the synagogue to the Jewish community. James specifically mentions them as those who are in 'every city' to show us that the Gentile believers wouldn't have any problem finding out the place and times of the synagogue meetings.

Acts 15:21 reveals what Yakov and the believing Jewish community had seen over the past eight to ten years concerning the Gentile. They had been going to the synagogues to learn about Messiah and the Law of Moses. It also presents that James assumed that future Gentile believers would also go to the synagogue to learn about Yeshua and the commandments. This means that Gentiles should still be learning Torah. This way they'll be able to walk in *all* the ways that are pleasing to Yeshua.[498]

Should the Gentile go to the traditional Jewish synagogue today?[499] Perhaps but the reason why Yakov directed them to the synagogue was to learn the Law of Moses. Today everyone has a Bible and can learn to walk in all the laws that apply to them. This is the essence of the verse.

James was concerned about the Gentile. Not being raised in the Law, the Gentile literally wouldn't know Adam from Eve, and certainly would be ignorant of many of God's specific rules on how to live a righteous life. Yakov wanted them to come to maturity in Messiah. How could they do that without the Word of God (the 'Old Testament; 2nd Tim. 3:14-17)? And *nothing* of the New Testament was even written when Acts 15 took place. Paul hadn't written any letters yet and the Gospels hadn't been written, etc.

In the days of Yakov, Peter and Paul, what Gentile would have had access to a Torah scroll? But we all have Bibles today and yes, Jewish and Christian Bibles are the same. The basic difference is that some of the books are

---

[498] Some might say that Acts 15:21 is not mentioned in the actual letter (vv. 15:22-32) but the Council sent two prophets (Acts 15:32) Judah and Silas, to relate by word of mouth (v. 27) *all* that was spoken of at the Council to the believers in Antioch. It's highly unlikely that they forgot to relate the essence of v. 21.

[499] With 2,000 years of Christian anti-Semitism and Jewish apologetics behind the Rabbis concerning Messiah Yeshua, the Synagogue today is extremely hostile and anti-Yeshua. Judaism has also taken into itself spirits of witchcraft in the form of Kabbalah. The important thing to ascertain from Yakov's admonition to the Gentile about going to the synagogue is that the Gentile is to learn the Torah the way Yeshua walked it out, and the way He desires for us to walk it out. There's a vast difference between learning and living Torah with Yeshua's Spirit, and learning about Judaism. One is a divine Treasure; the other can be a very deep and dangerous pit.

arranged in a different order but they're all there. The words in an English Christian 'Old Testament' are basically the same words that an English speaking Jew finds in his Tanach.[500]

Today believers can read the first five books of Moses (and the rest of the Tanach or Old Testament), asking the Spirit of Yeshua to open their eyes as to what God wants them to see and to walk in. There are many believing house assemblies and congregations rising up that keep the Sabbath and the Feast days, etc. One can learn many things there. It will give Gentile and Jewish believers a foundation from which to springboard off of. More on understanding the implications of this in the section *Reality Ramifications.*

---

[500] Jewish translators of the Hebrew Tanach into English steer around prophecies of the Messiah that directly point to Yeshua. At these places they may alter some words so the Jewish person won't be able to make a connection to Jesus. This is where their belief system 'takes over.' One place where this happens is Isaiah's virgin who would conceive the Messiah (Is. 7:14). It's dealt with under Jewish Newsletters: *Recognize This Man?* at http://www.seedofabraham.net/nltr23.html. Another Scripture is Ps. 22:16 which speaks of Messiah's hands and feet being pierced. It's addressed in the same section under *Lion Hands* at http://www.seedofabraham.net/nltr25.html. Aside from textual changes like these, the vast majority of the texts are identical in meaning, if not in actual word.

Someone might say that this is unfair and they'd be right. But this also happens with Christian translations of Greek New Testament texts that specifically point out the Law's validity. One such place is Heb. 4:9. Both the Textus Receptus and the Majority Text have the exact same words for the verse. The KJV and the NKJV speak of a 'rest' that remains for the people of God. The NASB and the NRSV, as well as others, correctly speak of 'a *Sabbath* rest' that remains for the people of God. The Greek word is sabbatismos, a technical term found in ancient literature for Sabbath observance.

Samuele Bacchiochi, in *The New Testament Sabbath* (Gillette, WY: *The Sabbath Sentinel* magazine, 1987), says that the writer of Hebrews is teaching that a '*Sabbath keeping* is left behind for the people of God.' The Greek word sabbatismos is found in 'Plutarch, *De Superstitione* 3 (Moralia 166A); Justin Martyr, *Dialogue With Trypho* 23, 3; Epiphanius, *Adversus Haereses* 30, 2, 2; *Apostolic Constitutions* 2, 36, 7.' And Andrew Lincoln admits that 'in each of these places the term denotes the *observance or celebration of the Sabbath.* This usage corresponds to the Septuagint usage of the cognate verb *sabbatizo* (cf. Exodus 16:30; Leviticus 23:32; 26:34f; 2nd Chronicles 36:21), which also has reference to *Sabbath observance.*'

All these speak of a literal Sabbath observance for New Testament believers and shouldn't be lightly brushed aside by saying that the text is only speaking 'spiritually.'

Acts 21:25 — Observe No Such Thing!

Acts 21:25 is the third and last place where the four rules appear. The KJV states that the Gentiles should 'observe no such thing'. There are two possible Hebraic interpretations of what James meant, and neither one of them negates the Law for the Gentile. The first interpretation is that the Nazarite Vow wasn't to be taken by a Gentile. The second is that the Gentile wasn't to be circumcised.

There are also two different English translations for the verse due to the two different Greek texts. Only the Textus Receptus (KJV, NKJV) has the phrase, *observe no such thing*. Without getting into which Greek text might be the one that Luke actually wrote, we'll deal with both of them.

First, the two texts will be written out, then a comment about the New American Standard Bible which doesn't have the phrase. After that the KJV translation will be flushed out because it seems to point to the Law's demise. These two Bibles reflect the differences in the Greek texts. The meaningful differences of the KJV are placed in *italics*:[501]

> NASB — Acts 21:25: 'But concerning the Gentiles who have believed, we wrote, having decided that they should abstain from meat sacrificed to idols and from blood and from what is strangled and from fornication.'

> KJV — Acts 21:25: 'As touching the Gentiles which believe, we have written and concluded that they *observe no such thing, save only* that they keep themselves from things offered to idols, and from blood, and from strangled, and from fornication.'

The NASB doesn't have the Greek phrase 'observe no such thing, save only' that the KJV (and basically the NKJV) has. The New Revised Standard Version reads much like the NASB and makes it very plain that

---

[501] The New American Standard Bible and the New Revised Standard Version use the 1881 Westcott-Hort Greek version of the New Testament. This has been revised and updated as the Greek New Testament, United Bible Societies' Third Corrected Edition, 1983 (Brown, *NGEINT*, p. iv; page number not printed). Page vii (also without Roman numerals) says this Greek text 'represents the best in modern textual scholarship.' Textual criticism determines what words were originally in the text and what were added or left out. This is important for Acts 21:25. The Textus Receptus, which the KJV and the NKJV rely on, differs for the verse in question from the UBS Greek text. It's worth reading *ISBE*'s section on the *History of Textual Criticism*, pp. 820-821 (Bromiley, *ISBE*, vol. four, 1979) to get an understanding of the two major Greek texts, and also pp. 814-820 to find out about the different Greek manuscripts and why some are considered more valuable than others.

there was a letter sent. This will figure into the proper understanding of the verse:

> NRSV—Acts 21:25: 'But as for the Gentiles who have become believers, *we have sent a letter* with our judgment that they should abstain from what has been sacrificed to idols and from blood and from what is strangled and from fornication.'

In both the NASB and the NRSV there's no phrase that seems to be saying the Gentiles have only four rules (save only). James is just reiterating the decision of Acts 15:20. There's nothing in the verse that lends itself to coming against a Torah lifestyle in the United Bible Societies' text.

With the KJV's 'observe no such thing, save only' the term *save only* seems to be saying that the four rules are the only rules that a Gentile has to keep.[502] The problem with this is the translation of the Greek phrase. It doesn't mean *save only*. It means *except* or *but*. The Greek words translated as save only are ει μη (ae may). Walter Bauer says it means *except, if not* or *but*.[503] Placing *if not* into the sentence doesn't make any sense,

> 'that they should observe no such thing, *if not* that they keep themselves from things offered to idols'.

Placing *except* within the verse, it reads like this,

> 'As touching the Gentiles which believe, we have written and concluded that they observe no such thing, *except* that they keep themselves from things offered to idols, and from blood, and from strangled, and from fornication.' (Acts 21:25)

Both the Greek *Interlinear* translation (for the Textus Receptus) of the Greek phrase[504] and the New King James Version use *except* in their translation of v. 25. Using *except* changes the tone of the verse from 'these are the *only* commandments a Gentile needs to do' to 'even though the Gentile can't observe *this* (observe no such thing v. 25), they can and should do the four rules.' That's a major shift in thinking from the Gentiles having only four rules.

Placing *but* within the statement further drives home the point that James

---

[502] Be that as it may, how many Christians keep the four rules or know anything about them, even as the Church interprets them?

[503] Bauer, *GELNT*, p. 220. Also Perschbacher, *NAGL*, p. 119.

[504] George Ricker Berry, Editor and Translator, *Interlinear Greek-English New Testament* (Grand Rapids, MI: Baker Book House, 2000), p. 380, Acts 25:10.

wasn't speaking of only four rules. He was reiterating what the Gentiles could do in relation to what he had just previously said to Paul:

> 'As touching the Gentiles which believe, we have written and concluded that they observe no such thing, *but* that they keep themselves from things offered to idols, and from blood, and from strangled, and from fornication.' (Acts 21:25)

Inserting *but* presents a different thought than *save only*. It seems that James wanted the Gentiles to know that even though they couldn't do whatever it was that he was speaking about before (observe no such thing) they could keep the four rules.

As for the longer phrase, that they *observe no such thing*, Bruce uses this phrase as a place to come against the Law. He writes,

> 'The elders added the assurance that they had no thought of going back on the terms of the apostolic decree, and imposing legal requirements on Gentile believers. So far as they were concerned, said the elders, all that was required of them was that they should abstain from eating flesh that had been sacrificed' etc. 'As for the Gentile believers, of course, we have already agreed that nothing is to be imposed on them apart from the abstentions detailed in the apostolic letter.'[505]

Bruce is certain that no other legal requirements (i.e. the Law), were necessary for the Gentile. *All* 'that was required of them' was that they keep just these four rules. Marshall takes a similar position:

> 'the fact that Paul was being asked to behave in this way in no sense implied that similar demands would be made of the Gentiles. The *fundamental freedom of the Gentiles from the law* had been established at the meeting described in chapter 15 whose decision is now reaffirmed. It seems strange that the Jerusalem decree should be repeated verbatim (cf. 15:20, 29) to Paul who was well aware of its contents.'[506]

Paul was entering into a Nazarite Vow but according to Marshall, Bruce insists that Paul couldn't have taken the Vow because it lasts for at least 30 days. Bruce thinks the vow of the four men was going to be complete

---

[505] Bruce, *The Book of the Acts*, p. 407.

[506] Marshall, *Acts*, p. 346.

in seven days.[507] He suggests that the four men had contacted some 'ritual uncleanness during their vow' and that Paul was going to pay for those

---

[507] Ibid., p. 345 note 1. Bruce is on the right track but heading in the wrong direction. Perhaps the controversy and enigma over what Paul entered into with those four Jewish men (Acts 21:23-24) would be solved by suggesting that the seven day purification rite (Acts 21:26-27) was just that; a seven day period that one had to walk in before they were able to actually enter into the 30, 60 or 100 day Nazarite Vow. In other words it was a preliminary purification or cleansing rite one did before they took the Nazarite Vow.

Acts 21:26-27 speaks of 'days of purification' not 'days of separation' as it does for the Vow in Num. 6:2, 4, 6, 8, 12, 13, 21 twice, with vv. 18-19 speaking of the consecrated or set apart head or hair (NKJV). One can only speculate as to why no information on a preliminary purification rite exists but the fact is that there's no record of a seven day Nazarite Vow either. A seven day purification rite, before taking the Nazarite Vow, is most likely what Paul entered into with the four men.

Another possibility is that it may have been a special time of purification for Jewish men coming from *outside* the land of Israel (Judah and Galilee). This would deal with their perceived uncleanness of being amongst the idolatrous Gentiles. But with more Jews living outside the land of Israel than inside, and many hundreds of thousands coming to Israel for each of the three annual holy Feasts (Passover, Pentecost, and Tabernacles), it would seem far too long a time for pilgrims to have to prepare for the Feast (as well as the sheer numbers of it making it an impossible practice).

If this was a seven day rite of purification that Paul initially embarked on, as it seems (Acts 21:26-27), both the concept and the sacrifice(s) that would have been offered for him and each of the four men at the end of their purification (Acts 21:24, 26), may have come from the Torah dealing with the Nazarite becoming defiled (Num. 6:9-12). A Nazarite became defiled when someone suddenly died in their presence (Num. 6:9). He would have to shave his hair 'on the seventh day' (Num. 6:9; Acts 21:24, 27) and on the eighth day, bring either two turtledoves or two young pigeons to the priest as a sin sacrifice and a burnt sacrifice (Num. 6:10-11), as well as a lamb for a guilt offering (Num. 6:12). Then he would begin his Vow anew. Here is not only a seven day time of purification from uncleanness (Num. 6:9; Acts 21:26-27) but also the shaving of the hair of the head on the seventh day, spoken of as the day of his cleansing (Num. 6:9; in Acts 21:24, 26, purified; NKJV). And with the sacrifices on the eighth day, the man's head became sanctified again (Num. 6:11, 18-19) and able to begin the Nazarite Vow afresh (or in the case of the four men and Paul, to begin it).

This seven day ritual of purification may very well have been adapted in Paul's day for any Jew wanting to take the Nazarite Vow. This understanding in no way alters a central point of Acts 21. Paul was entering into (the preliminary stage of) a Nazarite Vow (the shaving of the hair, Num. 6:9; Acts 21:24). And he would have offered sacrifice for both himself, and paid for the sacrifices of the others (Num. 6:10-12; Acts 21:24, 26) to show everyone that he still walked orderly and *kept the Law of Moses* (Acts 21:24) as a Christian.

expenses. But as I. Howard Marshall counters,

> 'Bruce apparently assumes that Paul could share in the
> rite although he had not shared in the defilement. This
> view does not explain the preliminary visit to the temple
> for' (Paul's) 'purification in verse 26.'[508]

Good point! Why would Paul need to be purified with them if he weren't
defiled or taking the Vow? If he were just paying the expenses for their
purification, he wouldn't need to be purified (note the past tense in Acts
24:18). Of course, even if Paul wasn't taking the Vow, he would still be
seen *supporting the Law and sacrifice* as the men were deeply involved in
both. If Paul thought the Law and sacrifice were done away with, his com-
pliance with the suggestion, to pay for the men and their sacrifices and be
purified with them, would certainly seem to have gone against his conscience, unless he didn't think the Law had ceased for believers.

If Paul didn't think that the Law was done away with, this would have
been a perfect place to have a showdown. Wouldn't it have been much
better for Paul to tell the truth to James and all the Jewish believers, that
Jesus had done away with the need for such things? If Jesus wants believers to walk in His Truth[509] and the *Jewish believers were walking in false-
hood about the Law*, why wouldn't Paul address the issue here in Acts
21:20-26? Paul wasn't shy when it came to standing up against Peter in
Antioch when he thought Peter was wrong (Gal. 2:11).

Most people today don't see Peter as Paul's equal, but in his day, Peter
was the *chief* Apostle and recognized as such by all the believers in
Jerusalem and beyond. Paul had enough fortitude with Peter in Antioch,
why not with James in Jerusalem if he thought the Law was wrong?

The men were under a Nazarite Vow as no other vow included the shaving
of the head (Num. 6:18; Acts 21:24). Although Marshall lines up with
Bruce in the 'only four and no more Camp' he says that for Paul to take
the Nazarite Vow was not out of line. *He sees Paul as having kept the
Law*. In relation to the Vow he states,

> 'Paul's action would make it clear that *he lived in obser-
> vance of the law*, but many scholars have doubted
> whether the historical Paul would have agreed to this pro-
> posal.'[510]

---

[508] Marshall, *Acts*, p. 345.

[509] Jn. 14:6; 15:26; Rom. 1:18; Eph. 4:24; 2nd Tim. 2:15; Heb. 10:26; 2nd Peter
1:2; 1st Jn. 1:6; 4:6; 5:6.

It seems very strange for Marshall to speak of a Law-free Gospel, base it on Paul's writings, and then turn around and say that Paul kept the Law. Be that as it may, many scholars disagree with 'the Paul' presented in Acts 15 and 21 saying *their* Paul would never have allowed or done such things. But the authority of James, the integrity of Luke, and the inspiration of the Holy Spirit stand behind the facts of Acts: the historical Paul kept the Law and he gave the four rules 'to his Gentiles.' He also took the Nazarite Vow which meant that he was going to offer *animal sacrifices* to God in the Temple at Jerusalem *about 25 years after the Resurrection.*

Many are shocked when they learn that Paul took a Nazarite Vow because of Church teaching against the Law. The observance of the Vow meant the sacrificing of three animals for each man (Num. 6:14-21). Paul would pay for all the sacrifices, both for him and the four men (Acts 21:23-24) at the conclusion of the purification rite, and the Vow.

Wycliffe also believes that Acts 15 meant the Gentiles were 'free from the Law' but should only keep the four rules so that no offense would be given to the Jewish believers. They say the four rules in Acts 21 were meant to emphasize that.[511]

Williams also states, 'it's clearly understood that what Paul was being asked to do had no implications for the Gentile believers.'[512] He says that,

> 'no legal requirement was to be laid upon the Gentiles as
> necessary for salvation'.

As true as that is, he then says that *only* the four rules would be required of them.[513] He too writes that it's odd and out of place that James would repeat the four rules verbatim, but says it may have been for those present with Paul, or a literary device of Luke's.

Knowling cuts to the heart of the problem by saying the Gentiles were 'on a different footing' than 'the born Jews who became Christians'[514] in that *they couldn't observe something* the Jews could. He says the repetition of the rules was James restating his commitment to the Decree, and that he expected Paul to show that he had 'no desire to disparage the law'.[515]

---

[510] Ibid., pp. 345-346.

[511] Pfeiffer, *WBC*, p. 1165.

[512] Williams, *Acts*, p. 366.

[513] Ibid.

[514] Knowling, *The Acts of the Apostles*, p. 450.

[515] Ibid., p. 451.

Stern rightly says the accusation against Paul (Acts 21:21) was a baseless lie. Paul was accused of teaching Jews *not* to circumcise their sons, and to stop observing the Law. Obviously, others were misinterpreting Paul's letters too. Stern offers three points to refute it. One, Paul kept the Law; he circumcised Timothy (16:3), observed the Feasts (20:16), says that he believed in the Law (24:14), and that 'he had committed no offense against the Law' (25:8). At the end of his life he stated that he had done nothing to offend the Jewish people or the Traditions of the Fathers (28:17).[516]

Two, Stern explains that Paul's teaching of the Gentiles not to observe Jewish Law was never given to the Jewish believers (1st Cor. 7:18; Gal. 5:2-6, etc.).[517] Here Stern wrongly sees that the Gentile was subject to a Law-free Gospel. Ah! Too bad for the Jew! He can't eat pork and must keep the Sabbath day holy but the Gentile can eat a ham sandwich on the Sabbath day while mowing his lawn.

Is this really what Grace is all about? Stern creates two totally different Flocks for the Shepherd who came to make both flocks one (Jn. 10:16). Shouldn't God's holy Instruction apply to every believer? Except for circumcision, Paul makes no distinction in his writings (Rom. 3:31; 7:7, 12, 14; 1st Cor. 7:17-19; 2nd Tim. 3:16-17). And the Apostles (Yakov in James 2:8-12; 4:11-12; John in Rev. 14:12, etc.), as well as the Lord Himself (Mt. 5:19) don't seem to differentiate between Jew and Gentile either. In other words, aside from circumcision, the Gentile and the Jew should observe the same laws. There's no section in Paul's writings that are just for Jews and another that's just for Gentiles in terms of *different* rules. If the Jews were keeping the Law and the Gentiles didn't have to, there'd seem to be a need for different sections addressed to each group.

With point three Stern presents the overlooked fact that the New Testament doesn't need to repeat *truths already evident* from the Old Testament. 'It assumes them' and so did Paul.[518] This is an excellent point. Just like a sequel to a good book, the New doesn't have to list all the laws of Moses in order for them to be valid. Many Christians though, think the New is 'completely different than the Old' and if it's not specifically stated in the New it doesn't apply to them.[519] But being grafted into Israel

---

[516] Stern, *JNTC*, p. 303.

[517] Ibid.

[518] Ibid.

[519] Witness the conservative branch of the denomination called The Church of Christ that won't have any musical instruments in their church because it isn't specifically mentioned in the New Testament.

(Rom. 11) means that the Gentile was meant to learn about his new Family history and *their* way of living (Torah, Prophets, Writings and New Covenant). The New Covenant wasn't made with the Gentile, but only with the House of Judah and the House of Israel (Jer. 31:31-34).

Stern believes that Paul's keeping of the Law was affirmed in Acts 21:24 with Paul's subsequent obedience to Yakov's suggestion of taking the Vow (v. 26).[520] Those that don't want to see this tacitly proclaim Luke to be a liar. As there's no indication that Luke was a liar, the text plainly reveals that the Apostle Paul kept the Law...as a Christian.

Stern writes that Mishna *Nazir* (Nazarite) says the time of the Nazarite Vow was 'one to three months in length.' And that,

> 'clearly, the four men were poor; otherwise they could
> have bought their own sacrificial animals and gifts.' Paul
> 'as patron must do more than merely pay the expenses; he
> too must be accepted by the cohanim' (priests of the Tem-
> ple) 'and be *ritually purified.*'[521]

As patron and participant[522] Paul was in agreement that both the Nazarite Vow and therefore sacrifice *after* the Resurrection of Jesus were valid. And this was his second Nazarite Vow recorded in Acts.[523] Hegg rightly

---

[520] Stern, *JNTC*, p. 304.

[521] Ibid.

[522] Paul was a participant in the Vow, walking alongside those who had just begun it. According to Acts 21:24 Paul was told to 'take them and *purify yourself* along with them' and in v. 26, 'Paul took the men and the next day, purifying himself along with them, went into the Temple giving notice of the completion of the days of purification until *the sacrifice was offered for each one of them.*' With the purification over, Paul would have begun the Vow with the other men. Williams, *Acts*, p. 366, also believes Paul was under the Vow. Knowling, *The Acts of the Apostles*, pp. 449-450 states that the Greek word 'certainly seems to demand that' Paul 'place himself on a level with the four men and take upon himself the Nazarite vow.' See also Acts 24:18.

[523] Acts 18:18 states, 'Paul, having remained many days longer, took leave of the brethren and put out to sea for Syria and with him were Priscilla and Aquila. In Cenchrea *he had his hair cut, for he was keeping a vow.*' Scholars are perplexed that Paul would do such a thing. Yet Marshall, *Acts*, pp. 344-345, believes it was a Nazarite Vow that Paul took in Acts 18:18, and Williams, *Acts*, pp. 321-322 says it was based on a Nazarite Vow. Stern, *JNTC*, pp. 290-291 doesn't think Paul's vow of Cenchrea was a strict Nazarite Vow saying that it could only be done in Jerusalem. But Williams overcomes Stern's objection by revealing that Josephus (*War* 2.309–314) writes that such a thing was possible. Marshall, *Acts* p. 300 citing Mishnah *Nazir* 3:6; 5:4 says the shaving of the hair for the Nazarite Vow was permissible outside Jerusalem and Israel.

says there were 'no competing values between the death of Yeshua and the offering of sacrifices in the Temple.'[524] With the Jerusalem believers keeping the Law (Acts 21:20), many would sacrifice and take the Nazarite Vow on a regular basis…to honor Jesus.

The Nazarite Vow pictured an especial consecration and devotion to God such as only the High Priest had (Lev. 21:10-11; Num. 6:6-7). And of course anyone taking the Vow was seen to hold *God's Law* in the highest esteem. *This is the reason* why James directed Paul to take the Vow; to prove to all the believers (and providentially to us today), that what they had heard about Paul was a slanderous lie, and that he still walked 'orderly, *keeping the Law*' (Acts 21:24; 1st Cor. 11:1).

The phrase *observe no such thing* doesn't refer to the nullification of the Law but possibly to the Nazarite Vow that Paul was about to take. If the Gentile was to walk in the Law of Moses, why would James tell them not to take the Nazarite Vow? Why shouldn't the Gentile be able to observe the Nazarite Vow and sacrifice?

Theoretically he could have. The Gentile should have been able to keep the Vow and to sacrifice. God ordained it in the days of Moses (Lev. 22:17-19; Num. 15:14-16), but now the Temple was in the hands of a wicked High Priest and Sanhedrin. They were extremely anti-Yeshua.[525] And they wouldn't recognize the believing Gentile as part of the House of Israel. Therefore the Gentile wasn't able to take the Nazarite Vow.

Upon completion of the Vow each person was to sacrifice at the Altar of the Temple three different animals (Num. 6:13-20). This is something the Gentile wouldn't be able to do, but not because sacrifice 'was done away with.' Obviously from this very event, sacrifice was still taking place among all the Jewish believers including James and the Apostles John, Peter and Paul at least twenty-four years after the Resurrection.[526]

The Nazarite Vow is one possibility as to what James meant when he said that the Gentile should *observe no such thing* for he had just directed Paul to take the Vow. The Gentile wasn't able to observe the Vow though. Yet in Yeshua's Kingdom of a thousand years on this Earth in Jerusalem, both

---

[524] Hegg, *The Letter Writer*, p. 289 note 564.

[525] Mt. 26:57-68; 27:1-2, 11-14, 17-20, 39-43, 62-66; 27:11-15; Acts 4:1-22; 5:17-42; 7:1-60; 9:1-2, etc.

[526] Bromiley, *ISBE*, vol. one, p. 692. For the '*Arrest of Paul in Jerusalem*' which takes place in Acts 21:26-36, *ISBE* states it was the year 54 A.D. Unger, *UBD*, pp. 486-488 has 58 A.D. And Douglas, *IBD*, Part 1, p. 281 has 59 A.D. when Paul returned to Jerusalem (which would make it 29 years after Yeshua rose from the dead).

Jew and Gentile will be able to sacrifice in His Temple (Ezk. 45–48; Zech. 14:16-21; Rev. 20:1-10).

In this case *observe no such thing* may point to the Nazarite Vow but certainly not to the dissolution of the Law. This understanding, coupled with the fact that 'save only' should be translated as 'except' or 'but' reveals that James didn't mean the Gentiles had only four rules. The emphasis shifts to the Nazarite Vow that the believing Gentiles *couldn't* observe. James wouldn't have directed them to the synagogue to learn the Law in Acts 15:21, only to reverse himself in 21:25 and not indicate why.

Having said all that, the correct interpretation of what James meant when he said *observe no such thing* refers to the prohibition against Gentile circumcision. The context, and the way the sentence reads, point directly to this.

The first indicator is the slander against Paul (that he was teaching Jews *not to circumcise* their sons; Acts 21:21). That, along with the fact that James says he had *already written a letter* about it, reveals that Gentile circumcision was the subject of what the Gentile shouldn't observe:

> 'As touching the Gentiles which believe, *we have written and concluded* that *they observe no such thing.*' (KJV, 21:25)

Written and concluded refers to the letter of Acts 15:29 that James wrote to the assembly at Antioch and which was circulated in all the believing assemblies or synagogues (Acts 16:4). The letter laid to rest the question of *Gentile circumcision* for salvation. Yakov's phrase, *we have written and concluded* points directly to his decision of Acts 15, that Gentiles weren't to be circumcised.

The slander against Paul was put to an end when he took the Nazarite Vow. It expressly reveals that he still kept the Law (and wanted the Gentiles to also; 1st Cor. 4:16-17), and specifically that circumcision was still required of the Jewish believer and his sons. *Observe no such thing* means that the Gentile believer and his sons *were not* to be circumcised.[527]

---

[527] This is a further refutation of Hegg's position of Gentile circumcision 'for the right reasons' (i.e. that the Gentile knows he's not being circumcised and following the Law in order to be saved; see p. 157 note 403). Yakov is again declaring in 21:25 that Gentiles weren't to be circumcised, period. Acts through Revelation covers a time span of about 70 years (30 A.D. to 100 A.D.). During this time Gentile believers were having many sons, yet there's not a single reference in any letter validating this position. It's hard to believe that an issue of this magnitude could be overlooked by *all* the writers of the New Testament 'if circumcision for the right reason' was a valid theological understand-

As for Yakov repeating the four rules in speaking with Paul, many have thought it out of place.[528] *On the contrary though* this is a most appropriate time for him to reiterate the rules. After having told Paul to take the Vow to declare that *Jewish* circumcision was still intact, James immediately lets us know that circumcision (*still*) didn't apply to the Gentiles but they had to keep the four rules. It was *extremely* appropriate for James to reiterate the four rules. He *clarified what was most incumbent* upon the Gentiles after he had just spoken what they *weren't* to do; circumcision.

The Gentile wasn't to be circumcised in order to become a Jew, and keep the Law for salvation. It's into the Kingdom of Yeshua that we both come and it's only to the Jew that circumcision was given for a sign of the covenant relationship that Father Abraham had with Yahveh, before the Law (Gen. 17:1-14, 23-27).

In a very real sense, we Jews are also adopted into the (new) Family of those who love Messiah, just as the Gentiles are (Acts 15:7-11; Rom. 8:15; Gal. 4:1-5; 6:15). It's by His Blood Sacrifice and His Grace that we enter. That's why Paul and Peter can say that circumcision wasn't necessary for the Gentile believer, but that all must keep the Commandments of God as they apply to them (Rom. 3:20, 31).

On the other hand, wouldn't the continued circumcision of believing Jewish boys create a problem if believing Gentile boys weren't? After all, if both were to keep the Law, how could one group be required to circumcise their sons while the other was forbidden?

One reason why God might not want the Gentile circumcised may be to preserve the racial Seed of Abraham, Isaac and Jacob for His end time purpose: to display His faithful forgiving loving-kindness to Israel after the flesh; to her and to the world (Is. 62:1-12; Rom. 11:25-32).

Another symbolic reason may also lie in the fact that in Israel at any one time, half the population wasn't circumcised...the women. The Gentile, like the believing wife, was to woo her husband (the Jew) to the Lord by her chaste and holy conduct (1st Pet. 3:1-2). God wanted the Gentile believer to be a godly witness to the Jew, to bring the Jew to Messiah (Rom. 10:1, 19; 11:1, 5-14). Would non-circumcision make the Gentile less than the Jew? Of course not (1st Cor. 7:17-19), especially as the Gentile had re-

---

ing. On the contrary though, Paul expressly comes against it when he says if you came uncircumcised, *remain that way* (1st Cor. 7:18; also Gal. 2:3). Gentile 'circumcision for the right reason' was never an option in Apostolic times.

[528] Marshall, *Acts*, p. 346; Williams, *Acts*, pp. 366-367; and Knowling, *The Acts of the Apostles*, p. 450, etc.

ceived the circumcision made without hands (Col. 2:11; Phil. 3:3) which could do to the heart what physical circumcision only symbolized; full surrender and a new heart like Messiah's (Dt. 10:16; 30:6; Ezk. 36:26). Physical circumcision wasn't sufficient to change the Adamic nature. It didn't matter spiritually if one were circumcised or not, only racially.

The wife was created to be the helpmate of the husband (Gen. 2:20-23). She was on equal footing with the husband as a human being before God They were *one* (Gen. 2:24; Mt. 19:6; Eph. 2:13-16). But she was *different* from her husband. Yet obviously the Jewish woman was still part of covenant Israel and required to keep the laws of Moses that applied to her.

Yeshua said He had *another* Flock and that the two would become one Flock (Jn. 10:16). Here's another possible hint of a 'marriage union' with the Gentile taking the place of the wife, to woo her husband to Messiah Yeshua by her prayers and holy conduct. It's happening today.

Observe no such thing refers not to the Nazarite Vow, and still less to the Law, but to Yakov's decision that the Gentile wasn't to be circumcised. It fits well with Paul being accused of teaching Jews not to circumcise their sons, and James saying that they had written and concluded something (the decision of Acts 15).

With the four rules being mentioned, it also reveals exactly what James was referring to. In other words, if the four rules hadn't been reiterated, some scholars would have said that there were *other* things 'written and concluded' that Luke didn't mention. It would have opened up endless speculation and further strange interpretations. Thank God that James reiterated the four rules!

Observe no such thing can't be used to teach that James gave *only* four rules to the Gentiles, or that they didn't have to keep the Law. On the contrary, James was making sure that everyone knew that Paul still kept the Law, and by extension, everyone else. He reemphasized the four rules of Acts 15 to make sure that the Gentiles knew what they *could* implement, in relation to what they *couldn't* do: circumcision.

Observe no such thing first focused on the Nazarite Vow to point out that sacrifices were still in effect for all the Apostles, 25 years after the Resurrection and theoretically, for the Gentile believer also. Just from this perspective of the Nazarite Vow, the the Law of Moses is confirmed for every believer today.[529]

---

[529] For more on why the sacrifices of Moses are still theologically in effect, see *Sacrifice in the New Testament* at http://www.seedofabraham.net/ntsac.html.

Acts 15:20, 29; 21:25 — Switched Rules

A brief profile of the three passages where the four rules are seen is both insightful and enigmatic. Insightful in that it also confirms blood as sacrificial blood that is drunk.[530] Enigmatic in that the order of the four rules changes after initially being spoken by Yakov in Acts 15:20.

Number two, cult prostitution and number four, blood, trade places after the ruling is first declared by Yakov in Acts 15:20:

Acts 15:20: 'but to write to them'

1. 'to keep away from the pollutions of idols'
2. 'and of cult prostitution'
3. 'and of things strangled'
4. 'and of blood.'

Acts 15:29:

1. 'to keep away from meat sacrificed to idols'
2. 'and blood'
3. 'and strangled things'
4. 'and cult prostitution, from which keeping yourselves you will do well. Goodbye.'

Acts 21:25: 'And concerning the Gentiles having believed, we wrote, having decided (that) they avoid *both*'[531]

1. 'the meat offered to idols'
2. 'and blood'
3. 'and strangled' (things)
4. 'and cult prostitution.'[532]

The word changes for the first rule in Acts 15:20 to a different Greek word in the letter of 15:29 and is reiterated in 21:25. The change emphasizes the point that it isn't just any food sacrificed or given to idols but that it's the sacrifice of animal flesh.[533]

---

[530] Eating blood at any time is sin. The differentiation here is between blood that would literally be drunk at a pagan sacrifice (idolatry), and that which is found in a rare hamburger or steak, etc. (a dietary regulation).

[531] The King James Version does not have the word *both*. It's not found in the Textus Receptus (which is the basis for the KJV).

[532] Brown, *NGEINT*, pp. 472-473, 499. The three passages have 'cult prostitution' instead of the innocuous 'sexual immorality.'

Any food (grain, vegetables, fruit, etc.) could be given or 'offered' to an idol (or a pagan priest as the idol's representative). The Greek word for 15:20's first rule could theoretically encompass those non-animal foods. But the Greek word for the first rule in Acts 15:29 and 21:25[534] specifically means *animals* sacrificed to idols. Yakov was speaking of a major idolatrous rite and not the mere giving of grain, fruit or baked goods by the offerer to a priest.

In the original order listed (Acts 15:20) number two (cult prostitution) and number four (blood) are switched in the letter of Acts 15:29 and when it's reiterated in Acts 21:25. Why does this happen? After Yakov declared it in Acts 15:20, he seemed to realize that a more natural order for it would be the way it was enacted in a pagan ritual. He placed the blood that would be drunk at a pagan sacrifice, immediately after the animal was sacrificed to the pagan god. It's the order of a pagan ceremony:

1. sacrifice the animal,

2. drink its blood and later, after it's roasted,

3. eat the meat of the sacrifice,

4. and 'worship' the god or goddess through the cult prostitutes.

The Greek word for *both* in Acts 21:25 is το (toe). It means both[535] in the sense that it,

> 'connects' 'clauses, thereby indicating a close relationship betw. them.'[536]

Yakov saw the close relationship or order of events between the animal sacrificed and its blood being drunk and wrote the letter and reiterated it accordingly. Yakov said to 'avoid *both*' the sacrificial meat *and* its blood. This excludes blood from meaning murder or blood in rare roast beef or

---

[533] Bruce, *The Book of the Acts*, pp. 299-300. A report by Eusebius, *HE* 5.1.26 reveals that later Christians understood blood in Acts 15:20 (15:29; 21:25) to refer to that which was drunk (rather than blood in rare meat, or not properly drained, or murder). It states that the martyrs Vienne and Lyon protested their accusation by saying 'How could Christians eat children when they are not allowed even to drink the blood of brute beasts?'

[534] In English the wording for the first rule in both Acts 15:29 and 21:25 is different but the Greek word is the same. It stresses that it's an animal sacrificed to idols with the meat being eaten *at the time of the pagan ceremony*. See Witherington, p. 20 above.

[535] Perschbacher, *NAGL*, p. 403.

[536] Bauer, *GELNT*, p. 807.

even blood within the meat of the sacrificial animal sold at the market-place. The term *blood* is intricately connected to rule one on sacrificial idolatry and speaks of the idolater drinking it after the animal was sacrificed.

Yakov could further be assuring believers of the idolatrous nature of the Decree by taking the two chief rules (animals sacrificed to idols and cult prostitution) and making them 'bookends.' This would *enclose* the 'lesser two' of the four rules, displaying all of them as a package deal or unit on sacrificial-sexual idolatry.

Switched Rules emphasizes that the four rules of Yakov are a conceptual unit on sacrificial-sexual idolatry. James seems to have switched rules two and four to portray the conceptual nature of the rules by showing their natural order in a sacrificial ceremony.

This new order also allows for the two most blatant sacrificial-sexual rules of the four, to enclose the other two, thereby ensuring that everyone would understand that the rules dealt with sacrificial-sexual idolatry. And with Yakov using *both*, the sacrificial blood that would be drunk is intimately tied into the animal that was just sacrificed.

This four rules of Yakov deal with sacrificial-sexual idolatry, not dietary regulations. They were given so the Gentile would immediately come to see the path he had to take in order for his faith in Jesus to be seen as genuine. The four rules weren't given for table fellowship between the Jewish and Gentile believers.

YAKOV'S CONCERN

Most theologians see the four rules of Acts 15:20 as taken from the Law of Moses with at least two rules being of a non-moral character (strangled and blood).[537] Others see the rules coming from the Noahide Laws. Both groups think the rules were given for table fellowship so the Gentile wouldn't offend his Jewish counterpart who was 'still attached to the Law.' The interpretation of table fellowship will be discussed first, then the Noahide people and then Yakov's concern: sacrificial-sexual idolatry.

Table Fellowship

Scholars center their interpretation of Acts 15:20 around table fellowship even though it presents a theological dilemma for them. They have to acknowledge that the rules come from the Law of Moses[538] and that some are 'just ceremonial.' This is justified by saying that it was to assuage the sensitivities of the Jewish believers who still walked in Torah.

Various Interpretations of the Rules: Acts 15:20, 29; 21:25

1. The First Rule: Pollutions of Idols

    1. meat sacrificed to idols and eaten at the sacrifice with the remains sold in the marketplace.[539]

    2. meat sacrificed to idols and eaten only at the cult sacrifice.[540]

2. The Second Rule: Pornay'ah

    1. sexual immorality[541]

    2. unchastity[542]

---

[537] Williams, *Acts*, p. 266. The Decree touches 'on both the ethical and ceremonial aspects of the law.'

[538] Marshall, *Acts*, p. 243: 'fellowship at table with Gentiles'. Williams, *Acts*, p. 266: so the Gentile and Jew could 'live in harmony with one another.' It'd be impossible for the Jew to 'have any dealing with the Gentile believers unless the latter observed these basic requirements.' Pfeiffer, *WBC*, p. 1152: 'fellowship between Jew and Gentile.'

[539] Bauer, *GELNT*, p. 221. Perschbacher, *NAGL*, p. 118. Friberg, *ALGNT*, p. 130. Marshall, *Acts*, p. 253. Bruce, *The Book of the Acts*, p. 295. *Wycliffe*, p.1152. Williams, *Acts*, p. 267. Stern, *JNTC*, p. 277.

[540] Witherington, *The Acts of the Apostles*, pp. 461-463.

[541] Brown, *NGEINT*, p. 472. Stern, JNTC, p. 277, and any other form of illicit sex including temple prostitution.

3. adultery[543]

4. fornication[544]

5. the prohibited marriages of Lev. 18:6-18[545]

6. cult prostitution.[546]

3. The Third Rule: Things Strangled

1. proper animal slaughter and the draining of the blood based on Lev. 17.[547]

2. prohibition against eating flesh with the blood still in it. Based on the 'Noachian decree of Gen. 9:4.'[548]

3. a pagan sacrifice that was strangled.[549]

4. The Fourth Rule: Blood

1. murder[550]

2. the eating of meat with blood in it[551]

3. the drinking of raw blood from a pagan sacrifice.[552]

---

[542] Marshall, *Acts*, p. 253. Unchastity, illicit sex or breaches of the Jewish marriage law.

[543] Unger, *UBD*, p. 378. Brown, *CED*, p. 602.

[544] KJV. Brown, *NGEINT*, p. 472; the NRSV margin translation has fornication.

[545] Marshall, *Acts*, p. 253. Bruce, *The Book of the Acts*, p. 295. Williams, *Acts*, p. 266. Williams also suggests idolatry 'may have been' 'intended' as 'idolatry often involved immorality'.

[546] Knowling, *The Acts of the Apostles*, pp. 324-325. Bivin, *Understanding the Difficult Words of Jesus*, p. 109: 'cult prostitutes.' Witherington, *The Acts of the Apostles*, pp. 463-464. Hegg, *The Letter Writer*, p. 279. Pfeiffer, *WBC*, p. 1152. *Wycliffe* lists it as a possibility along with 'illicit intercourse.'

[547] Friberg, *ALGNT*, p. 319. Bauer, *GELNT*, p. 680. Marshall, *Acts*, p. 253. Williams, *Acts*, p. 266. Pfeiffer, *WBC*, p. 1152. Stern, *JNTC*, p. 277. Hegg, *The Letter Writer*, p. 277.

[548] Bruce, *The Book of the Acts*, p. 296.

[549] Witherington, *The Acts of the Apostles*, p. 464. Hegg, *The Letter Writer*, p. 277.

[550] Stern, *JNTC*, p. 277. He also lists as possibilities, 'drinking animals' blood 'or failing to remove it from meat'. Witherington, *The Acts of the Apostles*, p. 464 note 426 lists this also as a second possibility.

[551] Marshall, *Acts*, pp. 243, 253. Bruce, *The Book of the Acts*, pp. 295-296. He says it comes from the Noahide Decree. Williams, *Acts*, p. 266. Knowling, *The Acts of the Apostles*, p. 325. Pfeiffer, *WBC*, p. 1152.

Most everyone correctly understands the first rule (although some add that it was to be avoided at the market, which Yakov didn't mean). Pornay'ah (#2) wasn't seen as cult harlotry and therefore rules three and four were assigned to food regulations.[553] The interpretation of the rules in this manner allowed theologians to present them as 'table fellowship' and continue to teach that the Law wasn't valid any longer.

If blood (#4) related to table fellowship (the prohibition against eating it in meat), then Yakov should have said which animal meat could be eaten and which couldn't, so as not to offend the Jewish believer. After all, this was supposedly the purpose of the rules. Eating pig would definitely offend a Jew. But no reference is ever made to which animals could be eaten.

In other words, if Yakov was getting that specific, in blood not being found within meat one was eating (a dietary regulation), and that the animal should be properly slaughtered and drained of its blood (i.e. not strangled #3), he clearly fails to tell the Gentile which animals were acceptable meat to eat and which weren't. Theoretically the situation arises that the Gentile could have butchered a pig according to acceptable slaughter practices by slitting the throat and draining the blood and then roasting it till it was 'well done.' But can you imagine a Gentile believer sitting down with his Jewish friend and offering him some hot pork chops? Great way to start a conversation!

It also begs the question that the pig is not the only meat or food that is forbidden by God that would obviously offend every Jew at the table. What if the Gentile were to offer shrimp? It doesn't have any blood or need to be slaughtered properly. God forbids this creature along with dogs, cats, ponies, catfish, squid and shark, etc. (see Lev. 11; Dt. 14).

Yakov never addresses this in either Acts 15 or Acts 21 or any other place. No foods are ever mentioned that might offend a Jew. This is why blood can't relate to dietary regulations of the Law (meat they might get from the market that wasn't properly drained of its blood). And this is why 'table fellowship' is an extremely poor interpretation of the rules. Blood must be seen as the pagan ritual of drinking it for pagan communion. So the very idea that the rules were given so as not to offend the Jews boomerangs right back into the faces of those who declare them to be for 'Jewish sensitivities.' Witherington sees this:

> 'The rules that James offers' he says, 'are *much too limit-*

---

[552] Witherington, *The Acts of the Apostles*, p. 464. Hegg, *The Letter Writer*, p. 276, also note 586.

[553] Knowling, *The Acts of the Apostles*, pp. 324-325. Marshall, *Acts*, p. 253.

ed to regulate matters of table fellowship, for, as Wilson says, "they do not even guarantee that no forbidden meat or wine (for example, pork or wine from libations) is used."'[554]

One might argue that the Gentiles would learn about the forbidden creatures as they went to the synagogue and heard the Law read (Acts 15:21). This too misses the point. Aside from most theologians shying away from having the Gentiles go to the synagogue in the first place, it might take six months or longer for the Gentile to even hear Lev. 11 or Dt. 14 read, to understand the dietary laws. It's not as though the Gentiles had their own Bibles and could read it whenever they wanted to. That's why the Gentile was going to the synagogue in the first place; to hear the Word of God and to learn the laws that applied to him.

But if the Gentile didn't hear about the dietary laws for six months, did it mean that he wasn't to fellowship with the Jewish believers for that length of time? And if so, where is there any hint of that written in Scripture? No, blood doesn't relate to the dietary laws. And as for blood equaling murder, every Gentile knew the punishment that Rome exacted for it. No believing Gentile needed to be admonished about murdering people.

In biblical law the eating of blood in rare meat is sin (Lev. 3:17; 7:26-27; 19:26; Ezek. 33:25) but not necessarily idolatrous. The 'eating' of blood that the Bible speaks of as idolatrous is seen as drinking it from a pagan sacrifice. Drinking the raw blood of an animal was part of the worship of pagan gods and goddesses. This was done to attain the characteristics of the god and the benefits thereof. And as Paul found out, there was much need for this rule (1st Cor. 10:20-21; also Rev. 2:14, 20 implied).

Blood and strangled are just two aspects of the four rules that have been misunderstood. Turning to rule two, some think that fornication means not to marry within the prohibited relations of Lev. 18:6-18.[555] But pornay'ah cannot be translated as pertaining to 'prohibited marriages' because it primarily means prostitution.

Witherington insightfully saw that Torah regulations found in Lev. 18 for 'prohibited unions between close relations' was *never* addressed in the Septuagint as pornay'ah.[556] This is another reason why the rule doesn't speak of the prohibited marriages. Because of this and the fact that the Gentiles aren't told which meats were clean or unclean, Witherington real-

---

[554] Witherington, *The Acts of the Apostles*, p. 465.

[555] Kittel, *TDNT*, vol. VI, p. 593. Marshall, *Acts*, p. 253.

[556] Witherington, *The Acts of the Apostles*, p. 465.

ized that rules three and four *couldn't* be food regulations.

Others see pornay'ah as *sexual immorality, unchastity* or *fornication* (popularly defined), but these water down the Greek word to the lowest common denominator and defy the meaning of biblical interpretation for the word, the context, and its historical environment. *Unchaste* can be made to mean anything sexual and consequently it specifically means nothing.

From both its Hebrew and Greek usage, cult prostitution was easily seen as the definition for pornay'ah, rule two. The history of ancient Israel and the world at large confirmed this, along with Yeshua's use of pornay'ah as the only biblical grounds for divorce between two believers. First Corinthians and Revelation further supported this understanding.

Why don't most scholars translate the second rule as cult prostitution? And then, placed right after the prohibition not to eat the meat of an idolatrous sacrifice, the context of sacrificial idolatry could have been recognized much sooner than it was. Witherington in 1998 seems to be the first to present the four as a *unit* on sacrificial-sexual idolatry.

The Church's anti-Law bias has blinded them. That's why pornay'ah, blood and strangled weren't properly understood. By separating and annulling Torah from the New Covenant, scholars didn't have the right tools for the job and fell into gross error. Their understanding wars against the Word of God. Theological blindness is not confined to the Pharisees and as such, it adversely effects hundreds of millions of believers today.

With most theologians thinking that they are 'free from the Law' it's hard to imagine how they can present any rules as coming from the Law. Knowling was quick to point this out. If the Law was done away with, how could Yakov do this, or more importantly, *how could Paul allow it*?! If the Law was done away with, why didn't Paul tell everyone? When would the Jewish believers learn this 'vital truth'? And if the rules were only to be kept in the presence of the Jews, the Jews would certainly be offended when they found out about this hypocrisy, especially the Jewish Apostles.

There are other theological and practical problems with interpreting the rules for table fellowship. One is that it creates two separate and distinct groups of believers within the Kingdom of God, with two *different* standards for sin. What day will the two peoples (in the same congregation) assemble on? Should majority rule or should they meet on both days? This is theologically absurd and in practical terms, impossible. The Jew must keep the Sabbath day holy and if he doesn't it's sin. But the Gentile can make any day holy he wants to? Welcome to the Wall of Separation...*in reverse* (Eph. 2:14). Is the Kingdom of Jesus a democracy? Who makes up the rules, God or the Church? God forbid if both groups want to have a picnic: 'No thanks, I'll pass on the shrimp and cocktail sauce.' And in December, 'Thank you very much for your Christmas gift!' Oh Joy unspeakable, full of Glory! If this wouldn't be offensive to a Jew, what would be?!

This is one reason why most Jews won't even consider Jesus a viable option for being the Messiah. They see Christianity as just another pagan religion, for only pagans keep Sunday and Easter. They know the Messiah of Israel wouldn't change Sabbath to Sunday and do away with Law of Moses. And isn't that exactly what Jesus states in Mt. 5:17-19?

Theologians get around the rules by saying that the Jewish believers didn't realize the Law was done away with. But this creates an even larger problem than they seemed to have solved. How could all the believing Jews in Acts 15, eighteen years after the Resurrection, still think the Law was to be obeyed?[557] Were they all, including the Apostles who walked with Jesus, just so slow to heed the teaching of the Holy Spirit in this vital area? And even Paul, the Church's champion, kept the Law to the point of *Nazarite Vow and sacrifice* (Acts 21:20-26) about 25 years after the Resurrection.[558] And nowhere in Acts do the Apostles *ever* renounce the Law.

Having two theologically different communities of faith is totally foreign to God and His Word. A major theme of Scripture is that,

> 'There shall be one law for the native born and the stranger among them.'[559]

How much more for the Gentile believer who has now become *one with Israel* in Yeshua? Messiah declares that even though there is another flock (i.e. the Gentiles), the *two shall be one* and have one Shepherd. He said,

> 'I have other sheep (Gentiles) which are not of this fold (Jews). I must bring them also and they will hear My Voice and *they will become one Flock* with one Shepherd.' (John 10:16)

Wouldn't it seem very strange for His Jewish sheep to observe the Sab-

---

[557] Unger, *UBD*, pp. 486-488 and Douglas, *IBD*, Part 1, p. 281 have Acts 15 in 48 A.D. Witherington, *The Acts of the Apostles*, p. 444 note 361 and Bromiley, *ISBE*, vol. one, p. 692 have 49 A.D. See also p. 183 note 478 above.

[558] Bromiley, *ISBE*, vol. one, p. 692 has it in 54 A.D. Douglas, *IBD*, Part 1, p. 281 has 59 A.D.

[559] See pp. 245-249 of the Appendix: *Two Different Kingdoms? The Stranger and the Native Born* for Scripture cites and a greater understanding of who the stranger was.

bath, but not His Gentile sheep? In this One Flock, would it be a sin for a Jewish believer to eat shrimp, but a Gentile Christian would be 'free' to eat it? What kind of a kingdom would that be? It'd be a *divided* kingdom with diametrically opposed rules *for what constitutes sin.*

It also makes God out to be the one erecting a 'middle wall of partition.' There's nothing in Rom. 11:17-21, 24-27 where the Gentile is grafted into the cultivated olive tree (Israel), and Eph. 2:12-22; 3:6 where the Gentile is part of the Commonwealth of Israel and made into 'one new Man' with the Jew, to support a different theological lifestyle for the Gentile.[560]

Table fellowship is not why Yakov gave the four rules. Nowhere is table fellowship mentioned in Acts 15. Nowhere is it the reason for them holding the Council. And nowhere in the Word of God is it said to be the reason for giving the four authoritative rules.[561] The commandments of Yakov[562] were given in relation to what a Gentile must do in order for his faith in Jesus to be seen as biblically genuine.

The Book of Acts tells us 'what happened.' It's very hard to argue with what it states about Paul and all the Jews keeping the Law of Moses 25 years after the Resurrection (Acts 21:20, 24). Some realize the futility of trying to bend those two verses. They're honest and say they don't understand it. How could Paul take the Nazarite Vow if the Law was 'no more'?

Others teach that Paul was only being 'a Jew to the Jews.'[563] He was just

---

[560] Don't let some translations of Eph. 2:15 mislead you; it speaks of the laws that *separated* Jews from Gentiles, not all the Law (Ex. 23:33; 34:12; Dt. 7:3-11; Josh. 23:11-15; Acts 10:28).

[561] Marshall, *Acts*, p. 255: 'the letter carries on with a firm tone of authority. The decision reached by the church was regarded as being inspired by the Spirit, who is throughout Acts the guide of the church in its decisions and actions.' Williams, *Acts*, p. 270: 'the council's decision had been reached under the guidance of the Holy Spirit (cf. 10:19; 13:2f.). This belief is made explicit in verse 28, where the form of expression does not mean that they put themselves on a par with the Spirit, but only that they were willing to submit to his guidance'. Bruce, *The Book of the Acts*, p. 299. 'The decree is regarded as binding in the letters to the seven churches of proconsular Asia (Rev. 2:14, 20). Toward the end of the second century it was observed by the churches of the Rhone valley (which had close links with those of Asia) and...Africa.'

[562] The biblical reality of the four rules of Acts 15:20 is that they are commandments from the Lord. Yakov didn't make these up on his own. And they're not suggestions. Just as the writings of Paul are to be obeyed, so too the four rules of Yakov. Paul says 'If anyone thinks he is a prophet or spiritual, let him recognize that the things which I write to you are the Lord's commandments' (1st Cor. 14:37). See also 2nd Cor. 8:8 (by inference), 1st Tim. 6:14; 2nd Pet. 3:2, 14-18.

observing the Vow so as not to offend the Jews. If this were the case, Paul would have been a chameleon, not an Apostle.

Others have the chutzpah (audacity) to think that Paul was 'afraid for his life' from Yakov and the Jewish believers! *This,* they say, was why Paul did something that he'd never have done on his own. But this makes Paul

---

[563] Knowling, *The Acts of the Apostles,* p. 451. Marshall, *Acts,* p. 346, citing Stahlin and including himself. Bruce, *The Book of the Acts,* pp. 406-408. Bruce argues that the Elders and James were lacking understanding as to *why* Paul followed their counsel and took the Vow: 'Therefore in their naïveté, they put a proposal to him' p. 406. Bruce says that Paul was only going along with them to be 'a Jew to the Jews'; 'Paul fell in with their suggestion' relieving 'them of embarrassment' (because of what they had heard about Paul teaching Jews not to circumcise their children, etc.). He writes that Paul did this as part of his 'stated policy' 1st Cor. 9:20. He ends by saying that Paul 'cannot be fairly charged with compromising his own gospel principles.'

Paul most certainly could be charged with unethical behavior if his reasons were as Bruce has stated. Paul expressly took the Nazarite Vow to show everyone that he kept the Law. Keeping Torah doesn't mean to keep it only when in Jewish society ('He himself was happy to conform to Jewish customs when he found himself in Jewish society' Bruce, p. 406), but in every society. Yet Bruce says that among the Gentiles, Paul would 'conform to Gentile ways' (p. 406). What does that mean? What is the 'way of the Gentile'? Did Paul sacrifice to idols? Did he eat pig? Did he desecrate the Sabbath?

Bruce's Paul seems to be a deceiver of the highest order, for the taking of the Nazarite Vow meant that Paul walked in Torah all the time, among both Jew and Gentile. One cannot imagine Paul saying to God that he would keep the Sabbath day holy among the Jews, but not among the Gentiles. It's ludicrous to think of Paul like that. Paul would have been extremely unscrupulous if he took the Vow *only to appease James,* the Jewish Apostles and the Elders, etc. The *stated reason* for Paul taking the Vow was so that '*all* will know that there is *nothing* to the things which they have been told about you, but that you yourself also walk orderly, *keeping the Law*' (Acts 21:24).

If Paul only took the Vow to appease James, *he was deceiving James* and all the other Jewish believers there. Paul kept Sabbath and Torah among the Gentiles (Acts 24:14; 25:8), and in Acts 20:16 and 1st Cor. 16:8 the Apostle to the Gentiles ordered his life around Shavu'ote (the Feast of Pentecost, Lev. 23:15-21; see also Acts 18:18, 21; 20:6; 27:9).

What being 'a Gentile to the Gentiles' meant for Paul was that he would *associate with them,* something he'd never have done as a Pharisee (Acts 26:5) before coming to Yeshua. This is why he rebukes Peter, for *not associating* with the Gentile believers when Peter knew better (Gal. 2:11-15; Acts 10:15, 28, 34-35). It doesn't mean that Paul or Peter ate unclean meat as some suggest. It also means that he'd relate to Gentiles on their terms, seeking to bring the Gospel to them in ways they'd understand. It didn't mean he'd sin against God in the process by breaking the Sabbath, eating pig, keeping the Feast of Ishtar (Easter) or 'living like a Gentile sinner' (Gal. 2:15; 1st Tim. 5:22).

out to be a very weak and unprincipled man, something the Scriptures don't bear out (Acts 9:20-29; 14:19-22; 2nd Cor. 11:23-12:21; 2nd Peter 3:14-18). It also makes James and the other Apostles out to be more like the James' Gang, than living examples of Yeshua's love and *way of life.*

Other scholars though simply say it didn't happen! It was just fanciful writing on Luke's part! He made it up! They say that *the Paul* they know would never have allowed it. And that's true. *Their image* of Paul would never have allowed it to happen. *Their Paul* set them 'free from the Law.' But the biblical Paul declares freedom from sin, not the holy Law of God.

With some of the letters of Paul, theologians are able 'to theologize the Law away' because they mistake Paul coming against the Law in relation to salvation and circumcision, for his entire view of the Law. They're not convincing though when they try to explain why Paul would elevate the Law (Rom. 3:31; 7:7, 12, 14; 1st Cor. 5:6-8; 7:19, etc.), and here in Acts the only recourse they have is to declare Luke a liar! Marshall says,

> 'many scholars have doubted whether the historical Paul would have agreed to this proposal. A. Hausrath put the objection most vividly by saying that it would be more credible that the dying Calvin would have bequeathed a golden dress to the mother of God' (Roman Catholicism's sinless and deified Mary), 'than that Paul should have entered upon this action. Luke, it is claimed, *has invented the incident* to show that Paul was a law-abiding Jew. Even Stahlin' 'argues that Paul would never have accepted verse 24b'.[564] (Acts 21:24 states that Paul took the Vow to show everyone that he kept the Law).

These scholars seem to think that Luke the Gentile had nothing better to do than to *fabricate* an Apostle Paul who kept the Law! Why would Luke do such a monstrous thing?!

If the Law was done away with, the *biblical Paul* would have certainly voiced his view against James. In that he doesn't, we know that it wasn't. The Apostle still kept the Law and exhorted Gentiles to do the same, as he himself writes of in his letters (Rom. 2:13; 3:31; 7:7, 12; 1st Cor. 5:6-8; 7:19; 9:8; 14:34, etc.).

David Williams, who espouses table fellowship, nevertheless writes that *Paul kept the Law all his life.* He also refutes those who say that Paul was

---

[564] Marshall, *Acts,* pp. 345-346. See *ISBE,* vol. one, pp. 43-44 for just how accurate Luke was in his historical details, which speaks of his overall accuracy. Luke, Ramsay states, 'should be placed among the very greatest of historians'.

against the Apostolic Decree of Acts 15:20-21 (by his not presenting it in his letters; e.g. Rom. 14 or 1st Cor. 8:10). He says 'there is nothing in all his writings to suggest that he disapproved of them'.[565] Paul,

> 'believed that his own teaching *upheld the law* (Rom 3:31), and his epistles are full of exhortations *to live by the letter* no less than by the spirit of the law (cf., e.g. Rom 13:8-10; Eph. 5:1,' etc.).[566]

> 'Of course he knew now that obedience to the law could no longer be regarded as the basis of salvation (cf. Gal. 2:15), but for Paul *the law remained the authoritative guide to Christian living*'. 'Broadly speaking, this was the conclusion reached by the Jerusalem council.'[567]

The Law of Moses is 'the authoritative guide to Christian living'. That's all God ever intended it to be (Dt. 4:5-8; Rom. 3:31). But if Paul didn't nullify the Law, who did? The concept of a 'Law-free Gospel' is the heretical teaching of the Catholic Church, not the New Testament. Protestants have followed this interpretation without so much as questioning it. The Catholic Church threw out God's holy Sabbath and castigated the Law 'as Jewish' and so began anti-Semitism. It was around 100 A.D.[568]

Yeshua declares the permanence of the Law for His Kingdom on Earth (Mt. 5:17-19; Lk. 16:17; Jn. 10:35). But this too is theologized away by most, saying that with His death, the Law of Moses was done away with because 'Jesus fulfilled it.' But it's evident from the Lord's own words in Mt. 5:17-19 that fulfilling the Law *cannot* mean that He did away with it (*'Do not think* that I came to abolish the Law'). What can *fulfill* mean?

1. *Fulfill* means that Yeshua taught the divine essence of the Law by His understanding of what it actually meant, thus complementing the written Law by revealing it's deeper heavenly dimension. Saying that those who hate their brother have broken the commandment to murder doesn't do away with the commandment on murder. It amplifies it and reveals how God understands the commandment. Even the Rabbis say that 'when the Messiah comes' he will teach us the Law (i.e. explain the deeper spiritual meanings of it). And that's exactly what Yeshua did. He didn't cancel the Law by His sacrifice for our sins, He canceled our sin indebtedness (Col.

---

[565] Williams, *Acts*, p. 260.

[566] Ibid., p. 261.

[567] Ibid.

[568] Bacchiocchi, *From Sabbath To Sunday*, pp. 152-157, 159-207, 211-212.

2:14), and He changed our nature to walk in the Law's holy ways (Rom. 6–8), just as He did (Jer. 31:31-34; 2nd Cor. 5:21 and 1st Pet. 1:20-24 by inference).

- Yeshua being the Passover Lamb doesn't do away with God's commandment to celebrate Passover (Ex. 12:14; 1st Cor. 5:6-8; Rev. 5:1-14). It enhances it tremendously. The First Passover paves the way for Yeshua to be the Second Passover. Here is the greater meaning of freedom from Egyptian slavery; freedom from the Kingdom of Darkness (Col. 1:13-14; 1st Pet. 2:9). Should we not celebrate this wonderful event that God has given to us on the day that He set up for us?

2. *Fulfill* also means that the prophecies in the Tanach about a suffering Messiah were realized or fulfilled in Yeshua. This would include prophecies concerning the Messiah who would be born in Bethlehem and beaten on the cheek with a rod (Mic. 5:1-2) and who would suffer and die an atoning death for Israel (Is. 53) etc. Yeshua expressly speaks of this understanding after His Resurrection in Luke 24:44:

- "Then He said to them, 'These are My words that I spoke to you while I was still with you; that *everything written about Me* in the Torah, the Prophets and the Psalms must be *fulfilled*.'"

3. Another area where Yeshua *fulfilled* the Law and the Prophets concerns the promises that God made to Fathers Abraham, Isaac and Jacob. With Yeshua, the promises were about to enter another phase. God promised that He would be the God of the Sons of Abraham, Isaac and Jacob and that He would circumcise their hearts and cause them to love Him and walk in His Torah (Dt. 30:6). God circumcising the hearts of Jews and Gentiles who believe in His Son (Phil. 3:3) doesn't nullify His Word to the Fathers or their sons (Rom. 11:26). It fulfills it.

- Yahveh spoke of giving Israel and Judah a New Covenant and forgiveness of sin (Jer. 31:31-34). His extending it to Gentiles (Is. 49:6) in no way negates His Word to Israel and Judah (Rom. 11:25-29). He expressly said He would give Israel a New Covenant and put His *Law* in their hearts (Jer. 31:33). How then could the New Covenant do away with the Law? It would be the exact antithesis of what Yahveh said about the New Covenant.

- Yahveh giving His Spirit to the Gentile who believes doesn't negate His Word to the flesh and blood Seed of Abraham, Isaac

216

and Jacob. The giving of His Spirit is for all those who walk with Him. Yeshua made it possible for Jews to have their hearts circumcised and to know the Father intimately by His Spirit, all things promised in the Tanach, being *fulfilled* in Yeshua *with no reference to the demise of the Law.*

4. Still another area where *fulfill* has application is Yeshua's very life. He fulfilled all the righteous demands of God's holy Torah and as such, became the ideal Israeli, Example par excellence of what it means to be a true Son of Israel. He's the Model that believers strive to emulate, by His Spirit. He was fully consecrated to His Father *and kept the Law from His heart* (Ps. 40:7-8). Should Christians strive for anything less (1st Cor. 11:1; 1st Jn. 2:6)? *Fulfill* doesn't mean God's Law is done away with.

Witherington saw the rules as a unit on sacrificial idolatry but unfortunately failed to grasp the theological significance of Acts 15:20-21. He says the rules were given so Jews outside Israel would not be offended by Gentiles continuing to practice idolatry 'by going to pagan feasts'.[569] But good church attendance didn't negate sacrificing to other gods and laying with cult harlots, as the letters of Paul testify to (1st Cor. 10; 2nd Cor. 6, etc.).

He also states that the rules were for 'fellowship'[570] and that it was 'important to James'[571] as a witness to non-believing Jews that the Gentiles were not practicing sacrificial idolatry any longer. How much of a witness it was to non-believing Jews is debatable, but fellowship can't be the reason for the rules, as he himself stated.[572]

Witherington also confuses the Judaizers with Peter, Paul and James by saying the Judaizers 'wanted Gentile Christians to be Torah observant'.[573] *The Jewish Apostles wanted* the Gentiles to be Torah observant! That's what Acts 15:20-21 is all about. It was the Judaizers who wanted the Gentiles to become Jews and *keep the Law in order to be saved.*

Hegg follows Witherington, seeing the rules as a 'prohibition of idol worship in the pagan temple.'[574] He too thinks they were for table fellowship between the two groups so there wouldn't be any 'accusations of idolatry'

---

[569] Witherington, *The Acts of the Apostles*, p. 463.

[570] Ibid., p. 439: 'so that both groups may be included in God's people on equal footing, fellowship may continue, and the church remain one.'

[571] Ibid., p. 463.

[572] Ibid. p. 465. See also pp. 208-209 and note 554 above.

[573] Ibid., pp. 647-648.

[574] Hegg, *The Letter Writer*, p. 269.

in the Jewish community, and that *strangled* also meant a dietary restriction (i.e. not to eat strangled meat with blood in it).[575] But James didn't give the rules for fellowship, non-believing Jewish approval, or as a food regulation. Hegg discerns though, that the Gentiles were to learn and observe the Law.[576]

Acts 15 deals with salvation issues, not table fellowship. The four rules revolve around sacrificial-sexual idolatry. They were given as a filter to the Gentile so that his faith in Jesus would be seen as biblically genuine.

Christian scholarship, in interpreting Acts 15:20-21, exposes their flawed theological presupposition. Devoid of Torah and actually anti-Law, they ingeniously pervert the Word of God and invent their own interpretations which seem very biblical. This happens quite frequently when theologians and translators come to passages in the New Testament that relate to the Law, and they are backed up by all the 'machinery of scholarship' and two millennia of traditional interpretation. When understood from its Hebraic perspective their theological error is all too easily seen.

The Church assigned the four rules to table fellowship and said these were the *only rules* that a Gentile had to keep.[577] But this places the Gentile outside the Torah observant *believing* Jewish community. The theological chaos this presents was seen at the picnic table.

The use of 'table fellowship' detaches or separates the Gentile from the Jewish believer (and the traditional Jew)[578] by placing him in a different category or walk with God. What God brought together, the Church cut asunder. Table fellowship was not what Yakov had in mind when he gave the four rules, as important a concept as that is.

---

[575] Ibid., p. 281: 'acceptance of Gentiles within the Torah community' speaks of table fellowship with Jewish believers and approval from the non-believing Jewish Community. Also p. 277 for not eating strangled meat with blood in it.

[576] Ibid., p. 73, 83, 288f.

[577] Marshall, *Acts*, pp. 242-243.

[578] If the Church had been walking in the Feasts and Sabbaths, etc., all these centuries, they would have truly seen the Jewish people as their relatives and not as enemies ('Christ killers!'). Persecution of the Jews would never have happened in the Name of Jesus and the Jewish people would have seen Gentiles keeping the Law of Moses and loving them. This would have led them into finding out more about Jesus as their Messiah. Tragically the very opposite has happened. In the Name of Jesus more Jews have been murdered than in all other names combined. The history of the Church toward the Jewish people has been very evil. Knowledge about this aspect of Church history can be gained from any book on Jewish history as 'Church history' seems to overlook it.

Noah and Acts 15:20

F. F. Bruce thought that Yakov's four rules came from the Noahide Laws.[579] This interpretation seeks to circumvent the possibility that Yakov was giving the Gentiles anything from the Law of Moses. But interesting questions and problems arise from this perspective on Acts 15:20.

First though, what are 'Noah's laws' for the Gentiles? The Gentiles were required to be,

1. 'practicing justice and
2. abstaining from blasphemy,
3. idolatry,
4. adultery,
5. bloodshed,
6. robbery and
7. eating flesh torn from a live animal' and 'also not to drink blood taken from a live animal.' (The last clause, 'not to drink blood taken from a live animal' was later added to the seventh.)[580]

All four rules of Yakov can be placed in Noah's third category of idolatry: eat no meat at the idolatrous sacrifice, don't practice cult prostitution or drink the blood of the sacrifice and keep away from strangled animal sacrifices. With a proper interpretation of the four rules one could hardly say that Yakov 'took' the rules from Noah, especially when they can all fit into one category. Unfortunately the Noahide people don't see the rules as a conceptual unit on sacrificial-sexual idolatry either.

If Yakov's first rule on not eating sacrificial meat was placed under idolatry (#3), and pornay'ah was seen as adultery (#4), and *blood* was seen as murder (#5), there's still no place to put *strangled* (unless it's in #3 idolatry which Noahide people don't see it relating to).[581] And in all this, only three of Noah's seven laws have been touched. But this is how Bruce and others might align Yakov's rules to Noah. Of course blood cannot be equated with murder so this negates it from being 'bloodshed' (#5), and pornay'ah isn't adultery (#4).

Some might suggest that *strangled* from Acts 15:20 be placed in Noah's 7th category. But the Rabbis created #7 to prohibit the Gentile from liter-

---

[579] Bruce, *The Book of the Acts*, pp. 295-296.

[580] Stern, *JNTC*, p. 278. The Noahide Laws are listed in the Talmud, *Sanhedrin* 56a.

[581] Some might try and place strangled in #7 but it's not a good fit.

ally severing a limb from a *living* animal and eating it raw. Strangled does not fit in here.

The additional comment to #7 (not to drink the blood from a *live* animal), referred not to drinking it at a pagan sacrifice per se, nor to eating the meat half-cooked with the blood still in it. It spoke of eating the blood in the severed limb of a **living** *animal*. Today though, it seems that the Rabbis interpret it to mean not drinking or eating blood which can be seen as both a dietary regulation and a prohibition against idolatry.[582]

Isn't it strange that James would seem to use only three of Noah's seven categories for the Gentiles? The Rabbis say that 'a righteous Gentile' was to do *all* of Noah's laws. James never mentions robbery (#6) and he doesn't include blasphemy (#2) either, etc. If the four rules were taken from the Noahide Laws, why didn't Yakov just give the Gentles all the Noahide laws? And why would the name of Moses be mentioned (v. 21), instead of Noah?

People who follow the Noahide Laws say that all Gentiles should observe them. Not that the laws of Noah are bad but this can't be justified from Acts 15:20 or anywhere else in the New Testament.[583] One has to really *stretch* Yakov's four rules into being *taken* from the Noahide Laws.

Unfortunately it's not possible to give any Scripture cites where Yahveh gave these laws to Noah for the Gentiles (except for murder and not eating blood from Gen. 9:4-6). That's because they come from the Talmud. The idea that God gave these seven laws to Noah, and therefore to the Gentiles so some could be righteous and go to Heaven, comes from the Rabbis.

Nowhere in Scripture are the Noahide Laws seen as having been given to Noah as say, God gave the Law to Moses for Israel. It's ironic though that

---

[582] JAHG—USA (Jews and Hasidic Gentiles—United to Save America) *The Noahide Laws* at http://www.noahide.com/lawslist.htm. Hasidic Gentiles is another term for Gentiles who keep the Noahide Laws.

[583] Gentiles who follow the Noahide Laws are deceived into believing that it's *all* a Gentile needs to do for eternal life. These people don't believe in Jesus as Savior. They're called Bnei Noach (Sons of Noah). This position, while rabbinic and false, found an adherent in Noahide leader Vendyl Jones, a former Baptist minister whom many label as apostate. Having met Mr. Jones in Jerusalem in 2005, I can attest to his apostasy. Among other things, he denies both the deity and the atoning work of Yeshua and actively seeks to take believers away from Messiah Yeshua.

Yeshua is God the Son (http://www.seedofabraham.net/yeshua.html) but this is considered blasphemy and idolatry by the Rabbis. Anyone who believes in the biblical Jesus cannot consider becoming a Bnei Noach.

the laws Noah did know, clean and unclean animals, are *not* part of the rabbinic Noahide Laws.[584] And Noah was a Gentile.

What is the theological purpose of Bruce and all those who espouse Yakov's rules as coming from Noah? Why do Yakov's rules have to come from the Noahide Laws? Placing the rules of Yakov within the framework of the Noahide Laws means that God gave certain rules for the Gentile (Noah), *before* the Law was given to Israel at Mt. Sinai. Hence, Yakov was only relating to the Gentile believers what they should be walking in. Theologically this means there'd be no need for them to keep the Law of Moses (Acts 15:21). But this is just another ingenious attempt at interpreting Acts 15:20, so the Gentile doesn't have to obey the Law of Moses.

When one starts from a false premise (that the Law is not for the Gentile or that it's no longer valid), and tries 'to fit Scripture into it' (Acts 15:20), the result is heretical teaching. Aside from the problems that have been seen with the four rules of Yakov trying to fit into the Noahide Laws, this is just table fellowship with a different twist. Instead of the four rules coming from the Law, which poses a problem for anti-Law theologians, here it comes from Noah, a Gentile who lived before the Law. But the same theological problems arise: there would be two totally different faith communities and 'law is still law.' If the Gentile is free from the Law, how can Bruce say that Gentiles are to keep some of, or all of, the *laws* of Noah? And of course the scene at the picnic table is a mess: 'Chitlins and gravy anyone?'

Although Edersheim spoke of the Noahide Laws being at the time of James,[585] but both Witherington and Hegg disagree and point out that the Noahide Laws weren't being given to Gentiles in the days of the Apostles.[586] This latter view would place Noahide interpretation of Acts 15:20 outside the realm of possibility. Some might say that James gave it to the Gentile believers first, before the Rabbis began giving it to the Gentiles. But it's hard to believe that the Rabbis would *follow* James the Jewish-Christian in this.

If properly interpreted the four rules of James can only be placed into one Noahide law, idolatry. If not properly interpreted, as Noahide people teach, the rules may be squeezed to fit into three or four Noahide laws at most.

---

[584] Gen. 7:2, 8; 8:20.

[585] Edersheim, *The Life and Times of Jesus The Messiah*, p. 1014.

[586] Witherington, *The Acts of the Apostles*, p. 464, also note 428. Hegg, *The Letter Writer*, pp. 266-268, also note 570.

Although this concept finds 'a way around' the Law of Moses as the origin of the rules, it doesn't account for the rules being made so as not to offend the Jew. The rules can't be assigned to table fellowship as is evident from the picnic table fiasco. And even though Noah knew clean from unclean animals, there are no rules about clean and unclean animals in the Noahide Laws. Even if one wanted to believe that all the rules of Noah were for the Gentile, it would still offend his Jewish believing friends who didn't eat unclean meats, let alone kept the Sabbath and Feast days holy.

Also, Noah's Laws are still *law*. Even if just a few were given to the Gentile, it would place the Gentile 'under law' and in a separate and certainly unequal category with his Jewish counterpart. This would make the Gentile a 'second class citizen,' something God never intended.

God's rules are either for both Jew and Gentile or they're for neither. Either Sabbath is still holy or it's not. It cannot be holy for the Jewish believer (Acts 21:20; Rom. 7:12; 1st Cor. 7:19), and 'just another day' for the Gentile believer. The Body of Christ is either one Flock called Israel (the Bride, etc.), with one Shepherd, or a middle wall of separation has been built by the Noahide people, as well as the Church.

God has always had his righteous remnant in Israel (1st Kgs. 19:1-18; Rom. 11:1-32). Jews and Gentiles that believe in Yeshua are part of this righteous remnant of Israel. There aren't two different sets of laws for them.

Sacrificial-Sexual Idolatry

Ben Witherington III writes that it's 'no exaggeration to say that Acts 15 is the most crucial chapter in the whole book.'[587] It is, but not only because the Gentile didn't have to be circumcised (become a Jew) and keep the Law for salvation, as important as that is. With a proper biblical interpretation of verses 20-21, the Law of Moses is seen as validated and authorized for every Gentile believer today.[588]

Sacrificial-sexual idolatry was the satanic scourge of the ancient world and the way of life for the Gentile. *Yakov dealt with the major issue first.* Eighteen years after the Resurrection[589] the assembly at Antioch sent Paul and Barnabas to Jerusalem (Acts 15:1-4), because of the conflict over what constituted Gentile salvation.

The Apostles and other Jewish believers assembled and listened to the arguments presented. After 'much dispute' (Acts 15:7) or arguing, Peter stood up and told his story about how the first Gentile, Cornelius, was saved (Acts 10:1-11:16). He said the Gentiles had received salvation in the same way as he had, 'through the Grace of the Lord Yeshua the Messiah' (15:11). Everyone was silent. The Lord had spoken through Peter. The rabbinic concept of keeping the Law for salvation was dealt the death blow it deserved. God never intended the Law to be used as a vehicle for eternal life.

Then Yakov, the literal half brother of Yeshua, arose and confirmed what Peter said, adding his own insight (Acts 15:13-18). God was raising up the fallen 'tabernacle of David' (the Kingdom of David that had laid in ruins for more than 900 years), through His/his Son and was inviting the Gentiles to be part of it (Is. 42:6; 49:6).

As Nasi (Prince) of the Council, Yakov sealed the decision (Acts 15:19) and issued the four rules (v. 20). Why the four rules? Why didn't he just declare that the Gentiles were saved by faith in Messiah Yeshua without needing to become circumcised and let it go at that?

Yakov was very concerned that these new Gentile believers might think they could continue to practice sacrificial pagan rites *along with* 'belief in Jesus.' This would seriously effect their salvation. The four rules that he presented to the believing Gentiles were the essence of idolatrous temple practices. Yakov exercised his judicial acumen and warned the Gentiles about something that would jeopardize their very salvation. Yakov's con-

---

[587] Witherington, *The Acts of the Apostles*, p. 439.

[588] Of course Jewish believers should observe the Law of Moses too.

[589] See p. 211 note 557 above for the time frame.

cern was extremely valid. The Apostle Paul had to deal with sacrificial-sexual idolatry among some of the Gentile believers in Corinth (1st Cor. 6:19-20; 10:21) as well as in other cities.[590] And the Risen Messiah had to rebuke two of the seven assemblies in Revelation for practicing it also (2:14, 20).

Gentile continuance in sacrificial-sexual idolatry was the concern of Yakov in issuing the four rules. It had absolutely nothing to do with table fellowship. As a Jew he knew the history of ancient Israel, and the past and current conditions in the pagan world. He also knew that Yahveh desired for His people to be totally devoted to Him through Yeshua. If Gentiles continued worshiping other gods along with belief in Yeshua, it would cost them their eternal life. The rules are a salvation issue.

The Hebrews committed cult prostitution with the women of Moab (Num. 25) yet they 'still believed' in Yahveh even after they had joined themselves to, and became 'one' with, Baal Peor through the sacrifices and orgies. It's this walking in the Camp of God and the Camp of Satan that Yakov addressed in Acts 15:20. In a very real sense, Yakov's ruling took care of the two *pluses*:

> He said that Jesus *plus* the Law couldn't earn salvation,
> and Jesus *plus* Zeus wouldn't be tolerated.

In the Ten Commandments the first thing God dealt with was idolatry. The first three commandments were directed against paganism. Other commandments revealed the punishment:

> 'The individual offender was devoted to destruction (Ex. 22:20); his nearest relatives were not only bound to denounce him and deliver him up to punishment (Dt. 13:2-10), but their hands were to strike the first blow when, on the evidence of at least two witnesses, he would be stoned (Dt. 17:2-5). To attempt to seduce others to false worship was a crime of equal enormity (Dt. 13:6-10).'[591]

Sacrificial-sexual idolatry was the only thing on Yakov's mind when he issued the four rules to the Gentiles who had come to believe in the Jewish Messiah. Yahveh addressed ancient Israel in a similar vein when He brought her out of the darkness of Egypt. The eating of unclean meat, as sinful as that is, was not the primary thing that made the Gentiles defiled

---

[590] Gal. 5:19; Eph. 5:3; Col. 3:5; 1st Thess. 4:3.

[591] Unger, *UBD*, p. 515.

in the eyes of the Jewish people. In Acts 10:28 Peter told Cornelius and the Gentiles gathered in his house, 'You yourselves know how unlawful it is for a man who is a Jew to *associate* with a Gentile or to visit him'.[592]

Peter speaks of the mere association with Gentiles as being off limits. This was not just a rabbinic tradition. It was their pagan 'worship' that truly defiled the soul of the Gentile. This made them unclean and would continue to defile Gentile believers if they practiced it, even if they said they 'believed in Jesus.' Witherington writes,

> 'Jews believed that the chief source of Gentile impurity was their contact with "the defilement of idols," not their contact with non-kosher food.'[593]

The four rules were to be observed immediately by the Gentiles in response to salvation, not for table fellowship with the Jewish believer. Was Gentile faith in Messiah Yeshua genuine? These rules would reveal that at a very crucial and basic level.

Most of the Gentiles coming into the Kingdom of Yeshua didn't have any idea Who the God of Israel was and what He required. Where would they find out that worshipping other gods was wrong? Where would they find out how God wanted them to walk out their new found faith? *This* is where the synagogue and the Law of Moses come in. Acts 15:21 assumes that the Gentile believer was to live a lifestyle of Torah so they could truly be one with the House of Israel[594] and not offend their believing Jewish brother...nor the God-Man who died for them.

There's a parallel in the Hebrews entering the Promised Land, and the Gentiles entering the Promised One. It has to do with worshipping God and God alone. This was the utmost concern for Yakov in giving the four rules. In the Ten Commandments it's written, 'You must have no other gods beside Me' (Dt. 5:7; see also Ex. 20:3; 22:20).

In Dt. 12 Yahveh begins to define what it means not to have any other

---

[592] It was this way from the beginning. Joshua said to Israel, 'Be strong then to keep and do all that is written in the Book of the Law of Moses so that you may not turn aside from it to the right hand or to the left, so that you will *not associate* with these nations, these which remain among you, or mention the name of their gods or make anyone swear by them or serve them or bow down to them. But you are to cling to Yahveh your God, as you have done to this day' (Joshua 23:6-8; see also Dt. 7:3).

[593] Witherington, *The Acts of the Apostles*, p. 462.

[594] The Gentile is grafted into Israel (Rom. 11:13-31), and part of the Commonwealth of Israel (Eph. 2:11-22). (See also p. 184 notes 481-482 above.)

gods. Among other things, the Hebrews weren't to have anything to do with pagan altars; only to destroy them (vv. 2-3). And they weren't to eat the blood (vv. 16, 23). In speaking of the pagan altars and the eating of blood, conceptually, the other rules can be placed right alongside them (the eating of the meat sacrificed to the god at the altar and the strangling of a sacrifice). And all four of them would be acted out around a pagan altar.[595]

When Yahveh was leading His people Israel into the Promised Land He wanted them to know what would jeopardize their covenantal relationship with Him. God was doing the same thing for the Gentiles through Yakov. This is further seen even to the extent in how Yahveh closes Dt. 12, and how Yakov closes his letter to the Gentiles. In Dt. 12:28 Moses says,

> 'Be careful to listen to all these words which I command you so that it may be well with you and your sons after you forever, *for you will be doing what is good and right in the sight of Yahveh your God.*'

In his letter to the Gentiles, James writes,

> 'that you abstain from things sacrificed to idols and from blood and from things strangled and from cult prostitution. *If you keep yourselves free from such things, you will do well.* Shalom to you!' (Peace to you! Acts 15:29)

The parallel between Dt. 12 and Acts 15:20 is seen in both what is commanded about sacrificial idolatry, and the closing, 'that it would be well' with each group to obey the commandments. Both Moses and Yakov were warning the people what would *not* be tolerated. Did it mean that God wasn't going to give any more commandments to Israel after Dt. 12? Or that Dt. 12 was all the commandments that God had for them? Hardly. Acts 15:20 is not the last of the commandments for the Gentile either.

Deuteronomy 12 is the first place in Deuteronomy where Yahveh explains or defines in a greater way, His commandment not to have any other gods except Him.[596] This is the reason why Yakov gave his ruling. The Gentiles

---

[595] See pp. 167-168 where the three major rules are seen before Deuteronomy.

[596] There is mention of breaking down altars (Dt. 7:5), and there's a warning not to forget Yahveh and bow down and follow other gods (Dt. 8:19), and of not being enticed to turn away from Yahveh (Dt. 11:16), before Dt. 12. But Dt. 12 begins the formal teaching of what it means to follow Yahveh in relation to other gods, as well as how to observe His other commandments. Before Dt. 12 God speaks of commandments, statutes, judgments and ordinances, preparing Israel to receive the Instruction, but He doesn't *explain* what His commandments, statutes, judgments and ordinances are. Of course in Dt. 5 there are the

were well known to have many gods and goddesses in their pantheon, and the inclusion of Jesus *would have posed no problem for many of them.* This was seen at Corinth, Pergamos and Thyatira. That's why these four rules were singled out. They must be obeyed, immediately. The rest of God's rules could be learned later. With the warning of James, they would understand that their faith must be in Yeshua and in Him alone. *ISBE* describes the pagan mindset of the Gentile believer:

> They 'would gladly have accepted Christ along with Mithra and Isis and Serapis'.[597] '*The same person* might be initiated into the mysteries of half a dozen pagan divinities and also be a priest of two or more gods. Some had not the slightest objection to worshiping Christ along with Mithra, Isis and Adonis.'[598]

Yakov knew this. Yeshua could breach no rivals. With knowledge of God's standard comes His wisdom and discernment as to what is pleasing to Him and what is sin (Dt. 4:5-8; Rom. 7:7, 12, 14; 1st John 3:1-5, etc.). When it's lacking, all sorts of heresies can enter (e.g. 'the Law is abolished,' 'the rules were given as a concession to Jewish sensitivities,' Sunday assembly instead of Sabbath holiness, etc.).

Without a standard from God in these areas, the way is open for pagan holy days and pagan ways to be 'baptized in the Name of Jesus.' And everyone actually does what *appears* to be right in their own eyes.[599] The Church has created its own holy days *in opposition* to those of God's. Baptizing a pagan celebration to an idol doesn't give it biblical legitimacy but it does make for a tradition of Man that nullifies God's Word. Moses sternly warned Israel about this:

> "Be careful to obey all these words that I command you today so that it may go well with you and with your children after you forever because you will be doing what is good and right in the sight of Yahveh your God. When Yahveh your God has cut off before you the nations whom you are about to enter to dispossess them, when

---

Ten Commandments where the first three speak of not worshipping any other gods, but in Dt. 12 and following it's more fully addressed.

[597] Bromiley, *ISBE*, vol. four, p. 214.

[598] Ibid.

[599] This phrase is used to denote Israel going astray after other gods (Dt. 12:8; Judges 17:6; 21:25). The opposite is to do what is right in God's eyes (Dt. 13:18; 1st Kings 15:5, 11; 2nd Kings 22:43, etc.).

you have dispossessed them and live in their land, *take care that you are not snared into imitating them* after they have been destroyed before you. *Do not inquire concerning their gods* saying, *"How did these nations worship their gods? I also want to do the same."'*

'*You must not do the same for Yahveh your God* because every abhorrent thing that Yahveh hates they have done for their gods. They even burn their sons and daughters in the fire to their gods. *You must diligently observe everything that I command you. Do not add to it or take anything away from it."* (Dt. 12:28-32)

What has the Church done in baptizing pagan Sunday, Easter, Thanksgiving and Christmas? They've taken celebrations to gods and goddesses and incorporated them into the worship of Jesus. The Church truly has a veil over her eyes and is blind to this dark reality. She's caught in her traditions that nullify God's Word and doesn't even realize it's sin. When it's brought to the attention of church officials, it's usually rationalized away: 'Oh, we don't worship Nimrod or Adonis. We worship the birth of Christ.' But *where has God given the Church authority* to make its own holy days?! Where does God say to celebrate the birth of His Son, or to change the day that He created and declared holy (Gen. 2:1-3)? The Church errs because it has thrown out God's Law.

The need for the Gentile to know what comprised salvation caused the Assembly in Jerusalem to meet. It was established that the Gentile was saved in the same way that the Jew was. Yakov declared the four rules and then uttered one verse of Scripture that reveals that believing Gentiles were already learning (and keeping) Torah.

It's very interesting that Yakov didn't *command* the Gentiles to go to the synagogue. Acts 15:21 is just 'a matter of fact' statement about Moses being in every city. For more than eight years Yakov had observed Gentile believers learning Torah in the congregations they worshiped in.[600] These

---

[600] An example of Gentile observance of the Law is seen in 195 A.D. All the congregations in what is now Turkey, Syria and Israel kept the Passover. This angered Bishop Victor of Rome (whose office would soon become that of the Pope). The Bishop *demanded* that those congregations celebrate Easter instead of the Jewish Passover. But Polycrates the bishop of all the assemblies in Turkey, 'claiming to possess the *genuine apostolic tradition* transmitted to him by the Apostles Philip and John, refused to be frightened into submission by the threats of Victor of Rome.' Bacchiocchi, *From Sabbath To Sunday*, p. 199 note 97, also pp. 198-207. If Gentiles weren't learning Torah in the days of Yakov, why would these congregations be keeping Passover?

congregations could also be called synagogues, especially by the Jewish believers. The assembly in Antioch would be seen by the Jewish and Gentile believers as a synagogue, and all Paul's 'house churches' could also be called 'house synagogues.' The Gentile believers were already going to synagogues and learning Torah in the eyes of Peter, Paul and James.

The church in Antioch, where the term Christian is first mentioned (Acts 11:26), was an assembly of Jewish and Gentile believers who obviously kept the Law (Acts 21:20; and 22:12 by inference). Paul's Gentiles assembled in 'house churches' and also learned the Law[601] along with their Jewish believing brethren.

All the assemblies of Paul met on the Sabbath day and celebrated Passover (1st Cor. 5:6-8; 7:19). This is ancient Church history. Sunday and Easter, ham and 'no Law' didn't enter the Body of Messiah for more than 30 years after Paul's death. No Gentile believer was assembling on Sunday or keeping Easter in Paul's day. None. That wouldn't begin till around 100 A.D.[602] These false and pagan traditions are easily seen in that there are no Scriptures stating that believers should observe any of those days.

Yakov's second rule in Acts 15:20 was seen in both the Hebrew and the Greek words to primarily mean prostitution, with the biblical emphasis on cult prostitution. The second rule, appearing immediately after the prohibition of eating sacrificial meat at the sacrifice, raised the theme of sacrificial idolatry for this rule also. Blood and things strangled followed suite.

Judah and Tamar revealed cult harlotry being practiced in Canaan in the days of the sons of Jacob and from the Baal Peor affair at the time of Moses. It made known how easily Israel was seduced, and the devastating consequences cult harlotry had upon the Sons of Israel.

In both Israel's history and that of the ancient world, cult harlotry was rampant. It was the sin that brought down both the House of Israel and the House of Judah. Yakov would certainly be aware of his own history and that of the pagans. He wouldn't want the Gentile believers to think that they could continue in sacrificial-sexual idolatry unscathed.

In the sections on Corinth and Revelation, both the Paul and Yeshua rebuked Gentile believers for practicing cult prostitution. Those Christians thought it was alright to do. And in the brief survey of pornay'ah and its derivatives in the New Testament, its use was overwhelmingly seen as cult prostitution and not common prostitution (and especially not adultery,

---

[601] Acts 20:20; Rom. 16:5; 1st Cor. 16:19; Col. 4:15; Philem. 1:2 (see also p. 184 notes 481-482 above.)

[602] Bacchiocchi, *From Sabbath To Sunday*, pp. 165-198.

sexual immorality, unchastity, the prohibited marriages of Lev. 18, common homosexuality or sex outside of marriage, etc.).

Once the smoke screen of traditional scholarship was blown away, the four rules of Yakov were seen as a conceptual unit on sacrificial-sexual idolatry. Yakov's admonition was very simple: tell the Gentiles what would sever them from Jesus (Acts 15:20), and encourage them to walk in God's ways by learning His Torah (Acts 15:21).

Today there aren't many Christians going about thinking that eating meat and drinking blood sacrificed to idols and lying with cult harlots would be acceptable to Jesus. But great is the importance of correctly understanding Acts 15:20-21. It can no longer be used by the Church to teach that Gentiles had only four rules to obey. And it cannot be spoken of as given for table fellowship out of Gentile consideration for the weaker Jewish believer. *Acts 15:20-21* exposes the satanic deception of a 'Law-free Gospel.'

Understanding the Hebrew Bible (Genesis through Revelation), from its Hebraic perspective is the goal.[603] God chose Abraham, not Socrates. He bound Himself (covenant), and interwove His ways (Torah, Prophets, Writings and New Testament), amongst Israel, not Greece. He revealed Himself in power (the Passover and Exodus; Yeshua crucified and resurrected) to Israel, not Rome. His reality and character are reflected in the *words* of the Hebrew Bible, not the Koran. *IBD* describes language as a reflection of a nation's cumulative experiences:

> 'it is an axiom of linguistics that any culture, no matter
> how primitive, develops that vocabulary which is perfect-
> ly adequate to express its thought and desires.'[604]

Only Israel encountered the God of Creation as a nation. Only Israel was freed from Egyptian slavery, walked through a split and dry-bed Red Sea, heard the Voice of Yahveh as a nation (Ex. 19:16f.), and was given the wisdom of God (Torah and Yeshua). No other nation was promised a land or entered into covenant with God (Dt. 10:15; 29:1), and both the New Covenant and the Messiah were promised...to Israel (Jer. 31:31-34). Hebrew is a very special language. The Hebrew Scriptures need to be understood for what they are saying as *The Lifting of the Veil* has revealed. The

---

[603] Our Hebraic perspective centers around the place of the Law of Moses in our lives (Rom. 3:31), as interpreted by Yeshua, not the Rabbis or Talmud or Halacha, etc. Yes, there are some insights that can be learned from them but many who study them, not grounded in Messiah, have taken a rocky detour on the Road of Life (Mt. 16:6-12; 23:1-33; Lk. 11:27-28, 37-54; Titus 1:9-16).

[604] Douglas, *IBD*, Part 1, p. 306.

Scriptures are Israel's privileged possession (Rom. 3:1-2; 9:1-5) and belong to every believer...

> 'Ask now about former ages, long before your own, ever since the day that God created human beings on the Earth. Ask from one end of the Heavens to the other: has anything so great as this ever happened or has its like ever been heard of? Has any people ever heard the voice of God speaking out of a Fire as you have heard and lived?'

> 'Or has any god ever attempted to go and take a nation for himself from the midst of another nation, by trials, by signs and wonders, by war, by a mighty hand and an outstretched arm and by terrifying displays of power, as Yahveh your God did for you in Egypt before your very eyes? *To you it was shown* so that you would acknowledge that Yahveh is God; there is no other besides Him! From the Heavens He made you hear His voice to discipline you. On Earth He showed you His great Fire while you heard His words coming out of the Fire. And because He loved your Fathers, He chose their sons after them.'

> 'He brought you out of Egypt with His own presence, by His great power, driving out before you nations greater and mightier than yourselves to bring you in, giving you their land for a possession as it is still today. So acknowledge today and take to heart that Yahveh is God in the Heavens above and on the Earth beneath; there is none other! *Keep His statutes and His commandments* which I am commanding you today *for your own well-being and that of your sons after you* so that you may long remain in the Land that Yahveh your God is giving you for all time.' (Dt. 4:32-40)

Yahveh gave His will to Israel when He gave her His Law. Keil says,

> the 'object of the glorious manifestation of His holy majesty upon Sinai' was the giving of 'the Law through Moses to the congregation of Jacob as a precious possession' and that 'Israel was distinguished above all nations by the possession of the divinely revealed Law.'[605]

In the beginning of Gentile salvation, the Gentiles learned Torah until the door was closed by what would become the Roman Catholic Church. But

---

[605] Keil, *The Pentateuch*, p. 875.

at the End, the Holy Spirit is opening the door that no church can shut.
The Gentile is learning Torah again. Praise God!

This understanding is a radical departure from Church theology but with a
proper Hebraic understanding of Acts 15:20-21, Church theology on the
demise of the Law is completely shattered. Many Gentiles have seen this
and are walking in their ancient Hebraic heritage as part of the Commonwealth of Israel (Eph. 2:11-22). Theologians can theologize Acts 15:20-21
away, but their efforts are being seen as very shallow.

Yeshua is lifting the veil of deception (Dan. 7:25; Acts 20:28-30) from the
eyes of His Bride, so she can more clearly see who He is. Thank God for
Yakov's Concern. Because of it believers are walking in the freedom of
God's perfect Law of Liberty:

> 'But one who looks intently at the perfect Law, the Law
> of Liberty (Freedom) and abides by it, not having become
> a forgetful hearer *but an effectual doer*, this man will be
> blessed in what he does.' (Yakov 1:25)

> 'May Your forgiving loving-kindnesses also come to me,
> Oh Yahveh, Your salvation according to Your word. So I
> shall have an answer for him who reproaches me, for I
> trust in Your word. Do not take *the word of Truth* utterly
> out of my mouth because I wait for Your *ordinances*. I
> will *keep Your Law* continually, forever and ever. And I
> will walk at *liberty* (freedom), for I seek Your precepts. I
> will also speak of Your *testimonies* before kings and shall
> not be ashamed. And I shall *delight* in Your *command-
> ments* which I love. I shall lift up my hands to Your com-
> mandments which I love, and I will meditate upon Your
> *statutes*.' (Psalm 119:41-48)

> Yeshua 'committed no sin, nor was any deceit found in
> His mouth'. (1st Peter 2:22)

> 'I would not have come to know sin except through the
> Law'. (Rom. 7:7c)

> 'whoever says "I abide in Him" *ought to walk just as He
> walked*.' (1st John 2:6)

There's much for us to learn about our God and Messiah in the Hebrew
Scriptures, both Old and New.[606]

---

[606] The underlying thought process of the New Testament is Hebraic in nature
and is the completion or fulfillment of God's promises to Israel.

REALITY RAMIFICATIONS

Many Christians love Jesus with all their heart but in ignorance eat pig, assemble on Sunday (and not God's holy Sabbath), keep Easter (and not Passover), etc. The Apostle Paul pleaded with the Corinthians involved in cult harlotry and didn't immediately cast them out because they were only babes in understanding the Word. They did it in pride and ignorance.

Today the Lord is calling all His people to stop all pagan practices and learn to walk in His Torah. The admonition in Revelation, 'to come out of her My People' reveals Yeshua's desire for His people to stop practicing the ways of darkness, thinking it's Light:

> 'And he cried out with a mighty voice saying, 'Fallen, fallen is Babylon the Great! She has become a dwelling place of demons and a prison of every unclean spirit and a prison of every unclean and hateful bird. For all the nations have drunk of the wine of the passion of her prostitution and the kings of the Earth have committed acts of harlotry with her and the merchants of the Earth have become rich by the wealth of her *sensuality*.'

> 'I heard another voice from the Heavens saying, 'Come out of her My People!, so that you will not participate in her sins and receive of her plagues, for her sins have piled up as high as the Heavens and God has remembered her iniquities.' (Rev. 18:2-5)

Understanding God's Word from His perspective brings greater discernment for what is right and what is wrong. His Torah allows the believer to see as He sees. The Father *is* getting the Bride ready for His Son:

> 'God is not a polygamist. He wants One People, One Bride. That's why Torah and the Sabbath are for the Gentile also. The Gentile coming into, and becoming one with Israel, not Israel going out and becoming pagan. The wild olive branch is grafted into the natural olive tree[607] not the other way around.'[608]

Many say that they don't have to keep the Mosaic Commandments. This is very unfortunate as the commandments of God are for personal blessing and safety. They are God's wisdom and knowledge. The Law is the verbal

---

[607] Rom. 11:15-29.

[608] Quote from Ruti Yehoshua, Jerusalem, Israel, Dec. 16th, 1996.

reflection of the One who gave it, and its authority is established (Dt. 4:5-8; 2nd Tim. 3:14-17).

Torah is for all followers of Yeshua, Jew and Gentile. For a biblical Gentile community to assemble together, they would all have to come together on the Sabbath. For them to celebrate the time when the Passover Lamb was slain for their freedom, they would have to celebrate Passover (1st Cor. 5:6-8). They would even come to the understanding that if they had a house with a flat roof (to walk on), they would need what is known as a parapet (a type of fence or railing that was made so people wouldn't accidentally fall over the edge.)[609]

Many Gentiles find themselves as the 'only one' that Torah is coming to. Spouse, friends and church haven't been touched by this yet. It's very lonely and disconcerting but this is similar to how Father Abraham felt when God told him to leave the things he knew behind (Gen. 12:1-4). Follow Yeshua and trust Him. It'll be a precious time of spiritual growth.

The Church needs to re-examine its theological structure concerning the Law and turn from their pagan traditions to the Word of God. Sunday, Easter and Christmas, etc., are pagan, anti-God and anti-Semitic. None of them has any biblical basis and should be thrown out and replaced with God's holy times and ways. This would cause Jews to take a second look.

Idolatry of any kind should not be practiced. Yeshua calls His people to be a holy people (1st Peter 1:13-19). The New Age movement dates all the way back to ancient Babylon. It's sorcery in modern clothes. As King Solomon once wrote, 'There's nothing new under the sun' (Eccl. 1:9). Transcendental meditation is sweeping the Western world with people ignorantly using mantras, invoking demons.

On some continents ancestor worship still exists among Christians. Reading the daily horoscope (astrology), Tarot cards, Ouija boards, crystals, beads, pyramids, and Eastern religions (Islam, Zen, Buddhism, etc.), are all part of the lure of the satanic Fisherman. Jewish mysticism (Kabbalah) is of the Devil.[610] These issues need to be addressed among the people of God. These sins need to be repented of and renounced 'by the Blood of Yeshua.' Ask Yeshua for His Blood to sever all connections with those people, spirits and practices, and to fill you with His Spirit and His ways.

---

[609] Dt. 22:8, 'When you build a new house, you shall make a parapet for your roof so that you will not bring blood guilt' (murder) 'on your house if anyone falls from it.'

[610] See *Kabbalah* at http://www.seedofabraham.net/kabbalah.html for why it's idolatry.

A Word About Torah

Some people might want to stone the blasphemer (Lev. 24:16) and other such acts of zealous righteousness. But there are a few considerations to take into account before the stone is thrown. The Law was given to a *nation* that was a *theocracy*. Yahveh literally directed Israel through His Torah, His High Priest, His mediator-king (Moses) and His Shekinah Glory Cloud. There was no authority but His. Under Joshua and King David it was similar. But not so in the days of Yeshua. The Jewish people were ruled by Rome. That's why the Sanhedrin needed *permission* from Rome to murder Yeshua. They didn't have authority to enact the death penalty.

For the person to be stoned in King David's day, the man would have to be brought to the town's elders to be judged first. It wasn't the responsibility of any one individual to take the law into their own hands. For instance, if a believing Gentile in Corinth had *speared* the believing Gentile who had been involved in incestuous cult prostitution (5:1), he would have been arrested, tried for murder in a Corinthian (Roman) court, found guilty and executed. They wouldn't have awarded him the Covenant of Shalom as Phineas received (Num. 25:11-12).[611]

The Apostle Paul gave the sinners time to repent (the ones accused of drinking the cup of demons; those involved with cult prostitution, etc.). But the one who had intercourse with his father's wife, Paul demanded that he be cast out of the congregation (1st Cor. 5:1-5; perhaps Paul only knew of this man?). If not repented of, it meant eternity in Hell for him.

This is just one example of how Torah is effected or 'shifts' in a nation that is non-Torah observant. But one must be equally aware that we're not to spiritualize the commandants (i.e. just to look for the principle 'behind' them, and do that instead of the commandments themselves).[612] For this isn't the primary reason why the commandments were given. The commandments are still in effect unless something overrides them, like circumcising a Jewish son on the Sabbath day (Jn. 7:21-24).

Yeshua came to reveal the deeper meaning or essence of Torah but He didn't do away with any of it.[613] He unveiled the commandment not to

---

[611] In killing Zimri and Cozbi, Phineas followed the judgement of God to Moses (Num. 25:4-5), and as a priest, he was also a judge (Dt. 17:8-13).

[612] For instance: to try and keep Sunday as the Sabbath by not working on it and resting, etc. The problem is that God never said one could change His holy day (Gen. 2:1-3; Ex. 20:8-11, etc.) by shifting its concept to another day.

[613] Mt. 5:17-19; 22:36-40; Lk. 16:16-17; John 10:35 'and Scripture cannot be

murder by revealing that hate was its essence. But the commandment not to murder still stands. Yeshua revealed the divine essence of the commandments. That's how Paul could say that the Law of Moses is very spiritual.[614] The commandments are spiritual pillars of righteousness.

The Ruach haKodesh (the Holy Spirit) is preparing the Bride: taking the veil away from her eyes to see the beauty of God's holy Torah which is a reflection of God Himself. That is why Acts 15:20-21 is beginning to be seen for what it is: *the* passage that brings the Gentile into Torah, that they might walk alongside their believing Jewish brethren who are doing the same thing. This is truly what makes Acts 15 epoch making in our day.

An Insight

This next set of quotes is an excerpt from a letter of Ruti Yehoshua. It clearly speaks of what God is desiring for His people Israel: a deeper walk in His Kingdom for both Jew and Gentile who love Messiah Yeshua:

> 'The Jewish person who comes to faith in Yeshua their Messiah has a dilemma. Where can they go for fellowship and remain true to the God of Israel and Hebraic understanding?'

> 'If they remain in the unbelieving Jewish community they are pulled and adulterated by the anti-Christ spirit that is throughout Rabbinic Judaism. This includes Jewish mysticism (Kabbalah) that is interwoven into the writings and the whole biased and manic-mitzvah[615] oriented belief system, which is a substitute for the Blood of Assurance' and the Ruach haKodesh.

> 'If on the other hand, they go into the Gentile Church (and this includes many of the so-called Messianic fellowships), they must enter a form of worship and practice that is foreign to Scripture, and anti-Semitic in attitude (in the Church).'

> 'Sunday, Easter, Thanksgiving[616] and Christmas are very

---

broken'; Rom. 3:31; 1st Cor. 7:17-19; Heb. 8:13; Rev. 12:17; 14:12, etc.

[614] Romans 7:14.

[615] Mitzva is the Hebrew word for commandment. The word has come to also mean a 'good deed.' Jewish people do 'mitzvas' in their desire to be seen as righteous and merit eternal life.

[616] See *Thanksgiving Day* at http://www.seedofabraham.net/thnksgiv.html.

pagan, as well as the symbols of the cross,[617] the fish,[618]

---

[617] Hislop, *The Two Babylons*, pp. 197-205.

[618] In Greek the word for fish is ιχθυς (ick-thoos). Each Greek letter has been made to represent a word (an acronym) meaning, Jesus Christ Son of God Savior. In Hebrew the word for the fish god was דָּגוֹן Dagon (dah-goan). Half fish and half man, it would fall down and break in pieces in front of the Ark of the Covenant (1st Sam. 5:1f.).

Dagon is identified with Bacchus who is also known as Ichthys (the fish god). Hislop, *The Two Babylons*, p. 247 and note * says that it was 'From about AD 360, to the time of the Emperor Justinian, about 550' 'that our Lord Jesus Christ began to be popularly called Ichthys, that is, "the Fish," manifestly to identify him with Dagon.' He was known by other names also. Hislop, p. 270 states, 'Saturn and Lateinos are just synonymous, having precisely the same meaning, and belonging equally to the same god. The reader cannot have forgotten the lines of Virgil, which showed that Lateinos, to whom the Romans or Latin race traced back their lineage, was represented with a glory around his head, to show that he was a 'child of the Sun.' Thus, then, it is evident that, in popular opinion, the original Lateinos had occupied the very same position as Saturn did in the Mysteries, who was equally worshipped as the 'offspring of the Sun.''

'Moreover, it is evident that the Romans knew that the name 'Lateinos' signifies the 'Hidden One,' for their antiquarians invariably affirm that Latium received its name from Saturn 'lying hid' there. On etymological grounds then, even on the testimony of the Romans, Lateinos is equivalent to the 'Hidden One'; that is, to Saturn, the 'god of Mystery.' Hislop, page 270 note ⁋ states, 'Latium Latinus (the Roman form of the Greek Lateinos), and Lateo, 'to lie hid,' all alike come from the Chaldee 'Lat' which has the same meaning.'

'The name 'lat,' or the hidden one, had evidently been given, as well as Saturn, to the great Babylonian god. This is evident from the name of the fish Latus, which was worshipped along with the Egyptian Minerva, in the city of Latopolis in Egypt, now Esneh (Wilkinson), that fish Latus evidently just being another name for the fish-god Dagon.'

'Ichthys, or the Fish, was one of the names of Bacchus; and the Assyrian goddess Atergatis, with her son Ichthys is said to have been cast into the lake of Ascalon.' 'That the sun-god Apollo had been known under the name of Lat, may be inferred from the Greek name of his mother-wife Leto, or in Doric, Lato, which is just the feminine of Lat. The Roman name Latona confirms this, for it signifies 'The lamenter of Lat,' as Bellona signifies 'The lamenter of Bel.'

Hislop on page 114 note * says: 'To identify Nimrod with Oannes, mentioned by Berosus as appearing out of the sea, it will be remembered that Nimrod has been proved to be Bacchus. Then, for proof that Nimrod or Bacchus,' 'on being overcome by his enemies, was fabled to have taken refuge in the sea, see Chap. IV, Sect. I. When, therefore, he was represented as reappearing, it was natural that he should reappear in the very character of Oannes as a Fish-god. 'Now, Jerome calls Dagon, the well known Fish-god, Piscem moeroris the Star of David,[619] and so-called 'pictures of Jesus,' etc.'

'Yeshua is leading the *called out* Jews and Gentiles to a Torah lifestyle rich in biblical Hebraic expression. God Himself is the Author of this Hebraic expression because it's His Essence and His Heart.'

'As we surrender ourselves to doing the will of the Father, which is Yeshua's heart, the Ruach haKodesh will lead us to leave both perverted Camps.'

'This doesn't mean that those Camps are devoid of helping us in our walk. But in these things we need to look to Him for His guidance, seeking only to please Him. We are no longer our own but have been bought by His Precious Blood and delivered out of darkness to serve Him in the newness of His Spirit in us.'

'I believe the Ruach' (Spirit) 'is showing us today that the Gentile believer is called also to serve the Jewish people.'

(Bryant, vol. iii. p. 179), 'the fish of sorrow,' which goes far to identify that Fish-god with Bacchus, the 'Lamented one'; and the identification is complete when Hesychius tells us that some called Bacchus, Ichthys, or "The fish"'. Hislop's theme is that the Catholic Church is a bastion of paganism and has replaced ancient Babylon as the enemy of God's people. His book thoroughly proves this.

There are some that say that the Philistine Dagon wasn't a fish god but a god of grain as the Hebrew word for grain דָּגָן (dah-gahn) and 'fish' דָּג (dahg) come from the same Hebrew verb which means 'to multiply.' Davidson, *AHCL*, p. 146 states that Dagon means a 'large fish' properly the 'name of an idol of the Philistines worshipped at Ashdod.' He says the word can also mean 'grain.' There was a Dagon in Mesopotamia who was a god of grain but it seems that the Philistines, who lived by the Mediterranean Sea, had Dagon as their fish god. Brown, *NBDBG*, p. 186; In 1st Sam. 5:4 when Dagon had fallen down, with hands and head cut off before the Ark of the Covenant, the trunk (body) of Dagon is literally called his 'fishy part' (as it was made in the form of a fish).

However one might understand this Dagon, the reality remains that Ichthys, under many different names, was known as the fish god and worshipped as such. His fish symbol is the same symbol that adorns many Christian car bumpers and Bibles, etc., who think it represents Jesus. But where in Scripture is Jesus ever symbolized as a fish?

[619] See *The Star of David* at www.seedofabraham.net/stardavd.html for an understanding of why believers shouldn't wear it, and *Jesus the Fish God?* at www.seedofabraham.net/fish.html for why believers shouldn't wear the fish symbol either. These two also negate the so-called 'Messianic Seal.'

'How is this walked out? By coming out of Babylonian (Church) practices and moving into obedience of the Torah of the God of Israel, led by His Spirit. This way the Jewish unbeliever who is coming to faith in Yeshua is not made to stumble but is rightly, truthfully restored to his or her God through His Son and Messiah. Yeshua does not look or act pagan. (This of course holds true for the Gentiles coming to Messiah as well, that they are not led into pagan practices also.)'

'We are created to reflect The Truth. Let us walk hand in hand as one people with the One who is Truth.'[620]

There's a desensitizing to pagan things when pagan holy days and ways are 'Christianized.' In other words, how can one tell if something is pagan or not? What is the *standard* by which to judge things?

Pagans were worshiping their gods a certain way one day, and the next, the Church took it and 'baptized' it for its people. Why do the followers of Jesus need to take anything from Satan? This is the problem when one throws out the standard of Jesus: Torah. It creates a vacuum and an ignorance for satanic things to come in.

The ancient Roman Church filled the vacuum with satanic 'holy days' and concepts and today, most Christians believe that these pagan days and ways are of God. When many find out otherwise, *tradition is so strong* that they can't or won't believe it. The veil is still over their eyes. The Torah of Yahveh is the standard from which to judge religion by. If people would read the Torah they'd know that God has given us His standard with His holy days and dietary laws, etc. And they'd see the conflict between what the Church teaches and what God commands for those that believe in Him.

Believers in Yeshua don't need to incorporate anything from Satan. God doesn't need 'to take anything back' from Satan that was never God's to begin with.

The God of Israel is not pleased with what the Church has done. This is easily seen in the admonitions He's given to Israel (Dt. 12:28-32; Acts 20:25-35; 2nd Tim. 3:16-17; 2nd Pet. 3:14-18; Rev. 18:2-5). What He has given to His people Israel is for the Gentile too. This way we can be a greater Light unto both the Jew and the Gentile that need Messiah Yeshua, as well as walk in His ways of life.

---

[620] Excerpted from a letter of Ruti Yehoshua, Jerusalem, Israel, Dec. 19th, 1996.

Some Advice

Our hearts continually wander from the attitude of serving and 'washing the feet of our brethren' which is Yeshua's Heart and His Attitude.[621] When we walk in this, the rest of Torah is easy to do. God doesn't expect us to walk in Torah overnight but He does expect us to begin. He wants us to grasp the concept that all the Law that applies to us is for us.[622] In keeping these commandments, in being aware when we break them or sin, we are saying to Abba El (Papa God), that we recognize His Authority to govern our lives. He knows what is good for us and what is sin. Walk in His Torah and let His Spirit lead you.

Torah is commanded, not suggested. If God demands it of us, we want to acknowledge this in our heart, and not give way to the teaching of the Church, or the 'wearing away' of our belief by 'well meaning' friends who think otherwise. This isn't forcing someone to do His commandments, that's not His way. It's being honest about what is required or expected of us. This is the target or the goal: to do His will in all areas of our life.

Fear of legalism is a stumbling block for many. Under the guise of caution there's little movement toward the *doing* of the commandments. Legalism is the strict enforcing or perversion of a law. Legalism is not equal to Law or Torah (except in the mind of the Church). If we're driving 61 miles per hour in a 60 mile per hour zone and a policeman gives us a ticket, that's legalism. But the law is good. The Law was given so there won't be chaos and accidents on the Highway of Life.

There were times that Yeshua had to correct us concerning a legalistic attitude. A heart that is open to Him will be led into His ways. If you're afraid of making a mistake or of becoming legalistic, you've already sinned by being afraid. Don't be afraid! (Mk. 5:35-36) Deal with the fear. Take it to our Father who is gracious in forgiving, and in granting wisdom and strength to overcome the fear.

Legalism is part of what we have to deal with in our lives. Legalism is part of our carnality. We are going to make mistakes. He allows this as

---

[621] John 13:14-17, 34-35.

[622] There are many commandments that apply to only certain individuals. The commandment of the parapet is only directed to those that have houses with a flat roof. If one doesn't have a house with a flat roof to walk on, one isn't expected to observe or to fulfill this commandment.

part of our experiential training in righteousness. We must come to Him and His Torah as little children. No one has all the answers but oh what joy there is in discovering (some of) them!

Keeping the Sabbath is not legalism. It's God's law for His chosen people Israel, both Jew and Gentile. Yeshua kept the Sabbath day holy all His Life and never did it legalistically. And He has given us His Spirit that we might follow His example, from the inside out.

Our understanding is faulty. That's why (His) Love covers a multitude of sins. We should be excited with Joy that He is teaching us His Torah (Genesis through Revelation). He will correct us as we walk with Him. He's a good Abba (Papa). Our learning Torah is like a child going with their Abba to the park on an adventure. He will take good care of us.

The teachings of the Rabbis can be insightful. They can flush out understanding of a commandment or a passage of Scripture. But realize that the Rabbis can be very wrong, extremely shallow and diabolically perverse (Mt. 16:5-12; 23:1-36). Pray before swallowing. Be careful.[623] If you're not sure or want another opinion, feel free to contact us.

We've seen too many sincere Christians fall into the tar pits of Judaism. A Judaism that has been anti-Christ since the Gold Calf. Without the infilling of His Spirit we all too easily fall prey to the spiritual Magician who loves to seduce and lead astray for damnation.

If you don't have the infilling of the Holy Spirit, seek it diligently. Study the Word. Learn Hebrew. It'll open up hidden treasures for you. Yes, we know it's hard but the rewards are sweet.

To abstain from all unclean meat is Torah. To 'keep kosher' the Jewish way is both Torah and rabbinical. There's a big difference. The Rabbis have added much to the Word and perverted it. God wants us to eat only meat that is clean according to His Torah.

Keeping kosher means different things to different sects within Orthodox and Conservative Judaism. God requires the one but not the other.[624] One of the differences is that in the observant Jewish community, one is not allowed to eat dairy and meat at the same meal. This is not scriptural. And one must have different dishes for dairy and meat meals.[625] A faulty rab-

---

[623] For a brief outline of some of the idolatrous and perverted things of Judaism see *Jewish Idolatry* at http://www.seedofabraham.net/jewidol.html.

[624] For instance, a clean animal, slaughtered properly by slitting the throat and draining the blood, is not considered kosher for Orthodox Jews unless certified by a rabbi. But it's kosher to God without rabbinic certification. See *Kosher: Jewish vs. Biblical* at http://www.seedofabraham.net/kosher.html.

binic interpretation of Ex. 23:19 (which is repeated in Ex. 34:26 and Dt. 14:21), has caused this.[626]

If you're led of the Lord, go to a synagogue service or two. Tell anyone at the synagogue who asks you why you're there, that Messiah Yeshua is leading you into keeping Torah. Perhaps you can learn Hebrew there.[627] Let the Holy Spirit lead you. You shouldn't encounter too many problems at first. And if they throw you out, realize that you're in good company (Yeshua and Paul, etc.).

Most Christians today don't fully understand how pervasive pagan wor-

---

[625] The eating of dairy with meat is strictly forbidden by the Rabbis but this is nowhere found in Scripture. This is very perverse as it sets up something as sin which God doesn't call sin. Also the separation of meat and dairy dishes, pots and pans, etc., stems from the ruling to separate meat from dairy. This is part of 'kosher the Orthodox Jewish way' but isn't found in God's Word. On the contrary, Father Abraham served God and two angels meat and dairy at the same time and they ate it (Gen. 18:8).

[626] The Jewish view is that one shouldn't eat meat and dairy together thus avoiding the possibility of eating the meat of the kid and the milk of the mother together. Of course the possibility exists that one can eat them at different times but the Rabbis don't address this. Carrying the rabbinic interpretation to all meat and dairy, one finds the impossible situation of chickens which don't give milk, but still cannot be eaten with dairy products.

The Rabbis have misunderstood the verse. It has nothing to do with the separation of meat and dairy but with an ancient pagan fertility rite. This prohibition comes 'on the heels' (Ex. 23:16, 19; 34:22, 26), or just before (Dt. 14:21-27), Yahveh's commandment concerning the end of the harvest year Feast of Tabernacles. The prohibition was aimed at stopping Israelis from copying the magical procedure of the pagans, in hoping that next year's crop would be bountiful.

Freeman, *Manners and Customs of the Bible*, p. 73, #133 states: this 'injunction is put in connection with sacrifices and festivals' (and not a dietary regulation). The seething of a kid in his mother's milk was an *idolatrous* practice done 'for the purpose of making trees and fields more fruitful the following year.' He says, 'on the authority of an ancient Karaite comment on the Pentateuch' 'it was an ancient heathen custom to boil a kid in the dam's milk, and then besprinkle with it all the trees, fields, gardens and orchards.'

Pfeiffer, *WBC*, p. 73 states, 'in the Ugarit literature discovered in 1930, it was learned that boiling a kid in its mother's milk was a Canaanite practice used in connection with fertility rites (*Birth of the Gods*, 1:14).' Harris, *TWOT*, vol. I, p. 285 states, 'Since a Ugaritic text (UT 16: Text no. 52:14) specifies, 'They cook a kid in milk,' 'the biblical injunction' was 'directed against a Canaanite fertility rite.'

[627] See www.seedofabraham.net/c&v.html for the Hebrew course and other teachings.

ship was in Yakov's day. *All the world* was deeply involved in it. From Ireland to India and from China to Chile, all the world was enslaved to pagan gods and their cruel practices. What ties them together was that they all stemmed from Babylon. The names of the gods and goddesses would change in each country, but the rites, practices, ceremonies, officials and doctrines were similar, if not the same. For an excellent detailed account of this, read Alexander Hislop's classic *The Two Babylons*.

By Yakov's time the keeping of the Law symbolized in circumcision had wrongfully attained the necessary status for salvation among the Jewish people. This perverse understanding of 'being Jewish' would be replaced by the Catholic Church with baptism (their unbiblical *sprinkling* vs. full immersion). Circumcision was given to Father Avraham as a *sign* of God's covenant *relationship* with him. But Avraham was already walking in salvation or covenant relationship with Yahveh (Gen. 15, 17).

Baptism in water is a spiritual reality of the death, burial and resurrection of the person, in imitation of Yeshua, for the removal of the sin nature (Rom. 6; death to self), and the infilling or indwelling of the Holy Spirit. It's also a typical reenactment of the dedication and consecration of the dwelling places for God (the Tabernacle, the Temple of Solomon, the Person of Yeshua at His baptism, and believing Israel; Num. 9:15-16; 1st Kg. 8:10-11; Mt. 3:16; Acts 2:1-4, 38 respectively).

The Roman Catholic Church perverted baptism. They claim that anyone sprinkled by them is 'guaranteed' Heaven despite their *lack of relationship* with Jesus and sinful lifestyle. They call it the waters of regeneration, a pagan concept also known as magic waters.[628]

We're called to walk in deep relationship with God, to keep His Torah and to teach our children to walk in it (Dt. 6:4-7). As we do this, we are their example. This way we are preparing them to worship the King, His way, when He comes to rule for 1,000 years upon the Earth in Israel from the Temple in Jerusalem:

> 'Blessed and holy are those who share in the first resurrection! Over these the second death has no power but they will be priests of God and of Messiah and they will reign with Him a thousand years.' (Rev 20:6)

> 'And it shall come to pass that everyone who is left of all the nations which came against Jerusalem, shall go up from year to year to worship the King, the Lord of Hosts and *to keep the Feast of Tabernacles*. And it shall be that

---

[628] Hislop, *The Two Babylons*, pp. 129-144.

whichever of the families of the Earth do not come up to Jerusalem to worship the King, the Lord of Hosts, on them there will be no rain.' 'Everyone who *sacrifices* shall come...and cook them there. There shall no longer be a Canaanite in the House of the Lord of Hosts.' (Zech. 14:16-17; 21; see also Ezk. 40-48)

'Circumcision is nothing and uncircumcision is nothing but *what matters is the keeping of the Commandments of God.*' (1st Cor. 7:19)

'So the Dragon was enraged with the Woman and went off to make war with the rest of her children *who keep the Commandments of God* and hold to the testimony of Yeshua.' (Rev. 12:17)

'Here is the perseverance of the holy ones who *keep the Commandments of God* and their faith in Yeshua.' (Rev. 14:12)

It's time for God's people Israel, both Jew and Gentile who love Jesus with all their heart, to come out of Babylon and all her ways of darkness:

'And I heard another voice from Heaven saying, "Come out of her My People!, so that you may not participate in her sins and that you may not receive of her plagues."' (Rev. 18:4)

'In days to come the Mountain of Yahveh's House shall be established as the highest of the mountains and shall be raised up above the hills. Peoples shall stream to it and many nations shall come and say, "Come! Let us go up to the Mountain of Yahveh, to the House (Temple) of the God of Jacob that He may teach us His ways and that we may walk in His paths." *For out of Zion shall go forth the Torah*, and the Word of Yahveh from Jerusalem.' (Mic. 4:1-2)

'but whenever a man turns to the Lord, *the veil is taken away*. Now the Lord is the Spirit and where the Spirit of the Lord is, *there is liberty*. But we all with *unveiled* face beholding as in a mirror the Glory of the Lord are being transformed *into the same image* from Glory to Glory, just as from the Lord, the Spirit.' (2nd Cor. 3:16-18)

APPENDIX

Two Different Kingdoms?

The Stranger and the Native Born

The following sections reinforce the themes that Yakov gave the four rules as a filter against sacrificial-sexual idolatry, and that the Law of Moses is for every believer in Yeshua.

There are five words in Hebrew for people that would reside within Israel who weren't from the Seed of Abraham, Isaac and Jacob. The Law would apply to only two of them: the slave (by circumstance), and the stranger.

Stranger is the English translation for 'ger' in the KJV, NKJV and NASB. The NIV uses alien and the NRSV uses resident alien.[629] The five designations are found in Ex. 12:43-48. It's the Passover chapter and the Lord is saying who could, and who could not, take part in it (yes or no).

1. foreigner	בֶּן-נֵכָר	(ben nay-har)	no	Ex. 12:43
2. hired worker	שָׂכִיר	(sah-here)	no	Ex. 12:45
3. temporary resident	תּוֹשָׁב	(toe-shav)	no	Ex. 12:45
4. slave	עֶבֶד	(eh-ved)	yes	Ex. 12:44
5. stranger	גֵּר	(ger)	yes	Ex. 12:48

Why one could or couldn't take part seems to revolve around what was in their heart toward God. The definition of the word tends to bring this out:

1. The foreigner *could not eat* of the Passover (Ex. 12:43). The noun means, 'what is strange, foreign.' The verb, 'to estrange, alienate' 'to seem strange' 'to reject'.[630] *TWOT* says it speaks of 'a foreign god (Dt. 32:12; Ps. 81:9)' and 'everything foreign (Neh. 13:30).'[631] This person worships other gods and *wants* to be alienated from Israel, her God and His Torah which appears 'strange' to him.

2. The hired worker *could not eat* of the Passover (Ex. 12:45). The

---

[629] Some translations like the KJV don't make a distinction between the stranger #5 and the foreigner #1. This is unfortunate as it seems that God is contradicting Himself (e.g. in Ex. 12:43, He says the *foreigner* (#1) can't keep the Passover. But if it's translated as stranger it seems to conflict with v. 48). The KJV people may have thought the terms were synonymous but they're not.

[630] Davidson, *AHCL*, p. 549.

[631] Harris, *TWOT*, vol. II, p. 580.

noun means a 'hired laborer, hireling.'[632] Yeshua said the hireling would run from trouble and leave the sheep to the wolf because he didn't care about the sheep (Jn. 10:12-13).

3. The temporary resident *could not eat* of the Passover (Ex. 12:45). This is a person who is also called a 'sojourner.'[633] He's a migrant, a 'temporary, landless wage earner.' The word can be 'a synonym for a hired servant (Lev. 22:10; 25:40).'[634]

4. The slave *could eat* of the Passover after he was circumcised (Ex. 12:44). The slave served his master, doing his will.[635] The slave seems to be 'one' with his Hebrew master (Gen. 17:9-13, 23-27).

5. The stranger *could eat* the Passover once he and all the males in his house were circumcised (Ex. 12:48). The verb means to 'dwell for a time'.[636] The stranger kept the Sabbath laws (Ex. 20:10; 23:12) and expressed the same loyalty to God as the native born (Lev. 20:2).[637]

- He was to hear the Law read (Dt. 31:12), and the Feasts applied to him (Ex. 12:19; Lev. 16:29; Num. 9:14; Dt. 16:14).

- His punishment was death if he sacrificed to a foreign god (Lev. 17:8f.), and he was forbidden to eat blood (Lev. 17:10-13). The special cleansing of the red heifer's ashes applied to him (Num. 19:10), as well as the laws of forbidden sexual unions (Lev. 18:26).

- It's written that Yahveh loves this *stranger*, giving him his food and clothing (Dt. 10:18). He wasn't to be oppressed by the Is-raeli and enjoyed the same rights as the native born (Ex. 22:21; Lev. 19:3; Jer. 7:6).[638] He was to be helped if he was poor (Lev. 19:10; Dt. 14:29; 16:11) and he could take of the gleanings of the olive trees and vineyards which were also reserved for the widow and the orphan (Dt. 24:20-21).

In essence the stranger (ger) who was circumcised was just like the native

---

[632] Davidson, *AHCL*, p. 715.

[633] Ibid., p. 352.

[634] Harris, *TWOT*, vol. I, p. 412.

[635] Davidson, *AHCL*, p. 583.

[636] Ibid., p. 134.

[637] Harris, *TWOT*, vol. I, p. 156.

[638] Ibid. Although the stranger (ger) is in a separate category from other foreign-ers who weren't native Hebrews, there are times when the word seems to be used as a general designation for anyone not of Israel (e.g. Dt. 10:19; 28:43).

born. Yahveh's Law extended to him. Basically there was to be only one law for both of them. If Yahveh's Law applied to the stranger in the midst of Israel under the Old Testament, *how much more* under the New Testament where the the Gentile has been circumcised by God (Col. 2:11)?

The Gentile comes into Israel through the New Covenant, the covenant that God gave to the House of Israel and the House of Judah (Jer. 31:31-34; Eph. 2:13). They are to learn the laws of the God of Israel that they might gain *greater* spiritual knowledge of Yahveh and walk in His ways with their Jewish believing brethren (Dt. 31:12-13; Acts 15:20-21).

The following is a partial list of cites which contain *ger* (#5, stranger)...

> Ex. 12:19: 'Seven days there shall be no leaven found in your houses for whoever eats what is leavened, that person shall be cut off from the Congregation of Israel, whether he is a *stranger* or a native of the Land.' (This pertains to Passover.)

> Ex. 12:43-45, 48: 'And Yahveh said to Moses and Aaron, "This is the ordinance of the Passover: No foreigner (#1) shall eat it. But *every man's slave* (#4) who is bought for money, when you have circumcised him then he may eat it. A temporary resident (#3) and a hired servant (#2) must not eat it."'

> 'And when a *stranger* (#5) dwells with you and wants to keep the Passover to Yahveh, let all his males be circumcised and then let him come near and keep it. *And he shall be as a native of the land.*'

> Lev. 16:29: 'This shall be a permanent statute for you: in the seventh month on the tenth day of the month you shall humble your souls and not do any work, whether the native or the *stranger* who sojourns among you'. (This is for the Day of Atonement.)

> Lev. 17:12: 'Therefore I said to the Sons of Israel, "No person among you may eat blood, nor may any *stranger* who sojourns among you eat blood."'

> Lev. 18:26: 'you are to keep My statutes and My judgments and shall not do any of these abominations, neither the native nor the *stranger* who sojourns among you'.

> Lev. 24:16: 'Moreover, the one who blasphemes the Name of Yahveh shall surely be put to death; all the Con-

gregation shall certainly stone him. The *stranger* as well as the native, when he blasphemes the Name shall be put to death.'

Num. 9:14: 'If a *stranger* sojourns among you and observes the Passover to Yahveh according to the statute of the Passover and according to its ordinance, so he shall do. *You shall have one statute both for the stranger* and for the native of the land.'

Num. 15:14-16: 'If a *stranger* sojourns with you or one who may be among you throughout your generations and he wishes to make a *sacrifice* by fire as a soothing aroma to Yahveh, *just as you do so he shall do.* As for the Assembly, there shall be one statute for you and for the stranger who sojourns with you, a *perpetual statute throughout your generations.* As you are, so shall the *stranger* be before Yahveh. There is to be *one law and one ordinance* for you and for the *stranger* who sojourns with you.'

Num. 15:29: 'You shall have one law for him who does anything unintentionally, for him who is native among the Sons of Israel and for the *stranger* who lives among them.'

Num. 15:30: 'But the person who does anything defiantly, whether he is native or a *stranger*, that one is blaspheming Yahveh and that person shall be cut off from among his people.'

Num. 19:10: 'The one who gathers the ashes of the heifer shall wash his clothes and be unclean until evening. And it shall be a perpetual statute to the Sons of Israel and to the *stranger* who lives among them.'

Num. 35:15: 'These six cities shall be for refuge for the Sons of Israel and for the *stranger* and for the sojourner among them. That anyone who kills a person unintentionally may flee there.'

Dt. 31:12: 'Assemble the people, the men and the women and children and the *stranger* who is in your town so that they may hear and learn and fear Yahveh your God and *be careful to observe all the words of this Law.*'

Josh. 8:33-35: 'All Israel, *stranger* as well as native born, with their Elders and officers and their judges, stood on opposite sides of the Ark in front of the Levitical Priests who carried the Ark of the Covenant of Yahveh. Half of them in front of Mount Gerizim and half of them in front of Mount Ebal as Moses the Servant of Yahveh had commanded, that they should bless the people of Israel. And afterward he read all the words of the Law, blessings and curses, according to all that is written in the Book of the Law. There was not a word of all that Moses commanded that Joshua did not read before all the Assembly of Israel and the women and the little ones and the *strangers* who resided among them.'

Ezk. 47:23: '"And *in the Tribe* with which the *stranger* stays, there you shall *give him his inheritance"* declares the Lord Yahveh.' (This speaks of the Millennial Kingdom. Ezk. 40–48 describes a Temple yet to be built.)

Isaiah 56:6-7: 'Also the *foreigners* who *join themselves* to Yahveh to minister to Him and to love the Name of Yahveh, to be His servants; everyone who keeps from profaning the Sabbath and holds fast My Covenant, these I will bring to My holy Mountain and make them joyful in My House of Prayer.'

'Their burnt offerings and their *sacrifices* will be accepted on My Altar for My House shall be called a House of Prayer for *all* peoples.'

This last cite in Isaiah doesn't speak of the stranger (ger) but of the ben nayhar (#1, the foreigner). It shows that Yahveh's compassion would extend to those who had been formerly excluded from the covenant. Now salvation is open to everyone who turns to Him through Messiah Yeshua.

Welcome to the Commonwealth of Israel, the Kingdom of God where the wall of partition has been broken down:[639]

'So then, you are no longer *strangers and foreigners* but you are fellow citizens with the holy ones and are of God's Household.' (Eph. 2:19)

'"And it shall be from New Moon to New Moon and from Sabbath to Sabbath, *all mankind* will come to bow down before Me" says Yahveh.' (Isaiah 66:23)

---

[639] Rom. 11:16-29; Eph. 2:1-22; 3:6.

The Blood

Lev. 17:10-14: 'And any man from the House of Israel or from the *strangers* who sojourn among them who eats any *blood*, I will set My face against that person who eats *blood* and will cut him off from among his people.'

'For the life of the flesh is in the *blood* and I have given it to you on the Altar to make atonement for your souls. For it is the *blood* by reason of the life that makes atonement. Therefore I said to the Sons of Israel, "No person among you may eat *blood* nor may any *stranger* who sojourns among you eat *blood*."'

'So when any man from the Sons of Israel or from the *strangers* who sojourn among them, in hunting catches a beast or a bird which may be eaten, he shall pour out its blood and cover it with earth.'

'As for the life of all flesh, its *blood* is identified with its life. Therefore I said to the Sons of Israel, "You are not to eat the *blood* of any flesh for the life of all flesh is its *blood*. Whoever eats it shall be cut off."'

The animal was caught and slaughtered, with the blood drained upon the Earth and covered. Hunters know that the blood needs to be drained immediately after the kill. This way the meat will not become contaminated with the blood in it. It is only with today's modern methods of mass slaughtering of cattle and chicken, etc., that many times the blood is not properly drained. Welcome to the 21st century.

'The *blood* however, you must not eat. You must pour it out on the ground like water.' (Dt. 12:16)

'Only be sure that you do not eat the *blood*. For the *blood* is the life and you must not eat the life with the meat.' (Dt. 12:23)

Eating the blood in one's roast beef is wrong. It's sin (Lev. 7:26; 19:26; 2nd Sam. 14:32-34; Ezk. 33:25). But Yahveh didn't want Israel eating (drinking) the blood from any slaughter, as the pagans did in their sacrificial worship, whether at the pagan shrine or in the field.

The Harlot

Lev. 17:7: 'They shall no longer sacrifice their sacrifices to the goat demons with which they *play the cult harlot.* This shall be a permanent statute to them throughout their generations.'

Lev. 20:6: 'As for the person who turns to mediums and to spiritists, to *play the harlot* after them, I will also set My face against that person and will cut him off from among his people.'

Dt. 22:21: 'then they shall bring out the girl to the doorway of her father's house and the men of her city shall stone her to death because she has committed an act of foolishness in Israel by *playing the harlot* in her father's house. Thus you shall purge the evil from among you.'

Dt. 23:18: 'You shall not bring the hire of a *cult harlot* or the wages of a dog (a *homosexual male cult harlot*) into the House of Yahveh your God for any votive offering, for both of these are an abomination to Yahveh your God.'

Dt. 31:16: 'Yahveh said to Moses, "Behold, you are about to lie down with your fathers and this people will arise and *play the cult harlot* with the strange gods of the land into the midst of which they are going and will forsake Me and break My Covenant which I have made with them."'

Judges 2:17: 'Yet they did not listen to their Judges for they *played the cult harlot* after other gods and bowed themselves down to them. They turned aside quickly from the way in which their Fathers had walked in obeying the commandments of Yahveh. They did not do as their Fathers.'

2nd Chron. 21:11: 'Moreover he made high places in the mountains of Judah and caused the inhabitants of Jerusalem to *play the cult harlot* and led Judah astray.'

Psalm 106:35-40: 'But they *mingled with the nations and learned their practices* and served their idols which became a snare to them. They even sacrificed their sons and their daughters to the demons and shed innocent blood, the blood of their sons and their daughters whom they sacrificed to the idols of Canaan. And the Land was polluted with the blood. Thus they became unclean in their practices and *played the cult harlot* in their deeds. Therefore the anger of Yahveh was kindled against His people and He abhorred His Inheritance.'

Isaiah 1:21: 'How the Faithful City has become a *harlot!* She who was full of justice! Righteousness once lodged in Her, but now murderers!'

Jer. 2:20: 'For long ago I broke your yoke and tore off your bonds. But you said, 'I will not serve!' For on every high hill and under every green tree you have lain down as a *cult harlot.*'

Jer. 3:6-10: "Then Yahveh said to me in the days of King Josiah, 'Have you seen what faithless Israel did? She went up on every high hill and under every green tree and she was a *cult harlot* there.' I thought, 'After she has done all these things she will return to Me' but she did not return and her treacherous sister Judah saw it."

"And I saw that for all the adulteries of faithless Israel, I had sent her away and given her a writ of divorce, yet her treacherous sister Judah did not fear but she went and was a *cult harlot* also. Because of the lightness of her *cult harlotry* she polluted the Land and committed adultery with stones and trees. Yet in spite of all this her treacherous sister Judah did not return to Me with all her heart but rather in deception' declares Yahveh."

Ezk. 16:15-17, 26: 'But you trusted in your beauty and *played the cult harlot* because of your fame, and you poured out your *harlotries* on every passerby who might be willing. You took some of your clothes, made for yourself high places of various colors and *played the cult harlot* on them which should never have come about nor happened. You also took your beautiful jewels made of My gold and of My silver which I had given you and made for yourself male images that you might *play the cult harlot* with them.'

'You also played the *cult harlot* with the Egyptians, your

lustful neighbors and multiplied your *cult harlotry* to make Me angry.'

Hosea 4:12-14: 'My people consult their wooden idol and their diviner's wand informs them. For a spirit of *cult harlotry* has led them astray and they have *played the cult harlot*, departing from their God. They offer sacrifices on the tops of the mountains and burn incense on the hills, under oak, poplar and terebinth because their shade is pleasant. Therefore your daughters *play the harlot* and your brides commit adultery.'

'I will not punish your daughters when they *play the harlot* or your brides when they commit adultery, for the men themselves go apart with *cult harlots* and offer sacrifices with *temple harlots*. So the people without understanding are ruined.'

Nahum 3:4: 'All because of the many *cult harlotries* of the Harlot, the Charming One, the Mistress of Sorceries who sells nations by her *cult harlotries* and families by her sorceries.'[640]

Rev. 17:1: 'Then one of the seven angels who had the seven bowls came and spoke with me saying, 'Come here! I will show you the judgment of the Great *Cult Harlot* who sits on many waters'!

Rev. 17:15-16: 'And he said to me, 'The waters which you saw where the *Cult Harlot* sits are peoples, multitudes, nations and tongues. And the ten horns which you saw, and the beast, these will hate the *Cult Harlot* and will make her desolate and naked and will eat her flesh and will burn her up with fire.'

---

[640] This is the Great Cult Harlot of Babylon. Hislop, *The Two Babylons*, p. 304: 'The first deified woman was no doubt Semiramis, as the first deified man was her husband' (Nimrod). Semiramis was known in Israel as Astarte, and worshiped in other countries under many other names: Diana, Rhea, Venus, and Cybele (Madonna), etc. She was called 'an incarnation of the one spirit of God, the great Mother of all' 'the Holy Spirit of God' (this is the designation the Roman Catholic Church places on their deified Mary).

The Fire of God

When Yahveh appears in Fire on Mt. Sinai (Ex. 3:1-6; 19:16-20), the identification of God with fire is seen. The Fire in the Altar of the Tabernacle of Moses was never to go out.[641] It symbolized the eternal God. It's also a picture of the Fire of God on the Heavenly Altar. This Fire is eternal for it says that our God is a consuming Fire.[642]

The Altar fire was seen as a cleansing agent. The sacrifices were consumed by what pictured the Fire of God (the Holy Spirit). Symbolically, the sinful person was destroyed through this Living Fire, and ascended in a life of flame and smoke — transformed and totally dedicated to Yahveh.

When Yahveh appeared to His people Israel, He came in divine Fire and that is the closest thing 'in the natural' that we have for describing Yahveh's spiritual 'substance':

> Ex. 19:16-18: 'So it came about on the third day, when it was morning, that there were Thunder and Lightning flashes and a thick Cloud upon the Mountain and a very loud Shofar' (Ram's horn) 'so that all the people who were in the Camp trembled. And Moses brought the people out of the Camp to meet God and they stood at the foot of the Mountain. Now Mount Sinai was all in *Smoke* because Yahveh descended upon it in *Fire* and its *Smoke* ascended like the smoke of a furnace and the whole Mountain quaked violently.'

> Ex. 24:17: 'And to the eyes of the Sons of Israel, the appearance of the Glory of Yahveh was like a *consuming Fire* on the Mountain top.'

When the Tabernacle of Moses was first inaugurated, after Aaron and his sons were fully consecrated, Yahveh sent Fire from the Heavens to light the Altar of Sacrifice. It was the Holy Spirit:

> Lev. 9:23-24: 'Moses and Aaron went into the Tent of Meeting. When they came out and blessed the people the Glory of Yahveh appeared to all the people. Then *Fire* came out from before Yahveh and consumed the Burnt Sacrifice and the portions of fat on the Altar and when all the people saw it, they shouted and fell on their faces.'

---

[641] Lev. 6:13: 'Fire shall burn continually on the Altar. It's not to go out.'

[642] Dt. 4:24; Heb. 12:29. Also Ex. 19:16f; Lev. 9:23-24; Lk. 12:49; Rev. 4:5.

2nd Chron. 7:3: 'All the Sons of Israel, seeing the *Fire* come down and the Glory of Yahveh upon the Temple, bowed down on the pavement with their faces to the ground and they worshiped and gave praise to Yahveh saying, "Truly He is good! Truly His forgiving loving-kindness is everlasting."' (For Solomon's Temple)

When the Holy Spirit was given to Israel in Acts 2, we see that same Fire inhabiting the Apostles and all who believe in the Son:

Acts 2:3: 'And there appeared to them tongues as of *Fire* distributing themselves and they rested on each one of them.'

This Fire will purge us on our journey to the New Jerusalem, test our faith in Yeshua, and transform us into His Image:

1st Cor. 3:13: 'each man's work will become evident for the Day will show it because it is to be revealed with *Fire* and the *Fire* itself will test the quality of each man's work.'

2nd Cor. 3:18: 'But we all with *unveiled* face beholding as in a mirror the *Glory* of the Lord are being transformed into the same image from Glory to Glory.'

1st Peter 1:7: 'so that the proof of your faith, *being more precious than gold* which is perishable, even though tested by *Fire*, may be found to result in praise and glory and honor at the revelation of Yeshua the Messiah'.

In the Book of Revelation the Fire is seen in the Holy Spirit, the heavenly Altar, and in the eyes of the Son of Man:

Rev. 4:5: 'Out from the Throne come flashes of Lightning and sounds and peals of Thunder. And there were seven Lamps of *Fire* burning before the Throne which are the seven Spirits of God.'

Rev. 8:5: 'Then the angel took the censer and filled it with the *Fire* of the Altar and threw it to the Earth and there followed peals of Thunder and sounds and flashes of Lightning and an earthquake.'

Rev. 19:12: 'His eyes are a flame of *Fire* and on His head are many crowns and He has a Name written on Him which no one knows except Himself.'

The Fire of Paganism

Dt. 12:31: 'You shall not behave thus toward Yahveh your God for every abominable act which Yahveh hates they have done for their gods. *For they even burn their sons and daughters in the fire* to their gods.'

2nd Kings 16:3: 'But he' (Ahaz, King of Judah) 'walked in the way of the Kings of Israel and even made his son pass through the *fire*, according to the abominations of the nations whom Yahveh had driven out from before the Sons of Israel.' (To 'pass through the fire' meant the infant died in the fire as a sacrifice, and was eaten by his father and mother, and the pagan priest.)

2nd Kings 17:17: 'Then they' (the Sons of Israel in the northern kingdom), 'made their sons and their daughters pass through the *fire* and practiced divination and enchantments and sold themselves to do evil in the sight of Yahveh, provoking Him.'

2nd Chron. 33:6: 'He' (Manasseh, King of Judah) 'made his sons pass through the fire in the Valley of the Son of Hinnom, and he practiced witchcraft, used divination, practiced sorcery and dealt with mediums and spiritists. He did much evil in the sight of Yahveh, provoking Him to anger.'

Jer. 7:31: 'They' (the people of Judah), 'have built the high places of Topheth which is in the Valley of the Son of Hinnom, to burn their sons and their daughters in the *fire* which I did not command. It never entered My mind.'

Jer. 19:5: 'and have built the high places of Baal to burn their sons in the *fire* as burnt sacrifices to Baal, a thing which I never commanded or spoke of, nor did it ever enter My mind'.

Jer. 32:35: 'They built the high places of Baal that are in the Valley of Ben-Hinnom to cause their sons and their daughters to pass through the *fire* to Molech, which I had not commanded them nor had it entered My mind that they should do this abomination, to cause Judah to sin.'

Ezekiel 20:31: 'When you offer your gifts, when you

256

cause your sons to pass through the *fire*, you are defiling yourselves with all your idols to this day. And shall I be inquired of by you, Oh House of Israel?! As I live!' declares the Lord Yahveh, 'I will not be inquired of by you.'

Ezk. 23:37: 'For they have committed adultery and blood is on their hands. Thus they have committed adultery with their idols and even caused their sons whom they bore to Me, to pass through the *fire* to them as food.'

Paganism

Everything in God's Kingdom has its perverted counterfeit in paganism. Sacrifice is the outward expression of surrender to God (or a god), with heart-felt submission being the inner reality. Pagans offered to their gods their best and their dearest as a sacrifice for sin, making their infants 'pass through the fire.' The Prophet Micah (742–687 B.C.), speaks of this when he rhetorically asks,

'Shall I present *my first-born* for my rebellious acts? The *fruit of my body* for the sin of my soul?' (Mic. 7:6b)

Gentile babies were burned alive, screaming, as their drunken parents and other 'worshippers' shouted, sang and wildly danced, drums and other instruments pounding away. They would eat the children as part of their worship to gods like Molech, Baal and Dagon, etc. Those gods *demanded* this sacrifice, a perversion of the Mosaic sacrificial system. In Lev. 20:1-8 it's written:

'Then Yahveh spoke to Moses saying, "You shall also say to the Sons of Israel, 'Any man from the Sons of Israel or from the strangers sojourning in Israel, who gives any of his sons to Molech, must surely be put to death. The people of the Land shall stone him with stones. I will also set My face against that man and will cut him off from among his people because he has given some of his children to Molech, so as to defile My Sanctuary and to profane My Holy Name.'"'

'If the people of the Land however, should ever disregard that man when he gives any of his sons to Molech, so as not to put him to death, then I Myself will set My face against that man and against his family and I will cut off from among their people, both him and all those who play the harlot after him, by playing the cult prostitute after

Molech. As for the person who turns to mediums and to spiritists, to play the harlot after them, I will also set My face against that person and will cut him off from among his people. You must consecrate yourselves and be holy, for I am Yahveh your God. You must keep My Statutes and practice them. I am Yahveh *who makes you holy.*'

Not all pagan worship required human sacrifice but collectively they form a perverse picture of Gentile worship. Pagans sought to reside in the 'safety and blessings' of their gods, to the destruction of their souls and children.

Paganism and cult harlotry went hand-in-hand. There were also other satanic things that attached themselves to this 'worship' like murder. *UBD* speaks about the goddess Asherah,

'who is found in the Ras Shamra epic religious texts discovered at Ugarit in northern Syria (1927–37) as Asherat, 'Lady of the Sea' and *consort of El.* She was chief goddess of Tyre with the appellation Kudshu 'holiness' and she appears as a goddess by the side of Baal, whose consort she came to be, among the Canaanites of the south. Her worship was utterly detestable to faithful worshipers' of Yahveh '(1st Kg. 15:13).'[643]

'Asherah was only one manifestation of a chief goddess of western Asia regarded as both wife and sister of the principal Canaanite god *El.* Other names of the deity were Ashtoreth (Astarte) and *Anath.* Frequently' she was 'represented as a nude woman bestride a lion'.[644]

Her 'male prostitutes consecrated to the cult of the Kudshu and prostituting themselves to her honor were styled Kedishim, "sodomites" (Dt. 23:8; 1st Kings 14:24).'[645]

'At Byblos (biblical Gebal), on the Mediterranean, north of Sidon, a center dedicated to this goddess has been excavated. She and her colleagues specialized in sex'.[646]

It's also noted that 'lust and murder were glamorized in Canaanite religion.'[647] 'On a fragment of the Baal Epic,

---

[643] Unger, *UBD*, p. 412.

[644] Ibid.

[645] Ibid.

[646] Ibid.

Anath appears in an incredibly bloody orgy of destruction. For some unknown reason she fiendishly butchers mankind, young as well as old, in a most horrible and wholesale fashion, wading ecstatically in human gore up to her knees—yea, up to her throat, all the while exulting sadistically.'[648]

This is a glimpse, not only into paganism but the very essence of Satan and his desire for Man: murder for the sheer glee of brutally extinguishing life, with sex aligned as 'worship' to entice the ignorant and unsuspecting. Is it any wonder that God commanded Joshua to destroy every Canaanite?

Astarte was a Canaanite goddess 'of sensual love.'[649] 'Licentious worship was conducted in honor of her'[650] and even 'Solomon succumbed to her voluptuous worship (1st Kings 11:5; 2nd Kings 23:13).'[651]

The Ras Shamra Tablets tell us that Baal 'was the son of El, the father of the gods and the head of the Canaanite pantheon'.[652] He is also 'the son of Dagon.'[653] And that the 'inhabitants of Canaan were addicted to Baal worship, which was conducted by priests in their temples'.[654]

'The cult included animal sacrifice, ritualistic meals and licentious dances'[655] which would end in sexual orgies. 'High places had chambers for sacred prostitution by male prostitutes (Kedishim) and sacred harlots (Kedeshoth) (1st Kings 14:23-24; 2nd Kings 23:7)'.[656]

UBD says the northern kingdom of Israel was also infested with Baal worship:

'Ahab, who married' (Jezebel) 'a Zidonian priestess' (cult harlot), 'at her instigation, built a temple and altar to Baal,

---

[647] Ibid.

[648] Ibid.

[649] Ibid.

[650] Ibid.

[651] Ibid., p. 413.

[652] Ibid., p. 415.

[653] Ibid.

[654] Ibid.

[655] Ibid.

[656] Ibid.

and revived all the abomination of the Amorites (1st Kings 21:25-26). Henceforth, Baal worship became so completely identified with the northern kingdom that it is described as walking in the way or statutes of the Kings of Israel (2nd Kings 16:3; 17:8)'.[657]

Yahveh would put an end to these idolatrous practices by sending Assyria to destroy the northern kingdom in 721 B.C. Idolatry and cult harlotry in Judah were just as detestable though. Yahveh states in Jer. 17:1 that,

'The sin of Judah is written down with an iron stylus. With a diamond point it's engraved upon the tablet of their heart, and upon the horns of their altars'.

The Ras Shamra texts speak of cult harlotry being associated with the sun goddess Shaphash. This is unusual as most deities of the sun were male. It reveals the high status and honor female goddesses exerted over pagan men. And of course in the worship of these various deities, 'prostitution was glorified.'[658] These women were 'professionals.' *UBD* states:

A '*class of women* existed among the Phoenicians, Armenians, Lydians and Babylonians' (Epistle of Jer. v. 43). They are distinguished from the public prostitutes' 'and associated with the performances of sacred rites.'[659]

This was the pagan religious infrastructure. The names of the various gods and goddesses throughout the pagan world would change to suit each country and culture but their rites and rituals identify them. What began at that Tower in Babylon spread over all the Earth. The gods and goddesses of Babylon are found throughout all ancient pagan peoples. The only real difference being their change of names.

The god Vulcan is an example of how the gods and goddesses evolve from one country to the next. The name Vulcan was popularized on the T.V. show Star Trek, but the god was a murderer and devourer of infants. He's also known as Hephaistos which means, 'to break in pieces or *scatter* abroad.' It signifies that Vulcan, whose other names included but weren't limited to, Janus, Bel (the Confounder), Chaos and Merodach (the great rebel). They were all associated or identified with Nimrod. Because of his apostasy, Nimrod caused the people of the Earth to be *scattered* after the destruction of the Tower of Babel.

---

[657] Ibid.

[658] Ibid.

[659] Ibid., p. 514.

The symbol of Vulcan was the hammer which came from the club of Janus or Chaos, the god of confusion. The word 'club' in Chaldee literally means 'to break in pieces or scatter abroad.'[660] In his identification with Nimrod, Vulcan possessed many of the titles and characteristics of Nimrod.[661] Hislop states, 'Everything in the history of Vulcan exactly agrees with that of Nimrod.' Just a few parallels are quite impressive:

> 'Vulcan was the head and chief of the Cyclops, that is, 'the kings of flame.'[662] 'Nimrod was the head of the fire worshipers.'[663]

> 'Vulcan was the forger of the thunderbolts by which such havoc was made among the enemies of the gods. Ninus, or Nimrod, in his wars with the king of Bactria, seems to have carried on the conflict in a similar way.'[664]

> 'Vulcan (was) the god of fire of the Romans, and Nimrod, the fire god of Babylon.'[665]

> 'Nimrod, as the representative of the devouring fire to which human victims, and especially children, were offered in sacrifice, was regarded as the great child devourer.'[666] 'As the father of the gods, he was' 'called Kronos; and everyone knows that the classical story of Kronos was just this, that "he devoured his sons as soon as they were born."'[667] (See Rev. 12:4b)

> As 'the representative of Moloch or Baal, infants were the most acceptable offerings at his altar.'[668]

> 'Hence, the priests of Nimrod or Baal were necessarily required to eat of the human sacrifices; and thus it has come to pass that 'Cahna Bal,'[669] 'the Priest of Baal' is the es-

---

[660] Hislop, *The Two Babylons*, pp. 27-28.

[661] Ibid., p. 229. Hislop's cite for this is *Heathen Mythology Illustrated*, p. 75.

[662] Ibid. 'Kuclops, from Khuk, "king," and Lohb, "flame." The image of the great god was represented with three eyes—one in the forehead; hence the story of the Cyclops with the one eye in the forehead.'

[663] Ibid.

[664] Ibid.

[665] Ibid., p. 230.

[666] Ibid., p. 231.

[667] Ibid. Hislop cites 'Lempriere, *Saturn*' as the source for his information.

[668] Ibid.

tablished word in our own tongue for a devourer of human flesh' (a cannibal).[670]

Vulcan was a vicious god, but only a picture of Nimrod deified. Nimrod (Gen. 10:8-12), was the prototype for most of the chief gods of the world. Nimrod's deception was designed by Satan to lead the people of the Earth away from the One True God in whose Son is our only Hope.

Of course the pagans had their 'holy days' and teachings. But how could the Church 'baptize' these things and call them Christian? When the Torah was thrown out and some words of Paul were falsely used to justify it, the door was opened for Satan to enter (Dan. 7:25).

Christianity is the only religion in the world that doesn't emulate its founder. Jesus never ate pork or shrimp, and always kept the Sabbath day holy. How is it that most Christians don't follow Him in these areas (Mt. 5:17-19; 1st Jn. 2:1-6)? Hopefully *The Lifting of the Veil* will help many believers to see the deception, turn from it, and walk back into God's Truth.

> 'Thus says Yahveh! Stand at the crossroads and look! Ask for the Ancient Paths' (Torah), 'where the Good Way lies and walk in it! And you will find rest for your souls'. (Jer. 6:16)

> 'Remember the Torah of My servant Moses! The statutes and ordinances that I commanded him at Horeb for all Israel. Behold! I will send you the Prophet Elijah before the great and terrible day of Yahveh.' (Mal. 4:4-5)

---

[669] Ibid., p. 232. The 'word Cahna is the emphatic form of Cahn. Cahn is 'a priest,' Cahna is 'the priest.'

[670] Ibid. 'From the historian Castor (an Armenian translation of Eusebius, pars. i. p. 81), we learn that it was under Bel, or Belus, that is Baal, that the Cyclops lived; and the Scholiast of Æschylus (p. 32, ante, note) states that these Cyclops were the brethren of Kronos, who was also Bel, or Bal, as we have elsewhere seen (p. 32). The eye in their forehead shows that originally this name was a name of the great god; for that eye in India and Greece is found the characteristic of the supreme divinity. The Cyclops then, had been representatives of that' god, 'in other words, priests of Bel or Bal. Now, we find that the Cyclops were well known as cannibals, Referre ritus Cyclopum, 'to bring back the rites of the Cyclops,' meaning to revive the practice of eating human flesh. (Ovid, *Metam.*, xv. 93, vol. ii. p. 132.)'

BIBLIOGRAPHY

Bacchiocchi, Samuele. **From Sabbath To Sunday** (Rome: The Pontifical Gregorian University Press, 1977).

The New Testament Sabbath (Gillette, WY: The Sabbath Sentinel magazine, 1987)

Bauer, Walter. Augmented by William F. Arndt, F. W. Gingrich and Frederick Danker. **A Greek-English Lexicon of the New Testament and Other Early Christian Literature** (London: The University of Chicago Press, 1979).

Berry, George Ricker. Editor and Translator. **Interlinear Greek-English New Testament** (Grand Rapids, MI: Baker Books, 2000).

Bible Master 3.0: NAS Computer Bible (Anaheim, CA: Foundation Press Publications, 1992).

Bivin, David and Roy Blizzard. **Understanding the Difficult Words of Jesus** (Shippensburg, Pennsylvania: Destiny Image Publishers, 2001).

Botterweck, G. Johannes and Helmer Ringgren, Editors. John Willis, Translator. **Theological Dictionary of the Old Testament** (Grand Rapids, MI: William B. Eerdmans Publishing Company, 1997).

Bromiley, Geoffrey W., General Editor. Everett F. Harrison, Roland K. Harrison and William Sanford LaSor, Associate Editors. **The International Standard Bible Encyclopedia** (Grand Rapids, MI: William B. Eerdmans Publishing Company, 1979).

Brown, Dr. Francis; Dr. S. R. Driver, Dr. Charles A. Briggs, based on the lexicon of Professor Wilhelm Gesenius. Edward Robinson, Translator. El Rodiger, Editor. **The New Brown, Driver, Briggs, Gesenius Hebrew and English Lexicon** (Lafayette, IN: Associated Publishers and Authors, 1978).

Brown, Robert and Philip W. Comfort, Translators. J. D. Douglas, Editor. **The New Greek-English Interlinear New Testament** (Wheaton, IL: Tyndale House Publishers, 1990).

Bruce, F. F., Author. Gordon D. Fee, General Editor. **The New International Commentary on the New Testament: The Book of the Acts** (Grand Rapids, MI: William B. Eerdmans Publishing Company, 1988).

Companion Bible, The. The Authorized Version of 1611 (Grand Rapids, Michigan: Kregel Publications, 1990).

Davidson, Benjamin. **The Analytical Hebrew and Chaldee Lexicon**

(Grand Rapids, Michigan: Zondervan Publishing House, 1979).

Douglas, J. D., M.A., B.D., S.T.M., Ph.D., Organizing Editor. **The Illustrated Bible Dictionary** (Leicester, England: Inter-Varsity Press, 1998).

Edersheim, Alfred. **The Temple: It's Ministry and Services** (Peabody, MA: Hendrickson Publishers, 1994).

> **The Life and Times of Jesus The Messiah** (Peabody, MA: Hendrickson Publishers, 2000).

Findlay, G. G., B.A., Author. W. Robertson Nicoll, Editor, M.A., LL.D. **The Expositor's Greek Testament: St. Paul's First Epistle to the Corinthians** (Peabody, MA: Hendrickson Publishers, 2002).

France, R. T., M.A., B.D., Ph.D., Author. The Rev. Canon Leon Morris, M.Sc., M.Th., Ph.D., General Editor. **Tyndale New Testament Commentaries: Matthew** (Leicester, England: Inter-Varsity Press 2000).

Freeman, Rev. James M. **Manners and Customs of the Bible** (Plainfield, NJ: Logos International, 1972; originally written in 1874).

Friberg, Timothy and Barbara Friberg and Neva Miller. **Analytical Lexicon of the Greek New Testament** (Grand Rapids, MI: Baker Books, 2000).

Gower, Ralph. **The New Manners and Customs of Bible Times** (Chicago: Moody Press, 1987).

Harris, R. L., Editor. Gleason Archer, Jr. and Bruce Waltke, Associate Editors. **Theological Wordbook of the Old Testament** (Chicago: Moody Press, 1980).

Hegg, Tim. **The Letter Writer: Paul's Background and Torah Perspective** (Israel: First Fruits of Zion, 2002).

Hislop, Alexander. **The Two Babylons** (Neptune, NJ: Loizeaux Brothers, 1959; originally published in 1858).

Jenni, Ernst and Claus Westermann, Authors. Mark E. Biddle, Translator. **Theological Lexicon of the Old Testament** (Peabody, MA: Hendrickson Publishers, 1997).

Keil, C. F. and F. Delitzsch. **Commentary On The Old Testament** (Peabody, MA: Hendrickson Publishers, 2001; originally published by T. & T. Clark, Edinburgh, Scotland, 1866–91).

Kittel, Gerhard and Gerhard Friedrich, Editors. Geoffrey W. Bromiley, Translator and Editor. **Theological Dictionary of the New Testament** (Grand Rapids, MI: Wm. B. Eerdmans Publishing Company, 1999).

Knowling, R. J., D.D., Author. W. Robertson Nicoll, M.A., LL.D., Editor. **The Expositor's Greek Testament: The Acts of the Apostles** (Peabody, MA: Hendrickson Publishers, 2002).

Kruse, Colin G., B.D., M.Phil., Ph.D., Author. The Rev. Canon Leon Morris, M.Sc., M.Th., Ph.D., General Editor. **Tyndale New Testament Commentaries: 2 Corinthians** (Leicester, England: Inter-Varsity Press, 2000).

Livingstone, E. A. **The Concise Oxford Dictionary of the Christian Church** (Oxford, England: Oxford University Press, 2000).

Marshall, I. Howard, M.A., B.D., Ph.D., Author. Professor R.V.G. Tasker, M.A., B.D., General Editor. **Tyndale New Testament Commentaries: Acts** (Leicester, England: Inter-Varsity Press, 2000).

Montefiore, C. G. and H. Loewe. **A Rabbinic Anthology** (New York: Shocken Books, 1974).

Morris, Leon, The Rev. Canon, M.Sc., M.Th., Ph.D. **Tyndale New Testament Commentaries: 1 Corinthians** (Leicester, England: Inter-Varsity Press, 2000).

Tyndale New Testament Commentaries: Revelation (Leicester, England: Inter-Varsity Press, 2000).

Mounce, Robert H; W. Ward Gasque, New Testament Editor. **New International Biblical Commentary: Matthew** (Peabody, MA: Hendrickson Publishers, 1995).

Mounce, William D. **The Analytical Lexicon to the Greek New Testament** (Grand Rapids, Michigan: Zondervan Publishing House, 1993).

Perschbacher, Wesley J., Editor. **The New Analytical Greek Lexicon** (Peabody, MA: Hendrickson Publications, 1990).

Pfeiffer, Charles F., Old Testament. Everett F. Harrison, New Testament. **The Wycliffe Bible Commentary** (Chicago: Moody Press, 1977).

Pritchard, James B. **The Harper Atlas of the Bible** (New York: Harper & Row, Publishers, 1987).

Ryken, Leland and James Wilhoit and Tremper Longman III, General Editors. **Dictionary of Biblical Imagery** (Leicester, England: InterVarsity Press, 1998).

Scherman, Rabbi Nosson and Rabbi Meir Zlotowitz, General Editors. **The Chumash** (Brooklyn: Mesorah Publications, Ltd., 1994).

Sinclair, J. M., General Consultant. Diana Treffry, Editorial Director.

Collins English Dictionary (Glasgow, Scotland: HarperCollins Publishers, 1998).

Stern, David. **Jewish New Testament Commentary** (Clarksville, MD: Jewish New Testament Publications, 1992).

תורה נביאים כתובים והברית החדשה (**Torah, Prophets, Writings and The New Covenant**), (Jerusalem: The Bible Society of Israel, 1991). (Translation of the New Covenant by Yosef Atzmon and Committee in 1976; revised in 1991).

Unger, Merrill F. **Unger's Bible Dictionary** (Chicago: Moody Press, 1976).

Vos, Howard F. **Nelson's New Illustrated Bible Manners and Customs** (Nashville, TN: Thomas Nelson Publishers, 1999).

Williams, David J., Author. W. Ward Gasque, New Testament Editor. **New International Biblical Commentary: Acts** (Peabody, MA: Hendrickson Publishers, 1999).

Wilson, William. **Wilson's Old Testament Word Studies** (Peabody, MA: Hendrickson Publishers, no publishing date given).

Witherington III, Ben. **The Acts of the Apostles: A Socio-Rhetorical Commentary** (Grand Rapids, MI: William B. Eerdmans Publishing Company, 1998).

Woolf, Henry Bosley, Editor in Chief. **Webster's New Collegiate Dictionary** (Springfield, MA: G. & C. Merriam Co., 1980).

Internet Sites

Encyclopedia Mythical at http://www.pantheon.org/articles/e/eros.html. Eros in mythology.

JAHG–USA (Jews and Hasidic Gentiles—United to Save America), **The Noahide Laws** at http://www.noahide.com/lawslist.htm.

McKnight, Scot. **Jesus Creed** at www.jesuscreed.org/?p=2686. Aug. 6th, 2007. A summary of Sanders, Dunn and Wright.

1. p=2687. Aug. 10th, 2007. Other aspects of the New Perspective on Paul.

2. p=2688. Aug. 7th, 2007. Sociological markers.

3. p=2689. Aug. 8th, 2007. The Law was given to the Jews to show them how to live; what was good and right in God's eyes. It wasn't legalism.

4. p=2690. Aug. 9th, 2007. Israel's election, covenant and Law.

Wikipedia: The Free Encyclopedia

http://en.wikipedia.org/wiki/E._P._Sanders. A summary of Sanders.

http://en.wikipedia.org/wiki/Fornication. The Latin definition of fornication.

Wright, Nicholas T. **New Perspectives on Paul** at http://www.ntwright-page.com/Wright_New_Perspectives.htm. August 26th, 2003. Wright's view on the works of the Spirit showing that one is in the Kingdom.

The Paul Page at http://www.thepaulpage.com/Conversation.html. Oct. 25th, 2004. Dunn's view on Judaism's New Perspective.

Paul in Different Perspectives at http://www.ntwrightpage.com/Wright_Auburn_Paul.htm. January 3rd, 2005. Wright's view on the Greek word, gar.

Yehoshua, Avram. **The Seed of Abraham** at www.seedofabraham.net

1. *Sam the Rock Thrower*

2. *Law 102*

3. Meet Avram Yehoshua

4. Under *Mosaic Sacrifice and Messiah*

    1. *The Mosaic Sacrifices and the Blood of Jesus*

2. *Sacrifice in the New Testament*

5. DVD's & CD's, etc.

   1. The Hebrew course

   2. Christ in the Passover

6. Under Jewish Newsletters (a partial listing)

   1. *Recognize This Man?*

   2. *Lion Hands*

7. *Goodbye Messianic Judaism!*

8. The Feasts of Israel

9. In the Articles section (partial listings)

   1. under Biblical:

      1. *Do as the Pharisees Say?! Mt. 23:2-3*

      2. *Kingdom Violence: Mt. 11:12*

      3. *No Longer Under the Law? Two Important Phrases*

      4. *Yeshua: God the Son*

   2. under Christian:

      1. *Jesus the Fish God?*

      2. *Thanksgiving Day: Pagan?*

   3. under Jewish:

      1. *Jewish Idolatry*

      2. *Kabbalah*

      3. *The Kipa*

      4. *Kosher: Jewish vs. Biblical*

      5. *The Star of David*

   4. under Misc:

      1. *Hislop Under Attack*

      2. Scripture Reading Schedule

      3. The Ordination Process

Contact Information

Avram Yehoshua
P.O. Box 10981
Ramat Gan 52009
Israel

www.seedofabraham.net
avramyeh@netvision.net.il

ISBN 142512328-7

9 781425 123284